Keep t
need it
your ca

About the American Hotel & Lodging Association (AH&LA)

Founded in 1910, AH&LA is the trade association representing the lodging industry in the United States. AH&LA is a federation of state lodging associations throughout the United States with 11,000 lodging properties worldwide as members. The association offers its members assistance with governmental affairs representation, communications, marketing, hospitality operations, training and education, technology issues, and more. For information, call 202-289-3100.

LODGING, the management magazine of AH&LA, is a "living textbook" for hospitality students that provides timely features, industry news, and vital lodging information.

About the American Hotel & Lodging Educational Institute (EI)

An affiliate of AH&LA, the Educational Institute is the world's largest source of quality training and educational materials for the lodging industry. EI develops textbooks and courses that are used in more than 1,200 colleges and universities worldwide, and also offers courses to individuals through its Distance Learning program. Hotels worldwide rely on EI for training resources that focus on every aspect of lodging operations. Industry-tested videos, CD-ROMs, seminars, and skills guides prepare employees at every skill level. EI also offers professional certification for the industry's top performers. For information about EI's products and services, call 800-349-0299 or 407-999-8100.

About the American Hotel & Lodging Educational Foundation (AH&LEF)

An affiliate of AH&LA, the American Hotel & Lodging Educational Foundation provides financial support that enhances the stability, prosperity, and growth of the lodging industry through educational and research programs. AH&LEF has awarded millions of dollars in scholarship funds for students pursuing higher education in hospitality management. AH&LEF has also funded research projects on topics important to the industry, including occupational safety and health, turnover and diversity, and best practices in the U.S. lodging industry. For more information, go to www.ahlef.org.

00367TXT01ENGE
PP-3632

The International SPA Association Foundation is the 501(c)3 foundation of the International SPA Association and was created in 1999 to serve the educational and research needs of the spa industry. The ISPA Foundation's mission is to improve and enhance the value of the spa experience; its vision is to advance spa culture to sustain health and well-being. The ISPA Foundation's objectives include being the educational source for the spa industry, establishing definitive research that validates spa industry–related topics, and creating an endowment that sustains the ISPA Foundation in perpetuity.

Since 1991, the International SPA Association has been recognized worldwide as the professional organization and voice of the spa industry, representing health-and-wellness facilities and providers in more than seventy countries. Members encompass the entire arena of the spa experience, from resort/hotel, destination, mineral springs, medical, cruise ship, club, and day spas to service providers such as physicians, wellness instructors, nutritionists, massage therapists, and product suppliers.

ISPA's mission is to advance the spa industry by providing invaluable educational and networking opportunities, promoting the value of the spa experience, and speaking as the industry's authoritative voice to foster professionalism and growth.

FINANCIAL MANAGEMENT FOR SPAS

Educational Institute Books

UNIFORM SYSTEM OF ACCOUNTS FOR THE LODGING INDUSTRY
Tenth Revised Edition

WORLD OF RESORTS: FROM DEVELOPMENT TO MANAGEMENT
Third Edition
Chuck Yim Gee

PLANNING AND CONTROL FOR FOOD AND BEVERAGE OPERATIONS
Seventh Edition
Jack D. Ninemeier

UNDERSTANDING HOSPITALITY LAW
Fifth Edition
Jack P. Jefferies/Banks Brown

SUPERVISION IN THE HOSPITALITY INDUSTRY
Fourth Edition
Raphael R. Kavanaugh/Jack D. Ninemeier

MANAGEMENT OF FOOD AND BEVERAGE OPERATIONS
Fifth Edition
Jack D. Ninemeier

MANAGING FRONT OFFICE OPERATIONS
Eighth Edition
Michael L. Kasavana/Richard M. Brooks

MANAGING SERVICE IN FOOD AND BEVERAGE OPERATIONS
Fourth Edition
Ronald F. Cichy/Philip J. Hickey, Jr.

THE LODGING AND FOOD SERVICE INDUSTRY
Seventh Edition
Gerald W. Lattin

SECURITY AND LOSS PREVENTION MANAGEMENT
Second Edition
Raymond C. Ellis, Jr./David M. Stipanuk

HOSPITALITY INDUSTRY MANAGERIAL ACCOUNTING
Seventh Edition
Raymond S. Schmidgall

PURCHASING FOR FOOD SERVICE OPERATIONS
Ronald F. Cichy/Jeffery D Elsworth

MANAGING TECHNOLOGY IN THE HOSPITALITY INDUSTRY
Sixth Edition
Michael L. Kasavana

HOTEL AND RESTAURANT ACCOUNTING
Seventh Edition
Raymond Cote

ACCOUNTING FOR HOSPITALITY MANAGERS
Fifth Edition
Raymond Cote

CONVENTION MANAGEMENT AND SERVICE
Eighth Edition
Milton T. Astroff/James R. Abbey

HOSPITALITY SALES AND MARKETING
Fifth Edition
James R. Abbey

MANAGING HOUSEKEEPING OPERATIONS
Revised Third Edition
Aleta A. Nitschke/William D. Frye

HOSPITALITY TODAY: AN INTRODUCTION
Seventh Edition
Rocco M. Angelo/Andrew N. Vladimir

HOSPITALITY FACILITIES MANAGEMENT AND DESIGN
Third Edition
David M. Stipanuk

MANAGING HOSPITALITY HUMAN RESOURCES
Fourth Edition
Robert H. Woods

RETAIL MANAGEMENT FOR SPAS

HOSPITALITY INDUSTRY FINANCIAL ACCOUNTING
Third Edition
Raymond S. Schmidgall/James W. Damitio

INTERNATIONAL HOTELS: DEVELOPMENT & MANAGEMENT
Second Edition
Chuck Yim Gee

QUALITY SANITATION MANAGEMENT
Ronald F. Cichy

HOTEL INVESTMENTS: ISSUES & PERSPECTIVES
Fourth Edition
Edited by Lori E. Raleigh and Rachel J. Roginsky

LEADERSHIP AND MANAGEMENT IN THE HOSPITALITY INDUSTRY
Third Edition
Robert H. Woods/Judy Z. King

MARKETING IN THE HOSPITALITY INDUSTRY
Fifth Edition
Ronald A. Nykiel

UNIFORM SYSTEM OF ACCOUNTS FOR THE HEALTH, RACQUET AND SPORTSCLUB INDUSTRY

CONTEMPORARY CLUB MANAGEMENT
Second Edition
Edited by Joe Perdue for the Club Managers Association of America

RESORT CONDOMINIUM AND VACATION OWNERSHIP MANAGEMENT: A HOSPITALITY PERSPECTIVE
Robert A. Gentry/Pedro Mandoki/Jack Rush

ACCOUNTING FOR CLUB OPERATIONS
Raymond S. Schmidgall/James W. Damitio

TRAINING AND DEVELOPMENT FOR THE HOSPITALITY INDUSTRY
Debra F. Cannon/Catherine M. Gustafson

UNIFORM SYSTEM OF FINANCIAL REPORTING FOR CLUBS
Sixth Revised Edition

HOTEL ASSET MANAGEMENT: PRINCIPLES & PRACTICES
Second Edition
Edited by Greg Denton, Lori E. Raleigh, and A. J. Singh

MANAGING BEVERAGE OPERATIONS
Second Edition
Ronald F. Cichy/Lendal H. Kotschevar

FOOD SAFETY: MANAGING WITH THE HACCP SYSTEM
Second Edition
Ronald F. Cichy

UNIFORM SYSTEM OF FINANCIAL REPORTING FOR SPAS

FUNDAMENTALS OF DESTINATION MANAGEMENT AND MARKETING
Edited by Rich Harrill

ETHICS IN THE HOSPITALITY AND TOURISM INDUSTRY
Second Edition
Karen Lieberman/Bruce Nissen

SPA: A COMPREHENSIVE INTRODUCTION
Elizabeth M. Johnson/Bridgette M. Redman

HOSPITALITY 2015: THE FUTURE OF HOSPITALITY AND TRAVEL
Marvin Cetron/Fred DeMicco/Owen Davies

REVENUE MANAGEMENT: MAXIMIZING REVENUE IN HOSPITALITY OPERATIONS
Gabor Forgacs

FINANCIAL MANAGEMENT FOR SPAS
Raymond S. Schmidgall/John R. Korpi

07/11

FINANCIAL MANAGEMENT FOR SPAS

Raymond S. Schmidgall, Ph.D., CPA
John R. Korpi

The International SPA Association Foundation is the 501(c)3 foundation of the International SPA Association and was created in 1999 to serve the educational and research needs of the spa industry. The ISPA Foundation's mission is to improve and enhance the value of the spa experience; its vision is to advance spa culture to sustain health and well-being. The ISPA Foundation's objectives include being the educational source for the spa industry, establishing definitive research that validates spa industry related topics, and creating an endowment that sustains the ISPA Foundation in perpetuity.

Disclaimer

This publication is designed to provide accurate and authoritative information in regard to the subject matter covered. It is sold with the understanding that the publisher is not engaged in rendering legal, accounting, or other professional service. If legal advice or other expert assistance is required, the services of a competent professional person should be sought.

—*From the Declaration of Principles jointly adopted by the American Bar Association and a Committee of Publishers and Associations*

The authors are solely responsible for the contents of this publication. All views expressed herein are solely those of the authors and do not necessarily reflect the views of the Internatioanl SPA Association Foundation (ISPA), American Hotel & Lodging Educational Institute (the Institute), or the American Hotel & Lodging Association (AH&LA).

Nothing contained in this publication shall constitute a standard, an endorsement, or a recommendation of ISPA, the Institute, or AH&LA. ISPA, the Institute, and AH&LA disclaim any liability with respect to the use of any information, procedure, or product, or reliance thereon by any member of the hospitality industry.

Published by
The AMERICAN HOTEL & LODGING
EDUCATIONAL INSTITUTE
2113 N. High Street
Lansing, Michigan 48906-4221

The Educational Institute of the American
Hotel & Lodging Association is a nonprofit
educational foundation.

Printed in the United States of America
1 2 3 4 5 6 7 8 9 10 13 12 11 10 11

ISBN 978-0-86612-360-0

We'd like to express our gratitude to the sponsors of this edition of *Financial Management for Spas*.

Based in Austin, Texas, Hospitality Financial and Technology Professionals (HFTP) is the global professional association for financial and technology personnel working in hotels, clubs, and other hospitality-related businesses. HFTP provides first-class educational opportunities, research, and publications to members globally, including the premiere hospitality technology conference, HITEC, which was founded in 1972. It produces GUESTROOM 20X, a bi-annual, hands-on model hotel room showcasing the most innovative technologies for the guestroom. HFTP also awards the only hospitality-specific certifications for accounting and technology —the Certified Hospitality Accountant Executive (CHAE) and the Certified Hospitality Technology Professional (CHTP) designations. For more information, visit www.hftp.org.

Following a vision that grew from the home workshop of a meticulous industrial designer, Precor, for nearly three decades, has been dedicated to helping people lead more active and richer lives.

Founded as a small business with a single product—a rowing machine for home use—Precor has grown into a global leader in fitness, designing and producing a range of equipment and services for home and commercial markets.

Precor strategically built its company by pioneering design to meet the market demand for a comprehensive fitness offering—from cardio and strength to entertainment and programming.

Today, Precor is a preferred brand by fitness-minded travelers and discerning guests of the world's finest hotels, resorts, and spas. With a sleek complement of cardio, strength, and entertainment equipment supported by a network experienced in servicing facilities worldwide, Precor is a global resource offering a turnkey solution for hospitality customers whose core business isn't fitness.

Leading the Precor lineup is the sleek and durable Experience Series™ of cardio equipment, including traditional choices of treadmills, elliptical cross-trainers, and cycles, as well as the breakthrough Adaptive Motion Trainer™ (AMT®). Cardio Theater personal viewing screens integrate into Precor cardio, keeping workouts interesting and entertaining.

In addition, Precor has recently introduced two new lines of contemporary strength equipment to its offering. Each is beautifully designed and engineered to fit facilities that place a priority on economy of space and ease of use.

Over the past decade, Precor has established a strong track record of progressive environmental stewardship, and gained industry and government recognition for environmental and manufacturing best practices. Throughout the organization, Precor has pursued opportunities to reduce hazardous substance use and hazardous waste, while increasing recycling and acceptable treatment methods.

Recognized worldwide for uncompromised quality and durability in equipment that delivers a fluid, natural motion, Precor is proud to be in premier hotels, resorts, and spas in more than ninety countries. You can contact Precor by visiting the company's website at www.precor.com, or by calling toll-free 1-800-786-8404.

Contents

Preface

The International SPA Association and the ISPA Foundation recognize that, with the rapid growth in the spa industry around the world, education is extremely important in order for the industry to continue to thrive and serve its clients. To help provide for the successful future of the industry, ISPA and the ISPA Foundation have created *Financial Management for Spas,* a course designed to provide spa professionals with the financial skills they need to succeed.

Financial Management for Spas represents an important step in the sustainability of the spa industry. The global spa industry has experienced a great deal of change. In some countries, the industry has seen phenomenal growth; in other areas, this growth is just beginning. As the industry continues to evolve, and as more and more consumers learn about the benefits of spas and health-and-wellness lifestyle changes, the industry needs to be ready to serve them. In order to sustain the spa industry, it is imperative that spa professionals possess the business tools necessary for their own spas' growth and vitality. Because of the industry's tremendous growth, informational tools and resources on subjects such as retail, financial management, compensation, consumer and industry research and trends, and standard operating procedures are imperative. These tools will allow spa managers to provide an even greater customer-service experience and allow spas to be even better prepared for their guests.

The *Financial Management for Spas* text was developed in response to spa industry self-assessment skills surveys that have found that spa professionals rank their area of greatest need to be education on the business side of the spa equation. Spa leaders have an excellent grasp on the mission of spas to improve the wellness of spa guests. They serve guests and manage their spas with passion to uplift the spirits and well-being of spa guests, creating an experience that transitions guests from the stresses inherent in today's world and places them in an environment of tranquility and renewal. On the other hand, the demands of achieving significant profitability and managing issues from compensation-program development to budgeting and variance reporting seem contrary to the purpose of spas. Yet, the realistic measurement of a spa's performance is always articulated in financial terms. Spa managers can help ensure the success and sustainability of their spa businesses by mastering the skills of financial management contained in this text.

This text is unique in its presentation of managerial accounting principles, as the academic concepts and practices are framed within the real-life, day-to-day business of a spa operation. Each chapter in the book begins with a story intended to engage readers and foster a clear understanding of how the financial principles presented in the chapter impact the everyday life of spa managers. The chapters are constructed in such a way as to move the reader from the practical applications of the accounting principles presented to a thorough academic discussion of the financial reporting process for each topic in the text.

Acknowledgments

Financial Management for Spas would not have been possible without the involvement of many spa industry experts whose passion and enthusiasm for this undertaking was remarkable. Many industry leaders have devoted their valuable time and knowledge for the development of this text, with the vision of providing spa professionals the opportunity for intellectual and professional growth.

The *Financial Management for Spas* Task Force

The ISPA Foundation would like to express special gratitude to **Calvin Martin,** CPA, Partner, Calvin Martin & Company, for his many contributions to this text, including practical application content for Chapters 1 and 2, his leadership in developing material for Chapter 9, "Cash Management," and his willingness to undertake a cover-to-cover final review of the entire book. The ISPA Foundation thanks and commends him and all of those who developed content for this text by sharing their knowledge and expertise and for their untiring commitment to the completion of the project. In addition to Calvin, the other individuals responsible for this inaugural edition include the following:

- **Edwin Neill III,** President, Neill Corporation; and **Louie Lago,** Neill Corporation, for their content contribution to Chapter 3, "Inventory."
- **Jack Morrison, CMA,** Managing Director, Elmcrest College of Applied Health Sciences & Spa Management, for his help with the development of content for Chapter 4, "Income Statement."
- **Amy Martin Galbraith,** Partner, Calvin Martin & Company; **Jaime Huffman,** Executive Spa Director, The Grove Park Inn Resort & Spa; and **Ann Brown,** Spa Director, Spa Shiki at Four Seasons Resort, for their collective contributions to the material in Chapter 6, "Pricing and Menu Engineering."
- **Paul Schmidt,** Owner, CEO, Living Energy Design; **Jeremy McCarthy,** Corporate Director, Spa Development & Operations, Starwood Hotels & Resorts Worldwide, Inc.; and **Frank Pitsikalis,** President, ResortSuite, for their collaboration to develop the content for Chapter 8, "Revenue Management."
- **Jeff Kohl,** National Vertical Accounts Manager, Precor, Inc., for his participation in the development of the content contained in Chapter 10, "Capital Budgeting and Lease Accounting."
- **Richard Dusseau,** CEO, Spatality, for his contribution to the material contained in Chapter 11, "Business Plan Development."
- **Elizabeth Johnson** and **Bridgette Redman** of the American Hotel & Lodging Educational Institute, for taking the rough drafts of each chapter's opening story and refining them into material that leads readers into the chapter content.
- **Ryan Crabbe,** Corporate Director of Spa, Hilton Hotels; **Jennifer Wayland Smith,** Spa Director, Golden Door Spa at the Boulders Resort; and **Katelyn Megill,** Spa Supervisor, Golden Door Spa at the Boulders Resort, for their assistance with the text.

The Authors

The ISPA Foundation is honored and grateful to have worked with Ray Schmidgall and John Korpi as the co-authors of this book. Their experience and knowledge in writing, editing, storytelling, and industry-specific textbooks have helped shape this publication into a valuable resource for the spa industry.

The Peer Review

The authors and a task force of experienced and dedicated industry professionals supplied their time and expertise to guide the development of this text. Once each chapter was drafted, the content was sent through a peer review process. A variety of professionals were asked to participate in the process and provide feedback on chapter content and how the material was presented. We thank them for their commitment to higher education and for helping create a strong foundation for the future of the spa world:

- **Debi Barnes,** President, Turtle Cove Spa at Mountain Harbor Resort
- **Ann Brown,** Spa Director, Spa Shiki
- **Ann Duliere,** Controller, The Golden Door
- **Joel Friedman,** Director of Sales and Marketing, Priverus Software Corp.
- **Jamie Huffman,** Executive Spa Director, the Grove Park Inn Resort and Spa
- **Jack Morrison,** Managing Director, Elmcrest College
- **Terry L. Price,** Executive IT Manager, The Grove Park Inn Resort and Spa and 2010 President, Hospitality Financial and Technology Professionals
- **Paul Schmidt,** Owner and CEO, Living Energy Design
- **Jane Segerberg,** President, Segerberg Spa Consulting, LLC

The Partners

This book would not have been possible without the support, vision, and wisdom of other important partners and resources.

The International SPA Association was a vital partner and proponent of the development of *Financial Management for Spas*. ISPA is recognized worldwide as the leading professional organization and voice of the spa industry, and its support and involvement with this text reinforces that position. The authors are grateful for the assistance of many members of ISPA's staff, including Laura Beiting, Becky Brooks, and Sarah Whitney Cox.

The ISPA Foundation would also like to thank the American Hotel & Lodging Educational Institute (EI) for editing and publishing this textbook. The ISPA Foundation is honored and grateful to have worked with George Glazer and Tim Eaton on this book. We are grateful for their continued support of the ISPA Foundation's initiatives and the spa industry.

The Sponsors

The ISPA Foundation would like to thank the sponsors of this book, Hospitality Financial and Technology Professionals (HFTP) and Precor. HFTP's and Precor's sponsorship, support, and involvement in this project were vital to its development and future.

Hospitality Financial and Technology Professionals (HFTP) is the global professional association for financial and technology personnel working in hotels, clubs, and other hospitality-related businesses.

Precor is recognized worldwide for uncompromised quality and durability in fitness equipment that delivers a fluid, natural motion. Precor is found in premier hotels, resorts, and spas in more than ninety countries.

The 2010 ISPA Foundation Board of Directors

- Jeff Kohl, President
- Cathy Cluff, Vice President
- Celeste Hilling, Secretary
- Calvin Martin, Treasurer
- Brent A. Bauer, M.D., Medical Advisor
- Jean Kolb
- Edwin H. Neill III
- Ruth Stricker
- Deborah Szekely, Honorary Board Member
- Deborah Waldvogel
- Shenyn Wang

The 2010 ISPA Board of Directors

- Jean Kolb, Chairman
- Deborah Waldvogel, Vice Chairman
- Thor Holm, Secretary/Treasurer
- Sharilyn Abbajay
- Ann Brown
- Kathryn Dundas, M.D.
- Andrew Gibson
- Jesper Hougaard
- Jaime Huffman
- Lori Hutchinson

- Jeff Kohl
- Jeremy McCarthy
- Frank Pitsikalis
- Paul Schmidt
- Peter Sng
- Ella Stimpson
- Jennifer Wayland-Smith
- Susan Wheeler
- Brent A. Bauer, M.D., ISPA Medical Advisor

ISPA Contact Information

International SPA Association Foundation
2365 Harrodsburg Road, Ste. A325
Lexington, KY 40504 USA
1-888-651-4772 or 1-859-226-4326
ispa@ispastaff.com
www.experienceispa.com

About the Authors

RAY SCHMIDGALL, PH.D., CPA, is the Hilton Hotels Professor of Hospitality Financial Management at Michigan State University's *The* School of Hospitality Business, and is the school's accounting and financial management expert. He serves on industry committees of the Hospitality Financial and Technology Professionals and the American Hotel & Lodging Association. He conducts managerial accounting seminars for CMAA, HFTP, and GCSAA.

The seventh edition of his *Managerial Accounting for the Hospitality Industry* was released in September 2010. He has written numerous accounting textbooks oriented to the hospitality industry, including basic texts on financial management, financial accounting, and managerial accounting, and an accounting text for the club industry. Ray also authored the ISPA Foundation book *Uniform System of Financial Reporting for Spas* in 2004.

Prior to his teaching career, Ray was the financial controller of the American Hotel & Lodging Educational Institute, and worked as an auditor with Ernst & Ernst.

JOHN R. KORPI has been the driving force behind the development of ISPA and ISPA Foundation educational resources. He served as task force chair for each of the four previously published texts—*Uniform System of Financial Reporting for Spas, Retail Management for Spas, Supervisory Skill Builders for the Spa Industry,* and *Spa: A Comprehensive Introduction*—and is now the co-author of *Financial Management for Spas.* John's twenty-five years of experience as general manager of several nationally prominent resorts with spa operations and his twenty years of involvement with the International SPA Association allowed him to frame this text's discussion of managerial accounting principles within the practical setting of everyday spa operations.

John received his bachelor's degree from the University of St. Thomas, St. Paul, Minnesota, in Philosophy, and in 1995 was designated a Certified Hotel Administrator by the American Hotel & Lodging Educational Institute. He and his wife Karen, formerly Vice President of Spas for The Ritz-Carlton Hotel Company, LLC, formed Korpi & Korpi Consulting, *Balancing Spa Profits and Purpose,* in 2009.

Chapter 1 Outline

Competencies

1. Identify and define several common accounting terms used in connection with the financial statements. (pp. 5–7)
2. Distinguish between cash and accrual basis accounting and explain the purpose of accrual. (p. 8)
3. Describe the concepts addressed in generally accepted accounting principles (GAAP). (pp. 8–12)
4. Explain the use of debits and credits in double entry bookkeeping. (pp. 12–13)
5. Describe daily operating summary reports and demonstrate how they affect the financial statements. (pp. 13–28)
6. Outline the nine steps of the accounting cycle. (pp. 28–35)

1

Introduction to Spa Financial Management

ERICA FLIPPED OFF THE LIGHTS in the relaxation lounge of The Spa at The Luxury Resort as she made her way to the office. Today was her turn as the assistant spa director to close the spa. The leadership team shared a weekly opening and closing schedule so that a supervisor was always at the spa each morning when it opened and each evening when it closed.

Having completed her walk-through to make sure that everything had been turned off, that the professional product dispensary was perfectly clean and secured, and that the locker rooms were properly supplied and tidy for the next morning, Erica turned her eye to paperwork. She reviewed the appointments for the next day to see if there were any last-minute details that should be noted in the guest reception log, made a list of a few tasks for the morning staff to tend to, and reviewed the therapist schedule to ensure all was in good order. It was 9:20 P.M. and the final thing to do before shutting off the lights and locking the door was to print the spa's Daily Operating Summary. As she waited for the printout, Erica thought about her father, a hotel and resort general manager who retired after thirty-four years in the business. She remembered how he told her—many times—about the first general manager he worked for and how the lessons he learned from him paved the way for his own success.

Ted, Erica's dad, had been hired as a management trainee for a national hotel chain. His first assignment was working at the front desk of one of the company's large airport properties in New York. On her father's eighth day at the hotel, the general manager called him into his office and told him that he was going to show Ted how to do the night audit the next night. The GM explained that if Ted was really serious about becoming a great manager, the most important thing he could learn was how the day's business activities were being summarized in the Night Clerk's Summary Report. This document translated all of the day's financial transactions into the all-important language of accounting: numbers.

What happened that next night and the impression it made on Ted's hotel career was a story all too familiar to Erica. The GM showed up at 11 P.M. and spent all night working with Ted. He showed him how, in a hotel where there were hundreds if not thousands of individual transactions posted by a myriad of people, it was the night auditor's responsibility to clearly understand how all of those cumulative transactions came together and to describe everything that happened that day in a simple summary report. This task was the one final opportunity each day to make sure all the financial transactions were correct before the information was given to the accounting office.

"If you let bad numbers slip by, they inevitably come back to bite you, so always remember this one basic principle: if good information goes in, good information comes out," the GM told Ted. Even in today's highly computerized world, postings are still all done by people. And while they may be 95 to 99 percent accurate, there will always be mistakes. Ted learned that night that the manager must be able to look at a report and pick out those numbers that just don't look right and, when a mistake was found, that both the manager and night auditor must understand the process well enough to be able to correct any error.

Throughout his career, Erica's father said that managers often described the day by telling him stories, such as "We had a great banquet tonight for the opera society," or "Guests love the new menu items at the steak house restaurant," or "The hotel came within two rooms of a perfect sell out," or "The meeting planner for the group that had just checked out was very complimentary of the service his group received from the hotel staff." Dad always stressed that, while those stories were interesting, in the final analysis the most important information must be how each of those situations affected revenues and profitability. Was the opera society banquet priced in such a way as to be profitable? Were the new menu items increasing the average guest check in the restaurant? Was the average room rate above or below budget? Is the meeting planner contemplating holding another event at the hotel in the near future?

Erica chuckled to herself. She heard the same types of comments in the spa. She often heard comments like, "The new lime and verbena bath salts in the retail area are flying off the shelves," or, "The new stress-relief facial received positive feedback from the three guests who had it yesterday," or, "The woman in charge of the bridal party in the salon was so pleased," or, "The new yoga instructor had a great class this afternoon." These were all interesting stories, but Erica knew that the reality of the business of spa meant that she had to ask the big question: how did each of those stories affect revenues and profitability?

Erica remembered her dad's simple advice when she started her spa career. "Erica, if you just want to be an average spa professional, you can glance at the various management reports for the spa and spend a few minutes looking at the monthly income statement and, if the bottom number is good, simply move on to other matters. Or, if you want to be a great spa professional and distinguish yourself, you will take the time and effort to learn what impact each number has on the operation. Study basic accounting practices and realize that, while accounting may seem like some foreign language or the responsibility of the accounting office, you must run the spa as if it were your own. Discipline yourself to remember that at the heart of all accounting information is the cornerstone financial question, 'What would I do if I were spending my own money?' The individuals who run their operations as if they were their own will be most successful."

She recalled his cautionary words, "Remember, you can have three great months and then suddenly, if you take your eye off the ball, you may end up with a month where revenues are flat or down and payroll and expenses are out of whack. You will go quickly from hero to chump. You must accept that in the eyes of the management or owners, *you are only as good as your last financial statement.*"

"I'm no chump, Dad," said Erica. She picked up the Daily Operating Summary and sat down for 20 minutes to examine each number for the day, reviewed the stats on a month-to-date basis, and compared the numbers against budget pace. Almost everything looked on target, but there were a few numbers that needed clarification, and she made notes to review with the spa director the next day. She then set the alarm system, turned off the lights, and locked the door. As she walked to her car, she made a mental note to call her dad and thank him for teaching her the fundamentals of financial management.

This text is intended to provide spa beginners and veterans alike with a better understanding of financial management. Our hope is that you will learn to embrace the accounting process and to understand that, while accounting is in many ways a science, there is also an art to financial management. In the end, you will be able to appreciate the beauty in numbers.

Questions you should be able to answer after reading this chapter include:

1. What is accounting?
2. What is the fundamental accounting equation?
3. What are some common assets?
4. What is the difference between cash and accrual accounting?
5. What is meant by double-entry accounting?
6. What is a normal balance?
7. How are debit and credit defined?
8. What are the common elements of the daily operating summary report?
9. What are the generally accepted accounting principles?
10. What are the nine steps in the accounting cycle?

Accounting Principles and Terminology

Spa professionals must realize that the spas they are leading were developed, constructed, and supplied with someone's money. If it is a small day spa facility, it might be the owner's life savings combined with some capital provided by family or a loan received from a bank. Major corporate resort spas must be funded by capital from the corporation, partners, venture capitalists, or stockholders. Whatever the case, the beautiful spa surroundings and equipment are all possible because someone provided capital. In virtually all of the cases, these people want a return on their investment. Always remember that you are first and foremost responsible for providing a reasonable return on the capital invested to make the spa a reality. While many spa leaders think of accounting as a necessary evil and devote only the minimum time to working with the numbers, the truly successful spa leaders are those who journey deep into the layers of accounting to better understand their business and better assist spa leadership in making key business decisions.

Accounting is simply the language of business. Regardless of size, a spa must record, classify, and summarize its economic events in specified documents and, ultimately, on its financial statements. Accounting is a standard means of communicating financial information in a form that interested parties clearly understand.

The computer and advancements in spa software have revolutionized the generation and processing of financial transactions. Just fifteen to twenty years ago, such transactions were posted, classified, and summarized by individuals sitting at a desk with a calculator and ledger paper. Now they are processed instantaneously by the computer. Yet, in spite of technological advancements, one thing remains unchanged: it is critical to learn the *why* as well as the *how* of accounting. Learning the why and how of accounting will not only enable a spa professional to produce accurate and useful business information, it will more importantly give spa leaders the capacity to use that financial information to make prudent decisions.

Like any language, accounting has its unique terms and rules. To learn how to interpret and make use of the financial information, the spa professional must first understand the language of accounting.

Let's start by defining several terms associated with one of the major financial statements, the **balance sheet**. The balance sheet has three basic categories of financial information. It presents assets, liabilities, and owners' equity.

Assets are property or items of value owned by a spa. Some examples of assets are:

- *Cash:* The balance of currency and coins on hand and funds held in checking, savings, and money market accounts.
- *Accounts Receivable:* A promise by customers to pay later for goods and services already provided. Providing an invoice to a customer who promises to pay at a later date or charging a group's activities to its corporate master account to be paid at the end of the month are activities that create **accounts receivable**.
- *Prepaid Expenses:* Payments toward an expense for which there is no benefit until some future date. For example, a semi-annual insurance premium paid today is considered a prepaid expense because it provides insurance coverage for six months into the future.
- *Inventory:* This is the value of inventory on hand. One obvious example is the cost of the retail inventory of products to be sold to spa guests. Other examples

might include items such as spa robes or massage table linens which are of significant value and inventoried on a regular basis.

- *Fixed Assets:* These include the spa building and land, along with tangible assets of material value expected to last over a year that enable the spa to provide services, such as the massage tables, equipment and furnishings.

Liabilities are outside financial claims against the assets of a spa, such as its debts and obligations to creditors. Examples include:

- *Accounts Payable:* The spa's obligation to pay a vendor for goods or services already received (for example, for professional products from suppliers such as the skincare line or grooming area products). Once these items are delivered, the spa generally has 30 days to pay the amount shown on the invoice.
- *Notes Payable:* Loans made to the spa. These are traditionally broken down into short and long term. Short-term notes are generally due in one year or less, while long-term notes are generally due after 12 months, sometimes many years into the future.
- *Withheld Taxes:* Taxes withheld from employees' wages.
- *Payroll Taxes Payable:* The employer's share of payroll taxes owed.
- *Deferred Revenue:* Cash collected now or accounts receivable due to the spa for services or goods to be provided later. Examples would be the unused months of a year's membership fee paid and unredeemed gift certificates.

Owners' equity represents the owners' claims to the business's assets. The claims of a single owner are called *owner's equity* or *net worth.* In the generally accepted accounting principles (GAAP) structure, equity is simply the difference between assets and liabilities. The owner of the spa has positive equity if assets exceed liabilities. If a spa has $100,000 of assets and $75,000 of liabilities, the $75,000 of liabilities are, in effect, claims of creditors on the assets of the spa. Equity is the difference between the assets and liabilities, or $25,000. Good revenue performance generates a solid economic condition. Profits generate equity, while losses eat up equity.

We can now state what is known as the **basic** or **fundamental accounting equation**:

$$\text{Assets} = \text{Liabilities} + \text{Owners' Equity}$$

It can also be rearranged and stated as Assets − Liabilities = Owners' Equity.

Two other basic terms you need to understand are revenues and expenses. **Revenues** are inflows of assets resulting from the sale of goods and services to customers, while **expenses** are costs incurred in providing the goods and services offered. The key point is that these terms are related to the actual provision of goods or services. Some cash inflows are not revenues because they are not (yet) related to specific goods or services. A common example is the sale of gift cards. The spa receives payment for the card, but the payment is not *earned* or *recognized* as revenue until the goods or services are provided.

Accrual and Cash Accounting

There are generally two choices a spa can make when setting up an accounting system. It can either report its financial business on a cash basis or an accrual basis.

Cash basis accounting is generally available only to small spas. This method of accounting requires the exchange of cash or cash equivalents before revenue or expenses can be recognized. For example, when a spa takes payment from a customer by way of cash, check, or credit card, it must recognize the revenue for the service or product sold at that time. However, if the service or product is billed to the customer for payment at a later date, the revenue may not be recognized until the invoice is paid. Likewise, if the spa receives a service or buys a product from a supplier and pays by cash, check, or credit card, the expense must be recognized at that time. If the supplier provides the spa with an invoice to be paid at a later date, the spa may not book the expense until the invoice has been paid.

The vast majority of spas will use accrual basis accounting. In fact, in the United States, the IRS requires a business to use the accrual method if it meets one or more of the following conditions:

- The business has inventory.
- The business is a C corporation.
- The gross sales exceed $5 million (although some exceptions to this rule apply).

Accrual accounting is based on when the transaction happens, regardless of whether cash changes hands at that time. Revenue is recorded when it is generated and expenses are counted when incurred. If a group charges today's spa services to a corporate account to be invoiced and paid at a later date, the total sales value of all of their services would be recorded as revenue at the end of the day, even though payment may not be received for several more weeks.

The objective of accounting reports is to accurately represent the financial transactions of a business. If you use the **cash accounting** method and also bill for your services, there can be a delay of weeks, sometimes months, between the delivery of the service and its eventual payment. This leads to a discrepancy between when the service was performed and when the revenue is allowed to be recorded. The accrual method of accounting is more representative of a spa's actual business pattern. For this reason, accountants recommend the accrual method even for most small businesses, including small day spas. However, if a spa is truly a cash operation, then the simpler cash basis accounting method may be suitable.

Fundamental Principles

In order to understand accounting methods, you must understand basic accounting principles. **Generally accepted accounting principles** (often referred to as *GAAP*) provide a uniform basis for preparing financial statements. Although not "etched in stone," accounting principles have become accepted over time through common usage and through the work of such major accounting bodies as the American Institute of Certified Public Accountants, the American Accounting Association, and the Financial Accounting Standards Board (FASB).

Students of spa accounting may often wonder why an accounting transaction is recorded in a particular way at a particular time or why some asset value is not changed at some point. Generally, the reasons relate to accounting principles. The following sections briefly discuss several key principals of *GAAP*.

Cost. The **cost principle** states that when a transaction is recorded, it is the transaction price or cost that establishes the accounting value for the product or service purchased. For example, if a spa buys a microdermabrasion unit, the agreed-upon price between the spa and the supplier determines the amount to be recorded. If the agreed-upon price is $5,000, then the microdermabrasion unit is initially valued at $5,000 in the spa's accounting records. The supplier may have acquired the microdermabrasion unit from the manufacturer for $4,000 and the spa may receive an offer of $5,500 for it the day it is purchased; however, it is the actual cost that establishes the amount to be recorded. If amounts other than cost (such as estimates or appraisals) were used to record transactions, then accounting records would lose their usefulness. When cost is the basis for recording a transaction, the buyer and seller determine the amount to be recorded. This amount is generally an objective and fair measure of the value of the goods or services purchased.

When the value of current assets is clearly less than the cost recorded on the books, this decline in value must be recognized. Thus, the *conservatism principle* (discussed later) overrides the cost principle. On the other hand, property and equipment (called **fixed assets**) are normally carried at cost less depreciated amounts and are not reduced to market value as long as management plans to retain them for their useful life. This treatment of property and equipment is based on the *going-concern principle* (also discussed later).

Business Entity. Accounting and financial statements are based on the concepts that (1) each business is a **business entity** that maintains its own set of accounts and (2) these accounts are separate from the other financial interests of the owners. For example, if a spa owner gives a manager a spa product to take home from the spa for personal use, the spa should charge the cost to the owner's account. Recording business activity separately from the manager's or owner's personal affairs allows a reasonable determination of the spa's profitability. Not only does separate recording provide excellent information for managing the spa, it is also necessary for properly filing tax returns.

Continuity of the Business Unit. According to the **continuity of the business unit principle**, in preparing the accounting records and reports, it is assumed that the spa will continue indefinitely and that liquidation is not in prospect—in other words, the business is a going concern. This assumption is based on the concept that the real value of the spa is its ability to provide services, rather than the value its assets would bring in liquidation. According to this concept, the market value of the property and equipment need not appear on the financial statements, and prepaid expenses are considered assets.

Unit of Measurement. Financial statements are based on transactions expressed in monetary terms. The monetary unit is assumed to represent a stable unit of value, so that transactions from past periods and the current period can be included on the same statement. For example, a U.S. spa that maintains bank accounts in

Exhibit 1 Types of Disclosure

Type of Disclosure	Example
Accounting methods use	Straight-line method of depreciation
Change in the accounting methods	A change from depreciating a fixed asset using the straight-line method to using the double declining balance method
Contingent liability	A lawsuit against the spa for alleged failure to provide adequate security for a member who suffered personal injury
Events occurring after the financial statement date	A fire destroys significant assets of the spa one week after the end of the year
Unusual and nonrecurring items	A spa in Colorado suffers significant losses due to an earthquake

both U.S. dollars and euros will need to convert its euros into U.S. currency at the time the financial statements are generated in order to maintain a constant unit of measure.

Objective Evidence. Accounting transactions and the resulting accounting records should be based on **objective evidence**. This evidence is an invoice and/or a canceled check. However, estimations must occur in the absence of such objective evidence. For example, suppose that the owner of a day spa contributes equipment, purchased several years ago for personal use, to the spa. The owner may believe the equipment is worth $2,000, while the original catalog shows the cost several years ago of $2,500 and an appraiser appraises the equipment at $1,000. In this example, the most objective estimate of its value today would be the appraiser's estimate of $1,000.

Full Disclosure. The financial statements must provide information on all the facts pertinent to the interpretation of the financial statements. This **full disclosure** is accomplished either by reporting the information in the body of the financial statements or in footnotes to the financial statements. Footnote disclosures might include the accounting methods used, changes in accounting methods, contingent liabilities, events occurring after the financial statement date and unusual and nonrecurring items. An example of each type of disclosure is presented in Exhibit 1.

Consistency. Several accounting methods are often available for reporting a specific kind of activity. Spa management chooses the method most appropriate under the circumstances. For example, there are several ways to determine inventory values, and there are several methods of depreciating fixed assets. The **consistency principle** requires that, once an accounting method has been adopted, it should be followed from period to period unless a change is warranted and disclosed.

The consistency principle allows a user of financial information to make reasonable comparisons between periods. Without consistent accounting, trends indicated by supposedly comparable financial statements might be misleading. When it becomes necessary to change to another method, the change must be disclosed and the dollar effect on earnings and/or the statement of financial position must be reported.

Matching. The **matching principle** refers to relating expenses to revenues. Suppose that a spa pays $12,000 for insurance for the year. Since the spa produces monthly financial statements, it would initially record the $12,000 payment as a prepaid asset (a balance sheet account) and on a monthly basis allocate $1,000 to insurance expense. This process is referred to as *matching* and is the basis for adjusting entries at the end of each accounting period. The matching principle is used when transactions are recorded on an accrual rather than cash basis.

Conservatism. The **conservatism principle** calls for recognizing expenses as soon as possible, but delaying the recognition of revenues until they are ensured. The practical result is to be conservative (low) in recognizing an increase in net assets for the current year. It is not proper to deliberately understate an increase in net assets; however, many accountants wish to be cautious in recognizing revenues and "generous" in recognizing expenses.

A good example of this is the accounting treatment of lawsuits. If a spa is a plaintiff in a lawsuit and its legal counsel indicates the case will be won and estimates the amount of settlement, the amount is not recorded as revenue until a judgment is rendered and collection is reasonably assured. On the other hand, if the same spa is a defendant in a lawsuit and its legal counsel indicated the spa will lose the lawsuit and most likely will pay a stated amount, this "expense" is recognized immediately.

Another example of conservatism is apparent in the valuation of inventory at the lower of cost or current market value and the recognition of customer deposits as a liability until the customer uses the spa's services.

Materiality. According to the **materiality principle**, events or information must be accounted for if they "make a difference" to the user of the financial information. An item is material in comparison to a standard. Some accountants have attempted to establish materiality by rules of thumb; for example, an item may be recognized as material if it exceeds a certain percentage of total assets or total income. However, this approach fails to address an item's relative importance over time. In addition, several immaterial items may be material when viewed collectively.

The materiality principle is often applied to property and equipment. Tangible items used to generate revenue with useful lives beyond one year are commonly recorded as property and equipment. However, when such items cost less than a certain amount (specified by the owners of the spa), they are expensed because the cost is considered immaterial. An example would be a wastebasket. A $39 wastebasket might have a useful life of ten years, but if the spa's owner has set a $100 limit for recording expenditures as equipment, the cost of the wastebasket would be immaterial and the wastebasket would be expensed when purchased.

When a spa provides footnotes to supplement its financial statements, only material or potentially material items are presented.

Debits and Credits

In accounting, the financial recording system in which each business transaction affects at least two accounts is called **double-entry accounting**. **Debits** and **credits** are used to record the increases and decreases in each account affected by a business transaction. To debit an account means to record an amount on the left side, while to credit an account means to record an amount on the right side. Asset accounts are increased with debits and decreased with credits and the normal balance is a debit. Under the double-entry system, each transaction results in an equal number of debits and credits to two or more accounts. To visualize this concept, imagine that each account is presented with the letter "T". First, let us look at asset accounts.

ASSET ACCOUNTS

Debit	Credit
+	−
Increase Side Balance Side	Decrease Side

A spa purchases a portable massage table for $800. A check is processed by the spa to pay for the table. The transaction would be recorded by debiting Fixed Assets and crediting Cash. Assume that there was $12,000 of cash in the bank prior to this transaction. The cash and equipment T-accounts would be impacted as follows:

Cash – Checking

12,000	
	800
balance 11,200	

Fixed Assets

800	
balance 800	

Both accounts are assets, as one asset (cash) was exchanged for another asset (massage table). The cash account is decreased with a credit of $800 while the fixed asset account is increased with a debit of $800.

The rules of debits and credits for both Liability and Owners' Equity Accounts are as follows:

Liability and Owners' Equity Accounts

Debit	Credit
−	+
Decrease Side	Increase Side Balance Side

A debit entry decreases Liability and Owners' Equity accounts, while credits increase them. The normal balance is a credit.

Assume a spa entrepreneur invests $100,000 of cash in his/her new spa. The investment would be recorded in the cash (asset) and equity accounts as follows:

Cash	
100,000	
balance 100,000	

Owner's Equity	
	100,000
	100,000 balance

Further assume the same spa entrepreneur borrowed $50,000 from the bank. The amount borrowed would be shown in the cash (asset) and notes payable (liability) accounts as follows:

Cash	
100,000 50,000	
balance 150,000	

Notes payable	
	50,000
	50,000 balance

The three accounts of this spa entrepreneur would be as follows:

	Balances	
	Debit	Credit
Cash (asset)	$150,000	
Notes payable (liability)		$50,000
Owner's equity		100,000
Total	$150,000	$150,000

The total of the liability and owner's equity accounts of $150,000 equals the total of the cash account, an asset.

Daily Operating Summary Reports

While the opening story suggests that there is a single "one size fits all" spa daily closing report, in fact there are dozens of options depending upon the spa software system and the particular reports selected by management. An abundance of choices exists for spa software management systems specializing in the spa and salon industry. While each software system touts various strengths and offers dozens if not hundreds of choices as far as management reporting options, at a minimum, the daily operating reports should adequately report and provide information for four key areas:

- Payment type

- Disposition of payments and spa banking transactions
- Revenue reporting
- Non-revenue reporting and discounts

For the purposes of this text, Exhibits 2 through 4 have been created to articulate the critical data used by management. Additionally, the exhibits will demonstrate the effect that daily transactions of the spa have on the financial statements, which includes the balance sheet and the income statement.

The data used in the **Daily Operating Summary** can originate from various sources; however, the majority are created by the spa front desk and reception employees. These personnel are responsible for direct contact with the spa guest and handle charges, credits, and payments by the guest. This transactional information is usually captured and recorded by the spa software **point-of-sale (POS) system** throughout the day. At the end of the business day, a spa supervisor is generally responsible for running the reports, balancing the spa employee cash deposits to cash on hand, and balancing and verifying payment transactions.

In the case of hotel/resort spas, the daily transaction information captured by the spa may be transmitted directly to the hotel's property management system, which collects financial data from all departments within the hotel. Accounting clerks will validate the data and make entries directly into the cash receipts journal or cash disbursements journal, which in turn distributes those entries into the general ledger system of the hotel/resort.

In the day spa world, it is typically the spa director, assistant, or perhaps the owner who will review the daily operating closing information and transfer it from the POS system into some form of general ledger software system such as QuickBooks or Peachtree. Spa POS systems can be interfaced into the general ledger system so the data is easily transferred. However, in some cases, an accounting clerk may be utilized to enter the data manually.

The exhibits and discussions to follow are provided to demonstrate the critical basics of documenting financial data from the original source through the Daily Operating Summary to the spa financial statements. Financial success in the spa world begins with a clear, concise understanding of the source and flow of the day's financial activities.

Exhibit 2 is designed to include the four key information areas mentioned earlier in this chapter. Manually prepared Daily Operating Summary reports used prior to the proliferation of spa POS software systems generally were designed in one report that included the four key data points. Current POS software systems generally require two or more reports to encompass the information included in Exhibit 2.

Exhibit 3 represents a balance sheet for The Spa and will be used in this chapter to demonstrate the effect of the Daily Operating Summary transactions on the spa's balance sheet. Simply defined, a balance sheet reports the assets, liabilities, and owners' equity of an entity, or, in other words, the financial health of the spa at a given moment in time. Much attention is given in accounting literature to balance sheet reporting for a specific closing period, such as end of month, end of quarter, or end of year. However, for purposes of this text, transactions will be presented

Exhibit 2 Daily Operating Summary for Saturday, August 2, 20X8

Payment Type	Amount
Cash	$ 2,612.96
Check	5,000.00
Visa/Master Card	6,698.25
American Express	7,584.25
Diners Club	289.95
Discover	548.95
Gift Card Redemption	2,510.00
Acct's Receivable Charges	
Resort Guests	10,689.94
Members	3,897.47
Group Master Accounts	4,181.52
Other	–
Total Payments/Charges	$44,013.29
Cash (Over)/Short	(10.00)
Payments Balanced Proof	**$44,003.29**

Revenue	Amount	Treatment Count
Massage & Body Works	$6,500.00	51
Skin Care	4,000.00	39
Hair	2,700.00	45
Nail	3,060.00	68
Fitness	800.00	10
Food and Beverage	223.20	12
Health and Wellness	500.00	10
Membership Sales	5,000.00	1
Membership Dues	2,000.00	7
Day Use Revenue	585.00	10
Retail		
Apparel	695.00	8
Gifts and Accessories	365.00	15
Products	3,160.85	55
Other	–	–
Rentals and Other	1,200.00	8
Total Revenue	**$30,789.05**	

Disposition of Payments	Amount
Deposit to Bank	$ 7,612.96
Batch Control Tickets to Credit Card Processors	15,121.40
Batch Report To Gift Card Processing	2,510.00
Accounts Receivable Detail	18,768.93
Disposition of Payments and Charges	**$44,013.29**

Other Payments and Discounts	Amount	Number
Gratuities collected	$ 3,110.00	220
Sales Tax collected	1,374.24	6.00%
Guest Deposits	6,000.00	12
Gift Card Sales	3,200.00	12
Other	–	–
Promotional Services	(345.00)	1
Guest Comp's	(100.00)	1
Employee Discounts	(25.00)	1
Other Payments	13,214.24	
Total Revenue & Other	**$44,003.29**	

Spa Cash Bank	
Currency	
$20 x 10	$ 200.00
$10 x 20	200.00
$ 5 x 20	100.00
$ 1 x 50	50.00
Assorted Change	50.00
Total Funds-Spa Bank	$ 600.00

as being much more fluid, almost instantaneous, so that the financial statements are constantly being updated with each transaction. Modern technology lends to the fluid nature of the financial statements in such a way that management can be aware of the entity's financial health at any point in time. Exhibit 2 reflects the balance sheet for The Spa at the Luxury Resort used in Exhibit 1.

Exhibit 4 represents a **statement of income** for The Spa and will be used in this chapter to demonstrate the effect of the transactions summarized on the Daily Operating Summary on the spa's statement of income. A statement of income is

Exhibit 3 Balance Sheet For the Day Ended August 2, 20X8

Assets

	Balance, August 1, 20X8	Daily Operating Summary Activity	Balance, August 2, 20X8	
Current Assets				
Cash in Bank	$ 245,600.00	$ 7,612.96	$ 253,212.96	Bank Deposit
Accounts Receivable				
Credit Cards	65,056.00	15,121.40	80,177.40	Batch Control Tickets to Processors
Members	200,000.00	3,897.47	203,897.47	Member Charges
Resort Guests	45,123.00	14,871.46	59,994.46	Guest and Group Master charges
Total Acct's Receivable	310,179.00	33,890.33	344,069.33	
Inventories				
Retail	104,586.00		104,586.00	
Professional	21,564.00		21,564.00	
Other	2,541.00		2,541.00	
Prepaid Expenses	45,127.00		45,127.00	
Deferred Income Taxes, Current	5,421.00		5,421.00	
Other Current Assets	1,000.00		1,000.00	
Total Current Assets	$ 736,018.00	$ 41,503.29	$ 777,521.29	
			–	
Property and Equipment			–	
Land	1,000,000.00		1,000,000.00	
Buildings	4,500,125.00		4,500,125.00	
Leaseholds and Leasehold Improvements	450,000.00		450,000.00	
Construction in Progress	145,236.00		145,236.00	
Furniture, Fixtures and Equipment	1,546,000.00		1,546,000.00	
Automobiles	46,851.00		46,851.00	
Total Property and Equipment	7,688,212.00		7,688,212.00	
Less: Accumulated Depreciation	(1,254,800.00)		(1,254,800.00)	
Net Property and Equipment	6,433,412.00		6,433,412.00	
			–	
Other Assets			–	
Security and Lease Deposits	65,000.00		65,000.00	
Loan Fees	–		–	
Intangibles	100,000.00		100,000.00	
Deferred Income Taxes, Noncurrent	45,125.00		45,125.00	
Other Assets	65,000.00		65,000.00	
Total Other Assets	275,125.00		275,125.00	
			–	
Total Assets	$7,444,555.00	$ 41,503.29	$7,486,058.29	

(continued)

used to report the revenue and expenses of an entity for a defined period of time. That period of time is usually defined as one month, one quarter, six months, or a year. As mentioned earlier, material in this chapter will be presented with entries immediately being shown on the chapter exhibits without regard to date or time frame. As a transaction is generated by the spa, that transaction will simultaneously flow to the Daily Operating Summary and then directly to the statement of income.

Exhibit 3 *(continued)*

Liabilities and Owners' Equity

	Balance, August 1, 20X8	Daily Operating Summary Activity	Balance, August 2, 20X8	
Current Liabilities				
Accounts Payable	$ 25,685.00		$ 25,685.00	
Sales Tax Payable	1,149.00	$ 1,374.24	2,523.00.24	Sales Tax Collected on behalf of taxing entities
Gratuities Payable	2,856.00	3,110.00	5,966.00	Gratuities collected on behalf of staff
Current Portion of Long-Term Debt	55,000.00		55,000,00	
Income Taxes Payable	85,000.00		85,000.00	
Accrued Expenses	45,235.00		45,235.00	
Deferred Revenue—Gift Certificates	210,300.00	690.00	210,990.00	Net of 3,200 sold—2,510 redeemed
Customer Deposits	45,600.00	6,000.00	51,600.00	Customer Deposits received
Deferred Income Taxes-Current	15,252.00		15,252.00	
Other Current Liabilities	5,635.00		5,635.00	
Total Current Liabilities	491,712.00	11,174.24	502,886.24	
			–	
Long-Term Liabilities			–	
Notes Payable	1,500,000.00	–	1,500,000.00	
Total Long-Term Liabilities	1,500,000.00		1,500,000.00	
			–	
Owners' Equity			–	
Common Stock	4,000,000.00	–	4,000,000.00	
Retained Earnings	1,452,843.00	30,329.05	1,483,172.05	Net Income for day carried forward from income statement
Total Owners Equity	5,452,843.00	30,329.05	5,483,172.05	
			–	
Total Liabilities and Owners' Equity	$7,444,555.00	$ 41,503.29	$7,486,058.29	

Payment Type

Guests enjoying services at either a day spa or hotel/resort spa compensate the spa for the services rendered and merchandise purchased in a variety of ways. In a hotel/resort environment, the guest usually has a choice of payment via cash, credit card, charging to their room, or, if they are part of a group, the group master account. As a general rule, day spa guests pay the spa immediately after receiving the service or purchasing merchandise. Types of payment include cash, check, credit cards, gift card redemptions, and accounts receivable or membership charges.

Some spas sell memberships, including those with an initiation fee and monthly dues, annual memberships sold for a period of one year, and some simply with the payment of monthly dues. Some memberships are acquired with the payment of a fee designated as an "initiation fee," which is revenue received via a one-time, non-refundable fee that a spa charges for activating a membership and

Exhibit 4 Statement of Income for the Day Ended August 2, 20X8

	Daily Operating Summary		
	August 1, 20X8	August 2, 20X8	Month to Date
Net Revenue			
Massage	$ 4,750.00	$ 6,500.00	$ 11,250.00
Skin Care	3,000.00	4,000.00	7,000.00
Hair	1,800.00	2,700.00	4,500.00
Nail	2,485.00	3,060.00	5,545.00
Fitness	700.00	800.00	1,500.00
Food and Beverage	285.00	223.20	508.20
Health and Wellness	600.00	500.00	1,100.00
Memberships	3,400.00	7,000.00	10,400.00
Retail	3,684.00	4,220.85	7,905.85
Rentals and Other	800.00	1,200.00	2,000.00
Other Operating Activities	415.00	585.00	1,000.00
Less: Guest and Employee Discounts & Comps		(125.00)	(125.00)
Total Net Revenue	$ 21,919.00	$ 30,664.05	$ 52,583.05
Cost of Goods and Direct Expenses			
Massage	–	–	–
Skin Care	–	–	–
Hair	–	–	–
Nail	–	–	–
Fitness	–	–	–
Food and Beverage	–	–	–
Health and Wellness	–	–	–
Retail	–	–	–
Other Operating Activities	–	–	–
Total Direct Expenses	–	–	–
Gross Margin	21,919.00	30,664.05	52,583.05
Indirect Expenses			
Indirect Operating Expenses		(10.00)	(10.00)
Indirect Support Labor	–	–	–
Total Indirect Expenses	–	(10.00)	(10.00)
Undistributed Operating Expenses			
General and Administrative	–	–	–
Marketing	–	345.00	345.00
Facility Maintenance and Utilities	–	–	–
Total Undistrib. Operating Expenses	–	345.00	345.00
Income Before Fixed Charges	21,919.00	30,329.05	52,248.05

Exhibit 4 *(continued)*

Fixed Charges			
Insurance	–	–	–
Management Fees	–	–	–
Rent	–	–	–
Real Estate/Personal Property Taxes	–	–	–
Total Fixed Charges	–	–	–
Income Before Depreciation, Amortization, Interest Expense, & Income Taxes	21,919.00	30,329.05	52,248.05
Depreciation and Amortization	–	–	–
Interest Expense	–	–	–
(Gain) and Loss on Disposal of Property	–	–	–
Total	–	–	–
Income Before Income Taxes	21,919.00	30,329.05	52,248.05
Income Taxes	–	–	–
Net Income	$ 21,919.00	$ 30,329.05	$ 52,248.05

orientating the new member. They are generally recognized as revenue when the membership is sold. However, if the profit from initiation fees represents a substantial portion of the overall profit to be earned from a member (from initiation fees, ongoing dues and service, and merchandise purchased) then the initiation fee shall be deferred and recognized over the weighted life of the membership rather than at the time the membership is sold. In certain cases, the spa membership may be refundable, based on years of membership, ability to resell, exclusivity, etc. For the purposes of this example, with the initiation fee of $5,000 the revenue will be recognized immediately and not deferred. If it were a larger amount, such as $15,000, The Spa would clearly record the membership sale on the balance sheet as an asset and report a specified amount of the fee each month as revenue over several months or years. These fees must be clearly identified as such on the membership agreement. The member is likely also responsible for a predetermined amount of monthly "dues" that covers certain uses of the spa, club, or resort. On this particular day, membership dues billed totaled $2,000.

Daily Operating Summary			**Statement of Income**	
Revenue			Net revenue	
Membership Sales	$ 5,000.00			
Membership Dues	$ 2,000.00		Memberships	$ 7,000.00

When a member uses a spa service, such as a personal trainer, or buys merchandise, his or her member account is charged for the purchases and he or she is billed monthly for all service provided and/or merchandise purchased. To remain in good standing and to continue receipt of services, the member must pay the monthly billing within a designated period of time. In many cases, the member is required to keep a credit card on file to guarantee payment of the monthly amounts due for services, merchandise, and dues. On this day the members are charged $3,897.00 to their accounts.

Daily Operating Summary			**Balance Sheet**	
Payment Type			Accounts Receivable	
Accounts Receivable Charges				
Members	$ 3,897.00		Members	$ 3,897.00

Many destination and resort spas require a deposit by check or credit card in order to book a one- or several-day spa packages. These charges represent prepaid deposits to the spa until the guest arrives and uses the package reserved. On August 2, there were twelve guest deposits totaling $6,000. Even though The Spa received the $6,000 on August 2, it may not record the amount as revenue until the package is used. Thus it is recorded as a Liability on the balance sheet.

Daily Operating Summary			**Balance Sheet**	
Payment Type			Current Liabilities	
Recorded within the proper credit card account	$ 6,000.00		Customer Deposits	$ 6,000.00

Please see Exhibit 2. Under Payment Type, on August 2, 20X8, The Spa reported receiving $2,612.96 in cash and $5,000.00 in checks.

Daily Operating Summary			**Balance Sheet**	
Payment Type			Current Assets	
Cash	$ 2,612.96		Cash in Bank	$ 7,612.96
Check	$ 5,000.00			

Credit card transactions for card types including Visa/Master Card, American Express, Diners Club, and Discover were processed in various amounts that totaled $15,121.40.

Daily Operating Summary			**Balance Sheet**	
Payment Type			Current Assets	
Visa/Master Card	$ 6,698.25			
American Express	$ 7,584.25			
Diners Club	$ 289.95			
Discover	$ 548.95		Credit Cards	$15,121.40

Gifts of spa services are very popular, particularly for certain holidays including Mother's Day, Valentine's Day, and Christmas. Generally, the donor purchases a specific prepaid amount, or the cost for a specific treatment or package, from the spa, and that amount is recorded on a certificate or an electronically formatted gift card. After receiving the spa services, the donor uses the gift card or certificate to pay the spa. On August 2, 20X8, The Spa redeemed $2,510.00 in electronically formatted gift card funds.

Daily Operating Summary			**Balance Sheet**			**Statement of Income**
Payment Type			Deferred Revenue			Revenues
			Gift Certificates			
Gift Card Redemption	$2,510.00			($2,510.00)		Redemption will be recorded as revenue

Most importantly, the sale of a gift certificate/card is not recorded as revenue at the time of sale. It is recorded instead as Deferred Revenue Gift Certificates on the balance sheet as a Current Liability. Upon rendering the services, the deferred revenue is reclassified as actual revenue as shown previously. On this particular day The Spa sold twelve gift certificates in the amount of $3,200.

Daily Operating Summary		**Balance Sheet**	
Payment Type: The amount paid would be recorded under the appropriate credit card, cash, or check line		Current Liabilities	
		Deferred Revenue—Gift	$ 3,200.00
		The redemption of $2,510 and the sale of $3,200 are net for a total of $690 on the balance sheet.	

The Spa is part of The Luxury Resort, which includes 350 guest rooms, a golf course, several restaurants, and memberships of local residents. Resort guests charged $10,689.94 to their guest room accounts on August 2. While some resort guests will settle their spa charges at the spa following their treatments using a credit card or other form of payment, others will choose to sign their charges to their guest room account and settle all charges incurred during their stay upon checking out.

Daily Operating Summary			**Statement of Income**	
Payment Type			Net Revenue	
Resort Room Charges	$10,689.94		Charges will be recorded in appropriate revenue line	

It is very common for a resort property to host groups such as XYZ Corporation providing an incentive trip for the top sales producers. The group organizers will establish a specifically coded Master Account to which attendees will charge room and tax and approved incidental charges including any spa treatment provided. On August 2, 20X8, XYZ group attendees charged $4,181.52 of spa services to the Master Account.

Daily Operating Summary			**Statement of Income**	
Payment Type			Net Revenue	
Group Master Accounts	$ 4,181.52		Charges will be recorded in appropriate revenue line	

At the end of each day, the spa employee responsible for running the end of day reports will print out a report detailing the above transaction activity. The Daily Operating Summary (Exhibit 2) is depicted in summary amounts; however, the employee will have available various detail reports that will describe every spa transaction for the day. For example, the receipt of the $2,612.96 in cash has detailed reports by guest, by service rendered, time of day, the spa employee who processed the transaction, and even which terminal the transaction was posted on, all of which support the Total Payments Charges on the Daily Operations Summary. Total payments by guests of The Spa amounted to $44,013.29 on August 2, 20X8. The disposition of the Payments section of the summary report describes the mechanics of disposing of those payments into the financial reporting system.

Contemporaneous with the running of the Payment Type Reports, the employee will count and verify the spa employee cash bank/banks and compare the actual cash deposited to the cash receipts reported. Depending on the size of the spa, cash banks will be handled in one of two ways: either each guest reception agent will have an assigned personal bank and work out of a separate cash drawer or the desk staff will receive cash and make change out of a single cash drawer bank. In the case of individual employee banks, each guest reception agent will run the cash report for their personal employee code and be responsible for matching payments to cash postings and preparing an individual deposit. In the case of a common spa cash bank, the closing employee will run a summary cash report and count the cash and checks. In a small day spa a deposit ticket will be prepared to transmit the cash deposit to the spa's local retail bank. The employee will then drop the deposit into a night safe, or may transport the deposit directly to a night deposit at the spa's retail bank. In a hotel spa situation, the spa deposits will be dropped in the hotel general cashier drop box. The general cashier will then verify each employee deposit envelope from the hotel front desk, restaurants, spa, and so on, and prepare an overall bank deposit and store the funds in the vault to be picked up by an armored car service. In either case, a discrepancy in the physical bank count and cashiers report(s) will be researched at length and if unresolved will be reported as Cash Over/Short. The Spa reported an overage of $10, which carried to the statement of income—Indirect Operating Expenses.

Daily Operating Summary			**Statement of Income**	
Payment Type				
Cash (Over)/Short	$ (10.00)		Indirect Operating Expenses	$ (10.00)

Disposition of Payments and Spa Banking

Please see Exhibit 3. Note the deposit amount of $7,612.96 in the Daily Operating Summary Activity column on the line item Cash in Bank. Cash in Bank total was increased by that amount.

Credit card payments that are processed by the spa for payment are pre-approved electronically by a credit card processing vendor. At the end of the business day, all charges approved must be processed in a "batch" and remitted to the vendor for collection and payment to the spa's retail bank. The vendor charges the spa an agreed-upon fee for the approval, collection, and remittance function. On August 2, 20X8, The Spa batched and transmitted $15,121.40 to its credit card vendor for collection. It is important to understand that until the credit card processor collects the funds and deposits those funds to the spa's retail bank, the credit card payments are an account receivable. This amount was transmitted on August 2, 20X8 and appears under the Daily Operating Summary Activity column for the day.

Gift cards can either be handled and accounted for by the spa itself or outsourced to a gift card–processing vendor that will maintain an inventory of active cards, card balances, etc. If handled by the spa, most POS software systems are able to track the sale and redemption of gift cards. Regardless of the method used to track the sale and redemption, the redemption reclassifies Deferred Revenue—Gift Certificates to Revenue. On August 2, 20X8, The Spa redeemed $2,510 in gift cards. The $2,510 is recorded on the balance sheet, effectively reducing the liability and increasing revenue. On the same day The Spa sold $3,200 in new Gift Card sales. You will note that the balance sheet reflects the net of $2,510 redeemed and $3,200 of new gift certificates sold. If a gift card vendor is used, the spa employees will forward the names, contact information, and amounts to the processing vendor.

Daily Operating Summary			**Balance Sheet**	
Disposition of Payments			Current Assets	
Deposit to Bank	$ 7,612.96		Cash in Bank	$ 7,612.96
Batch Control Tickets to Credit Card Processor	$15,121.40		Accounts Receivable	
			Credit Cards	$15,121.40
Batch Report to Gift Card Processing	$ 2,510.00		Current Liabilities	
Gift Card Sales	$ 3,200.00		Deferred Revenue	
			Gift Certificates	$ 690.00

All accounts receivable charges, whether Resort Guests, Members, or Group Master Accounts, are detailed by guest and charged to their individual accounts on the appropriate accounts receivable ledger. The total of the charges carried to the balance sheet of the spa on August 2, 20X8, as additions to Current Assets, were $3,897.47 in Member Charges and $14,871.00 in Resort Guest Charges.

Daily Operating Summary			**Balance Sheet**	
Acct.'s Receivable Charges			Current Assets	
			Accounts Receivable	
Members	$ 3,897.47		Members	$ 3,897.47
Group Master Acct.	$ 4,181.52			
Resort Guests	$10,689.94		Resort Guests	$14,871.46

An additional section of the Disposition of Payments portion of the Daily Operating Summary is the Spa Bank. The spa or each employee who is "banked" will retain a certain amount of coin and paper currency in the individual or check-out bank. The Spa Bank cash-on-hand amounts are established as part of the internal controls of the spa. Variations of the report include starting cash balance, additional cash received during the day, less any disbursements from the spa employee cash bank (in day spas and some hotel spas it will be customary to implement a "petty cash" process to pay cash for small deliveries as a "paid out" voucher from the individual employee bank/s rather than writing frequent small checks for incidental purchases). The amount remaining consists of the ending balance of the spa cash banks, paid out vouchers, plus any cash (over)/short.

Spa Cash Bank	
Currency	
\$20 × 10	\$200.00
\$10 × 20	200.00
\$ 5 × 20	100.00
\$ 1 × 50	50.00
Assorted Change	50.00
Total Funds Spa Bank	\$ 600.00

Revenue Reporting

The *Uniform System of Financial Reporting for Spas* establishes numerous classifications of revenue and will be presented to meet the needs of each individual spa. It is important to understand that the information detailed under the "Revenue" section of Exhibit 2 is reported in many different manners by various POS software systems. Many ratios will be calculated from the data to provide management with meaningful information. The well-rounded, experienced spa director will be adept at understanding and managing all four sections of the Daily Operating Summary.

Total revenue of The Spa for August 2, 20X8, was \$30,789.05. Included in the various classifications are spa treatment revenues of \$10,500 (total massage and skin care), salon revenues of \$5,760 (hair and nail services), the sale of a membership initiation fee of \$5,000, and member dues paid of \$2,000. Note that the revenue reported on the Daily Operating Summary is recorded on the statement of income for The Spa for the line items under Net Revenue in the column Daily Operating Summary for August 2, 20X8 (Exhibit 3).

Non-Revenue Reporting and Discounts

In the course of daily operations, discounts will be given to employees, spa guests, occasional VIPs, or journalists. These miscellaneous adjustments are captured in the Other Payments and Discounts section of the Daily Operating Summary.

Daily Operating Summary			Statement of Income	
Revenue			Net Revenue	
Massage & Bodywork	$ 6,500.00		Massage	$ 6,500.00
Skin Care	$ 4,000.00		Skin Care	$ 4,000.00
Hair	$ 2,700.00		Hair	$ 2,700.00
Nail	$ 3,060.00		Nail	$ 3,060.00
Fitness	$ 800.00		Fitness	$ 800.00
Food and Beverage	$ 223.20		Food and Beverage	$ 223.20
Health and Wellness	$ 500.00		Health and Wellness	$ 500.00
Membership Sales	$ 5,000.00		Membership Sales	$ 5,000.00
Membership Dues	$ 2,000.00		Membership Dues	$ 2,000.00
Apparel	$ 695.00			
Gifts and Accessories	$ 365.00			
Products	$ 3,160.85		Retail Sales	$ 4,220.85
Day Use Revenue	$ 585.00		Day Use Fees	$ 585.00
Rentals and Other	$ 1,200.00		Other Revenue	$ 1,200.00
			Less Guest & Employee	
			Discounts and Comps	$ (125.00)
Total Revenue	$30,789.05			
Less:				
Guest Comps	$ 100.00			
Employee Discount	$ 25.00			
Total Revenue	$30,664.05		Total New Revenue	$30,664.05

Gratuities and Service Charges

The receiving of gratuities by spa therapists from spa guests is very common in the world of spa and represents a significant portion of a therapist's compensation. The method of giving and accounting for the gratuity is varied. It can include cash gratuities, addition to the bill at the discretion of the guest, or a mandatory fixed percentage of the service, known as an automatic service charge. Regardless of the methodology, the spa serves as a repository of the non-cash gratuity until subsequently paid to the therapist. Exhibit 2 details $3,110 in gratuities collected on behalf of The Spa therapists. That balance sheet (Exhibit 3) reflects the addition of the $3,110 to current Liabilities—Gratuities Payable.

Operational Summary			Balance Sheet	
Other Payments and Discounts			Current Liabilities	
Gratuities Collected	$ 3,110.00		Gratuities Payable	$ 3,110.00

It will vary by location, but generally state, municipal and local governments impose a sales tax upon retail and service establishments, including spas, that operate within their jurisdiction. The spa is responsible for levying and collecting sales taxes on services and merchandise sales that are subject to the tax. The tax collected at the point of sale is held "in trust" until a designated tax filing and payment date mandated by law. Either prior to or on the due date, the sales tax funds that have been held "in trust" are paid to the appropriate governmental agency. Exhibit 2A reflects Sales Tax collections of $1,374.24 on August 2, 20X8. The corresponding entry to the balance sheet (Exhibit 3) is shown as an addition to Current Liabilities—Sales Tax Payable.

Daily Operating Summary			**Balance Sheet**	
			Current Liabilities	
Sales Tax Collected	$ 1,374.24		Sales Tax Payable	$ 1,374.24

Revenue from any service provided by a spa service provider will be recorded in the Revenue Portion of the Daily Operating Summary and in the appropriate therapy classification of the statement of income. There are, however, times that the spa may provide services free of charge to a person visiting the hotel for a site inspection as it considers the hotel/resort for a future event or for journalists who may be publishing a story about the spa. On this date The Spa provided promotional services, in the amount of $345, to a regional newspaper journalist who was working on a spa vacations story.

Operational Summary			**Undistributed Operating Expenses**	
Other Payments and Discounts				
Promotional Services	$ (345.00)		Marketing	$ 345.00

Exhibit 2 shows that Guest Deposits were collected totaling $6,000 on August 2, 20X8, as a result of guests reserving blocks of time at the resort spa. The balance sheet (Exhibit 3) carries the $6,000 as an addition to Current Liabilities—Customer Deposits. When the guest completes his or her visit to the spa, the Customer Deposit amount will be credited against charges for services.

The Spa sold $3,200 in gift cards on August 2, 20X8. The balance sheet (Exhibit 3) nets the sales against the redemptions of $2,510 on the line item Deferred Revenue—Gift Certificates. Additionally, the spa employees will remit the names, contact information and amounts to the gift card processing vendor, if needed.

On August 2, 20X8, The Spa provided promotional services to a local news reporter in the amount of $345, gave a complaining guest a "comp" of $100, and the spa director received a $25 discount on the purchase of merchandise (see Exhibit 2).

The discount and comp totaling $125 are carried to the statement of income—Net Revenue line Less: Guest and Employee Discounts & Comps. The

Exhibit 5 Documents and Transactions

	Documents	
Type of Transaction	Prepared by Spa	Prepared Outside of Spa
Sales of products and services	Guest check	–
Cash receipts	Cash register tape	Checks
Purchases of products and services	Purchase order	Suppliers' invoices
Payroll	Time cards	–
	Payroll checks	
Cash disbursements	Check	–

$345 in services for the news reporter is reported in the statement of income under Undistributed Operating Expenses—Marketing Expenses (Exhibit 4).

The Accounting Cycle

In every accounting period (generally one month), an **accounting cycle** begins, starting with recording transactions and ending with a post-closing **trial balance**, explained in step 9 below. Each step in the cycle will be defined and discussed briefly. For purposes of clarity, the steps are presented as if each step were being performed manually. However, most of today's accounting software is capable of performing all steps instantaneously. Additionally, the accounting period can be thought of as a day, a week, a month or any desired period, because the software has the capability to record, process and post transactions in real time.

There are five common transactions in a spa operation:

1. Sales of products and services—Usually captured by a POS software system that integrates and posts seamlessly into the accounts.
2. Cash receipts—Usually captured by a POS software system that integrates into the accounts with automatic or semiautomatic posting.
3. Purchases of products and services—Originates with a Purchase Order/Inventory system that integrates into the **accounts payable** system, POS system and accounts of the spa.
4. Payroll—Usually originates from a payroll system module that integrates into the accounts.
5. Cash disbursements—Accounts payable system integrates and posts to the accounts.

With each transaction, documents are prepared and/or received from which the responsible person will record the transaction. These types of transactions are generally known as *original entry transactions*, because they originate from an original document or transaction. Accountants and spa staff should focus on the accuracy of the original entry documents in order to eliminate adjustments at a later date. Exhibit 5 lists a few key documents for each type of transaction.

Step 1 in the accounting cycle is recording the transactions in journals. **Journals** are simply books used for initially recording individual transactions. There is generally a separate journal (generically called a specialized journal) for each type of transaction. Examples include a cash receipts journal and a cash disbursements journal. In addition, each establishment maintains a general journal for recording entries not recorded in specialized journals. The process of recording requires that each transaction be analyzed and that a minimum of two accounts be affected, as mentioned earlier in our discussion of "T" accounts. For example, a cash sales transaction results in an increase to the cash account (debit) and an increase to the sales account (credit).

Step 2 in the accounting cycle is transferring the amounts from the journals to the ledger accounts. The ledger accounts, commonly known as the *general ledger,* comprise all the accounts that are used in the spa's accounting system. A discussion and illustration of the General Ledger accounts is included in Section 12 in the *Uniform System of Financial Reporting for Spas*. Another way of thinking about the general ledger is that it contains every account that makes up the assets = liabilities + owners' equity equation. A simple listing of the accounts is known as the *chart of accounts*. This process, called posting, changes the balance of individual accounts. For example, assume that cash at the beginning of the period is $1,000, cash receipts for the month total $50,000 (per the cash receipts journal), and cash disbursements equal $45,000 (per the cash disbursements journal). The general ledger cash account after these postings would show the following:

CASH

Date	**Posting Reference**	**Debit**	**Credit**	**Balance**
Bal.		1,000		1,000
EOM	CR	50,000		51,000
EOM	CD		45,000	6,000

Normally, the columns of each specialized journal are totaled and these totals are posted to the proper accounts at the end of the month (EOM). Software systems often give the option of posting totals or posting individual transactions to the accounts. Amounts recorded in the general journal, however, are posted individually. The example shows posting references of CR for the cash receipts journal and CD for the cash disbursements journal. The beginning cash balance of $1,000 increased to $6,000 by the end of the month because $50,000 was received and $45,000 disbursed.

Step 3 in the accounting cycle is preparing a trial balance. The trial balance is simply a listing of all account balances, with debit balance accounts and credit balance accounts in separate columns. The totals of each column should be equal and prove the equality of debits and credits. Exhibit 6 presents the hypothetical The Spa trial balance for the period ending August 2, 20X8. Notice that the debit and credit columns both total $8,699,355.

Step 4 in the accounting cycle is preparing adjusting entries. Adjusting entries are required to adjust accounts to reflect the proper account balances or to adjust accounts that are not automatically posted from various subsidiary ledgers, such

Exhibit 6 The Spa Trial Balance

The Spa at the Luxury Resort Trial Balance As of August 1, 20X8		
	Debits	**Credits**
Cash in Bank	$ 245,600.00	
Accounts Receivable		
Credit Cards	65,056.00	
Members	200,000.00	
Resort Guests	45,123.00	
Inventories		
Retail	104,586.00	
Professional	21,564.00	
Other	2,541.00	
Prepaid Expenses	45,127.00	
Deferred Income Taxes, Current	5,421.00	
Other Current Assets	1,000.00	
Land	1,000,000.00	
Buildings	4,500,125.00	
Leaseholds and Leasehold Improvements	450,000.00	
Construction in Progress	145,236.00	
Furniture, Fixtures, and Equipment	1,546,000.00	
Automobiles	46,851.00	
Less: Accumulated Depreciation		$1,254,800.00
Security and Lease Deposits	65,000.00	
Loan Fees	–	
Intangibles	100,000.00	
Deferred Income Taxes, Noncurrent	45,125.00	
Other Assets	65,000.00	
Accounts Payable		25,685.00
Sales Tax Payable		1,149.00
Gratuities Payable		2,856.00
Current Portion of Long-Term Debt		55,000.00
Income Taxes Payable		85,000.00
Accrued Expenses		45,235.00
Deferred Revenue—Gift Certificates		210,300.00
Customer Deposits		45,600.00
Deferred Income Taxes—Current		15,252.00
Other Current Liabilities		5,635.00
Notes Payable		1,500,000.00
Common Stock		4,000,000.00
Retained Earnings		1,430,924.00

Exhibit 6 *(continued)*

Revenue		
Massage		4,750.00
Skin Care		3,000.00
Hair		1,800.00
Nail		2,485.00
Fitness		700.00
Food and Beverage		285.00
Health and Wellness		600.00
Memberships		3,400.00
Retail		3,684.00
Rental and Other		800.00
Other Operating Activities		415.00
Less: Guest and Employee Discounts & Comps		
Cost of Sales		
Massage		
Skin Care		
Hair		
Nail		
Fitness		
Food and Beverage		
Health and Wellness		
Retail		
Other Operating Activities		
Indirect Operating Expenses		
Indirect Support Labor		
General and Administrative		
Marketing		
Facility Maintenance and Utilities		
Insurance		
Management Fees		
Rent		
Real Estate/Personal Property Taxes		
Depreciation and Amortization		
Interest Expense		
(Gain) and Loss on Disposal of Property		
	$8,699,355.00	$ 8,699,355.00

as payroll, accounts payable, etc. The adjusting entries are recorded in the general journal at the end of the accounting period. The major categories of adjusting entries, along with examples, are shown in Exhibit 7.

Step 5 is posting the adjusting entries. All adjusting entries are posted individually from the general journal. All adjustments are different, so there are no common accounts affected by the adjustments (in contrast to the entries recorded in specialized journals).

Exhibit 7 Major Categories of Adjusting Entries

Category	Examples	Accounts Debited	Accounts Credited
1. Prepaid expense	a. Reduction of prepaid insurance	Insurance Expense	Prepaid Insurance
	b. Reduction of prepaid rent	Rent Expense	Prepaid Rent
2. Accrued expense	a. Accrual of payroll	Payroll Expense	Accrued Payroll
	b. Accrual of interest expense on a note payable	Interest Expense	Interest Payable
3. Unearned revenue	Reduction of deferred rent	Deferred Rent	Rental Revenue
4. Accrued revenue	Accrual of interest earned on note receivable	Interest Receivable	Interest Income
5. Estimated items	Depreciation expense	Depreciation Expense	Accumulated Depreciation, Property, and Equipment
6. Inventory adjustment	Recording of ending inventory value from physical inventory. (Note: Other account balances such as Purchases are also transferred to the Cost of Goods Sold account.)	Inventory end of month	Cost of Goods Sold

Step 6 in the accounting cycle is preparing an adjusted trial balance. After the adjusting entries are posted to the accounts, an adjusted trial balance is prepared to once again test the equality of debit and credit accounts. This process may be facilitated by using a worksheet (see Exhibit 8).

Step 7 is the preparation of the financial statements. Using a worksheet approach, the accountant simply extends all figures from the adjusted trial balance to the proper columns on the statement of income and balance sheet. Exhibit 8 reveals the difference between the debit and credit columns under the statement of income, which results in an increase in net assets. For The Spa revenues of $52,718 exceeded expenses of $1,345, resulting in an increase in net assets of $51,373. The increase in net assets of $51,373 added to the total credits of $8,689,360 (balance sheet columns) equals total debits of $8,740,733 (balance sheet).

Again, it is very important to understand that software systems generally process the above steps automatically. The "original entry" is entered into the journal and post to subsidiary ledgers, such as payroll and to the general ledger account. Trial balances and working trial balances are then updated.

Exhibit 8 Working Trial Balance

The Spa
at the Luxury Resort
Working Trial Balance
As of August 2, 20X8

Account Title	August 1 Trial Balance		Daily Summary Transactions—August 2		August 2 Trial Balance		Adjustments			Adjusted Trial Balance		Statement of Income		Balance Sheet	
	Debits	Credits	Debits	Credits	Debits	Credits	Debits	Credits		Debits	Credits	Debits	Credits	Debits	Credits
Cash in Bank	$ 245,600		$ 7,612		$ 253,212	$ –				$ 253,212	$ –			$ 253,212	$ –
Accounts Receivable					–	–				–	–			–	–
Credit Cards	65,056		15,121		80,177	–				80,177	–			80,177	–
Members	200,000		3,897		203,897	–				203,897	–			203,897	–
Resort Guests	45,123		14,873		59,996	–				59,996	–			59,996	–
Inventories					–	–				–	–			–	–
Retail	104,586				104,586	–				104,586	–			104,586	–
Professional	21,564				21,564	–				21,564	–			21,564	–
Other	2,541				2,541	–				2,541	–			2,541	–
Prepaid Expenses	45,127				45,127	–		125	(a)	45,002				45,002	–
Deferred Income Taxes, Current	5,421				5,421	–				5,421	–			5,421	–
Other Current Assets	1,000				1,000	–				1,000	–			1,000	–
Land	1,000,000				1,000,000	–				1,000,000	–			1,000,000	–
Buildings	4,500,125				4,500,125	–				4,500,125	–			4,500,125	–
Leaseholds and Leasehold Improvements	450,000				450,000	–				450,000	–			450,000	–
Construction in Progress	145,236				145,236	–				145,236	–			145,236	–
Furniture, Fixtures, and Equipment	1,546,000				1,546,000	–				1,546,000	–			1,546,000	–
Automobiles	46,851				46,851	–				46,851	–			46,851	–
Less: Accumulated Depreciation		1,254,800			–	1,254,800		750	(b)	–	1,255,550			–	1,255,550
Security and Lease Deposits	65,000				65,000	–				65,000	–			65,000	–
Loan Fees					–	–				–	–			–	–
Intangibles	100,000				100,000	–				100,000	–			100,000	–
Deferred Income Taxes, Noncurrent	45,125				45,125	–				45,125	–			45,125	–
Other Assets	65,000				65,000	–				65,000	–			65,000	–
Accounts Payable		25,685			–	25,685				–	25,685			–	25,685
Sales Tax Payable		1,149		1,374	–	2,523				–	2,523			–	2,523
Gratuities Payable		2,856		3,110	–	5,966				–	5,966			–	5,966
Current Portion of Long-Term Debt		55,000			–	55,000				–	55,000			–	55,000
Income Taxes Payable		85,000			–	85,000				–	85,000			–	85,000
Accrued Expenses		45,235			–	45,235				–	45,235			–	45,235
Deferred Revenue—Gift Certificates		210,300	2,510	3,200		210,990				–	210,990			–	210,990
Customer Deposits		45,600		6,000	–	51,600				–	51,600			–	51,600
Deferred Income Taxes—Current		15,252			–	15,252				–	15,252			–	15,252
Other Current Liabilities		5,635			–	5,635				–	5,635			–	5,635
Notes Payable		1,500,000			–	1,500,000				–	1,500,000			–	1,500,000
Common Stock		4,000,000			–	4,000,000				–	4,000,000			–	4,000,000
Retained Earnings		1,430,924			–	1,430,924				–	1,430,924			–	1,430,924

(continued)

Exhibit 8 *(continued)*

Account Title	August 1 Trial Balance		Daily Summary Transactions—August 2		August 2 Trial Balance		Adjustments			Adjusted Trial Balance		Statement of Income		Balance Sheet	
	Debits	Credits	Debits	Credits	Debits	Credits	Debits	Credits		Debits	Credits	Debits	Credits	Debits	Credits
Revenue					–	–				–	–				
Massage		4,750		6,500	–	11,250				–	11,250	–	11,250		
Skin Care		3,000		4,000	–	7,000				–	7,000	–	7,000		
Hair		1,800		2,700	–	4,500				–	4,500	–	4,500		
Nail		2,485		3,060	–	5,545				–	5,545	–	5,545		
Fitness		700		800	–	1,500				–	1,500	–	1,500		
Food and Beverage		285		223	–	508				–	508	–	508		
Health and Wellness		600		500	–	1,100				–	1,100	–	1,100		
Memberships		3,400		7,000	–	10,400				–	10,400	–	10,400		
Retail		3,684		4,221	–	7,905				–	7,905	–	7,905		
Rental and Other		800		1,200	–	2,000				–	2,000	–	2,000		
Other Operating Activities		415		585	–	1,000				–	1,000	–	1,000		
Less: Discounts & Comps			125		125	–				125	–	125	–		
Cost of Sales					–	–				–	–	–	–		
Massage					–	–				–	–	–	–		
Skin Care					–	–				–	–	–	–		
Hair					–	–				–	–	–	–		
Nail					–	–				–	–	–	–		
Fitness					–	–				–	–	–	–		
Food and Beverage					–	–				–	–	–	–		
Health and Wellness					–	–				–	–	–	–		
Retail					–	–				–	–	–	–		
Other Operating Activities					–	–				–	–	–	–		
Indirect Operating Expenses				10	–	10				–	10	–	10		
Indirect Support Labor					–	–				–	–	–	–		
General and Administrative					–	–				–	–	–	–		
Marketing			345		345	–				345	–	345	–		
Facility Maintenance and Utilities					–	–				–	–	–	–		
Insurance					–	–	125		(a)	125	–	125	–		
Management Fees					–	–				–	–	–	–		
Rent					–	–				–	–	–	–		
Real Estate/Personal Property Taxes					–	–				–	–	–	–		
Depreciation and Amortization					–	–	750		(b)	750	–	750	–		
Interest Expense					–	–				–	–	–	–		
(Gain)/ Loss on Disposal of Property					–	–				–	–	–	–		
												1,345	52,718	8,740,733	8,689,360
												51,373			51,373
	$8,699,355	$8,699,355	$ 44,483	$ 44,483	$8,741,328	$8,741,328	$ 875	$ 875		$8,742,078	$8,742,078	$ 52,718	$ 52,718	$8,740,733	$8,740,733

Note: All amounts are shown in this exhibit to the nearest $1.

The accountant then prepares a formal statement of income and balance sheet in accordance with GAAP (especially the full disclosure principle). This process may include footnotes to the statements and additional financial statements, such as the statement of cash flows.

In step 8, after preparation of the financial statements, the revenue and expense accounts are closed. These temporary owners' equity accounts are closed into the appropriate owners' equity account. The closing entries either increase the appropriate owners' equity account (if the spa operation earned a profit) or decrease the appropriate owners' equity account (if a loss was suffered). The closing entries result in zero balances in all revenue and expense ledger accounts. The closing entries are recorded in the general journal and posted to the proper accounts. The closing of the revenue and expense account is performed only at the end of the spa's accounting year. The final step is the preparation of a posting closing trial balance. This trial balance reflects the balances of all permanent accounts (assets, liabilities, and owners' equity); and, of course, the total of the accounts with debit balances must equal to the accounts with credit balances.

Summary

The major objectives of this chapter have been to provide a review of basic accounting procedures and concepts. A daily operating summary report was used to show the financial details of daily revenue activities. The impact on both the balance sheet and the statement of income were illustrated. Spas, although different in several respects from firms in many other industries, maintain their accounts according to the same basic principles. A spa manager should therefore be well versed in general accounting and the special accounting considerations of a spa operation.

In order to reflect accurately the operations of spas and to ensure consistent recording between periods and properties, spa accountants follow generally accepted accounting principles. The cost principle stipulates that items be recorded at the amount for which they are purchased. The continuity of the business unit principle assumes that the spa is a going concern that is not threatened by having to liquidate immediately. The property must be treated as an entity separate from its owners according to the business entity principle. Other requirements are that accountants use objective evidence whenever possible and fully disclose financial items of significance to the users of the financial statements. If these principles are adhered to, the resultant statements will more accurately report the property's operations and financial position.

This chapter also provided a brief overview of basis accounting mechanics. Assets are items owned by the property and have debit balances; liabilities are amounts the property owes and have credit balances. The difference between assets and liabilities is owners' equity—the amount of residual claims owners have on assets. The chapter included a brief description of the nine steps of the accounting cycle.

Key Terms

accounting cycle—Sequence of principal accounting procedures of a fiscal period: analyzing transactions, journal entry, posting to ledger, trial balance, adjustments, preparation of periodic financial statements, account closing, post-closing trial balance.

accounts payable—The spa's obligation to pay a vendor for goods or services already received (for example, for professional products from suppliers such as the skin care line or grooming area products).

accounts receivable—A promise by customers to pay later for goods and services already provided (for example, providing an invoice to a customer who promises to pay at a later date or charging a group's activities to its corporate master account to be paid at the end of the month).

accrual accounting—A method of accounting in which revenues and expenses are reported in the period in which they are considered to have been earned or incurred, regardless of the actual time of collection or payment.

assets—Resources available for use by the spa; that is, anything owned by the spa that has monetary value.

balance sheet—Statement of the financial position of the spa at a given date, giving the account balances for assets, liabilities, and owners' equity.

basic accounting equation—The fundamental equation of assets = liabilities + owners' equity. Also known as the fundamental accounting equation.

business entity—An accounting principle that requires that a business maintain its own set of accounts that are separate from the other financial interests of the owner(s).

cash accounting—A method of accounting in which revenues and expenses are reported at the time they are collected or paid.

consistency principle—The generally accepted accounting principle that requires that once an accounting method has been adopted, it should be followed from period to period in the future unless a change in accounting methods is warranted and disclosed.

conservatism principle—The generally accepted accounting principle that requires accounting procedures that recognize expenses as soon as possible, but delay the recognition of revenues until they are ensured. For example, non-refundable deposits for future services should be recognized as liabilities until the services are actually performed.

continuity of the business unit principle—The generally accepted accounting principle that requires the assumption in preparing the accounting records and reports that the business will continue indefinitely and that liquidation is not in prospect—in other words, that the business is a going concern. Also called the going concern principle.

cost principle—The generally accepted accounting principle which holds that, when a transaction is recorded, it is the transaction price or cost that establishes the accounting value for the product or service purchased.

credit—Decrease in an asset or increase in a liability or capital, entered on the right side of an account; such amounts are said to be credited to the account.

Daily Operating Summary—A daily report used to show the financial details of a spa's daily revenue activities.

debit—Increase in an asset or decrease in a liability or capital, entered on the left side of an account; such amounts are said to be debited or charged to the account.

double-entry accounting—The financial recording system in which each business transaction affects at least two accounts.

expenses—Costs incurred in providing the goods and services.

fixed assets—Spa property or equipment used to generate revenue for a period beyond one year.

full disclosure—The generally accepted accounting principle that requires that financial statements must provide information on all the significant facts that have a bearing on the statements' interpretation. Types of disclosures include the accounting methods used, changes in the accounting methods, contingent liabilities, events occurring subsequent to the financial statement date, and unusual and nonrecurring items.

generally accepted accounting principles (GAAP)—Accounting principles that have become accepted over time through common usage and also through the work of major accounting bodies. They provide a uniform basis for preparing financial statements.

journals—Accounting records of business transactions.

liabilities—Obligations of a business; largely indebtedness related to the expenses incurred in the process of generating income.

matching principle—The generally accepted accounting principle that requires recording expenses in the same period as the revenues to which they relate.

materiality principle—The generally accepted accounting principle that requires that events be recognized and recorded by accounting procedures if they make a difference as determined by some relative standard of comparison. For example, materiality may be established by a rule of thumb that states that an item is recognized if it exceeds *x* percent or more of total assets or income.

objective evidence—The preferred basis of accounting transactions and the resulting accounting records.

owners' equity—Financial interest of the owners of a business; assets minus liabilities.

point-of-sale (POS) system—A network of electronic cash registers and computers that records a spa's sales transactions.

revenues—Inflows of assets resulting from the sale of goods and services.

statement of income—A report on the profitability of spa operations, including revenues earned and expenses incurred in generating the revenues for the period of time covered by the statement.

trial balance—A listing of all account balances, with debit balance accounts and credit balance accounts in separate columns; the totals of each column should be equal and prove the equality of debits and credits.

Review Questions

1. What is an example of a prepaid expense and why is the expenditure recorded as a prepaid expense rather than simply as an expense for the accounting period?
2. What is the difference between short term and long term notes?
3. When is revenue recognized when a spa keeps its books on a cash basis?
4. What part of a spa's operating activities is reflected in its daily operating summary report?
5. According to GAAP, what is the proper accounting for gift card certificates when purchased by a customer and later when they are used?
6. When does the conservatism principle trump the cost principle?
7. What are four types of disclosure and what is an example of each?
8. Why is an expenditure of $80 for a steel file often expensed when purchased rather than recorded as a fixed asset?
9. What are the five common types of transactions in a business operation?
10. What are three types of adjusting entries and what principle of accounting is the basis for recording adjusting entries?

Chapter 2 Outline

Spa Payroll
    Elements of a Spa Compensation Plan
Independent Contractors
Payroll Controls
Payroll Records
Regular Pay and Overtime Pay
Preparing Payroll Checks Manually
Payroll Journal Entries
    The Entry to Record Payroll
    The Entry to Record Payroll Taxes
Reporting Tips
Accruing Unpaid Wages

Competencies

1. Discuss the importance of containing payroll costs, and describe the elements of a spa's compensation plan. (pp. 43–47)
2. Discuss the issue of independent contractors in spas. (pp. 47–49)
3. Summarize payroll controls used by spas, identify payroll records, and discuss issues surrounding overtime pay. (pp. 49–55)
4. Outline factors involved in preparing payroll checks manually, and describe two major journal entries involving payroll. (pp. 55–64)
5. Describe issues involved in the reporting of employee tips, and explain how unpaid wages are accrued using adjusting entries. (pp. 64–71)

2

Accounting for Payroll

IT IS 2 P.M. AND ERICA, the assistant spa director, has just finished her rounds at The Spa. The Spa books 50-minute treatments with 10 minutes to turn over the treatment rooms for the next appointments, so Erica makes a point of periodically leaving her office and walking the treatment room corridor to check in with the therapists to see how their day is going and if they are having any issues. Therapists spend most of their time at the spa behind closed doors providing treatments, and Erica realizes that if she does not get out once an hour to visit with them, it would be possible to go all day without even seeing some of her staff.

She stops by the registration counter and all is quiet, so she returns to her office to begin work on the payroll. The work week at the resort is from 12:00 A.M. on Saturday morning to 11:59 P.M. on Friday evening. Payroll is paid bi-weekly and must be turned in to the resort accounting office by noon on Monday for checks to be distributed on Thursday. Sunday afternoon is the perfect time to do payroll, as it is the quietest time of the week with the fewest interruptions—the weekend guests have all departed and the business/group guests will not start checking in until Sunday evening. The Spa is not very busy, so Erica knows she will be able to concentrate on payroll input.

Erica would not admit that she hates doing payroll, but it is one of her least favorite responsibilities. After all, no one ever comes up to you on payday to say, "Thank you for getting my check right." However, if there is an error or perceived error, employees will be knocking at your door immediately—unless of course the error is in their favor! Erica understands the importance of treating payroll very seriously, as she has had mistakes on her own paycheck and remembers how upsetting it was. A spa is in the business of selling the healing hands of each therapist, so, to keep her therapists stress-free and happy, Erica always strives to have no problems or discrepancies once payroll is turned in to the accounting department.

Erica considers herself to be meticulous and remembers the standard carpentry advice to "measure twice and cut once" to reinforce the importance of double-checking her work. Spa payroll is complicated. The Spa has 68 full- and part-time staff members, so it is a daunting task to get everything 100 percent perfect. But she knows that controlling labor costs is vital to ensure financial success. By their very nature, spas are labor-intensive businesses that must carefully manage payroll costs to achieve long-term financial sustainability.

Erica sometimes thinks how easy it is for the resort front desk manager or executive housekeeper to do payroll. The employees of those departments have an hourly wage that is multiplied by the number of hours they worked, and that's it—simple. In the spa, though, the therapist compensation is a combination of several calculations. Erica's full-time therapists have an hourly rate between $6.00 and $9.00, based on seniority and the number of services they are certified to perform; there is also a percentage commission for the revenue each therapist produces during the pay period, which varies depending on the treatment. The Spa also charges an 18 percent service charge on all services as a convenience for guests, so they do not have to calculate gratuities. Of course, some guests wish to add to this standard gratuity, often paying the additional gratuity by adding it to their guestroom charge or credit card voucher—this must be accounted for as well. The service provider is given 15 percent of the 18 percent service charge; the remaining 3 percent is distributed to the guest reception and reservation agents based on the number of hours they have worked during that specific pay period, as they essentially act as salespeople for the therapists. Finally, each therapist receives commissions for the retail sales he or she generates, which are calculated on a sliding scale. Thus, for a staff of nearly 70 employees, there are hundreds of calculations that must accurately be recorded to build the payroll input. Thankful for her computer, Erica thinks to herself, "How in the world did people do this manually?"

Erica learned early in her career that most therapists treat their work as their own little business and will keep personal records of every treatment they provide. At The Spa, each therapist can log onto his or her own commission report any time at the computer station in the employee breakroom, and almost everyone keeps a careful eye on their service history. If a therapist discovers that a treatment that a guest extended from a 50-minute to a 75-minute treatment was charged as a 50-minute service, the therapist can write a note about the discrepancy and give it to one of the supervisors. Erica knows, though, that you can't simply take the therapist's word for it. Each discrepancy must be researched throughout the week.

Erica's payroll work is interrupted only a couple of times over the next few hours: once to meet with a guest who did not like her massage, and once by Anna, one of the therapists, who forgot to punch in after her lunch break. This required Erica to do a "punch edit" to manually correct the mistake, a mistake that happens almost every day. Erica spends the next few hours completing the payroll input. As she is putting everything away, she thinks about her good friend Monica, who runs The Day Spa downtown. Monica uses a payroll service, but still has to do all of the payroll calculations that Erica has to do, plus she has to be deeply involved with each of the transactions to pay state and federal taxes and administer the spa's benefit program. "I'm so happy I have an accounting staff to deal with all of those issues," thinks Erica.

Of course, completing the payroll input is not the end of the payroll story. Erica spends time every day monitoring payroll expenses against budget and makes certain that the labor cost percentage is in line with budget for each of the departments of the spa. She watches any overtime like a hawk, because that can ruin a monthly income statement so fast that it is almost impossible to salvage a good financial statement.

The purpose of this chapter is to give you an understanding of how some spa compensation programs are designed, the financial consequences of wage and salary decisions, and an overview of each of the federal and common state employer tax regulations and employment laws. Finally, various strategies to monitor and control labor—the largest single expense in a spa business—are explored.

After reading this chapter, you should be able to answer the following questions:

1. What is the difference between base pay and variable pay?
2. What are the major components of an employee's compensation?
3. How is the effective compensation rate determined?
4. What are five factors that can be used to determine if a person is an independent contractor or an employee?
5. What is meant by "segregate payroll functions whenever possible," and what are five payroll functions?
6. What are the four things covered by the Federal Wage and Hour Law?
7. What is the difference between the payroll journal and the employees' earnings records?
8. What are the major tax withholdings?
9. Under what circumstance must wages be accrued at the end of the month?
10. What are the two elements of the FICA tax?

Spa Payroll

Payroll represents the largest expense for any spa. According to the International SPA Association's *ISPA 2010 U.S. Spa Industry Study*, payroll and related costs for spas surveyed in 2009 was 47 percent of total spa revenues. When set against the estimated $12.3 billion of revenue generated by the spa industry in 2009, the payroll share of revenues translates into $5.76 billion in wages and salaries paid to persons employed in the industry.

According to PKF Consulting research released in 2008, from 2006 to 2007 spa department labor costs for the hotels in the survey increased by 6.6 percent, while total department revenue for the spas in the survey grew 5.0 percent. The increase in labor costs was driven in part by the mounting burden of benefits, which was reflected in the 8.7 percent growth in payroll-related expenses. It is simple to understand why labor costs are the largest expense for any spa when you consider that every guest of a spa receives extensive one-on-one services from a spa therapist. Thus, control of payroll costs is the largest factor influencing overall spa profitability. In 2004, the ISPA Foundation teamed up with Compensation Consulting Consortium (3C) to develop a publication entitled *Compensation Workbook for the Spa Industry*. In Section III: Compensation Economics, it states:

> In reviewing the total compensation expenses (base pay, variable pay, and benefit costs) for service firms as a percentage of annual revenue, those that find a balance between costs and growth are typically the most

profitable and are able to pay the most to their employees. If we consider total compensation in the range of 50 to 60 percent of annual revenue to be the desired positioning—with additional income from business expenses and profit typically used to provide owners or shareholders with a reasonable return on their investment and income to invest in the future of the spa—the organization then must increase revenue in order for the employees to increase their income.

Few organizations will be able to sustain their profitability and grow their businesses over the long term if total compensation costs for all employees combined consistently exceed 60 percent of revenue, and few service providers will be able to attract and retain qualified staff if they share less that 45 percent of the annual revenue in the form of compensation. Once a balance is achieved between sharing enough revenue in the way of total compensation to attract and retain qualified employees and also remain financially sound, the key becomes the spa's ability to increase revenue through its pricing structure, an increased number of clients, and higher revenue per client.

There are two very important issues that a spa professional must master with respect to labor cost in order for their spa to be successful: the development of a sustainable and competitive compensation plan and the skills to manage payroll expenses to achieve a reasonable spa profit.

The *total compensation system* is the term that encompasses all of the compensation programs offered by a spa. A total compensation system typically includes a base-wage program, one or more variable pay programs, and benefits and other non-cash compensation. It is not the intention of this chapter to cover in detail the full development of a spa compensation plan. For a complete and detailed discussion of the decisions and financial impacts involved in the development of a comprehensive compensation program for a spa, see the *Compensation Workbook for the Spa Industry,* which can be ordered from ISPA headquarters. This 120-page workbook discusses in significant detail all of the factors involved with the development of a compensation program that will help ensure the financial sustainability of a spa operation.

Elements of a Spa Compensation Plan

The chapter's opening story suggests that spa payroll has several components that make the calculations for payroll input a challenge for spa managers that requires their precise attention. In a hotel/resort spa or destination spa, there will be human resources and accounting departments that will manage the process of adding new employees to the payroll register and process the payroll accounting entries. In a day spa, these responsibilities will typically be handled by the spa director or, in some cases, even the spa owner. A day spa director or owner often will engage a payroll service or an outside accounting service to process the payroll details, but even then, day spa operators must be more versed in all of the accounting required to record payroll than their counterparts in hotel/resort spas or destination spas. Nonetheless, in all spas, payroll is not simply a matter of taking the employees' base hourly wages and multiplying them by the number of hours worked.

A wide range of compensation models are used in spas, especially when it comes to therapist pay. The *Compensation Workbook for the Spa Industry* identifies the following elements that generally are included in an overall spa compensation plan:

- *Base pay (or base salary).* This is the fixed amount of pay an individual employee receives that would typically be paid every two weeks or twice monthly. Spa employees who are paid on an hourly basis might see their base pay vary from one pay period to the next, depending on the number of hours worked. Staff who are paid on a salaried basis receive the same amount of pay each pay period unless there is an extenuating circumstance such as taking an unpaid leave of absence.
- *Variable pay (or incentive pay).* As the name implies, variable or incentive pay is not guaranteed. It fluctuates, usually with the performance of the spa and/or the individual employee. Variable pay covers such items as annual merit increases, commission payments, and incentive payments.
- *Commissions:* This type of variable pay program is typically provided to therapists who perform treatments and sell retail products, with the therapists' earnings determined by the revenue they generate. When a therapist is compensated through commission only, the pay delivery is usually referred to as "full commission." It is very common, however, to compensate employees using a blend of commission and base hourly rate. There are two common variations of the commission model:
    - *Percentage commission.* In this model, therapists are paid a fixed percentage of the revenues they generate—for example, a 35 percent commission of total revenues generated during the pay period. It is not uncommon to have different commission percentages for individuals on the spa staff, based on length of employment or the therapist's ability to perform a broader repertory of treatments through additional treatment certifications. Commission percentages can also vary by department. An esthetician or hair stylist may be given a higher commission percentage, for example than a massage therapist (this is largely dictated by labor market conditions).
    - *Fee-for-service.* With a fee-for-service compensation arrangement, the spa will assign a fixed dollar amount for each individual service instead of a percentage of revenue. For example, the spa may set a $24 fee-for-service for a 50-minute Swedish massage treatment. This method, as opposed to percentage commission, does not automatically result in an increase in pay rates every time the spa increases its prices. From this perspective it offers a greater level of control over payroll costs.
- *Service charges/gratuities/tips:* Regardless of the term used, service charges, gratuities, or tips (hereafter referred to as tips) have been traditionally paid by spa guests directly to the service provider. There are two pertinent questions related to tips in a spa: Should therapists be permitted to keep all of their tips? Or should a portion of the tips be shared with others on staff who assist

or generate treatment sales and might not be tipped directly by spa guests, such as the guest reception/reservations staff and spa attendants? There are also varying schools of thought among spa operations concerning whether an automatic service charge should be added to a client's bill to cover the tip, as opposed to leaving the amount of the tip up to the client. There appears to be a trend toward adding a service charge equal to 15 to 20 percent of the cost of the spa service. The arguments for assessing an automatic service charge are (1) with an automatic service charge, tipping is one less thing spa guests have to think about, (2) it makes accounting for tip income easier, and (3) it makes the billing transaction easier. It is critical to note that the IRS has determined that automatic/non-discretionary service charges are spa revenue and must be reported as such. Sales taxes must be paid on the service charge amount, and service charges distributed to employees are reported as a payroll expense under Distributed Service Charges in accordance with the *Uniform System of Financial Reporting for Spas.* It is important for spa managers and owners to recognize that tips are a significant part of the therapist compensation package. Additionally, in the United States, tips are considered part of wages, and the employee and employer are each required to pay FICA taxes of 7.65 percent (the rate in effect at the time of this writing) on tip income, which represents an additional direct labor cost for the spa. FICA taxes include both Social Security and Medicare taxes, which will be discussed in detail later in the chapter.

- *Retail commissions.* It is also common for spas to pay a commission to therapists and retail sales employees for the sale of retail products. In some cases, guest reception agents receive a percentage of the sales price of retail products if they encourage and close the retail product sales. Like all pay, this commission is subject to income tax withholding and FICA taxes in the United States, with the employer and employee each paying their share of the FICA taxes according to law. There are several variations on how retail commissions are paid. Sometimes employees are paid a straight-percentage commission for all retail sales they generate. Sometimes retail commissions are paid on a sliding scale, based on the achievement of predetermined retail sales levels. At other times, they are paid based on whether the spa exceeds sales objectives.

- *Incentive pay.* Incentive pay is a variable pay program that may be paid at least once a year and sometimes more frequently. Incentive plans often are linked to the financial performance and/or guest satisfaction scores achieved by the spa. These incentives are generally included in the compensation program for spa leadership positions, but there are an increasing number of spas that reward the performance of individual employees as well and usually pay on a curve, with a partial payout made if a minimum performance level is reached and an above-target payout made when spa financial performance exceeds budgeted levels. The theory for including all spa employees in the incentive program is that it will focus the entire spa team on achieving the spa's overall financial targets. The recent popularity of incentive programs is driven in large part by the desire of many spa managers to shift some of their spas' fixed costs to variable costs that will be contingent on their spas' financial success.

When staff members understand how their behavior and actions impact the spa's overall financial performance, and when the incentive payout is realistic and fair, the results are often quite impressive.

- *Merit pay.* This refers to annual adjustments to employees' base-pay levels that are typically determined as a budgeted amount for the spa (e.g., 3.5 percent of base pay) according to the market conditions affecting compensation and the financial performance of the spa. Merit pay is given to employees based on their individual performance and contribution levels.

In addition to direct payroll costs, a spa must structure a benefit program to remain competitive within the marketplace. Benefits are an additional expense and must be calculated when determining the overall labor costs of the spa's compensation program. Benefits are generally classified into three major categories: health and welfare benefits, which include health, life, and disability insurance and other related programs; retirement benefits, which include traditional pension plans and 401(k) savings plans; and paid time off, which includes vacation time, sick leave, and holidays.

The natural tendency for spa leaders is to focus on their employees' base wage/hourly rates or commission percentages instead of the spa's total compensation structure. Thus, they may believe that if they set a commission percentage of 35 percent of service revenue for therapists, the labor cost percentage is 35 percent. However, managers should keep in mind the spa's benefit package as well and determine the effective compensation rate (ECR) by adding the costs for all of the other components of compensation to determine the actual labor expense. Exhibit 1 provides an example of how an effective compensation rate is determined. As you can see, what at first review might appear to be a simple 35 percent commission on a treatment and 10 percent commission on a retail sale actually results in a labor cost of close to 50 percent.

Independent Contractors

Spas routinely use independent contractors to fill in gaps and to help with special projects or when a spike in business volume occurs. Sometimes, there is a belief that the use of independent contractors is a strategy to avoid payroll and benefit expenses. In the United States, independent contractors are not employees and therefore are not eligible for benefits, including the employer-paid portion of Social Security and Medicare taxes. Leadership in U.S. spas must be aware of the specific requirements outlined by the Internal Revenue Service to maintain an independent contractor–client relationship, as opposed to an employer-employee relationship. The Internal Revenue Service defines an independent contractor as a worker responsible for paying taxes to the IRS using Form 1040-ES. Independent contractors are in business for themselves and must make quarterly estimated tax payments for both income tax and self-employment tax. Self-employment tax is equivalent to both the employee and employer portions of the Social Security and Medicare taxes. Employers do not have to withhold or pay taxes on payments to independent contractors. In addition, when a spa uses an independent contractor, the spa has the right to control or direct only the result of the work done, not the

Exhibit 1 Determination of Effective Compensation Rate

Client Fee for 50-Minute Massage	$120.00	
Automatic Service Charge (18%)	$21.60	
Additional Client Cash Tip	$10.00	
Client Retail Purchase	$20.00	
Total Client Revenue	$161.60	(excludes cash tip)
Therapist Service Commission	$42.00	(35% of client fee)
Distributed Service Charge	$21.60	
Employer Portion of FICA	$5.63	(7.65% of $73.60*)
Healthcare Average Costs per Treatment	$4.29	
Paid-Time Off per Treatment	$3.85	
Retail Commission	$2.00	(10% of $20.00)
Employer Portion of FICA	$ .15	(7.65% of $2.00)
Sub-Total Retail Commission Rate	$2.15	
Total Compensation Paid (Excludes Cash Tip)	$79.52	
ECR for Total Client Revenue: $79.52 ÷ $161.60 =	49.2%	

*$42 + $21.60 + $10 = $73.60

means or methods the independent contractor uses to accomplish the result. An employer must report payments to an independent contractor by filing Form 1099-MISC, Miscellaneous Income, if the following four conditions are met:

1. Employer made a payment to someone who is not his/her employee;
2. Employer made a payment for services of its trade or business;
3. Employer made a payment to an individual, partnership, estate, or (in some cases) a corporation; and
4. Employer made payments to the payee of at least $600 during the year.

There are three main factors that spa managers should take into consideration when determining worker status: behavioral control, financial control, and relationship of the parties:

1. *Behavioral control.* A worker is an employee when the business has the right to direct and control the worker. When less extensive instructions are given on what should be done (not how it should be done), the worker may be classified as an independent contractor.
2. *Financial control.* A worker may be an independent contractor if he/she has a significant investment in his/her work, does not get reimbursed for some or all business expenses, and can realize a profit or incur a loss.

3. *Relationship of the parties.* A worker may be an independent contractor if he/she does not receive benefits.

Exhibit 2 outlines the IRS's 20-factor test for identifying independent contractors, with an explanation of what constitutes independent contractor status and employee status for each factor. If a spa engages independent contractors, it must be able to identify the relationship as such for most of these items. If more than a few items point toward the individual having employee status rather than independent contractor status, the spa should either change the control level of the relationship to better reflect the independent contractor–client relationship, or reclassify the individual as an employee.

Another somewhat unique condition that exists in spas (and is more likely in day spas) is called booth rental or chair rental. This is a circumstance in which the spa will rent a stylist chair or treatment room to an individual who basically runs his or her own business from the spa. The revenue generated by someone who has a booth rental is not run through the spa's financial records; the spa will instead simply record the amount of rent paid by the renter as Other Income on the spa's income statements. The practices of hiring independent contractors and/or using booth/chair rentals are very prevalent in the nail salon and barber shop industries. Seven percent of nail salon establishments have employees on the payroll, while only three percent of barber shop establishments have paid employees. Eighty-seven percent of beauty salon and spa establishments are non-employers, meaning they have no payroll employees. With the exception of unpaid family workers, individuals who work at non-employer establishments are classified as self-employed booth renters or independent contractors.

Payroll Controls

With respect to payroll controls, spas can sit at polar opposites on the spectrum of how payroll is processed. On one end of the spectrum is a large hotel/resort spa or destination spa that is part of a much larger operation that has a human resources department and a full accounting office with employees responsible for the payroll for all hotel/resort departments. On the opposite end of the spectrum, a small day spa will likely have a limited staff where the spa director or perhaps even the owner is responsible for payroll processing in conjunction with a payroll service, outside CPA, or accounting service.

The processes and controls contained in the remainder of this chapter are obviously being done by someone; who it is can vary from spa to spa, but the information and practices remain the same. The content will be presented without attempting to point out variations and distinctions between a hotel/resort spa, destination spa, or day spa. It is essential that all spa leaders fully understand the payroll controls and accounting entries required to process payroll, regardless of who is responsible for each task.

All spas should have several important payroll control features in place. To begin with, the following payroll functions should be segregated whenever possible:

Exhibit 2 IRS 20-Factor Test

Factor	Indicates Employee Status	Indicates Independent Contractor Status
Instructions	Worker is subject to control of and must comply with company's significant instructions	Worker determines when, where and how the work is performed
Training	Worker required to undergo on-the-job training	Worker is already highly skilled and receives no training from company
Integration	Worker's services are an integral part of the overall business; worker's services parallels work done by regular full-time employees	Worker's services are not integral to the success or continuation of the business; worker performs services separate and distinct from work done by regular full-time employees
Services Rendered	Worker must render the services personally	Worker need not render services personally and has helpers
Hiring/Supervision	Company hires, supervises and pays workers	Worker hires, supervises and pays helpers under a contract requiring him/her to provide materials and labor
Employment Relationship	Continuing relationship between worker and company	Relationship exists only until specific project is completed
Work Hours	Company sets work hours	Worker sets own work hours
Full-Time Effort	Worker must devote full-time effort to the company	Worker determines when and for whom he/she chooses to work
Location	Work is performed on company premises	Work is performed elsewhere
Order/Sequence	Company sets order or sequence of work performed	Worker follows his/her own pattern or schedule of work
Reports	Worker must submit regular oral or written reports	Regular reports not required
Payment Method	Worker is paid hourly, weekly or monthly	Worker is paid by the job or by straight commission
Expense Reimbursement	Company reimburses worker for business or traveling expenses	Worker pays his/her own expenses
Tools and Materials	Company provides worker's tools and materials	Worker furnishes his/her own tools and materials
Significant Investment	Worker does not invest in facilities and/or equipment used to provide services	Worker makes significant investment in facilities and or equipment he/she uses in performing services
Profit or Loss	Worker cannot make a profit or loss	Worker can realize a profit or loss under the contract
Employed by More than One Firm	Worker provides services to one company	Worker provides services to multiple related companies at the same time
Service Availability	Worker does not regularly make services available to the general public	Worker regularly makes services available to the general public
Firing	The right to discharge is an indicator of employer-employee relationship	Worker may not be fired if work is produced according to contract specifications
Quitting	Each party has right to terminate the relationship without incurring liability	Worker may terminate the relationship only upon completion of contract or breach of contract by other party

Source: www.employersassoc.com/FOD/1001.pdf.

- *Authorization of employment and establishment of wage rates for employees.* It is a good practice to have two levels of authorization for hiring and setting or changing wage rates for spa staff. In a hotel, the process for hiring new spa employees will typically include the spa director submitting an *employee requisition* to the human resources department, which will be signed by the property general manager or a designate. Once the employee has been hired, the hire-package documents will be signed by a senior property executive. In a day spa, spa leadership could have the owner or his or her designate serve as a second level of authorization.
- *Reporting of hours worked by employees.* In most cases, a spa will use a time clock or have the employees clock in and out on the spa computer system, but there are still small spa operations that use manual sign-in sheets or a time book to record employees hours worked. It is a good practice to have employee sign-in sheets include a line for employee signature verifying the correctness of hours indicated and also initialed by another staff member as a witness to the record of time indicated. In electronic timekeeping systems, any employee errors, omissions, or corrections must be edited by spa management. For control purposes, overtime hours should be approved in advance. It is also important to compare employees' punch clock times with their official shift times. Most employees will punch in a few minutes before their shift, but others may turn up and punch in an hour before their shift and spend the hour in the staff room socializing, relaxing, and/or eating. Time clocks should be placed in an area within view of a supervisor to discourage improper checking in and out.
- *Actual preparation of the payroll.* Payroll information is processed by the payroll clerk in the accounting department of a hotel spa. The gross pay less tax withholdings and voluntary deductions equals the net pay. The payroll check amount is the net pay. In a day spa, a payroll service will often be used. The outside service will print the checks and provide the payroll information for tax purposes and for recording in the spa's accounting records. A number of spas use direct bank deposit instead of physical checks. In these cases, each employee receives a detailed pay notice showing all calculations, deductions, and the net amount that was deposited to his or her bank account.
- *Signing of the payroll checks.* The checks are often signed by the controller or at least someone other than the payroll clerk. In a small spa, the checks will often be signed by the owner, who is fully aware of all spa employees.
- *Distribution of checks to employees.* Employee checks should not be distributed by the individual who prepares the payroll checks. In many large spas with many employees, it is a good practice to periodically use what is called the *payoff test,* whereby employees receiving the checks are asked to show identification so that the spa can make sure the individuals for whom the checks are made out actually exist and work at the spa. This procedure is decreasing due to the increasing use of direct deposit for handling employee checks.
- *Reconciliation of payroll bank accounts by an independent party.* The spa's payroll account balance on its books should be reconciled monthly to the balance

shown on the payroll account bank statement. The most common reconciling items are outstanding checks. The reconciliation should be prepared by someone who does not prepare the payroll or signs the checks, except in the case of the owner of a small day spa.

Employees should be paid by check or direct deposit only, not in cash. In addition, a special **imprest payroll account** should be used—also referred to as a payroll clearing account. An imprest payroll account is one into which only the exact amount of a given payroll period is deposited. Once all of the checks clear the bank, there is nothing left in the account.

Payroll input sheets and employee paychecks should be independently checked. In this and all other similar parts of the process, the documents being checked should be initialed by each individual as evidence it has been checked.

Any unclaimed payroll checks should be returned immediately to the controller or spa director, who will hold them until the employees return to work and pick up their checks directly from spa leadership or the controller's office.

Payroll Records

Most spas now use a computerized payroll system or outsource this function. It is essential that only spa leadership have access to employee personnel files and payroll records. In a hotel, these documents are generally held in the human resources or accounting office. In a small day spa, provisions must be made to prevent employee access to personnel and payroll records.

The Fair Labor Standards Act (FLSA), commonly known as the Federal Wage and Hour Law, covers such things as equal pay for equal work, record keeping requirements, minimum wage rates, and overtime pay. Most spas, except for very small operations, are subject to this act. The two tests to determine whether a spa is required to pay federal minimum wage and overtime under the FLSA are:

1. If the spa has revenues, or projects revenues, in excess of $500,000 per year, or if the spa was operating prior to April 1, 1990, and revenues were in excess of $362,500 on that date, the spa is subject to FLSA requirements.
2. Even if revenues are below $500,000 per year, a spa may be required to pay minimum wage and overtime to some employees. For example, if any employee is engaged in interstate communications, he or she is covered by the law.

If neither of these tests is met, the spa director should still consult with the state government to determine whether state minimum wage and overtime laws apply to the spa. When states have different rules than the FLSA, the more demanding rule must be met. For example, if the FLSA requires an hour minimum wage of $7.50 and the state law requires $8.00, then $8.00 is the required minimum hourly wage.

To comply with the FLSA, employers must keep records of the time worked by hourly employees. Time cards or time sheets are generally used to satisfy this requirement. The time cards or sheets can be completed manually or through an electronic time clock.

Exhibit 3 IRS Form W-4

Form **W-4**
Department of the Treasury
Internal Revenue Service

Employee's Withholding Allowance Certificate

▶ Whether you are entitled to claim a certain number of allowances or exemption from withholding is subject to review by the IRS. Your employer may be required to send a copy of this form to the IRS.

OMB No. 1545-0074
2010

1 Type or print your first name and middle initial. | Last name | 2 Your social security number

Home address (number and street or rural route) | 3 ☐ Single ☐ Married ☐ Married, but withhold at higher Single rate.
Note. If married, but legally separated, or spouse is a nonresident alien, check the "Single" box.

City or town, state, and ZIP code | 4 If your last name differs from that shown on your social security card, check here. You must call 1-800-772-1213 for a replacement card. ▶ ☐

5 Total number of allowances you are claiming (from line **H** above **or** from the applicable worksheet on page 2) 5
6 Additional amount, if any, you want withheld from each paycheck . . . . 6 $
7 I claim exemption from withholding for 2010, and I certify that I meet **both** of the following conditions for exemption.
• Last year I had a right to a refund of **all** federal income tax withheld because I had **no** tax liability **and**
• This year I expect a refund of **all** federal income tax withheld because I expect to have **no** tax liability.
If you meet both conditions, write "Exempt" here . . . . ▶ 7

Under penalties of perjury, I declare that I have examined this certificate and to the best of my knowledge and belief, it is true, correct, and complete.

Employee's signature
(Form is not valid unless you sign it.) ▶ **Date ▶**

8 Employer's name and address (Employer: Complete lines 8 and 10 only if sending to the IRS.) | 9 Office code (optional) | 10 Employer identification number (EIN)

For Privacy Act and Paperwork Reduction Act Notice, see page 2. Cat. No. 10220Q Form **W-4** (2010)

Spas will typically keep a **master payroll file** of records that contains important employee information. The information in the file would include employees' full names, addresses with zip codes, dates of birth (if less than 19 years of age), gender, occupation, time and day when their workweek starts, rate of pay, hours worked each day and week, regular earnings, overtime earnings, additions to and deductions from pay, total wages paid, pay date, and pay period.

All employees must complete Internal Revenue Service (IRS) Form W-4 and provide it to the employer.[1] The front of a W-4 form is shown in Exhibit 3. This form helps the employer calculate the amount of taxes withheld from the individual employee's payroll check. In addition, spas are required to have employees complete the U.S. Department of Homeland Security Eligibility Verification Form I-9, shown in Exhibit 4. Employers must provide IRS Form W-2 (see Exhibit 5) to employees annually for filing along with their income tax forms.

Another payroll record is the **payroll journal**. This lists a record of each payroll check issued by the day spa or the controller's office in a hotel, along with the corresponding gross pay and various deductions for federal, state, city, and FICA taxes; employee health care contributions; and miscellaneous contributions. An **employee's earnings record** is also kept for each employee of the spa. This record is used to compile information for government reporting of employees' wages. Some taxes apply to earnings up to a certain dollar amount only, and this record is used to make sure that those caps are not exceeded.

Regular Pay and Overtime Pay

According to the FLSA, regular pay for an employee is based on a 40-hour workweek. *Regular hourly rate* refers to the rate per hour that is used to compute regular pay. The FLSA requires that overtime pay be given for any hours worked in excess of 40 hours in a week; *overtime hourly rate* refers to the rate per hour used to compute overtime pay. The FLSA requires that overtime be paid at the rate of 1.5 times the employee's regular hourly rate. The regulations with regard to overtime pay

Exhibit 4 U.S. Employment Eligibility Verification Form I-9

OMB No. 1615-0047; Expires 06/30/08

Department of Homeland Security
U.S. Citizenship and Immigration Services

Form I-9, Employment Eligibility Verification

Please read instructions carefully before completing this form. The instructions must be available during completion of this form.

ANTI-DISCRIMINATION NOTICE: It is illegal to discriminate against work eligible individuals. Employers CANNOT specify which document(s) they will accept from an employee. The refusal to hire an individual because the documents have a future expiration date may also constitute illegal discrimination.

Section 1. Employee Information and Verification. To be completed and signed by employee at the time employment begins.

Print Name: Last	First	Middle Initial	Maiden Name
Address *(Street Name and Number)*		Apt. #	Date of Birth *(month/day/year)*
City	State	Zip Code	Social Security #

I am aware that federal law provides for imprisonment and/or fines for false statements or use of false documents in connection with the completion of this form.

I attest, under penalty of perjury, that I am (check one of the following):
- ☐ A citizen or national of the United States
- ☐ A lawful permanent resident (Alien #) A ________
- ☐ An alien authorized to work until ________
  (Alien # or Admission #) ________

Employee's Signature	Date *(month/day/year)*

Preparer and/or Translator Certification. *(To be completed and signed if Section 1 is prepared by a person other than the employee.) I attest, under penalty of perjury, that I have assisted in the completion of this form and that to the best of my knowledge the information is true and correct.*

Preparer's/Translator's Signature	Print Name
Address *(Street Name and Number, City, State, Zip Code)*	Date *(month/day/year)*

Section 2. Employer Review and Verification. To be completed and signed by employer. Examine one document from List A OR examine one document from List B and one from List C, as listed on the reverse of this form, and record the title, number and expiration date, if any, of the document(s).

	List A	OR	List B	AND	List C
Document title:					
Issuing authority:					
Document #:					
Expiration Date *(if any)*:					
Document #:					
Expiration Date *(if any)*:					

CERTIFICATION - I attest, under penalty of perjury, that I have examined the document(s) presented by the above-named employee, that the above-listed document(s) appear to be genuine and to relate to the employee named, that the employee began employment on *(month/day/year)* ________ **and that to the best of my knowledge the employee is eligible to work in the United States. (State employment agencies may omit the date the employee began employment.)**

Signature of Employer or Authorized Representative	Print Name	Title
Business or Organization Name and Address *(Street Name and Number, City, State, Zip Code)*		Date *(month/day/year)*

Section 3. Updating and Reverification. To be completed and signed by employer.

A. New Name *(if applicable)*	B. Date of Rehire *(month/day/year) (if applicable)*

C. If employee's previous grant of work authorization has expired, provide the information below for the document that establishes current employment eligibility.

Document Title: ________ Document #: ________ Expiration Date (if any): ________

I attest, under penalty of perjury, that to the best of my knowledge, this employee is eligible to work in the United States, and if the employee presented document(s), the document(s) I have examined appear to be genuine and to relate to the individual.

Signature of Employer or Authorized Representative	Date *(month/day/year)*

Form I-9 (Rev. 06/05/07) N

in other countries vary. In Canada, for example, for work on a statutory holiday, employees are paid double time for the hours worked plus holiday pay, so effectively they receive three times their regular pay.

Exhibit 5 IRS Form W-2

22222	a Employee's social security number	OMB No. 1545-0008	
b Employer identification number (EIN)		1 Wages, tips, other compensation	2 Federal income tax withheld
c Employer's name, address, and ZIP code		3 Social security wages	4 Social security tax withheld
		5 Medicare wages and tips	6 Medicare tax withheld
		7 Social security tips	8 Allocated tips
d Control number		9 Advance EIC payment	10 Dependent care benefits
e Employee's first name and initial Last name Suff.		11 Nonqualified plans	12a Code
		13 Statutory employee / Retirement plan / Third-party sick pay	12b Code
		14 Other	12c Code
			12d Code
f Employee's address and ZIP code			

15 State Employer's state ID number	16 State wages, tips, etc.	17 State income tax	18 Local wages, tips, etc.	19 Local income tax	20 Locality name

Form **W-2** Wage and Tax Statement 2010

Department of the Treasury—Internal Revenue Service

Copy 1—For State, City, or Local Tax Department

Another situation affecting overtime pay that arises in a hotel/resort property occurs when a spa employee works part of the week in the spa and in another hotel department for additional hours during the week. For example, a spa attendant may work some days at the spa and other days in the hotel's housekeeping department. The total hours worked in both positions that week must be counted to determine whether overtime pay is due. When the two jobs involved pay different regular rates, the overtime rate is calculated using a weighted average of the two rates. In some states, there is also a "seven-day rule," where employees are paid time-and-a-half on the seventh consecutive day of work.

Preparing Payroll Checks Manually

At times it may become necessary for spa managers to prepare payroll checks manually. For illustration purposes, let us assume that on the day to distribute checks it is discovered that the payroll clerk in the accounting office overlooked the payroll reports for three spa employees and no pay checks were prepared for them, requiring that manual checks be prepared. Employee A is a front desk supervisor, Employee B is a massage therapist, and Employee C is an esthetician. Details of each employee's components of compensation and deductions follow:

- Employee A (front desk supervisor): Employee A has a salary of $35,000 annually, plus a retail sales override commission of one-half percent on all product sales. Product sales for the twelve days of the biweekly payroll period were $50,562. Employee A is single, claims one exemption, and does not participate in the spa's cafeteria plan for benefits or in the spa's 401(k) retirement plan.

Exhibit 6 Sample Payroll Calculations and Payroll Journal Entries—Employee A

Employee A Payroll Calculation

Biweekly Salary—Annual Salary of $35,000 ÷ 26 pay periods		$1,346.15
Product Sales Commission	$50,562.00 × 0.5% =	$ 252.81
Gross Pay		$1,598.96
	Rate	
Social Security	6.20%	$ (99.14)
Medicare	1.45%	$ (23.18)
Federal Income Tax withholding from IRS Tables		$ (203.00)
Net Pay		$1,273.64

Payroll Journal for Employee A Payroll

		Debit	Credit
Salaries & Wages—Guest Reception		$1,346.15	
Commissions—Guest Reception		252.81	
Payroll Tax Expense—Social Sec.	Employer's matching amount.	99.14	
Payroll Tax Expense—Medicare		23.18	
Federal Unemployment (FUTA)	Employee's ytd income is over limit	–	
State Unemployment Tax (SUTA)		–	
Federal Withholding Payable			$ 203.00
Social Security & Medicare Payable			244.64
Cash in Bank			1,273.64
		$1,721.28	$1,721.28

Exhibit 6 shows the payroll calculations and payroll journal entries necessary to process a check for Employee A.

- Employee B (message therapist): Employee B has an hourly rate of $7.00 per hour, plus 35 percent of massage service revenue as a commission. Employee B also receives a 10 percent commission on her individual sale of products. During the biweekly period, Employee B worked 71 hours, her massage revenue was $5,100, and her sales were $485. Employee B is married, claiming two exemptions, and participates in the spa's 401(k) plan. Her contribution to the plan is 6 percent of her gross income. For each contribution Employee B makes to the 401(k) plan, the spa contributes a match of 50 percent, limited to a maximum of 3 percent of annual earnings. Exhibit 7 shows the payroll calculations and payroll journal entries necessary to process a check for Employee B.

Exhibit 7 Sample Payroll Calculations and Payroll Journal Entries—Employee B

Employee B Payroll Calculation

Hourly Wage	71 hours × $7.00 per hour =	$ 497.00
Commission on Massage Revenue	$5,100.00 × 35% =	$1,785.00
Product Sales Commission	$485.00 × 10% =	$ 48.50
Gross Pay		$2,330.50
	Rate	
Social Security	6.20%	$ (144.49)
Medicare	1.45%	$ (33.79)
Net pay before 401(k) deduction		$2,152.22
401(k) Deduction—6% of $2,330.50	6.00%	$ (139.83)
Net pay for income tax withholding		$2,012.39
Federal Income Tax withholding from IRS Tables	(Based on payroll of $2,012.39)	$ (185.00)
Net Pay		$1,827.39

Payroll Journal for Employee B Payroll

		Debit	Credit
Salaries & Wages—Massage		$2,282.00	
Commissions—Massage		48.50	
Matching Contribution—401(k)		69.92	
Payroll Tax Expense—Social Sec.	Employer's matching amount.	144.49	
Payroll Tax Expense—Medicare		33.79	
Employee 401(k) Deferral Payable			$ 139.83
Employer 401(k) Match Payable			69.92
Federal Withholding Payable			185.00
Social Security & Medicare Payable			356.56
Cash in Bank			1,827.39
		$2,578.70	$2,578.70

- Employee C (esthetician): Employee C has an hourly rate of $8.00 per hour. She worked 45 hours the first week and 42 hours the second week for a total of 87 hours. She is paid a 40 percent commission on her skin care revenue of $6,585.00 and a 5 percent commission on the first $1,000 of product sales in a biweekly period; on any product sales exceeding $1,000, she is paid a 10 percent commission. Her product sales for the biweekly period were $2,505.75. Employee C is married, claims one exemption, participates in the spa's cafeteria

(Section 125) plan, and contributes 10 percent of her compensation to the 401(k) retirement plan.

The Spa furnishes group health and dental coverage to all full-time employees after they have worked at the spa for 90 days at no cost to the employee. However, if family coverage is desired by the employee, the employee is required to pay for the additional insurance cost. The spa has adopted an IRC Section 125 Plan, commonly called a "cafeteria plan," that allows the payment from the employee to be made pre-tax. Employee C's biweekly deduction for health insurance is $200. Exhibit 8 shows the payroll calculations and payroll journal entries necessary to process a check for Employee C.

Payroll Journal Entries

There are two major journal entries involving payroll. These two separate and distinct entries are referred to as *the entry to record payroll* and *the entry to record payroll taxes.*

The Entry to Record Payroll

It may be useful to think of the payroll entry as a "check stub" entry; if we had only one employee and that employee's check stub were in front of us, we could use the stub's information to journalize the entry. The following items would be included in the payroll entry:

1. *Gross pay.* Gross pay is calculated by multiplying the hours the employee worked for the pay period by the hourly rate where applicable, including any overtime premium. Additionally, gross pay would include service commissions or fee-per-service amounts, distributed service charges, reported tips, and any retail commissions earned. In the case of salaried employees, gross pay would be the annual salary divided by the number of pay periods in the year (typically 24 with semi-monthly or 26 for biweekly systems) plus any incentive pay earned.
2. *Federal income tax.* Exhibit 9 is an example of the type of withholding tables employers refer to for this deduction. The withholding amounts for federal income tax vary depending on gross pay, marital status, number of withholding allowances, and pay period.
3. *FICA taxes.* FICA taxes include both Social Security taxes and Medicare taxes resulting from the **Federal Insurance Contributions Act (FICA).** At the time of this writing, the rate for FICA taxes is 7.65 percent. This rate is actually a combination of two rates: 6.2 percent on the first $106,800 of income (as of the year 2010), plus 1.45 percent on all income.
4. *State income tax.* States vary widely in the amount of state income tax assessed, ranging from zero percent in several states to North Dakota's rate of about 12 percent.
5. *Miscellaneous deductions.* Other deductions from an individual's pay might include local income tax, the employee's contribution to health care benefits,

Exhibit 8 Sample Payroll Calculations and Payroll Journal Entries—Employee C

Employee C Payroll Calculation

Hourly Wage—Straight Time	87 hours × $8.00 per hour =	$ 696.00
Hourly Wage—Overtime	7 hours × $4.00 per hour =	$ 28.00
Commission on Skin Care Revenue	$6,585.00 × 40% =	$2,634.00
Product Sales Commission—1st 1M	$1,000.00 × 5% =	$ 50.00
Product Sales Commission—after 1M	$1,505.75 × 10% =	$ 150.58
Gross Compensation Available		$3,558.58
Less: Cafeteria plan deduction	Deduction before taxes	$ (200.00)
Gross Pay		$3,358.58
	Rate	
Social Security	6.20%	$ (220.63)
Medicare	1.45%	$ (51.60)
Net pay before 401(k) deduction		$3,086.35
401(k) Deduction—10% of $3,558.58	10.00%	$ (355.86)
Net pay for income tax withholding		$2,730.49
Federal Income Tax withholding from IRS Tables	(Based on payroll of $2,730.49)	$ (311.00)
Net Pay		$2,419.49

Payroll Journal for Employee C Payroll

		Debit	Credit
Salaries & Wages—Skin Care		$3,358.00	
Commissions—Skin Care		200.58	
Matching Contribution—401(k)		106.76	
Payroll Tax Expense—Social Sec.	Employer's matching amount.	220.63	
Payroll Tax Expense—Medicare		51.60	
Cafeteria Plan Payable			$ 200.00
Employee 401(k) Deferral Payable			355.86
Employer 401(k) Match Payable			106.76
Federal Withholding Payable			311.00
Social Security & Medicare Payable			544.46
Cash in Bank			2,419.49
		$3,937.57	$3,937.57

Exhibit 9 Sample Withholding Table

MARRIED Persons—**BIWEEKLY** Payroll Period
(For Wages Paid Through December 2010)

And the wages are–		And the number of withholding allowances claimed is—										
At least	But less than	0	1	2	3	4	5	6	7	8	9	10
		The amount of income tax to be withheld is—										
$0	**$540**	$0	$0	$0	$0	$0	$0	$0	$0	$0	$0	$0
540	**560**	2	0	0	0	0	0	0	0	0	0	0
560	**580**	4	0	0	0	0	0	0	0	0	0	0
580	**600**	6	0	0	0	0	0	0	0	0	0	0
600	**620**	8	0	0	0	0	0	0	0	0	0	0
620	**640**	10	0	0	0	0	0	0	0	0	0	0
640	**660**	12	0	0	0	0	0	0	0	0	0	0
660	**680**	14	0	0	0	0	0	0	0	0	0	0
680	**700**	16	2	0	0	0	0	0	0	0	0	0
700	**720**	18	4	0	0	0	0	0	0	0	0	0
720	**740**	20	6	0	0	0	0	0	0	0	0	0
740	**760**	22	8	0	0	0	0	0	0	0	0	0
760	**780**	24	10	0	0	0	0	0	0	0	0	0
780	**800**	26	12	0	0	0	0	0	0	0	0	0
800	**820**	28	14	0	0	0	0	0	0	0	0	0
820	**840**	30	16	2	0	0	0	0	0	0	0	0
840	**860**	32	18	4	0	0	0	0	0	0	0	0
860	**880**	34	20	6	0	0	0	0	0	0	0	0
880	**900**	36	22	8	0	0	0	0	0	0	0	0
900	**920**	38	24	10	0	0	0	0	0	0	0	0
920	**940**	40	26	12	0	0	0	0	0	0	0	0
940	**960**	43	28	14	0	0	0	0	0	0	0	0
960	**980**	46	30	16	2	0	0	0	0	0	0	0
980	**1000**	49	32	18	4	0	0	0	0	0	0	0
1000	**1020**	52	34	20	6	0	0	0	0	0	0	0
1020	**1040**	55	36	22	8	0	0	0	0	0	0	0
1040	**1060**	58	38	24	10	0	0	0	0	0	0	0
1060	**1080**	61	40	26	12	0	0	0	0	0	0	0
1080	**1100**	64	42	28	14	0	0	0	0	0	0	0
1100	**1120**	67	45	30	16	2	0	0	0	0	0	0
1120	**1140**	70	48	32	18	4	0	0	0	0	0	0
1140	**1160**	73	51	34	20	6	0	0	0	0	0	0
1160	**1180**	76	54	36	22	8	0	0	0	0	0	0
1180	**1200**	79	57	38	24	10	0	0	0	0	0	0
1200	**1220**	82	60	40	26	12	0	0	0	0	0	0
1220	**1240**	85	63	42	28	14	0	0	0	0	0	0
1240	**1260**	88	66	45	30	16	2	0	0	0	0	0
1260	**1280**	91	69	48	32	18	4	0	0	0	0	0
1280	**1300**	94	72	51	34	20	6	0	0	0	0	0
1300	**1320**	97	75	54	36	22	8	0	0	0	0	0
1320	**1340**	100	78	57	38	24	10	0	0	0	0	0
1340	**1360**	103	81	60	40	26	12	0	0	0	0	0
1360	**1380**	106	84	63	42	28	14	0	0	0	0	0
1380	**1400**	109	87	66	45	30	16	2	0	0	0	0
1400	**1420**	112	90	69	48	32	18	4	0	0	0	0
1420	**1440**	115	93	72	51	34	20	6	0	0	0	0
1440	**1460**	118	96	75	54	36	22	8	0	0	0	0
1460	**1480**	121	99	78	57	38	24	10	0	0	0	0
1480	**1500**	124	102	81	60	40	26	12	0	0	0	0
1500	**1520**	127	105	84	63	42	28	14	0	0	0	0
1520	**1540**	130	108	87	66	45	30	16	2	0	0	0
1540	**1560**	133	111	90	69	48	32	18	4	0	0	0
1560	**1580**	136	114	93	72	51	34	20	6	0	0	0
1580	**1600**	139	117	96	75	54	36	22	8	0	0	0
1600	**1620**	142	120	99	78	57	38	24	10	0	0	0
1620	**1640**	145	123	102	81	60	40	26	12	0	0	0
1640	**1660**	148	126	105	84	63	42	28	14	0	0	0
1660	**1680**	151	129	108	87	66	45	30	16	2	0	0
1680	**1700**	154	132	111	90	69	48	32	18	4	0	0
1700	**1720**	157	135	114	93	72	51	34	20	6	0	0
1720	**1740**	160	138	117	96	75	54	36	22	8	0	0
1740	**1760**	163	141	120	99	78	57	38	24	10	0	0
1760	**1780**	166	144	123	102	81	60	40	26	12	0	0
1780	**1800**	169	147	126	105	84	63	42	28	14	0	0
1800	**1820**	172	150	129	108	87	66	45	30	16	2	0
1820	**1840**	175	153	132	111	90	69	48	32	18	4	0
1840	**1860**	178	156	135	114	93	72	51	34	20	6	0
1860	**1880**	181	159	138	117	96	75	54	36	22	8	0
1880	**1900**	184	162	141	120	99	78	57	38	24	10	0
1900	**1920**	187	165	144	123	102	81	60	40	26	12	0
1920	**1940**	190	168	147	126	105	84	63	42	28	14	0
1940	**1960**	193	171	150	129	108	87	66	45	30	16	2
1960	**1980**	196	174	153	132	111	90	69	48	32	18	4
1980	**2000**	199	177	156	135	114	93	72	51	34	20	6
2000	**2020**	202	180	159	138	117	96	75	54	36	22	8
2020	**2040**	205	183	162	141	120	99	78	57	38	24	10
2040	**2060**	208	186	165	144	123	102	81	60	40	26	12
2060	**2080**	211	189	168	147	126	105	84	63	42	28	14
2080	**2100**	214	192	171	150	129	108	87	66	45	30	16
2100	**2120**	217	195	174	153	132	111	90	69	48	32	18
2120	**2140**	220	198	177	156	135	114	93	72	51	34	20
2140	**2160**	223	201	180	159	138	117	96	75	54	36	22
2160	**2180**	226	204	183	162	141	120	99	78	57	38	24
2180	**2200**	229	207	186	165	144	123	102	81	60	40	26
2200	**2220**	232	210	189	168	147	126	105	84	63	42	28

Publication 15 (2010) Page 47

union dues taken by the employer and later remitted to the union, or a payroll deduction for items such as charitable contributions and 401(k) contributions. All of these current liabilities are eventually remitted to the appropriate agencies. From the time they are deducted from employee wages until they are remitted to the agencies, they are considered current liabilities for the spa and recorded on the balance sheet.

6. *The amount of the employee's net pay.* Net pay is simply gross pay minus the various deductions. It is the amount of the payroll check.

The Entry to Record Payroll Taxes

The second major entry involving payroll is the one recording the employer's payroll taxes. **Payroll taxes** represent additional taxes paid by the employer based on employee wages. The three major elements of payroll taxes are the employer's FICA tax contribution and its contributions under the **Federal Unemployment Tax Act (FUTA)** and the **State Unemployment Tax Act (SUTA)**.

We have already discussed FICA taxes in relation to the first payroll entry. FICA also states that the employer must match the dollar amount of the credit to FICA Tax Payable in the first journal entry (that is, the entry to record the payroll will be the same dollar amount in this second journal entry). Employers are required to report the amounts of FICA taxes for employees on Federal Form 941, which is filed quarterly. The first page of Federal Form 941 is shown in Exhibit 10. Employers are now able to report FICA taxes electronically by touchtone telephone with Form 941 Telefile, and online via the Electronic Federal Tax Payment System website at www.eftps.gov.

The Federal Unemployment Tax Act (FUTA) establishes a tax that pays unemployment wages to people who have lost their jobs. This fund is financed through taxes levied on employer payrolls. The federal unemployment tax is 6.2 percent on employee wages up to $7,000. This tax is no longer levied on an employee's wages after the first $7,000.

States must contribute dollars into the federal unemployment fund. To do so, they levy their own state unemployment tax rates. These rates vary by state, but whatever that rate is, employers are allowed to use the state tax rate as a credit against the federal rate. For example, assume that a state levied a 5.4 percent state unemployment rate while the federal rate was 6.2 percent. This would result in a federal unemployment tax rate of 0.8 percent (that is, 6.2 percent minus 5.4 percent).

With the information given in the earlier example of calculating three employees' paychecks manually, and using a federal unemployment rate of 6.2 percent and a state rate of 5.4 percent, the spa would make the following journal entry (assuming no employee had earned $7,000 yet) to record its payroll taxes:

FUTA Expense	$58.30	
SUTA Expense	$393.55	
FUTA Payable		$58.30
SUTA Payable		$393.55

The amount of Payroll Tax Expense is simply the total of the three credits to the liability accounts. (The annual unemployment tax return for reporting federal taxes is Form 940. The first page is shown in Exhibit 11.)

The only connection between the two separate required entries is the FICA tax payable credit amount, which should be the same in both journal entries. Note

Exhibit 10 Federal Form 941

Form **941 for 2010: Employer's QUARTERLY Federal Tax Return** 951110
(Rev. April 2010) Department of the Treasury — Internal Revenue Service OMB No. 1545-0029

(EIN) Employer identification number ☐☐ - ☐☐☐☐☐☐☐

Name (not your trade name)

Trade name (if any)

Address
Number Street Suite or room number
City State ZIP code

Report for this Quarter of 2010 (Check one.)

☐ 1: January, February, March
☐ 2: April, May, June
☐ 3: July, August, September
☐ 4: October, November, December

Read the separate instructions before you complete Form 941. Type or print within the boxes.

Part 1: Answer these questions for this quarter.

1	Number of employees who received wages, tips, or other compensation for the pay period including: *Mar. 12* (Quarter 1), *June 12* (Quarter 2), *Sept. 12* (Quarter 3), or *Dec. 12* (Quarter 4)			1	
2	Wages, tips, and other compensation			2	.
3	Income tax withheld from wages, tips, and other compensation			3	.
4	If no wages, tips, and other compensation are subject to social security or Medicare tax				☐ Check and go to line 6e.
		Column 1	*Column 2*		
5a	Taxable social security wages*	. × .124 =	.		*Report wages/tips for this quarter, including those paid to qualified new employees, on lines 5a–5c. The social security tax exemption on wages/tips will be figured on lines 6c and 6d and will reduce the tax on line 6e.
5b	Taxable social security tips*	. × .124 =	.		
5c	Taxable Medicare wages & tips*	. × .029 =	.		
5d	Add *Column 2* line 5a, *Column 2* line 5b, and *Column 2* line 5c			5d	.
6a	Number of qualified employees *first* paid exempt wages/tips this quarter				See instructions for definitions of qualified employee and exempt wages/tips.
6b	Number of qualified employees paid exempt wages/tips this quarter				
6c	Exempt wages/tips paid to qualified employees this quarter	. × .062 =		6d	.
6e	Total taxes before adjustments (line 3 + line 5d – line 6d = line 6e)			6e	.
7a	Current quarter's adjustment for fractions of cents			7a	.
7b	Current quarter's adjustment for sick pay			7b	.
7c	Current quarter's adjustments for tips and group-term life insurance			7c	.
8	Total taxes after adjustments. Combine lines 6e through 7c			8	.
9	Advance earned income credit (EIC) payments made to employees			9	.
10	Total taxes after adjustment for advance EIC (line 8 – line 9 = line 10)			10	.
11	Total deposits, including prior quarter overpayments			11	.
12a	COBRA premium assistance payments (see instructions)			12a	.
12b	Number of individuals provided COBRA premium assistance				Complete lines 12c, 12d, and 12e only for the 2nd quarter of 2010.
12c	Number of qualified employees paid exempt wages/tips March 19–31				
12d	Exempt wages/tips paid to qualified employees March 19–31	. × .062 =		12e	.
13	Add lines 11, 12a, and 12e			13	.
14	Balance due. If line 10 is more than line 13, enter the difference and see instructions			14	.
15	Overpayment. If line 13 is more than line 10, enter the difference	.			Check one: ☐ Apply to next return. ☐ Send a refund.

► You MUST complete both pages of Form 941 and SIGN it. Next ►

For Privacy Act and Paperwork Reduction Act Notice, see the back of the Payment Voucher. Cat. No. 17001Z Form **941** (Rev. 4-2010)

the total cost of employees to the employer; that is, in this example, it costs the employer the gross wages of $5,000 plus the payroll taxes of $693 for a total cost to the employer of $5,693.

Exhibit 11 Federal Form 940

Form **940 for 2009: Employer's Annual Federal Unemployment (FUTA) Tax Return** 850109

Department of the Treasury — Internal Revenue Service OMB No. 1545-0028

(EIN)
Employer identification number ☐☐ - ☐☐☐☐☐☐☐

Name *(not your trade name)*

Trade name *(if any)*

Address Number Street Suite or room number

City State ZIP code

Type of Return
(Check all that apply.)

☐ **a.** Amended
☐ **b.** Successor employer
☐ **c.** No payments to employees in 2009
☐ **d.** Final: Business closed or stopped paying wages

Read the separate instructions before you fill out this form. Please type or print within the boxes.

Part 1: Tell us about your return. If any line does NOT apply, leave it blank.

1 If you were required to pay your state unemployment tax in ...

1a One state only, write the state abbreviation . . . . **1a** ☐☐

- OR -

1b More than one state (You are a multi-state employer) . . . . **1b** ☐ Check here. Fill out Schedule A.

2 If you paid wages in a state that is subject to CREDIT REDUCTION . . . . **2** ☐ Check here. Fill out Schedule A (Form 940), Part 2.

Part 2: Determine your FUTA tax before adjustments for 2009. If any line does NOT apply, leave it blank.

3 Total payments to all employees . . . . **3** .

4 Payments exempt from FUTA tax . . . . **4** .

Check all that apply: **4a** ☐ Fringe benefits **4c** ☐ Retirement/Pension **4e** ☐ Other
4b ☐ Group-term life insurance **4d** ☐ Dependent care

5 Total of payments made to each employee in excess of $7,000 . . . . **5** .

6 Subtotal (line 4 + line 5 = line 6) . . . . **6** .

7 Total taxable FUTA wages (line 3 – line 6 = line 7) . . . . **7** .

8 FUTA tax before adjustments (line 7 × .008 = line 8) . . . . **8** .

Part 3: Determine your adjustments. If any line does NOT apply, leave it blank.

9 If ALL of the taxable FUTA wages you paid were excluded from state unemployment tax, multiply line 7 by .054 (line 7 × .054 = line 9). Then go to line 12 . . . . **9** .

10 If SOME of the taxable FUTA wages you paid were excluded from state unemployment tax, OR you paid ANY state unemployment tax late (after the due date for filing Form 940), fill out the worksheet in the instructions. Enter the amount from line 7 of the worksheet . . . . . . **10** .

11 If credit reduction applies, enter the amount from line 3 of Schedule A (Form 940) . . . . . . **11** .

Part 4: Determine your FUTA tax and balance due or overpayment for 2009. If any line does NOT apply, leave it blank.

12 Total FUTA tax after adjustments (lines 8 + 9 + 10 + 11 = line 12) . . . . **12** .

13 FUTA tax deposited for the year, including any overpayment applied from a prior year . . **13** .

14 Balance due (If line 12 is more than line 13, enter the difference on line 14.)
- If line 14 is more than $500, you must deposit your tax.
- If line 14 is $500 or less, you may pay with this return. For more information on how to pay, see the separate instructions . . . . **14** .

15 Overpayment (If line 13 is more than line 12, enter the difference on line 15 and check a box below.) . . . . **15** .

Check one: ☐ Apply to next return. ☐ Send a refund.

▶ You **MUST** fill out both pages of this form and **SIGN** it.

Next ➡

For Privacy Act and Paperwork Reduction Act Notice, see the back of Form 940-V, Payment Voucher. Cat. No. 11234O Form **940** (2009)

Employees often do not realize what the costs of their employment actually are to the employer. In this case, there is a 14 percent difference between the gross wages of the employees and the total payroll cost to the employer (and this does not include the cost of any additional benefits the employer provides to its employees). Since employee benefits and payroll taxes can be costly, spas may outsource or hire independent contractors rather than use employees to perform certain services—such as accounting, data processing, computer and software maintenance, and janitorial or equipment service—and save on payroll taxes. Payroll tax expenses and employee benefits are expensed directly to the individual departments, i.e., Skin Care, Massage, etc. Alternatively, payroll tax expense and employee expenses can be grouped on a single schedule. Exhibit 12 shows the recording of the three manual payroll checks discussed earlier on the Schedule of Payroll Taxes and Employee Benefits from the *Uniform System of Financial Reporting for Spas*.

Payroll expenses, including wages, commissions, taxes, and benefits, are recorded directly to the individual department income statements and summarized on the summary statement of income. Exhibit 13 reflects the payroll information for Employee C, the esthetician from our earlier example. The summary statement of income combines the payroll expenses included on the Skin Care—Schedule 2L into one line item (see Exhibit 14). The Spa's balance sheet demonstrates the effect of the manual payroll check paid to Employee C for the payroll period ended August 15, 20X8 (see Exhibit 15).

Reporting Tips

Most employees of spas receive tips from their clients. There are both federal and state regulations on tip reporting, and the calculation of tip reporting can be complex. (For additional information on the calculation of tip reporting, see IRS Publication 531, Reporting Tip Income.)

Tips are voluntary contributions by clients to a spa's employees. By law, they belong to the spa's employees. When clients use their credit cards to pay their charges and add tips for their therapists, the tip amount must be paid to the therapists. The spa must recognize the amount tipped for FICA purposes and pay both the therapist's and the spa's share of FICA tax on the tip. (This was part of the discussion for determining the effective compensation rate earlier in the chapter.) Technically, the tip received by the spa is a liability of the spa until paid.

When clients are charged an automatic service charge, it must be recognized as revenue. In Exhibit 13, the service charge as revenue would be shown under Other—Service Charge. When the service charge is paid to the spa's staff, the amount is recorded as Distributed Service Charges and shown as payroll and related expenses (also on Exhibit 13). The related FICA taxes for service charges were discussed in determining ECR earlier in the chapter.

Accruing Unpaid Wages

Wages are paid periodically to spa employees—on a biweekly basis, for example. However, the two-week pay period seldom ends on the last day of an accounting period. Therefore, to record all wages for the month, wages must be accrued using an adjusting entry. The accrual recognizes both Wages Expense and the liability Wages Payable.

Exhibit 12 Schedule of Payroll Taxes and Employee Benefit

The Spa
The Luxury Resort
Payroll Taxes and Employee Benefits—Schedule 19S-19L
For the two weeks ended August 15, 20X8

	Jayne Clark	Joan Breedlove								Rhonda Brown				
	Sched 1L Massage	Sched 2L Skin Care	Sched 3L Hair	Sched 4L Nail	Sched 5L Fitness	Sched 6L Food & Beverage	Sched 7L Health & Wellness	Sched 9L Retail	Sched 10L Other Operating Departments	Sched 12L Support Labor	Sched 14L Admin & General	Sched 15L Marketing	Sched 16L Facility Maintenance and Utilities	Total
Payroll Taxes														
Federal Retirement (FICA)	144	221								99				464
Federal Unemployment (FUTA)	–	–								–				–
Medicare (FICA)	34	52								23				109
State Disability	–	–												–
State Unemployment (SUTA)	–	–												–
Total Payroll Taxes	178	272	–	–	–	–	–	–	–	122	–	–	–	573
Employee Benefits														
Auto Allowance														–
Childcare														–
Contributory Savings Plan (401[k])	70	107												177
Dental Insurance														–
Disability Pay														–
Group Life Insurance		(200)												(200)
Health Insurance														–
Meals														–
Profit Sharing														–
Stock Benefits														–
Workers' Compensation														–
Other														–
Total Employee Benefits	70	(93)	–	–	–	–	–	–	–	–	–	–	–	(23)
Total Payroll Taxes and Employee Benefits	248	179	–	–	–	–	–	–	–	122	–	–	–	550

Exhibit 13 Payroll Information for Employee C

The Spa
The Luxury Resort
Skin Care—Schedule 2L
For the two weeks ended August 15, 20X8

	Two weeks ended 8/15/20X8	
Revenue		
Facial Treatments		
Standard Facials		
Specialty Facials	–	
Total Facial Treatments		
Waxing Services		
Body Hair Removal		
Face Hair Removal	–	
Total Waxing Services		
Other		
Breakage		
Service Charge		
Other Revenue	–	
Total Other		
Total Revenue	–	
Allowances		
Net Revenue	–	
Direct Expenses		
Payroll & Related Expenses		
Salaries & Wages	3,358	
Commissions	201	
Contract		
Distributed Service Charges		
Payroll Taxes & Employee Benefits	272	P/R Taxes and Benefit Sch.
Total Payroll & Related Expenses	3,831	
Other—Professional Products & Supplies		
Total Direct Expenses	3,831	
Departmental Contribution	(3,831)	

Schedule depicts the payroll expenses only for Employee C for the biweekly payroll period ended August 15, 20X8. This schedule is included in the Summary Income Statement.

Assume The Spa pays its employees every two weeks, and the last payday in January is January 24. Wages for the period of January 25–31 must be accrued. For simplicity's sake, let's assume that all employees' wages total $10,000 every 14 days. Since the January 25–31 period covers seven days, the accrual should be $5,000. The adjustment would be recorded as follows:

Exhibit 14 Summary Statement of Income

The Spa
The Luxury Resort
STATEMENT OF INCOME
For the period ended August 15, 20X8

	Month to Date	Manual Payroll for Joan Breedlove August 15, 20X8	Month To Date	
Net Revenue				
Massage	$ 4,750		$ 4,750	
Skin Care	3,000		3,000	
Hair	1,800		1,800	
Nail	2,485		2,485	
Fitness	700		700	
Food and Beverage	285		285	
Health and Wellness	600		600	
Memberships	3,400		3,400	
Retail	3,684		3,684	
Rental and Other	800		800	
Other Operating Activities	415		415	
Less: Guest and Employee Discounts & Comps			–	
Total Net Revenue	$ 21,919		$ 21,919	
Cost of Goods and Direct Expenses				
Massage	–	–	–	
Skin Care	–	3,738	3,738	Skin Care Schd. 2L
Hair	–	–	–	
Nail	–	–	–	
Fitness	–	–	–	
Food and Beverage	–	–	–	
Health and Wellness	–	–	–	
Retail	–	–	–	
Other Operating Activities	–	–	–	
Total Direct Expenses	–	3,738	3,738	
Gross Margin	21,919	(3,738)	18,181	
Indirect Expenses				
Indirect Operating Expenses	–		–	
Indirect Support Labor	–		–	
Total Indirect Expenses	–	–	–	
Undistributed Operating Expenses				
General and Administrative	–	–	–	
Marketing	–	–	–	
Facility Maintenance and Utilities	–	–	–	
Total Undistributed Operating Expenses	–	–	–	
Income Before Fixed Charges	21,919	(3,738)	18,181	

(continued)

Exhibit 14 *(continued)*

Fixed Charges			
Insurance	–	–	–
Management Fees	–	–	–
Rent	–	–	–
Real Estate/Personal Property Taxes	–	–	–
Total Fixed Charges	–	–	–
Income Before Depreciation, Amortization, Interest Expense & Income Taxes	21,919	(3,738)	18,181
Depreciation and Amortization	–	–	–
Interest Expense	–	–	–
(Gain) and Loss on Disposal of Property	–	–	–
Total	–	–	–
Income Before Income Taxes	21,919	(3,738)	18,181
Income Taxes	–	–	–
Net Income	$21,919	$(3,738)	$18,181

Wages Expense	$5,000	
Wage Payable		$5,000
To record accrued wages at the end of January.		

In addition, the related payroll tax expenses must be recorded. For simplicity's sake, we will focus only on the FICA accrual. The FICA accrual is calculated as follows:

$$\$5{,}000 \times .0765 = \$382.50$$

The adjustment would be recorded as follows:

FICA Expense	$ 382.50	
FICA Payable		$ 382.50
To record accrued FICA expenses at the end of January.		

These accruals are made simply to record the expense for the proper accounting period (in this case, January) and the related liability following GAAP. When the pay period is complete, the employees will be paid the amounts earned and related payroll expenses will be recorded. To make the accounting easier in the following month (in this case, February), the payroll for the first biweekly period can be recorded as discussed previously. However, when this payroll is recorded, the payroll expense is overstated for the following month because it includes amounts accrued for the prior month. To correct the overstatement, reversing entries must be recorded in the month following the month of the accrual. Because payroll in a spa represents such a significant expense, failing to make proper accrual entries

Exhibit 15 Balance Sheet

The Spa
The Luxury Resort
Balance Sheet
For the period ended August 15, 20X8

Assets

	Balance, August 15, 20X8	Manual Payroll for Joan Breedlove	Balance after Posting Payroll Information	
CURRENT ASSETS				
Cash in Bank	$ 245,600	(2,419)	243,181	Net Payroll Check
Accounts Receivable				
Credit Cards	65,056		65,056	
Members	200,000		200,000	
Resort Guests	45,123		45,123	
Total Acct's Receivable	310,179	–	310,179	
Inventories				
Retail	104,586		104,586	
Professional	21,564		21,564	
Other	2,541		2,541	
Prepaid Expenses	45,127		45,127	
Deferred Income Taxes, Current	5,421		5,421	
Other Current Assets	1,000		1,000	
Total Current Assets	$ 736,018	$(2,419)	733,599	
			–	
PROPERTY AND EQUIPMENT			–	
Land	1,000,000		1,000,000	
Buildings	4,500,125		4,500,125	
Leaseholds and Leasehold Improvements	450,000		450,000	
Construction in Progress	145,236		145,236	
Furniture, Fixtures and Equipment	1,546,000		1,546,000	
Automobiles	46,851		46,851	
Total Property and Equipment	7,688,212		7,688,212	
Less: Accumulated Depreciation	(1,254,800)		(1,254,800)	
Net Property and Equipment	6,433,412		6,433,412	
OTHER ASSETS			–	
Security and Lease Deposits	65,000		65,000	
Loan Fees	–		–	
Intangibles	100,000		100,000	
Deferred Income Taxes, Noncurrent	45,125		45,125	
Other Assets	65,000		65,000	
Total Other Assets	275,125		275,125	
			–	
TOTAL ASSETS	$7,444,555		$7,442,136	

(continued)

Exhibit 15 *(continued)*

Liabilities and Owners' Equity

	Balance, August 15, 20X8	Manual Payroll for Joan Breedlove	Balance after Posting Payroll Information
CURRENT LIABILITIES			
Accounts Payable	$ 25,685		$ 25,685
Sales Tax Payable	1,149		1,149
Gratuities Payable	2,856		2,856
Current Portion of Long-Term Debt	55,000		55,000
Income Taxes Payable	85,000		85,000
Accrued Expenses	45,235		45,235
Payroll Taxes Payable—Income Taxes		311	311
FICA and Medicare Taxes Payable		545	545
401(k) Deferrals and Matching Payable		463	463
Cafeteria Plan Payable		200	200
Deferred Revenue—Gift Certificates	210,300		210,300
Customer Deposits	45,600		45,600
Deferred Income Taxes-Current	15,252		15,252
Other Current Liabilities	5,635		5,635
Total Current Liabilities	491,712	1,519	493,231
			–
LONG-TERM LIABILITIES			–
Notes Payable	1,500,000	–	1,500,000
Total Long-Term Liabilities	1,500,000		1,500,000
			–
OWNERS EQUITY			–
Common Stock	4,000,000	–	4,000,000
Retained Earnings	1,452,843	(3,938)	1,448,905
Total Owners' Equity	5,452,843	(3,938)	5,448,905
			–
TOTAL LIABILITIES AND OWNERS' EQUITY	$7,444,555	$(2,419)	$7,442,136

can have a significant and very misleading impact on reported performance for a reporting period. In fact, if an accrual is missed, it will cause current expenses to be understated and the subsequent period's expenses to be overstated.

Continuing with our example, the spa's reversing entries recorded on February 1 will be as follows:

Wages Expense	$5,000	
Wage Payable		$5,000
FICA Expense	$ 382.50	
FICA Payable		$ 382.50
To reverse the adjustments at the end of January.		

The T-account for Wages Expense after the payment of the first payroll in February would appear as follows:

Wages Expense

Debit		Credit	
		Feb. 1 (reversing entry)	$5,000
Feb. 7 (actual payroll entry)	$10,000		
Bal.	5,000		

The $5,000 balance in the Wages Expense T-account reflects the actual wages expense for the first week of February—$10,000 in total was paid to the employees.

Summary

Payroll, along with all its related tax liabilities, represents the largest expense of a spa. The major components are salary/wages, fringe benefits, and payroll taxes.

The calculation of an employee's gross wages is often fairly complex due to the numerous elements that may be included, such as base pay, variable pay, tips, retail commissions, and merit pay. To determine the actual labor expense per treatment, an effective compensation rate should be calculated.

Spas will often use independent contractors to provide various treatments. To avoid being assessed interest and penalties for wrongly classifying a employee as an independent contractor, the spa director should carefully use the IRS 20 Factor Test to make a proper classification determination.

In order to proper control payroll expense, the following payroll functions are required:

1. Authorization of employment and establishment of wage rates for employees
2. Reporting hours worked by employees
3. Preparation of payroll
4. Signing of payroll checks
5. Distribution of checks to employees
6. Reconciliation of payroll bank account

U.S. spa managers must be aware of the Fair Labor Standards Act and its coverage of equal pay for equal work, record keeping requirements, minimum wage rates, and overtime pay rules. Spas keep a master payroll file, and accounting for payroll is facilitated with a payroll journal and employees earnings records.

In the United States, tips received from customers must be properly accounted for following IRS regulations. At the end of each year, employees are issued W-2s in accordance with the Internal Revenue code.

Wages earned during an accounting period, such as a month, that are not paid to the employees during that month must be accrued. The related payroll taxes must also be recognized.

Since labor costs are significant, spa directors must make sure the accounting personnel handling payroll are diligent and detailed in properly accounting for these costs.

Endnote

1. All IRS forms and publications discussed in this chapter may be downloaded free of charge from the Internal Revenue Service's website at www.irs.gov/formspubs/index.html.

Key Terms

employee's earnings record—An individual record kept for each employee during the calendar year that shows gross wages earned and amounts withheld and deducted. Used at the end of the year to prepare IRS Form W-2.

Federal Insurance Contributions Act (FICA)—An act that levies employment taxes on employers and employees as part of the federal Social Security program. Employers must deduct FICA taxes from employees' wages.

Federal Unemployment Tax Act (FUTA)—A federal law imposing a payroll tax on employers for the purpose of funding national and state unemployment programs.

imprest payroll account—A payroll account for which a predetermined, fixed amount of funds are maintained or replenished as part of typical control procedures.

master payroll file—A payroll file containing employee information, including employee names, addresses, Social Security numbers, wage rates, and payroll deduction information.

payroll journal—A journal containing a record of each payroll check issued, along with the corresponding gross pay and various deductions for taxes, health care, and so on.

payroll taxes—Additional taxes, paid by the employer, which are based on employee wages. The three major payroll taxes are a result of the Federal Insurance Contribution Act (FICA), the Federal Unemployment Tax Act (FUTA), and the State Unemployment Tax Act (SUTA).

State Unemployment Tax Act (SUTA)—An unemployment tax rate levied by individual states. The rate varies by state, and employers may use the state tax rate as a credit against the federal rate.

Review Questions

1. How significant are the labor costs of a spa?
2. What basic items should be included in a payroll master file?
3. What information is provided in a payroll journal?
4. What information is provided by an employee earnings record?
5. What are the differences between the entry to record the payroll and the entry to record the payroll taxes?

6. What does the acronym "FICA" stand for, and is the FICA tax an employer tax or an employee tax?
7. How is the effective compensation rate determined?
8. Are FUTA and SUTA taxes paid by the employer, the employee, or both?
9. What is usually the most difficult timekeeping area for a spa to control? What is the recommended way to deal with this area?

Chapter 3 Outline

Competencies

1. Describe types of spa inventory and outline the perpetual and periodic inventory systems. (pp. 77–79)
2. Describe and compare the three different inventory valuation methods. (pp. 79–84)
3. Demonstrate how to estimate inventory values using the gross profit method and the retail inventory method. (pp. 84–87)
4. Explain the LCM requirement and discuss how different types of costs vary with inventory decisions. (pp. 87–88)
5. Identify and differentiate between the different types of inventory monitoring systems. (pp. 88–89)
6. List some recommendations on performing cycle counts, avoiding out-of-stocks, and avoiding shrinkage. (pp. 89–91)

3

Inventory

AS MONICA IS DRIVING into work at the Day Spa, she says to herself, "Where did the month go? Here it is March 31 already and the end of the first quarter of the year." She knows what that means—it is inventory night. Not her favorite thing to do, but she knows that monthly financial statements are supposed to accurately reflect the events that occurred during the month, both good and bad. Taking regular inventories is important for accurate and consistent financial statements.

Over the years, Monica has learned that not all accountants want to record expenses in the same way. There are some who do not like inventory management and believe that when the spa places an order, it should be expensed right away. Well, that's acceptable for Q-tips and other disposables, but how about when the spa orders $3,000 in new robes, or when the locker room shower supplies are purchased in gallon sizes with four gallons per case and a six case minimum? The spa doesn't want to have $3,000 in robe expense one month and none for the next few months. When expensing the entire cost upon delivery, the spa can end up with one month when expenses are high and the next month when expenses are very low. This can create inconsistent operating results and make it difficult to tell if there is an inventory control problem or not. Such inconsistency can result in many frustrating, often unproductive hours going through accounting entries, invoices, and other documents trying to explain the reason for the inconsistency of one month when compared to another month or when compared to budget.

The spa's current accountant is a believer in inventory management and has developed a written policy that establishes the criteria and determines what gets inventoried and how frequently the category is to be counted. It's not that he wants small consumable items like copy paper inventoried, but he recognizes that operating supplies are used every day and wants the month-end statements to be an accurate reflection of that month's expenses. For significant items like linens and robes, marketing brochures, spa menus, and professional products, it is best to complete regular inventories for the purpose of recording accurate consumption of operating supplies. Controlling inventory allows the spa management team to learn about the operation. Additionally, it provides excellent information for decision-making and alerts management to problems.

Monica remembers her worst inventory nightmare —working for a spa director who took retail inventory only once every six months. The accountant would book the budgeted cost of goods sold percentage each month and then reconcile the entries against the physical inventory that was taken every six months. During that six-month period, the spa was experiencing a lot of retail inventory shrinkage. Therapists would simply take a retail product to use for treatments if they were out of the product in their professional inventory. Retail items were taken from the shelves and given to a frequent client as a way of saying thank you without having the spa desk staff record the gift as Sales and Promotion. The result was an 88.3 percent retail cost of goods sold for the month, which created a huge stir with the spa's owner. Monica remembers spending days trying to reconstruct inventory variances and trying to explain what happened to the owner without criticizing the accountant who had not set any policies and procedures with respect to taking inventories. Although that experience was a good lesson, it's something Monica never wants to go through again. She has since been committed to regular inventory counts and inventory management and control policies.

The Day Spa conducts a monthly inventory of all retail merchandise, professional treatment products, and grooming area products that it buys in bulk. Additionally, as is part of the inventory policy, at the end of the quarter Monica organizes the inventory of spa linens and robes. She has also taken the advice given to her by her friend Erica, who told her about her father's inventory practice from working in a hotel kitchen in the old days. In addition to taking the regular monthly food and beverage inventories, her father did daily "steak counts." The kitchen manager would count the high-price items such as the steaks, lobster tails, caviar, and saffron, and then match the counts against starting inventory. New product received the previous day was matched against what was sold on the daily sales report to make sure that everything was accounted for, almost like maintaining a perpetual inventory.

In today's spas, there are jars or bottles of spa products that can cost \$100–\$200 and must be treated like gold, so a supervisor is assigned to take a daily inventory of these goods to ensure that nothing goes missing. After all, if you lose a few jars of expensive product, it directly affects the cost of goods sold and profitability performance.

Monica arrives in the spa parking area knowing that she can begin her day by taking inventory of the retail storage room. It will be a long evening, as most of the inventories must be taken after the spa has closed for the day and the inventory stops moving. Monica recognizes that taking physical counts is not the end of the inventory process. Everything has to be extended and the total value from the physical inventory must be reconciled with what is recorded on the general ledger accounts and balance sheet. If the difference (variance) is significant, it will have to be investigated, which could mean many more tedious hours of work.

This chapter deals with various types of inventory, inventory valuation, and how inventory decisions and processes affect retail cost of goods sold, monthly operating expenses, and the spa monthly department profit.

You should be able to answer these questions after studying this chapter:

1. How is inventory defined?
2. What are the three types of inventory maintained by a spa?
3. What is a perpetual inventory system?
4. What is a periodic inventory system?
5. What do LIFO and FIFO mean?
6. During periods of rising costs, which inventory valuation method results in the highest cost of sales?
7. What are two advantages of LIFO?
8. What is gross profit?
9. How is cost of sales determined using the gross profit method?
10. What are three inventory holding costs?

Inventory Management

Inventory can be defined both as the stock of items on hand at a particular time and as a listing of those products and how many of each is on hand. Taking inventory means counting the items in inventory and updating the list of what is on hand.

Inventory may be purchased for resale or for use in the spa. Separate inventories are maintained for resale items and professional use items. For example, shampoo is purchased for resale and used by hair stylists for washing clients' hair; in most cases, the unit size, packaging, and cost of the retail shampoo will be smaller, more eye-catching, and more expensive than the shampoo purchased (generally in bulk) for use in the spa. The cost of the shampoo is recorded initially as inventory on the balance sheet. When sold or used, it will be recorded as Cost of Goods Sold or Hair Professional Product expense.

Spas have three types of inventory: retail, professional, and operating supplies. **Retail inventory** includes products that are sold directly to the consumer. These may include:

- Apparel: footwear, women's, men's/unisex, robes and terry
- Gifts and accessories: books and media, fashion accessories, home products
- Spa products: bath/body products, hair products, make-up products, nail products, private label products, skin care products
- Other retail inventory: snacks and beverages, sundries, miscellaneous retail items

Professional inventory includes products used to perform services for clients. These may include:

- Hair products: shampoo and conditioning products, color products, chemical products, styling products

Exhibit 1 Periodic versus Perpetual Inventory Systems

Perpetual Inventory System	Periodic Inventory System
Inventory account and the balance of Costs of Goods Sold exist throughout year.	The inventory account and Cost of Goods Sold are nonexistent until the physical count at the end of the period.
No individual Purchases account is used; however, the purchases are recorded in the Inventory account.	A Purchases account is used to record purchases.
No individual Purchase Returns account is used; however, the purchases returned are recorded as reductions in the Inventory assuming they had been initially recorded as Inventory before being returned.	The Purchase Return account is used to record purchase returns.
Cost of Goods Sold is recorded and inventory is reduced when there is a sale.	Cost of Goods Sold is computed from the ending inventory figure.
Returns from customers are recorded by reducing the Cost of Goods Sold and adding back into inventory.	There are no inventory entries for goods returned by customers unless they are unopened and resalable.

- Skin care products: facial products, chemicals for medically supervised peels, microdermabrasion supplies, tissue fillers
- Massage inventory: body treatment products and massage treatment products
- Nail inventory: foot care products and hand care products
- Skin care inventory: facial treatment products and hair removal products

Operating supplies inventory includes items that a spa would order in larger quantities to be used over several months. Examples would include gift wrap and packaging, logo paper, and plastic bags. Marketing and collateral materials are typically printed in large quantities that must be inventoried. Examples might include spa brochures, menus of services, thank-you cards, and guest intake forms. Grooming area products (often purchased in 30–55 gallon drums or cases of four one-gallon containers) might include shampoo and conditioner used in guest showers or the salon shampoo station back bar, shower gel in showers, body lotion, and sunscreen lotion.

Inventory Classification Systems

The two generally accepted inventory classification systems that a spa may use are the **perpetual inventory system** and the **periodic inventory system** (see Exhibit 1).

The format of an inventory system may vary according to the requirements of the individual spa business practices.

Under the perpetual inventory system, records are kept of the quantity and cost of individual inventory items throughout the year as soon as the items are purchased/received from vendors and as soon as inventory items are sold to customers or consumed in operations. It is an ongoing running tally of the quantity and value of what should be on hand at any point in time. The cost of goods sold is recorded as goods are transferred (sold) to customers as Cost of Goods Sold or used in operations as an operating expense, and the inventory balance is kept current at all times. A perpetual inventory system does not eliminate the need for periodic physical inventory counts, which are needed to ensure the perpetual inventory records are a true reflection of inventory on hand at the end of the accounting period. Adjusting/reconciling entries may sometimes be needed on the perpetual inventory records to bring them into line with actual physical inventory. See Exhibits 2 and 3 for examples of the perpetual inventory system.

Under the periodic inventory system, a physical inventory is taken at the end of an accounting period (e.g., monthly, quarterly, semi-annually, or annually.) Detailed records of physical inventory movement and inventory on hand at any point in time are not maintained during the period. The Cost of Goods Sold is computed after the physical inventory is taken. See Exhibits 2 and 3 for examples of the periodic inventory system.

Inventory Valuation Methods

An inventory valuation allows a company to provide a monetary value for items that make up its inventory stock. Inventory is sometimes a business's largest current asset. Proper valuation is necessary to ensure accurate financial statements. If inventory is not properly valued, expenses cannot be properly matched to revenues, and a company could be at risk for making poor business decisions because of misleading information.

The three most common valuation methods directly affect cost of goods sold, and thus gross margin, differently. The three are known as weighted average; first-in, first-out (FIFO); and last-in, first-out (LIFO). We will go over examples of each of these valuation methods using the information in the following table:

	Number of Items	Unit Purchase Cost	Total Cost
Beginning Inventory	200	$12.00	$2,400
Purchase #1	400	13.00	5,200
Purchase #2	300	13.70	4,110
Purchase #3	350	14.20	4,970
Goods Available for Sale	1,250		$16,680
		Unit Selling Price	**Total Sales**
Units Sold During Month	870	$20	$17,400
Units on Hand at End of Month	380		

Exhibit 2 Spa A: Retail Merchandise

On May 1, 20X9, Spa A purchased on account 100 units of retail merchandise at $30 per unit.

Perpetual Inventory System

5/1/X9	Debit	Credit
Retail Merchandise Inventory	$3,000	
Accounts Payable		$3,000

Periodic Inventory System

5/1/X9	Debit	Credit
Retail Merchandise Purchases	$3,000	
Accounts Payable		$3,000

Under the periodic inventory system, all purchases during the accounting period are recorded in the Purchases account.

On May 6, 20X9, Spa A sold 20 units of retail merchandise at $50 per unit and received cash.

Perpetual Inventory System

5/6/X9	Debit	Credit
Cash	$1,000	
Retail Sales		$1,000
Cost of Goods Sold	$ 600	
Retail Merchandise Inventory		$ 600

Under the perpetual inventory system, changes in merchandise inventory are recorded after each transaction, that is, after each purchase and each sale.

Periodic Inventory System

5/6/X9	Debit	Credit
Cash	$1,000	
Retail Sales		$1,000
5/31/X9		
Retail Merchandise Inventory	$2,400	
Purchases		$2,400

Under the periodic inventory system, the second journal entry is recorded at the end of an accounting period.

Quantity of Merchandise Inventory

100 units purchased – 20 units sold = 80 units

Cost of Merchandise Inventory

80 units × $30/unit = $2,400

5/31/X9	Debit	Credit
Cost of Goods Sold	$ 600	
Retail Purchases		$ 600

Total purchased – ending balance of merchandise inventory

100 units × $30/unit – 80 units × $30/unit

Ending Inventory = Beginning Inventory + Purchases during the Period – Cost of Goods Sold
= $0 + $3,000 – $600
= $2,400

Cost of Goods Sold = Beginning Inventory + Purchases During the Period – Ending Inventory
= $0 + $3,000 – $2,400
= $600

Exhibit 3 Spa B: Retail Merchandise

On June 5, 20X9, Spa B purchased on account 60 units of merchandise at $35 per unit.

Perpetual Inventory System

6/5/X9	Debit	Credit
Retail Merchandise Inventory	$2,100	
Accounts Payable		$2,100

Periodic Inventory System

6/5/X9	Debit	Credit
Retail Merchandise Purchases	$2,100	
Accounts Payable		$2,100

Under the periodic inventory system, all purchases during the accounting period are recorded in the Purchases account.

On June 16, 2009, Spa B sold 40 units of merchandise at $55 per unit on credit.

6/16/X9	Debit	Credit
Cash	$2,200	
Retail Sales		$2,200
Cost of Goods Sold	$1,400	
Retail Merchandise Inventory		$1,400

Under the perpetual inventory system, changes in merchandise inventory are recorded after each transaction, that is, after each purchase and each sale.

6/16/X9	Debit	Credit
Cash	$2,200	
Retail Sales		$2,200
6/30/X9		
Retail Merchandise Inventory	$ 700	
Purchases		$ 700

Under the periodic inventory system, the second journal entry is recorded at the end of an accounting period.

Quantity of Merchandise Inventory

60 units purchased – 40 units sold = 20 units

Cost of Merchandise Inventory

20 units × $35/unit = $700

6/30/X9	Debit	Credit
Cost of Goods Sold	$1,400	
Retail Purchases		$1,400

Total purchased – ending balance of merchandise inventory

60 units × $35/unit – 20 units × $35/unit

Ending Inventory = Beginning Inventory + Purchases during the Period – Cost of Goods Sold
= $0 + $2,100 – $1,400
= $700

Cost of Goods Sold = Beginning Inventory + Purchases During the Period – Ending Inventory
= $0 + $2,100 – $700
= $1,400

Weighted Average Method

In the **weighted average method of inventory valuation**, value is determined by averaging the costs of items in the beginning inventory with the cost of items purchased during the period. First, an average cost is determined by dividing total costs by total units. The average cost is then multiplied by the number of units remaining at the end of the period to determine the ending inventory. Cost of Goods Sold and Gross Margin are then calculated using the following formulas:

Cost of Goods Sold = Goods Available for Sale − Ending Inventory
Gross Margin = Net Sales − Cost of Goods Sold

Using the information provided in the previous table, average cost and ending inventory are calculated as follows:

Average Cost = $16,680 ÷ 1,250 = $13.34   Ending Inventory = 380 × $13.34 = $5,070.72

Goods Available for Sale	$16,680.00	Net Sales	$17,400.00
Ending Inventory	−5,070.72	Cost of Goods Sold	−11,609.28
Cost of Goods Sold	$11,609.28	Gross Margin	$ 5,790.72

First-In, First-Out Method

The **first-in, first-out (FIFO) method of inventory valuation** is commonly used in the spa industry. If you assume that the items purchased first were sold first, then those remaining in inventory would be the more recent items purchased. This makes sense from a physical flow standpoint, particularly when dealing with inventoried items that have expiration dates, like many skin care products. For inventory valuation purposes, however, it does not matter if the actual physical products purchased first are issued from inventory first; what matters is that the *cost* of the earliest purchase is used for issues. The FIFO method values the ending inventory as if you sold first the items purchased first.

	Number of Items	**Unit Cost**	**Total Cost**
Remaining Units:			
From Purchase #3	350	$14.20	$4,970
From Purchase #2	30	13.70	411
Ending Inventory	380		$5,381

Using the formulas provided in the previous section discussing the weighted average cost method, the Cost of Goods Sold and Gross Margin are calculated as follows:

Goods Available for Sale	$16,680	Net Sales	$17,400
Ending Inventory	− 5,381	Cost of Goods Sold	−11,299
Cost of Goods Sold	$11,299	Gross Margin	$6,101

Alternatively, the cost of goods sold can be determined by totaling the costs of units sold as follows:

	Number of Items	Unit Cost	Total
Beginning Inventory	200	$12.00	$2,400
Purchase #1	400	$13.00	$5,200
Purchase #2	270	$13.70	$3,699
Total	870		$11,299

Last-In, First-Out Method

In the **last-in, first-out (LIFO) method of inventory valuation**, the costs for the items purchased last are used first. Those items remaining in inventory at the end of the accounting period would be the earlier item purchased. Although this does not usually make sense from a physical product flow standpoint, it does not matter from an accounting perspective—the actual product flow does not need to match the one chosen for determining the cost of goods sold. That is, you can issue the oldest product in inventory, but value it at the most recent purchase price.

	Number of Items	Unit Cost	Total Cost
Remaining Units:			
From Beginning Inventory	200	$12.00	$2,400
From Purchase #1	180	$13.00	$2,340
Ending Inventory	380		$4,740

The Cost of Goods Sold and Gross Margin are calculated as follows:

Goods Available for Sale	$16,680	Net Sales	$17,400
Ending Inventory	– 4,740	Cost of Goods Sold	– 11,940
Cost of Goods Sold	$11,940	Gross Margin	$ 5,460

The cost of goods sold could also again be determined by multiplying the cost of the units by units assumed to be sold as follows:

	Number of Items	Unit Cost	Total
Purchase #3	350	$14.20	$4,970
Purchase #2	300	$13.70	$4,110
Purchase #1	220	$13.00	$2,860
Total	870		$11,940

Key Points

Note that the three valuation methods produce quite different results.

	Weighted Average	FIFO	LIFO
Gross Margin	$5,790.72	$6,101	$5,460
Ending Inventory	$5,070.72	$5,381	$4,740
Cost of Goods Sold	$11,609.28	$11,299	$11,940

There are several points to keep in mind with regard to these valuation methods. When prices are rising, LIFO results in the lowest gross margin and FIFO in the highest gross margin; the reverse is true when prices are declining. The LIFO gross margin is the closest to measuring the cost of goods sold as the cost to replace the inventory. When prices are rising, FIFO gives the best measure of the cost of the ending inventory at current prices; the reverse is true when prices are declining. Weighted average numbers for gross margin, ending inventory, and cost of goods sold fall between the same numbers determined by using LIFO and FIFO.

Once a particular inventory valuation method is chosen, it cannot arbitrarily be changed. In the unusual event that a company decides to change its inventory valuation method, a complete detailed explanation, including the financial impact due to the change, must be disclosed in the notes to the financial statements.

The following table presents a brief list of the advantages and disadvantages of each inventory valuation method:

Method	Advantages	Disadvantages
Weighted average	• Hard to manipulate • Easy to calculate	• Averages may not reflect inflation
FIFO	• Hard to manipulate • Makes physical sense • Ending inventory valuation reflects actual costs of inventory	• Produces "inventory" profits when prices are rising in that the cost of goods sold is based on noncurrent prices • Does not minimize taxes
LIFO	• Minimizes taxes during inflationary times • Reflects current replacement cost of goods sold	• Easy to manipulate • Physical flow unrealistic • Ending inventory valuation is lower than reality if the physical flow is FIFO • Cannot use in foreign operations following International Financial Reporting Standards (IFRS)

Estimating Inventory Values

Spas sometimes need to determine the value of inventory when a physical count is impossible or impractical. For example, a spa may need to know how much inventory was destroyed in a fire. Spas using the perpetual system simply report the inventory account balance in such situations, assuming it was all destroyed, but those using the periodic system must estimate the value of the destroyed inventory. Two ways of estimating inventory levels are the gross profit method and the retail inventory method. In using these methods it is important to distinguish between the value of only the destroyed inventory and the value of all inventory; no matter the system used, a physical count of undestroyed or usable inventory will be required. In the following examples, we address the issue of estimating the value of all ending inventory. By reducing the estimated value of all ending inventory by the value of all remaining usable inventory after the fire, we can reasonably estimate the value of inventory lost in the fire.

Gross Profit Method

The **gross profit method** estimates the value of inventory by applying the spa's historical gross profit percentage to current-period information about net sales and the cost of goods available for sale. It is calculated using the following formulas:

Gross Profit = Net Sales − Cost of Goods Sold

Gross Profit Margin = Gross Profit ÷ Net Sales

For example, if a spa had net retail sales of $400,000 during the previous year and the cost of goods sold during that year was $260,000, then gross profit was $140,000 and the gross profit margin was 35 percent.

Net Sales	$400,000
Cost of Goods Sold	−$260,000
Gross Profit	$140,000

Gross Profit Margin = $140,000 ÷ $400,000 = 35%

If gross profit margin is 35 percent, then cost of goods sold is 65 percent of net sales.

Suppose that one month into the current fiscal year, the spa decides to use the gross profit margin from the previous year to estimate inventory. Net sales for the month were $50,000, beginning inventory was $5,000, and purchases during the month totaled $30,000. First, the spa multiplies net sales for the month by the historical gross profit margin to estimate gross profit.

Gross Profit = Net Sales × Gross Profit Margin

$17,500 = $50,000 × 35%

Next, estimated gross profit is subtracted from net sales to estimate the cost of goods sold.

Net Sales	$50,000
Gross Profit	− $17,500
Cost of Goods Sold	$32,500

Alternatively, cost of goods sold may be determined by multiplying net sales by 65 percent (100 percent − gross profit margin of 35 percent). Therefore, cost of goods sold equals $50,000 × 0.65 = $32,500.

Finally, the estimated cost of goods sold is subtracted from the cost of goods available for sale to estimate the value of inventory.

Beginning Inventory	$ 5,000
Purchases	+ $ 30,000
Cost of Goods Available for Sale	$ 35,000
Less Cost of Goods Sold	− $ 32,500
Ending Inventory	$ 2,500

The gross profit method produces a reasonably accurate result as long as the historical gross profit margin still applies to the current period. However, increasing competition, new market conditions, and other factors may cause the historical gross profit margin to change over time.

Retail Inventory Method

Traditional retail businesses such as Macy's or Nordstrom track the inventories at the retail sales price of inventory. This information provides another way to estimate ending inventory, which is known as the **retail inventory method**. Suppose a retail store wants to estimate the cost of ending inventory using the information shown below.

	Cost	Retail
Beginning Inventory	$ 49,000	$ 80,000
Purchases	$209,000	$350,000
Goods Available for Sale	$258,000	$430,000
Net Sales		$400,000

The first step is to calculate the retail value of ending inventory by subtracting net sales from the retail value of goods available for sale.

	Cost	Retail
Beginning Inventory	$ 49,000	$ 80,000
Purchases	$209,000	$350,000
Goods Available for Sale	$258,000	$430,000
Net Sales		$400,000
Ending Inventory (Retail)		$ 30,000

Next, the cost-to-retail ratio is calculated by dividing the cost of goods available for sale by the retail value of goods available for sale.

	Cost	Retail
Beginning Inventory	$ 49,000	$ 80,000
Purchases	$209,000	$350,000
Goods Available for Sale	$258,000	$430,000
Net Sales		$400,000
Ending Inventory (Retail)		$ 30,000
Cost-to-Retail Ratio	$258,000 ÷ $430,000= 60%	

Then, the estimated cost of ending inventory is found by multiplying the retail value of ending inventory by the cost-to-retail ratio.

	Cost	Retail
Beginning Inventory	$ 49,000	$ 80,000
Purchases	$209,000	$350,000
Goods Available for Sale	$258,000	$430,000
Net Sales		$400,000
Ending Inventory (Retail)		$ 30,000
Cost-to-Retail Ratio		× 60%
Ending Inventory Cost		$ 18,000

One limitation of the retail inventory method is that a store's cost-to-retail ratio may vary significantly from one type of item to another, but the calculation simply uses an average ratio. If the items that actually sold have a cost-to-retail ratio that differs significantly from the ratio used in the calculation, the estimate will be inaccurate. Another limitation in a spa environment is that this method would only apply to retail inventory and only where both cost and retail prices are tracked. It would not apply to the inventory of professional products or other inventories maintained by the spa.

Lower of Cost or Market Requirement

The market value of each item on hand as of the inventory date is determined and compared to the cost of each item. The lower of the two is used to value that inventory. GAAP requires spas and other businesses to reduce their inventory to market value when the market is less than the cost.

When you use the **lower of cost or market (LCM)** requirement, you must value each item of inventory (or groups of items that are the same) separately. You then take the lower amount between cost (determined using one of the cost-based valuation methods) and market value for each item, and add them together to arrive at the total inventory value. Do not compare the total cost to the total market value of total inventory and then take the lower amount.

Say a spa has three items in inventory, with the following costs and market values:

- Product A has a cost of $10 and a market value of $12.
- Product B has a cost of $15 and a market value of $14.
- Product C has a cost of $18 and a market value of $11.
- The total cost of the three is $43 and the total market value of the three is $37.

The spa's valuation of each product by the lower of cost or market requirement results in:

- Product A: $10 (cost)
- Product B: $14 (market value)
- Product C: $11 (market value)
- The total is $35.

Thus, the value of the inventory is set at $35.

Cost Behaviors for Different Inventory Decisions

When assessing the cost effectiveness of an inventory policy, it is helpful to measure the total inventory costs that will be incurred during some reference period of time. The time period most frequently used for comparing costs is one year. Over that span of time, there will be a certain need, demand, or requirement for each inventory item. In that context, the following describes how the annual costs in each category will vary with changes in the inventory lot-sizing decision.

Item Costs. For items that are ordered from external sources, the per-unit item cost is predominantly the purchase price paid for the item. On some occasions, this cost may also include additional charges, like freight charges, duties, or insurance.

Holding Costs. Any items that are held in inventory will incur a cost for their storage. This cost will comprise a variety of components, an obvious one being the cost of the storage facility. There are other more subtle expenses that add to the holding cost (also called the carrying cost), including insurance on the held inventory and damage to, theft of, deterioration of, or obsolescence of the held items. The order-size decision has an impact on the average level of inventory that must be carried. If smaller quantities are ordered, on average there will be fewer units being held in inventory, resulting in lower annual inventory holding costs. If larger quantities are ordered, on average there will be more units being held in inventory, resulting in higher annual inventory holding costs. While these costs are real, they should be balanced against shortage costs caused by out-of-stocks when determining inventory levels. Product carrying costs at a spa are generally low due to the relatively high number of inventory turns spas experience.

Shortage Costs. Companies incur shortage costs whenever demand for an item exceeds the available inventory. These shortage costs include lost sales, loss of goodwill, customer irritation, backorders, expediting charges, etc. Spas are less likely to experience shortages if they have high levels of inventory. The order-size decision has a direct impact on the average level of inventory. Larger orders mean more items are being acquired than are immediately needed, so the excess will remain on inventory, thus increasing the amount of capital tied up in the inventory account. Smaller order quantities lead to lower levels of inventory and, correspondingly, a higher likelihood of shortages and associated shortage costs. The bottom line is this: larger order sizes will lead to lower annual shortage costs and higher holding costs.

Inventory Monitoring

Different approaches exist for monitoring inventory and deciding when and how much to order when items need replenishment. These include continuous review systems, periodic review systems, and min-max systems.

Continuous Review System

The continuous review system maintains a constant order size, but allows the time between order placements to vary. This method of monitoring inventory is sometimes referred to as a perpetual review method, a fixed quantity system, a two-bin system, or a par level system. When the inventory is depleted to the reorder point, a replenishment order is placed. This system provides close control over inventory items, since the inventory levels are under perpetual scrutiny.

Periodic Review System

A periodic review system maintains a constant time between the placement of orders, but allows the order size to vary. This method of monitoring inventory is sometimes referred to as a fixed interval system or fixed period system. It requires that inventory levels be checked at fixed intervals. The amount that is ordered at a particular time is the difference between the current inventory level and a predetermined target inventory level (also called an order-up-to level). If demand has been low during the prior interval, inventory levels will be relatively high, and the amount to be ordered will be relatively low. If demand has been high during the prior interval, inventory levels will have been depleted to low levels, and the amount to be ordered will be higher. Spas using this method run a greater risk of running out of an item in a period of abnormal demand or usage, since the order time is driven by a date rather than a minimum quantity trigger. For items with an expiration date, this method also runs the risk of having expired items in inventory in a period of abnormally low demand or usage.

Min-Max System

A min-max system allows both the order size and the time between order placements to vary. This method of monitoring inventory is sometimes referred to as an optional replenishment system. It is a hybrid system that combines elements of both the continuous review system and the periodic review system. It is similar to the periodic review system in that it only checks inventory levels at fixed intervals, and it has a target inventory level. When a review period arises, the system does not automatically place an order. An order is placed only if the size of the order would be sufficient to warrant placing the order. This determination is made by incorporating the reorder point pars from the continuous review system. At the review period, the inventory level on hand is compared to a reorder par level for the item. If inventory has not fallen below the par level, no order is placed; however, if the inventory level has dropped below the reorder par level, an order is placed. The size of the order is the difference between the inventory on hand and the par inventory level, including a factor for the number of units expected to be sold between the date the order is placed and the supplier-provided delivery date.

Inventory Best Practices

Spa inventories are essential to efficient operations. Poorly organized inventory management efforts can lead to unfortunate consequences and both tangible and intangible business costs. On the other hand, well-designed inventory management efforts can improve efficiency, profitability, and guest satisfaction. To better achieve these desired results, spa managers should pay attention to this critical area and implement recognized best practices.

Cycle Counts

In the busy environment of a spa, with its often long operating hours over a seven-day operating week, full inventory counts can be difficult to schedule and manage. One solution to this challenge is to perform periodic cycle counts. A **cycle count** is a partial count of a certain defined set of inventory items. This count should happen frequently, with different items counted each time. For example, the first week of the month might be designated for a count of skin care items. The items would be physically counted, matched against either the perpetual inventory or the count reflected on the last physical inventory plus items received less items sold, and any adjustments made accordingly. The next week, gift items would be counted, and so on, until staff had counted and adjusted each domain of inventory.

Counting a few items often reduces the hassle of a complete physical inventory and increases staff satisfaction. Counting in this way also has the benefit of sending a recurring message that management is paying close attention to the items on hand, which helps to deter theft. Each cycle count might occur on a designated day of the week, when the spa is the least busy and staff is available to perform the work.

Avoiding Out-of-Stocks

Nothing is more disheartening to staff (or the owner!) than being unable to make a sale due to items being out of stock. For example, many estheticians are paid a commission on retail sales, and to the owner they often represent the highest yielding margin of any spa sales. Retail products are essential to the guest's home care regimen, which allows them to take the benefit of the spa experience home and gives them a reason to return to the spa to replenish their product supply. An out-of-stock on a key product leads to unhappy staff, an unhappy owner, and an unhappy guest.

On the other hand, hotel managers and spa owners are constantly focused on keeping inventory levels in check. While this makes sense for slower-moving items, much can be gained by keeping higher levels of key items. We find that the top 20 items in a spa's retail inventory often account for close to half of the spa's retail sales. By maintaining higher levels of these items, for say six weeks rather than the standard four for other items, out-of-stock items can be minimized. (Take care with items that have expiration dates of less than six weeks out).

Another key tool in avoiding items being out of stock is to balance inventory based on product movement. The minimum and maximum inventory levels are not static. They are based upon product movement. A movement report on stock keeping units (SKU), which are alphanumeric identification codes for each product, should be run periodically to ensure that the minimums and maximums are still set at the proper level for each item.

Another area where out-of-stocks can really cost a spa money is in professional products that are essential to providing a service. For a spa that provides hair services, hair color is the best example. A guest who is told that the spa is out of the color needed to highlight her hair is likely to never return. Similarly, many spas market and book appointments for particular product treatments such as masks and peels, and running out of these products can lead to unhappy customers. This problem can be avoided by keeping extra stock of these essential professional products. The inventory carrying cost is more than paid for by the ability to deliver booked services.

Avoiding Shrinkage

A final best practice relates to minimizing **shrinkage**, which is the unauthorized reduction of inventory. While theft (one contributor to shrinkage) occurs at some point in every retail business, much shrinkage relates to people simply being hurried and not following procedures. For example, if a staff member is rushed to get a professional product, he or she might fail to note its use in the computer, which means that product is taken out of inventory without being recorded; this results in an apparent shortage in physical stock when compared to perpetual book records. Strict enforcement of rules for accounting for professional products can help. Another idea that works well is to store all professional products under lock and key in a dispensary. The products should be placed in lockable cabinets with shelves labeled for ease of inventory tracking. A sign-out sheet can be placed near the shelf so that, if there is no time to enter the product into the computer, a note can be made by hand and the adjustment made later. In very busy, high-volume spa operations, there may be justification for a person stationed at the dispensary, whose job is preparing and filling staff product requirements and properly recording each release.

Summary

Although inventory as a percentage of total assets is often relatively low for most spas, its impact on profits can be great. Therefore, inventory must be accounted for and carefully controlled. The two primary types of inventory systems are the periodic and the perpetual systems.

Three basic methods for valuing ending inventory are weighted average; first-in, first-out (FIFO); and last-in, first-out (LIFO). Each of these methods provides a slightly different valuation of inventory and, as a consequence, cost of goods sold and gross margin. Therefore, for the sake of consistency, the firm should use the same method each period, unless it has a valid reason for changing it. If a change is necessary, it should be fully documented in the notes to the financial statements.

Sometimes it may be necessary to estimate the value of inventory, such as when a fire destroys the inventory and its value must be estimated for insurance purposes, or when a physical inventory would be inconvenient or too costly. Two methods used to estimate the value of inventory are the retail method and the gross profit method.

Occasionally, obsolescence, deterioration, or a drop in the current market prices of inventory may cause a firm to lower the value of inventory on its books to comply with the accounting principle of conservatism.

Inventory monitoring can be done using the continuous system, perpetual system, or min-max system. The continuous system allows time between order placements to vary. The perpetual system allows order size to vary. The min-max system allows both factors to vary.

Performing cycle counts can ease the burdens of a full physical inventory. Out-of-stocks can sometimes be avoided by maintaining higher levels of top products, continually balancing inventory, and keeping back-stock for particular products. Shrinkage may be minimized by ensuring all procedures are followed, and in some cases by storing products in a dispensary.

With the growth of technology, many firms are switching to a perpetual inventory system wherein the value of inventory on hand is updated continuously through the firm's computer systems. Even when a perpetual inventory system is used, adjustments might be needed to bring the books into compliance with the physical inventory.

Key Terms

first-in, first-out (FIFO) method of inventory valuation—A method of valuing inventory in which the first units into inventory are considered sold first; hence, ending inventory consists of the latest purchases.

cycle count—A partial count of a certain defined set of inventory items.

gross profit method of inventory valuation—A method of estimating ending inventory based on a historical gross profit percentage for the firm.

last-in, first-out (LIFO) method of inventory valuation—A method of valuing inventory in which the last units into inventory are considered sold first; hence, ending inventory consists of the earliest purchases.

lower of cost or market (LCM)—An accounting procedure for valuing ending inventory based on the generally accepted accounting principle of conservatism.

operating supplies inventory—Inventory that includes items that a spa would order in larger quantities to be used over several months.

periodic inventory system—A system of accounting for inventory under which cost of goods sold must be computed. There are no continuous inventory records kept, so a physical count of the storeroom is required to determine the inventory on hand.

perpetual inventory system—A system of accounting for inventory that records receipts and issues and provides a continuous record of the quantity and cost of merchandise in inventory.

professional inventory—Inventory that includes products used to perform services for clients.

retail inventory—Inventory that includes products that are sold directly to the consumer.

retail method of inventory valuation—A method of estimating ending inventory based on the relationship between cost and retail price.

shrinkage—Unauthorized reductions to inventory; can be due to theft or carelessness and failure to follow proper issuing procedures.

weighted average method of inventory valuation—A method of valuing inventory in which the value is determined by averaging the cost of items in the beginning inventory with the cost of items purchased during the period.

Review Questions

1. What are the differences between the periodic and perpetual inventory systems?

2. How do the LIFO and FIFO methods of inventory valuation differ? How do these methods affect gross profit?
3. What are some advantages and disadvantages of the weighted average method of valuation?
4. What is the gross profit method of estimating inventory? When would it be necessary to use this method?
5. What special records must be maintained to implement the retail method of estimating inventory?
6. What is meant by the lower of cost or market?
7. What are inventory holding costs?
8. What three systems are used to monitor inventory levels?
9. What is a cycle count?

Chapter 4 Outline

Competencies

1. Identify the users of income statements and outline the income statement's relationship with the balance sheet. (pp. 97–99)
2. Describe major elements of the income statement and explain differences between income statements for internal and external users. (pp. 99–117)
3. Describe the *Uniform System of Financial Reporting for Spas* and discuss internal income statements (departmental schedules). (pp. 117–120)
4. Distinguish indirect expenses from undistributed operating expenses. (pp. 120–123)
5. Discuss the elements of fixed charges, and payroll taxes and employee benefits. (pp. 123–125)

4

Income Statement

IT IS THE FIFTH OF MAY AND Erica has a 2 P.M. meeting with the hotel controller to discuss the "first run" of the April financial statements for The Spa. The resort converted its spa reporting and general ledger account numbers in 2007, following the publication of the *Uniform System of Financial Reporting for Spas*. This conversion resulted in a significant improvement in the format and interpretation of financial data for the spa operation. Erica has been given a copy of the spa department schedules and will block out some time in the morning to review the results and write her list of questions for the controller.

It is the practice at the hotel to run a preliminary income statement just five days after the month-end closing and for the controller to meet with the food and beverage director, rooms executive, and other key members of the hotel executive committee to review the first run before he completes and distributes the final income statement on or about the 10th of the month.

As Erica begins her review, she thinks to herself, "Thank goodness the spa had another great month. Revenues for the month and year to date are ahead of budget and the spa departmental profit is significantly above both last year's numbers and the budget." She does, however, remember her father's advice: "Even when financial results are very good, you do not simply file away the income statement and move on to other day-to-day operational issues." Erica has learned that invariably there are issues and entries that require research before the statements are published.

The first thing Erica checks are the payroll numbers. She does a daily payroll report for the spa and, while the month-end numbers on her daily payroll summary are reasonably close to those on the first statement, she will want to share her month-end numbers with the controller, who may adjust his payroll accrual to her actual numbers. She also thinks that the retail cost of goods sold percentage is too high, so she pulls out her month-end retail inventory value extensions and the month-end retail sales abstract to take to her session with the controller.

In the meeting, the controller starts by questioning the nail revenues. While the overall spa revenues exceeded budget, the nail department revenue is 14 percent below budget. Erica explains that the spa had two nail technicians who left at the beginning of the month. Although she was able to fill both positions, the nail department operated short-handed for two weeks, which adversely affected nail revenues. With regard to payroll expense, since the current month ended on a Wednesday and the payroll week ended the previous Friday, the controller had to accrue five days of payroll this month. Erica pointed out that there was an unusually busy weekend when the spa had to bring in extra staff, which accounted for the spike in payroll for that weekend. The controller has, over time, gained a high level of confidence in the accuracy of Erica's payroll records. Therefore, he is comfortable in adjusting the payroll expense, based on her records, to best reflect the actual labor costs for the spa. He knows that Erica is very detailed with her payroll calculations and that her numbers are generally accurate. However, he reminds her that if she underestimates her payroll one month, it will come back to bite her the next month when he records the actual payroll and reverses his accrual entry. Erica already understood the basics of accrual accounting, so she knew that if she were to low-ball the payroll one month just to look good, it would catch up with her and overstate the payroll on the following month's statement.

Erica also notes that the Guest Supplies expense item seems high and asks to review the entries in the general ledger to see what purchases were recorded. Since the spa has only one major resource partner from whom they buy a lot of supplies, Erica has her assistant review each individual vendor invoice to confirm it was recorded to the proper general ledger account number. As part of her normal accounting routine, the assistant writes the general ledger expense account number alongside each item on the invoice to help the accounting clerk input the invoice. In this case, the entire invoice amount was mistakenly recorded to Guest Supplies when a significant number of the products were disposables used in nail services and should have been posted to Nail—Professional Products and Supplies. The controller agreed to make the correction on the final run.

Finally, after some research and double-checking, Erica and the controller determine that the retail cost of goods sold percentage is in fact higher than the spa would typically run. Erica recalls that The Spa ran a special "gift with purchase" promotion during the month of April. The promotion involved a complimentary eight-ounce SPF 15 day cream with any purchase of three skin care products. The promotion worked very well and the spa sold more than two hundred of these retail gift packages at a cost of $129 each, but adding the special gift did increase the cost of sales percentage. Erica and the controller both chimed in at almost the same time with the old line, "You can't put percentages in the bank." That is, although the promotion caused the cost percentage to go up slightly, the volume of sales it generated certainly added incremental retail revenue.

Erica left the meeting to return to the spa and thought, "I really like these sessions. It is so good to have another set of eyes look at the financial results to make sure I didn't make any significant mistakes during the month."

This chapter explains how the financial results for a spa operation are organized and reported on the monthly departmental statements. Financial statements are the end result of the accounting cycle. Data is recorded, accumulated, analyzed, summarized, and reported in meaningful formats to users of financial statements.

The financial statement used to convey operating performance is the **income statement**. It is also sometimes referred to as the *statement of operations*, the *profit and loss statement* (or simply the *P&L*), and various other titles. The income statement reports sales and expenses that ideally result in net income, but sometimes in a net loss, for an accounting period. If a spa is part of a hotel/resort, the spa's income statement represents one of many departmental schedules that are integrated into an overall income statement for the entire hotel/resort. This information is generally provided in abbreviated statements to interested outsiders such as bankers and other lenders, but is presented in considerable detail to internal users such as the spa's owner, director, and various department heads as appropriate.

In this chapter, we will discuss the income statement's major users and major components. We will also discuss earnings per share, external versus internal statements, and the *Uniform System of Financial Reporting for Spas*. After reading this chapter, you should be able to answer the following questions:

1. Who are the internal and external users of a spa's financial information?
2. When is revenue recorded, based on the accrual method of accounting?
3. What are the two major elements of the income statement?
4. What is the relationship of the income statement to the balance sheet?
5. How is the Cost of Goods Sold determined?
6. How is the gain or loss on sale of equipment determined?
7. What is the distinction between indirect expenses and undistributed operating expenses in the income statement?
8. What are four major fixed charges shown on the income statement?
9. Why do tax and book depreciation often differ?
10. What is the purpose of a separate payroll taxes and employee benefits schedule?

Users of Income Statements

Owners, potential owners, managers, financial institutions, and creditors such as suppliers are all users of a spa's financial information. In general, users are divided into two groups: internal and external users. Internal users of financial statements are the managers of the business. External users of financial statements include potential investors, creditors, and owners not active in managing the spa. The information needs of these two groups are generally quite different.

External users are given a statement that reflects the basics—that is, total sales and a few categories of expenses. Internal statements contain more detailed information supported by schedules that provide breakdowns by department and comparisons to operating budgets. Managers need this detail to manage their departments effectively. The information is often provided in accordance with the *Uniform System of Financial Reporting for Spas (USFRS)* and, of course, **generally accepted accounting principles (GAAP).**

Each user of financial statements seeks operational information for his or her own reasons. By far, the greatest number of spa operations are sole proprietorships whose owners and potential owners are interested in profitability as an indicator of the company's ability to sustain itself and earn a reasonable return on investment (ROI). They are also interested in profitability as a measure of the performance and effectiveness of the spa's senior management.

In a corporate structure where the spa property is a part of a larger, publicly traded corporation, the owners/shareholders are interested in profitability as an indicator of the potential for cash dividends and an increase in the market price for publicly traded stocks (ROI). Creditors are interested in profitability as an indicator of the spa's ability to pay its debts.

The amount of detail that external users and some owners require is usually not extensive. However, these users will likely request additional detail, analysis, and explanation when their objectives and expectations are not being met. The frequency with which information is distributed is another factor that normally varies between users. External users and inactive owners are likely to require financial information only annually, semi-annually, or quarterly. Greater frequency might be requested in cases where performance is below expectations and they want to see what actions management is taking to improve the financial performance and protect their investment.

Management wants the operating results to indicate the degree of success in managing operations. Spa managers expect the operating results to reveal problem areas so they can take corrective action to ensure that the spa generates profits in accordance with the operating plan and the owners' expectations. Managers also need to see specific areas of overachievement so they can try to repeat such performance in the future. A great deal of detail is required in order for the financial information to represent an effective management tool. For example, knowing that total direct expenses were 10 percent higher than the budget is of limited, if any, use to a spa manager. The manager needs to know what department or service center generated the extra expenses. The manager needs to see if the 10 percent overage was the combined result of one department being 30 percent over budget on direct expenses and another being 20 percent below budgeted expenses. Managers need to be able to see within each department what specific line item(s) of direct expenses gave rise to the negative variance. Only by being able to specifically identify the source(s) of negative and positive variances can the spa manager take appropriate action.

In most cases, from a management perspective, the value of the detailed financial results diminishes with time. It may be very difficult for managers to take effective corrective action for a situation that they learn about two months after the fact. Timeliness can be just as critical as accuracy and detail. For key financial areas like revenues, labor expenses, major direct expense components, and the like, it is not uncommon for the spa manager to monitor these elements on a daily or weekly basis and to request confirmation of any significant variances almost immediately, so corrective action can be implemented in a timely manner.

Relationship with the Balance Sheet

The income statement covers a period of time, while the balance sheet is prepared as of the last day of the accounting period – a single point in time. Thus, the income statement reflects operations of the spa for the period between balance sheet dates, as shown below:

The result of operations—net income (or net loss)—for the period is added to (or subtracted from) the owners' equity account and shown on the balance sheet at the end of the accounting period.

Major Elements of the Income Statement

Revenue is normally the first listed major element of the income statement. With an accrual basis accounting system, revenues are recorded when they are earned. For example, when a spa guest receives a treatment, the service revenue is recorded as earned regardless of when the spa guest pays for that treatment. When funds that are not required for operations are invested in a bank certificate of deposit, revenue in the form of interest is generally earned over time, while the interest may be earned on a daily basis, payment will likely not occur until the maturity date. Excess funds might occur during peak gift certificate sales periods, but it may be the practice of the spa to not record these sales as revenue until they are actually earned. So, there are circumstances where funds are received before revenue is earned and where revenue is earned before funds are received. This makes the timing of recording revenues very important. Generally, with sales and interest, revenue is recorded (accrued) before cash is received. Conversely, when a spa guest purchases a gift certificate, the amount is initially recorded as a liability rather than revenue because the spa has not yet performed the service for which it has been paid. In the future, when a guest redeems all or a portion of the gift certificate for a service, the liability will be reduced and revenue increased for the value of the service.

The revenues shown on an income statement generally are net revenues; that is, the total amounts charged (gross revenue) less any allowances (such as discounts or credits) granted at the time of or after the sale. As noted earlier, the amount of revenue details shown on the financial statement may vary by user.

The next major income statement element is expenses. Expenses recorded include outflows related to the accounting period and outflows that relate to the revenue earned in the same accounting period. Expenses related to the period are expenses incurred even though revenues may not have been directly earned by their incurrence. For example, insurance on a building is a fixed expense that provides risk coverage for a period of time and is unrelated to sales activity. Assuming a standard annual premium is billed, the total insurance bill is recorded as Prepaid Insurance on the balance sheet (not the income statement); then, the prepaid insurance is reduced periodically (usually monthly) by moving appropriate amounts to Insurance Expense on the income statement based on time, not revenue. Many other expenses are incurred in direct relation to revenue.

Adjusting entries at the end of the accounting period are recorded to match expense to revenue. For example, assume that all revenue earned in the period has been properly recognized at the end of that period. However, using the example in the opening story, if the last payroll period of the month ends five days before the last day of the period, an adjusting entry that accrues payroll for those five days is made to record that expense. This will ensure that the cost/expense of these five days of labor is properly matched to the revenue that was recorded and included for those five days. While each case must be individually assessed, it is very common that such adjusting/accrual entries at the end of one period are reversed at the beginning of the following period. Using the same labor scenario, when the next actual payroll is processed, it will include the five days of the previous period, so a reversing entry equal to the previously accrued amount ensures that the labor cost of those five days is charged only to the period that matches it correctly to the related revenue. Here are sample journal entries to illustrate:

Massage Department Direct Labor Expense	$5,000.00	
Skin Care Department Direct Labor Expense	$5,000.00	
Nail Department Direct Labor Expense	$1,000.00	
Hair Department Direct Labor Expense	$2,000.00	
Accrued Payroll Payable		$13,000.00
To accrue payroll to the end of the period.		

This entry demonstrates that it is important to accrue payroll by operating department so that departmental schedules under the *USFRS* can be supported. The *USFRS* is explained in detail later in the chapter.

The reversing entry at the beginning of the subsequent period would be as follows:

Accrued Payroll Payable	$13,000.00	
Massage Department Direct Labor Expense		$5,000.00
Skin Care Department Direct Labor Expense		$5,000.00
Nail Department Direct Labor Expense		$1,000.00
Hair Department Direct Labor Expense		$2,000.00
To reverse payroll accrual of prior period.		

Sales

The sale of goods or services occurs between the seller (the spa) and the buyer (the spa guest). The goods or services are provided by the seller in exchange for the guest's cash or promise to pay at a later date, which is referred to as *accounts receivable.*

Services are recorded as sales at the time the services are provided. For example, when a spa guest receives a service, a sale is recorded when the service has been completed. Likewise, retail products and food/beverage sales are recorded at the time of the sale. In the case of food and beverage, the server's check is the source document for the sale of goods. The revenue from the sale is recorded at the time of the sale (regardless of when the spa requires the guest to pay) for the following reasons:

1. Legal title to the goods (retail merchandise) has passed from the seller to the buyer.
2. The selling price was established in advance.
3. The seller's obligation has been completed.
4. The goods have been exchanged for another asset, such as cash or accounts receivable.

Each time sales are made, the appropriate sales/revenue accounts are credited and Cash or Accounts Receivable debited. Sales are recorded at the agreed-upon or posted price. When the spa guest is dissatisfied with the goods or services, a discretionary allowance may be made; that is, the guest may be given partial credit. For example, assume a guest is displeased with a $75 facial treatment and the spa manager decides to give the guest a $50 allowance (discount off the regular price). In this case, the relevant Revenue—Facial Treatments account is credited for $75, the skin care Allowances account is debited $50, and the guest's cash payment or Accounts Receivable is debited $25, the amount the guest actually owed for the service. In effect, net skin care service revenue becomes $25 ($75 published price less the $50 allowance) in this instance, since service allowances are offset against service revenues in determining net service revenue to be shown on the spa's income statement.

It is worth acknowledging that many, if not most, spa operations operate on a cash-at-time-of-service basis and seldom, if ever, extend credit to their clients. Where credit or payment terms are never offered to clients, there will be little use of accounts receivable. However, some spas that are part of hotels/resorts may allow guests to charge their spa services to their room accounts and not have to pay until they check out. In another situation, a spa that normally does not extend credit may do so in the case of a group booking by a company of several treatments at the spa. In this case, the spa agrees to invoice the company for goods and services after the group has visited the spa and the actual total charges are known. In these and other similar situations, the use of accounts receivable will ensure that revenue is properly recorded in the period it was earned, even if payment is received in a subsequent period. Even payments made by credit card are a form of accounts receivable, as there is a lag time between the posting of the credit card charges and the payments received by the spa.

When a spa sells goods not consumed on the premises, such as spa products or spa retail shop merchandise, there may be some returns. For example, the merchandise may have been damaged at the time of the sale but the spa guest may not have been aware of this until the merchandise was later removed from its packaging. Adjustments for returns will usually, but not always, be given to spa guests in the same manner in which they paid for the merchandise – if they paid cash, they will likely be given a cash refund; if they paid by credit card, they will likely be given a credit to their credit card. (How such returns are adjusted for the client is a matter of the particular spa's policy and not a matter of *USFRS* or GAAP.) For example, in a situation where a spa guest paid cash for a $100 jar of cream (plus 10 percent sales tax) but later legitimately returned it and was given a $110 cash refund (product value and sales tax), this refund would be recorded as follows:

Retail Skin Care Product Sales Returns	$100.00	
Sales Tax	$ 10.00	
Cash		$110.00
To record defective product returned by guest.		

If the spa was part of a facility that provided lodging and the guest had charged the purchase to his or her room but returned the product before checking out, then the allowance/credit could go to the guest's hotel account and the entry would look like the following:

Retail Skin Care Product Sales Returns	$100.00	
Sales Tax	$ 10.00	
Accounts Receivable		$110.00
To record defective product returned by guest.		

Note that in both of these examples, the return is recorded in a separate contra-sales Returns account rather than by directly reducing the sales account. This allows managers to monitor the volume of such activity and take appropriate action, such as talking to the supplier about the defective products and returning them to the supplier for credit. Keeping returns separate also allows the spa manager to see any significant fluctuations in the number or value of returns and to investigate the reasons for these returns in a timely manner to ensure their legitimacy.

Some spas use one account for both returns and allowances, while others maintain two (or more) separate accounts. A spa may maintain separate accounts for returns and allowances within each key revenue center or department. The choice depends on volume and the degree of control the manager feels is warranted and necessary based on individual circumstances. As with any other element of financial data, the more material an item is and the more control the manager feels is warranted, the more detailed the breakdown of that data is likely to be.

Cost of Goods Sold

Let's begin with some commonsense fundamentals on the use of the term **cost of goods sold**. For our purpose, we are adhering to the methodologies of the *USFRS*, which are highly recommended and explained later in the chapter.

The only place the term Cost of Goods Sold is used in the *USFRS* is in Schedule 9—Retail. In that context, it makes sense to think of Cost of Goods Sold as being appropriate only where goods (not services) are sold. Further, only the cost of the merchandise purchased for resale, freight charges, and any governmental duty charges are charged to the line item Cost of Goods Sold. Direct Expenses, including labor, merchandise displays, and buying trips, are kept separate from

Exhibit 1 Partial USFRS Retail—Schedule 9

Any Spa
Partial Retail Schedule (to Cost of Goods Sold line)
For the Month Ending March 31, 20XX

Revenue	
Apparel	
Footwear	$ 417
Men's/Unisex	2,650
Robes and Terry	2,667
Women's	7,517
Total Apparel	13,251
Gifts and Accessories	
Books and Media	1,075
Fashion Accessories	3,583
Home	2,508
Total Gifts and Accessories	7,166
Products	
Bath and Body Products	6,042
Hair Products	1,458
Make-Up Products	1,083
Nail Products	667
Private Label Products	2,833
Skin Care Products	12,083
Total Products	24,166
Other Retail	
Snacks and Beverages	1,833
Sundries	833
Other	667
Total Other Retail	3,333
Total Revenue	47,916
Revenue Adjustments	
Employee Discounts	3,583
Merchandise Returns	1,200
Allowances	167
Total Revenue Adjustments	4,950
Net Revenue	42,966
Cost of Goods Sold	22,333

Cost of Goods Sold. Exhibit 1 is an example of *USFRS* Schedule 9 down to the Cost of Goods Sold line.

At the time goods are purchased for resale, they are recorded as Inventories—Retail on the balance sheet. When the goods are sold, an accounting entry is made to transfer the costs of those goods from the balance sheet (inventory) to a Cost of

Goods Sold account on the income statement, thus matching costs to related revenues. The costs may be transferred at the time of the sale, or they may be recorded at the end of the accounting period. For simplicity's sake, we will assume that all goods purchased for resale are charged to a Retail Goods Purchases account that represents an inventory sub-account. Let's look at an example where skin care cream, at a delivered cost of $50, is purchased for resale (similar entries would be made for all of the goods that are purchased for resale during the period):

Account	Debit	Credit
Retail Skin Care Product Purchases (*inventory asset*)	$50.00	
Accounts Payable or Cash (as appropriate)		$50.00
To record purchase of product for resale.		

At the end of the accounting period, a physical inventory of all retail goods is taken and the cost of that inventory is determined. Using that valuation, the Cost of Goods Sold for the period is determined as follows:

Inventories—Retail, beginning of the period	$35,000
Plus: Retail Goods Purchases during the period	25,000
Equals: Retail goods available for resale during the period	60,000
Less: Inventories—Retail, end of the period	37,667
Equals: Cost of Goods Sold	$22,333

This example assumes that no inventoried items were used for any purpose other than resale. In reality, this is often not the case. Items in inventory might be given to staff as prizes or awards for reaching certain performance goals, given away as part of a promotional campaign, transferred from retail for use in delivery of a treatment, given to VIPs as a gift, etc. In these and any other situation where inventory is knowingly depleted, such transactions should be properly documented, accounted for, and incorporated into the Cost of Goods Sold calculation. What follows is an example where inventory was also used for staff rewards and promotions:

Inventories—Retail, beginning of the period	$35,000
Plus: Retail Goods Purchases during the period	25,000
Equals: Retail goods available for resale during the period	60,000
Less: Inventories—Retail, end of the period	37,117
Equals: cost of goods used	22,883
Less: cost of staff reward prizes (skin care department)	300
Less: cost of promotional give away	250
Equals: Cost of Goods Sold	$22,333

The journal entries (two of them) to record the Cost of Goods Sold, other uses of inventory, and ending inventory in this example would be as follows:

Account	Debit	Credit
Cost of Goods Sold	$22,883	
Inventories—Retail	$ 2,117	
Retail Goods Purchases		$25,000
To record cost of retail goods sales and to adjust Inventory to match the ending physical count inventory.		

This entry debits Inventories—Retail by $2,117, effectively increasing that account to $37,117 (it was $35,000 to open), the same as the physical count. The $22,883 debit to Cost of Goods Sold and the $2,117 debit to Inventories—Retail are offset by the $25,000 credit to Retail Goods Purchases, reducing that account to zero.

The other entry required is the record of the cost of the employee incentives and promotional giveaway campaign, which would be recorded as follows:

Account	Debit	Credit
Employee Benefits–Other (Skin Care Department)	$300	
Promotional Expenses	$250	
Cost of Goods Sold		$550
To record retail goods used in operations.		

This entry records the expense of using retail items in operations (as opposed to using them for retail sales) for employee incentives and promotional campaigns by transferring the inventory values out of Cost of Goods Sold into the appropriate expense accounts. In so doing, the Cost of Goods Sold account is credited to reflect the cost of retail products that were not sold, but used elsewhere within the spa. A number of other inventory movements can take place; each should be properly recorded. For example, consider a case in which the spa sells a professional-use-size jar of cream to a staff member. That jar would not have been intended for resale and therefore would not be part of retail inventory, so you would need to determine where the purchase of that product was recorded in order to understand how to properly record this sale to the staff member. (Most likely, in this example, the original purchase of the product would have been recorded as professional skin care product inventory and the jar in question would be part of professional product usage expense, prior to the accounting entry adjusting for the sale to the employee.)

While the examples in this section give an accurate and simple understanding of the principles behind the Cost of Goods Sold calculation, they also represent a gross over-simplification of most actual processes.[1] Even these simple examples, however, point to the necessity of developing procedures and tight controls to handle all movements and transfers of retail inventory.

There are a number of generally accepted methods of valuing inventory. Spas should maintain separate inventories for each of the retail product classifications, as well as Cost of Goods Sold calculations for each major category or group of retail product they sell. There should be a separate physical count and valuation for every stock-keeping unit (product); products should be grouped into categories like skin care products, apparel, gifts, and accessories. The same is true of professional-use product inventories.

Many spas will want to maintain a "book," "perpetual," or "running" inventory to determine the number of items they calculate to be on hand at any point in time, so they can match this to the quantities identified by the physical count. This is particularly important for high-unit-cost retail items. This allows the spa manager to identify and investigate significant variances between the running book counts and the physical counts. Proper and consistent inventory and cost of goods

Exhibit 2 Partial *USFRS* Retail—Schedule 9 (Remainder)

Any Spa
Partial Retail Schedule (from Cost of Goods Sold Line)
For the Month Ending March 31, 20XX

Cost of Goods Sold	$ 22,333
Gross Margin	20,633
Direct Expenses	
Payroll and Related Expenses	
Salaries and Wages	6,008
Commissions	1,083
Payroll Taxes and Employee Benefits	1,958
Total Payroll and Related Expenses	9,049
Other Expenses	
Buying Trips	500
Contract Services	42
Gift Wrap and Packaging	375
Licenses and Fees	42
Merchandise Displays and Accessories	208
Merchandise Tags	83
Operating Supplies	250
Packaging and Freight	167
Professional Development	50
Telecommunications	75
Uniforms	58
Other Retail Expenses	42
Total Other Expenses	1,892
Total Direct Expenses	10,941
Departmental Income (Loss)	$ 9,692

sold policies and practices can have a significant impact on the accuracy and reliability of a spa's financial statements.

Expenses

Expenses other than those included in Cost of Goods Sold include day-to-day operational expenses such as supplies and labor. For a day spa, they will also include depreciation, interest, and income taxes. Before we look at other departments, let's look at Exhibit 2 for an example of what the bottom half of the schedule shown in Exhibit 1 might look like.

Direct expenses are generally recorded for each revenue department. For example, labor costs related to skin care therapists are recorded as expenses of the skin care department, while, as shown in Exhibit 2, labor costs of the retail staff are recorded in the retail department. Labor costs include three major areas: (1)

salaries and wages, (2) commissions, and (3) payroll taxes and employee benefits. Not all spas will have the same mix of departments because of differences in the scope of services they provide. The *USFRS* provides twelve sub-schedules meant to cover the majority, if not all, of the potential mixes of services a spa might offer.

Drawing from a few of the department schedules provided in the *USFRS*, assume a spa's payroll for the month included the following wages:

Massage Department Employees		
Salaries & Wages	$ 7,500	
Commissions	34,333	
Contract Employees	3,167	
Distributed Service Charges (Gratuities Paid)	11,667	$56,667
Skin Care Department Employees		
Salaries & Wages	2,625	
Commissions	12,333	
Contract Employees	1,125	
Distributed Service Charges (Gratuities Paid)	4,458	20,541
Hair Department Employees		
Salaries & Wages	958	
Commissions	4,400	
Contract Employees	417	
Distributed Service Charges (Gratuities Paid)	1,650	7,425
Nail Department Employees		
Salaries & Wages	1,017	
Commissions	4,667	
Contract Employees	442	
Distributed Service Charges (Gratuities Paid)	1,733	7,859
Fitness Department Employees		
Salaries & Wages	5,500	
Commissions	7,000	
Contract Employees	917	
Distributed Service Charges (Gratuities Paid)		13,417
Food and Beverage Department Employees		
Salaries & Wages	2,925	
Commissions		
Contract Employees		
Distributed Service Charges (Gratuities Paid)		2,925
Total		$108,834

Further assume the related payroll taxes were as follows:

Massage Department Employees	$ 9,417
Skin Care Department Employees	3,417
Hair Department Employees	1,358
Nail Department Employees	1,458
Fitness Department Employees	2,575
Food and Beverage Department Employees	708
Total	$18,933

Finally, assume the only employee benefit is health insurance, which is assigned to departments based on the premiums related to their respective employees:

Massage Department Employees	$3,000
Skin Care Department Employees	1,000
Hair Department Employees	250
Nail Department Employees	300
Fitness Department Employees	750
Food and Beverage Department Employees	100
Total	$5,400

The total labor costs by department would be summarized as follows:

	Massage Dept.	Skin Care Dept.	Hair Dept.	Nail Dept.	Fitness Dept.	F&B Dept.
Salaries/Wages	7,500	2,625	958	1,017	5,500	2,925
Commissions	34,333	12,333	4,400	4,667	7,000	
Contract	3,167	1,125	417	442	917	
Distributed Service Charges	11,667	4,458	1,650	1,733		
Payroll Taxes	9,417	3,417	1,358	1,458	2,575	708
Fringe Benefits	3,000	1,000	250	300	750	100
Totals	$69,084	$24,958	$9,033	$9,617	$16,742	$3,733

In addition to labor expenses, spa businesses record other direct expenses to their related departments. For example, professional skin care products used to provide skin care services are a direct expense of the skin care department. Athletic equipment and supplies are direct expenses of the fitness department. Departments that generate and record revenues from guests, such as the massage department, skin care department, and retail department, are commonly called operating departments or **profit centers**. Departments that provide services to profit centers, such as support labor (reception, housekeeping, supervision, etc.), marketing, administrative and general services, and facility maintenance and utilities are sometimes called **service centers**. Several other expenses are not directly related to any one specific department and are simply recorded in separate (non-departmental) schedules (this will be addressed later in the chapter). These expenses usually relate to the operation as a whole rather than to individual departments. They include depreciation, interest, insurance, rent, and property taxes.

Each department schedule has several accounts for recording its various expenses. Cumulatively, these accounts are referred to as the *chart of accounts*. These classifications are typically based on the detailed chart of accounts referred to as the uniform system of accounts (discussed later in the chapter) and facilitate the preparation of the income statement. The uniform system of accounts also prescribes an extensive expense dictionary. In combination, the chart of accounts and the expense dictionary ensure a high degree of consistency and accuracy in recording financial data. They add to the reliability of the statements produced from that data. The chart of accounts and expense dictionary prescribed under the *USFRS* have been developed and prepared with flexibility in mind, recognizing that one spa may require or desire far more detail in any given schedule than another spa. In these cases, additional expense categories can simply be added to the chart of accounts to provide that additional detail.

Gains and Losses

Gains and losses are not something that most spa directors are responsible for; in fact, it would be unusual if they were. Subjects like gains and losses, income taxes, extraordinary items, and earnings per share are matters normally dealt with by a spa's top finance person, an outside accountant, or the owner. However, it has been said that outstanding managers run the spa as if it were their own. Thus, it is incumbent on spa directors to be generally familiar with the terminology and principles related to this subject matter and the relevance of gains and losses to the spa's financial statements and overall financial health.

For clarity in reporting financial performance, gains and losses are differentiated from profit and loss resulting from operations. **Gains** are defined as increases in assets, reductions in liabilities, or a combination of both. Gains result from a spa operation's incidental transactions and from all other transactions and events affecting the operation during the period, except those that count as revenue or investments by owners. Simply stated, a gain results when an activity incidental to the spa's operation occurs that generally results in an increase in assets. For example, there may be a gain on the sale of equipment. The spa uses equipment to provide services, and when the equipment is sold, only the excess proceeds over its net book value (purchase price less accumulated depreciation) is recognized as a gain.

For example, assume a spa sold a hydraulic treatment bed for $2,000 that had been used to provide skin treatments to guests. Furthermore, assume the bed cost $5,000 when purchased and had accumulated depreciation of $4,000 at the time of sale. Its net book value (NBV) would be determined as follows:

Cost	$5,000
Accumulated depreciation	–4,000
Net book value	$1,000

The gain on the sale is the result of the selling price exceeding the NBV as follows:

Selling price	$2,000
Net book value	–1,000
Gain on sale	$1,000

Losses are defined as decreases in assets, increases in liabilities, or a combination of both resulting from a spa operation's incidental transactions and from other transactions and events affecting the operation during a period, except those that count as expenses or distributions to the owner. Simply put, most losses result when activities incidental to the spa result in a loss on disposal of assets. In the earlier equipment example, if the proceeds were less than the equipment's net book value, a loss would occur and would be recorded as Loss on Sale of Equipment. A key point to remember in this example is that we have assumed the sale of equipment is not part of this spa's core daily business operations; that is, the spa is not in business to sell beds. So, in this case, the gain or loss is regarded as incidental and reported separately as a gain or loss, rather than included in the operating profit or loss of the spa. However, in a business whose core is buying and selling equipment, the sale of the equipment would, in fact, represent a revenue component in that company's operating profit and loss. When equipment is purchased for resale by a business, it is recorded as inventory and it is *not* depreciated. Cost of Goods Sold is charged for the cost of equipment and inventory is reduced when the equipment is sold.

Another example would be a loss from an act of nature, such as a tornado or a hurricane. The loss recorded is the reduction of assets less any insurance proceeds received.

In income statements for spa operations, revenues and gains are reported separately, and expenses are distinguished from losses. These distinctions are important in determining management's success in operating the spa. Management is held accountable primarily for operations (revenues and expenses) and only secondarily (if at all – usually only to the extent that management was able to control or influence the outcome) for gains and losses. In other words, management is accountable for those outcomes over which it has or should have some control. Let's look a bit deeper into an act of nature in which losses are regarded as the value of lost assets less insurance proceeds received. While management obviously has no control over nature, it does have control over ensuring that appropriate insurance is in place. Risk management is a management responsibility.

Income Taxes

Let's review and summarize how we arrive at income before taxes. In a simple retail business environment, the order of elements presented on the income statement is conventionally shown as follows:

Revenue (sales)
Less: Cost of goods sold
Less: Labor expenses
Less: Other expenses
Equals: Operating income (loss)
Plus: Gains
Less: Losses
Equals: Income before taxes
Less: Income taxes
Equals: Net income (loss)

This format suggests that all activities flow directly from the journal entries to the income statement without the use of supporting schedules. The presentation of Cost of Sales further suggests that the revenue is primarily retail-oriented. However, spas generally earn the majority of their revenue from services, where use of the term Cost of Goods Sold is not appropriate. Furthermore, under the *USFRS*,

Exhibit 3 ***USFRS* Statement of Income—Short Version**

Any Spa
Statement of Income (Short Version)
For the Month Ending March 31, 20XX

Net Revenue	$ 285,058
Total Direct Expenses	181,116
Gross Margin	103,942
Total Indirect and Undistributed Expenses	69,908
Income Before Fixed Charges	34,034
Fixed Charges	7,417
Income Before Depreciation, Amortization, Interest Expense, & Income Taxes	26,617
Depreciation and Amortization	6,667
Interest Expense	2,500
(Gain) and Loss on Disposal of Property	(4,167)
Income Before Income Taxes	21,617
Income Taxes	6,250
Net Income	$ 15,367

transactions are first recorded to departmental schedules and then combined on the spa's Summary Income Statement.

Exhibit 3 shows the *USFRS* format and order of elements for the short version of a spa's income statement. Exhibit 4 is the longer, more detailed version of the *USFRS*-based income statement. The detailed information in Exhibit 4 is obtained from the various supporting departmental and other schedules. The information in Exhibit 3 simply flows from the subtotal lines of Exhibit 4.

The income tax expense shown on the income statement is based on relevant revenues and expenses on the income statement. Government acts, legislation, and textbooks have been written on the complex and specialized topic of income taxes; however, for our purposes, it is sufficient to say that the income taxes shown on the income statement are seldom the same taxes shown on the firm's income tax return. The major reason for this is the difference between the accounting method used for financial statement purposes and that for income tax return purposes.

Consider a hypothetical spa that has $100,000 of annual pre-depreciation income. Assume that the only additional expense to be considered before the

Exhibit 4 *USFRS* Statement of Income—Expanded Version

Any Spa
Statement of Income(Expanded Version)
Fof the Month Ending March 31, 20XX

Net Revenue	
Massage	$ 120,500
Skin Care	43,583
Hair	17,166
Nail	16,650
Fitness	16,567
Food and Beverage	8,250
Health and Wellness	–
Memberships	14,500
Retail	42,967
Rental and Other	4,875
Other Operating Activities	–
Total Net Revenue	285,058
Cost of Goods and Direct Expenses	
Massage	72,833
Skin Care	28,375
Hair	10,492
Nail	9,583
Fitness	18,650
Food and Beverage	7,908
Health and Wellness	–
Retail	33,275
Other Operating Activities	–
Total Direct Expenses	181,116
Gross Margin	103,942
Indirect Expenses	
Indirect Operating Expenses	15,833
Indirect Support Labor	21,267
Total Indirect Expenses	37,100
Undistributed Operating Expenses	
General and Administrative	13,883
Marketing	8,258
Facility Maintenance and Utilities	10,667
Total Undistributed Operating Expenses	32,808
Income Before Fixed Charges	34,034

Exhibit 4 *(continued)*

Fixed Charges	
Insurance	2,000
Management Fees	–
Rent	834
Real Estate/Personal Property Taxes	4,583
Total Fixed Charges	7,417
Income Before Depreciation, Amortization, Interest Expense, & Income Taxes	26,617
Depreciation and Amortization	6,667
Interest Expense	2,500
(Gain) and Loss on Disposal of Property	(4,167)
Total	5,000
Income Before Income Taxes	21,617
Income Taxes	6,250
Net Income	$ 15,367

calculation of income taxes is depreciation. Many companies use accelerated methods of calculating depreciation on equipment for tax purposes because this helps to reduce their tax burden, but they most likely use the straight-line method for book purposes. The fundamental point here is that *book* methodologies and calculations are designed to spread the total cost of the asset reasonably evenly over its useful life. In contrast, *tax* methodologies and calculations are designed to minimize taxes payable. Now, assume that this spa with $100,000 of pre-depreciation income has $40,000 of depreciation expense for book purposes for a given year based on the straight-line method, and $60,000 of depreciation expense for tax purposes for the same year. In this case, the income tax expense for book purposes and for tax purposes, assuming a tax rate of 25 percent, would be as follows:

	Book Purposes	Tax Purposes
Pre-Depreciation Income	$100,000	$100,000
Depreciation Expense	40,000	60,000
Taxable Income	60,000	40,000
Tax Rate	25%	25%
Taxes (Income Tax Expense)	$15,000	$10,000

This spa would record $15,000 as income taxes on its income statement (books) and $10,000 payable on its tax return. The difference between the tax expense recorded for book purposes and the income tax paid on the tax return is recorded as a *deferred tax liability*. The journal entry to record income taxes in this case is as follows:

Account	Debit	Credit
Income Tax Expense	$15,000	
Income Tax Payable		$10,000
Deferred Income Taxes Payable		$5,000

At the risk of over-simplification, deferred tax is meant to represent and acknowledge that if assets were to be disposed of at their NBV, a gain on disposal could be generated for tax purposes, resulting in the liability to pay tax on that gain. The estimated tax on the gain would be roughly equal to the deferred tax liability amount being carried on the spa's books. So, deferred tax arising from depreciating fixed assets is a provision on the books that is meant to represent the potential tax liability if all of the spa's assets were disposed of at NBV. Once an asset has a net book value of zero for both book purposes and tax purposes, deferred tax liability is no longer an issue—provided the asset has no significant disposal value, in which case a taxable gain could be assessed if it were to be sold.

Extraordinary Items

In addition to the typical income statement elements discussed to this point, a spa may very infrequently report an **extraordinary item** on its income statement. Extraordinary items are reported at the bottom of the income statement after income taxes and just above the bottom line of net income. To show an item as extraordinary, the event must meet two major criteria:

1. Unusual nature–the underlying event should posses a high degree of abnormality and be clearly unrelated to the ordinary and typical current period activities of the spa.
2. Infrequent–the underlying event should not reasonably be expected to recur in the foreseeable future.

If an event does not meet both criteria, it is not reported as an extraordinary item. Of course, what is extraordinary for one spa may not be for another. A spa in California suffering loss from an earthquake may not consider that loss to be extraordinary, while a Michigan spa suffering loss from an earthquake would probably consider that loss to be extraordinary.

Extraordinary items are reported net of tax. That is, if an extraordinary loss results in taxes saved, the tax savings are offset against the loss before reporting the net loss as the extraordinary item. For example, consider a spa that has an extraordinary loss of $40,000 and a tax rate of 25 percent. Because of the $40,000 loss, $10,000 in taxes is saved. The extraordinary loss is shown on the income statement as a net loss amount of $30,000.

Earnings per Share

Most spas operate as proprietorships or single shareholder corporations. Owners and potential spa investors are most interested in the bottom line of the income statement—that is, net income. However, the net income amount by itself often lacks meaning in those cases where the spa is part of a larger corporate structure.

To provide a more meaningful number, accountants include **earnings per share (EPS)**. EPS in its simplest form is determined with the following equation:

$$\text{EPS} = \frac{\text{Net Income}}{\text{Common Shares Outstanding}}$$

EPS is calculated only for spa businesses organized as corporations or limited liability companies, since proprietorships and partnerships do not issue shares of stock. If a spa corporation has types of stock other than common outstanding stock, net income is reduced by the amount of income that belongs to non-common stockholders. EPS must be shown on the income statement before extraordinary items and net income.

Differences Between Income Statements for Internal and External Users

As mentioned at the beginning of the chapter, spas prepare income statements for both internal and external users. These statements can differ substantially; the significant differences between the income statements shown in Exhibit 3 and Exhibit 4 are examples of this. The income statements provided to external users are relatively brief (Exhibit 3), providing only key summary detail about the results of operations, such as the following:

Net revenue
Less: Total direct expenses
Equals: Gross margin
Less: Total indirect and undistributed expenses
Less: Fixed charges
Less: Depreciation/amortization plus interest plus gain/(loss) on disposal of property
Equals: Income before taxes
Less: Income tax
Equals: Net income

Footnotes, which generally appear after the financial statements in the financial report, are critical to interpreting the numbers reported on the income statement. Although the amount of operating information shown in Exhibit 3's income statement along with any accompanying footnotes (not shown) may be adequate for external users, management requires considerably more information (Exhibit 4), on a more frequent basis, than outsiders do. In general, the more frequent the need to make decisions, the more frequent and urgent the need for timely financial information. While spa managers' needs are met to some extent by the income statements, they are also heavily reliant on the detailed information contained in the supporting departmental and other schedules. In addition, following the *USFRS* recommended schedules, a Departmental Summary Monthly Statement of Income is produced specifically for management purposes (see Exhibit 5). Exhibit 5 is designed to provide the actual operating results for the operating period in question. However, reporting on only the current month's actual results is limiting in terms of representing a valuable management tool. In order to enhance the value of this data, management also needs to see comparative data, such as the

Exhibit 5 *USFRS* Departmental Summary Monthly Statement of Income–Expanded Format

Any Spa
Departmental Summary Monthly Statement of Income
For the Month Ending March 31, 20XX

Spa Departments	Net Revenues	Cost of Sales	Payroll and Related Expenses	Other Expenses	Income (Loss)
Massage	$ 120,500		$ 69,083	$ 3,750	$ 47,667
Skin Care	43,583		24,958	3,417	15,208
Nail	16,650		9,033	550	7,067
Hair	17,167		9,617	875	6,675
Total Spa Contributions	197,900		112,691	8,592	76,617
Indirect Expenses					
Indirect Support Labor			22,700		22,700
Indirect Operating Expenses				15,833	15,833
Total Indirect Expenses			22,700	15,833	38,533
Spa After Indirect Expenses	197,900		135,391	24,425	38,084
Memberships	14,500				14,500
Other Operated Departments					
Fitness	16,567		16,742	1,908	(2,083)
Food and Beverage	8,250	$ 2,675	3,733	1,500	342
Retail	42,967	22,333	9,050	1,892	9,692
Rentals and Other Income	4,875				4,875
Total Operated Departmental Contributions	72,659	25,008	29,525	5,300	12,826
Income Before Undistributed Expenses	285,059	25,008	164,917	29,725	65,408
Undistributed Operating Expenses					
Administrative and General			8,442	5,442	13,884
Marketing			2,850	5,408	8,258
Facilities Maintenance and Utilities				10,667	10,667
Total Undistributed Operating Expenses			11,292	21,517	32,809
Income Before Fixed Charges	$ 285,059	$ 25,008	$ 176,209	$ 51,242	32,601
Fixed Charges					7,417
Income Before Depreciation, Amortization, Interest, and Income Taxes					25,183
Depreciation and Amortization					6,667
Interest Expense					2,500
Gain or Loss on Disposal of Property					(4,167)
Income Before Income Taxes					20,183
Income Taxes					6,250
Net Income					$ 13,933

budgeted numbers for the same period, the figures for the same period last year, the current year-to-date totals, and the budgeted year-to-date totals.

In addition, some spa businesses revise their budgets and show the latest forecast of results if they expect a major difference between the year-to-date numbers and the originally budgeted numbers. Management can then compare actual results against the most recent forecasts. In addition to the monthly operating statement, a common report prepared for management is the weekly or daily operations report (DOR).

By analyzing variances (the differences between actual, budget actual, forecast actual, and prior period) through the use of this comparative data, the spa manager is better equipped to put together an action plan to recover or limit negative variances and ensure that positive variances are maintained and maximized.

Uniform System of Financial Reporting for Spas

The *USFRS* is a standardized accounting system prepared specifically for the spa industry. In addition to being an accounting system, the *USFRS* is also the title of a book on the subject that comes with a CD of financial statement and schedule templates. Other similar uniform systems have been prepared for other industries, such as the *Uniform System of Financial Reporting for Clubs*. The uniform system provides a turnkey system for new entrants into the spa industry by offering detailed information about accounts, classifications, formats, contents, uses of financial statements, supporting schedules, and reports. For example, the *USFRS* contains not only the basic financial statements, but also more than twenty supplementary departmental operating sub-schedules and a section covering ratio analysis and statistics. It also includes an extensive expense dictionary that serves to advise users about what account particular expense items should be charged to. This ensures internal consistency and reliability with respect to expense allocations.

The *USFRS* also allows for more reasonable comparison of the operational results of similar spa operations. When similar establishments follow a uniform system of accounts, the differences in accounting among these spas are minimized, thus ensuring meaningful comparability.

Uniform systems are time-tested systems. The first edition of the *Uniform System of Accounts for Hotels (USAH)* was published in 1926 by the Hotel Association of New York City. Since then, the *USAH* has been revised many times by committees, in the beginning by New York City accountants and, most recently, by accountants from across the United States. The Tenth Revised Edition of what is now known as the *Uniform System of Accounts for the Lodging Industry (USALI)* was prepared by the Financial Management Committee of the American Hotel & Lodging Association and representatives from the Hospitality and Financial Technology Professionals organization. The *USFRS* was modeled closely after the time-tested *USALI* and was published in 2005 as a joint initiative between the American Hotel & Lodging Educational Institute, the ISPA Foundation, and the Hospitality Financial and Technology Professionals.

The uniform system of accounts for spas can be adapted for use by large and small spa operations. The *USFRS* makes provision for more accounts and classifications than a single spa will generally use. It also provides for longer, detailed versions and shorter, abbreviated versions of various departmental operating statements. It contains the flexibility for spas to develop their own additional specialty sub-schedules without compromising the consistency and integrity of the principal system. Each spa can select the schedules and accounts that it requires and ignore the others.

The majority of the *USFRS* is designed to be used at the internal operations management level rather than for external users. The expanded format of the income statement (Exhibit 4) and the expanded format of the departmental summary monthly statement of income (Exhibit 5) are based on the principles that support **responsibility accounting**; that is, the presentation is organized to focus attention on departmental results for departments such as massage, skin care, nails, etc. The *USFRS* clearly recognizes and provides for the fact that corporate and external readers are interested only in abbreviated summary data – they don't want to run the business, they just want assurance about their return on investment. The income statements prepared at the corporate level, where more than one spa property is owned by the same corporation, would most likely be considerably different. They would likely include sale of properties, corporate overhead expenses, and other items that would not necessarily appear on an individual spa property's income statement.

Internal Income Statements

This section looks at the functionality of the *USFRS* departmental schedules. One schedule is maintained for each significant operating department/profit center. The *USFRS* provides **departmental schedules** for:

- Massage
- Skin Care
- Nail
- Hair
- Fitness
- Food & Beverage
- Health & Wellness
- Membership Dues and Fees
- Retail
- Other Operating Departments

Exhibit 6 is an example of a departmental schedule for the massage department. Departmental schedules for other spa departments are similar. It should be noted that the Other Operating Departments item listed above is meant as a catch-all schedule in recognition that many spas offer unique programs or profit centers that may not be accommodated by the other schedules. Examples might include things such as art programs, adventure experiences, beach services, kid's club programs, and tennis and equestrian services.

Exhibit 6 Sample Spa Departmental Schedule–Massage Department

Any Spa
Massage Department Contribution Schedule
For the Month Ending March 31, 20XX

Revenue	
Massage	
Relaxation and Therapeutic	$ 71,250
Specialty	23,750
Total Massage	95,000
Body Treatments	
Hydrotherapy	833
Wraps and Scrubs	6,667
Specialty Body Treatments	3,750
Total Body Treatments	11,250
Other	
Breakage	417
Service Charges	14,167
Other Revenue	833
Total Other	15,417
Total Revenue	121,667
Allowances	1,167
Net Revenue	120,500
Direct Expenses	
Payroll and Related Expenses	
Salaries and Wages	7,500
Commissions	34,333
Contract	3,167
Distributed Service Charges	11,667
Payroll Taxes and Employee Benefits	12,417
Total Payroll and Related Expenses	69,084
Other—Professional Products and Supplies	3,750
Total Direct Expenses	72,834
Departmental Contribution	$ 47,666

Each of a spa's departmental schedules provides a detailed analysis of revenues, allowances, and direct expenses, in which:

Total departmental revenues
Less allowances
Less direct expenses
Equals departmental contribution/income (loss) – i.e., the contribution

The contribution made by each operating department is transferred to the departmental summary monthly statement of income (Exhibit 5), with net revenues and direct expenses being transferred to the income statement (Exhibit 4). For purposes of the departmental summary monthly statement of income (the internal management tool), massage, skin care, nail, and hair are reported separate from the other departments. This presentation recognizes that many day spas, which make up the majority of the industry, provide services only under these four classifications. These departments are not separated for presentation on the published and more traditional income statements such as the one shown in Exhibit 4.

As noted earlier, departmental schedules can be used as the basis for management accountability. While it may be difficult to hold the manager of the massage department accountable for revenues in the period, the manager could be held accountable for maintaining payroll and other direct expenses at or below a prescribed percentage of revenue. Spa department managers may also have accountability for client retention and other factors that affect revenue.

Net departmental revenue less **direct operating expenses** equals total **departmental contribution (income)**, which is the contribution by profit centers to both overhead expenses and net income.

Indirect Expenses

Indirect expenses are broken into two main groupings, with a *USFRS* schedule to provide details on both: Schedule 8 covers support labor, while Schedule 9 covers indirect operating expenses. Whereas direct expenses can be specifically tied to the activities of a particular service department, indirect expenses, while still being generally tied to the provision of guest services, are difficult to associate with any one or more particular guest services departments. For example, the labor cost expenses related to providing reception and hostess services in the spa relate to the overall experience of all spa guests, regardless of the services they receive. Similarly, it would be impractical to monitor and assign the precise cost of robes to those guests having a massage versus a facial, or to determine which guests had complimentary herbal teas and fruits in the relaxation lounge, except by some arbitrary allocation of the expenses to each revenue department and recorded separately as indirect operating expenses. See Exhibit 7 and Exhibit 8 to get a better idea of the types of spa expenses that represent indirect expenses.

Undistributed Operating Expenses

While indirect expenses are closely connected to the provision of guest services, **undistributed operating expenses** are more closely aligned to the business side of the spa operation. The use of undistributed operating expenses follows the principles of *USALI.* For the hotel/resort spa, the spa departmental statement ends with the support labor and indirect operating expenses; departmental profit is then rolled forward to the overall property income statement. Prior to the publication of the *USFRS,* most day spa income statements had several pages of individual line item expense categories with little systematic organization. Under the *USFRS,* there are three main groupings of expenses that constitute undistributed operating expenses: (1) Administrative and General, (2) Marketing, and (3) Facilities

Exhibit 7 *USFRS* Support Labor Schedule

Any Spa Support Labor Schedule For the Month Ending March 31, 20XX	
Salaries and Wages	
Guest Reception	$ 4,242
Host(ess)/Attendant	4,108
Housekeeping	1,208
Reservations	2,550
Supervision	4,000
Distributed Service Charges	800
Payroll Taxes and Employee Benefits	5,792
Total Support Labor	$ 22,700

Exhibit 8 *USFRS* Indirect Operating Expenses Schedule

Any Spa Indirect Operating Expenses Schedule For the Month Ending March 31, 20XX	
Ambience	$ 592
Contract Services	2,933
Dues and Subscriptions	175
Equipment Rental	117
Guest Clothing	625
Guest Supplies	2,542
Hospitality	783
Laundry	3,592
Licenses and Fees	92
Linen	1,633
Operating Supplies	1,658
Professional Development	517
Telecommunications	183
Uniforms	225
Other	167
Total Indirect Operating Expenses	$ 15,834

Maintenance and Utilities. Exhibits 9, 10, and 11 show the schedules recommended by the *USFRS* for collecting and reporting undistributed operating expenses.

The grouping and reporting of undistributed operating expenses into these schedules, and in fact all of the *USFRS* schedules, can be thought of in terms of grouping activities and expenses into unique areas of responsibility. This is very

Exhibit 9 *USFRS* Administrative & General Schedule

Any Spa
Administration & General Schedule
For the Month Ending March 31, 20XX

Payroll and Related Expenses	
Management Salaries	$ 6,667
Payroll Taxes and Employee Benefits	1,775
Total Payroll and Related Expenses	8,442
Accounting Expenses	
Audit and Other External Expenses	300
Payroll Processing Expenses	250
Other Accounting Expenses	200
Total Accounting Expenses	750
Other Expenses	
Bank Charges	83
Cash Over/Short	(16)
Credit and Collection	167
Credit Card Commissions	1,583
Donations	83
Dues and Subscriptions	250
Human Resources	525
Information Systems	583
Legal and Professional	167
Licenses and Fees	50
Loss and Damage	42
Meals and Entertainment	83
Operating Supplies	200
Postage	50
Professional Development	58
Provision for Doubtful Accounts	250
Security	200
Telecommunications	108
Travel	142
Other	83
Total Other Expenses	4,691
Total Administrative and General Expenses	$ 13,883

helpful from a management perspective, as it forms the framework of the responsibility accounting system inherent in the *USFRS*. In many spa operations there is a departmental management structure in place. In addition to service department managers, there may be a facilities manager, a marketing manager, an administration manager, and a general manager overseeing all of these areas. In smaller operations, one person may manage more than one department. Collecting and reporting financial information that clearly reflects the key areas of management responsibility facilitates accurate financial performance assessments.

Exhibit 10 *USFRS* Marketing Schedule

Any Spa Marketing Schedule For the Month Ending March 31, 20XX	
Payroll and Related Expenses	
Salaries and Wages	$ 2,250
Payroll Taxes and Employee Benefits	600
Total Payroll and Related Expenses	2,850
Other Expenses	
Advertising Broadcast	1,083
Advertising Print	1,667
Collateral Materials	725
Complimentary Guests	250
Direct Mail	375
Dues and Subscriptions	83
In-House Promotions	208
Meals and Entertainment	200
Postage	42
Professional Development	59
Special Events	333
Telecommunications	50
Trade Shows	200
Travel	83
Other Marketing	50
Total Other Expenses	5,408
Total Marketing Expenses	$ 8,258

Fixed Charges

Fixed charges generally represent expenses over which operational management of the spa has little or no direct discretionary influence or control. Examples of fixed charges under the *USFRS* include: rent, real estate taxes, business taxes, insurance, and **management fees.** On the *USFRS* schedule for fixed charges, depreciation and amortization, interest expense, and gain or loss on disposal are also individually reported, but on their own separate total lines. This group schedule is referred to as the Fixed Charges Schedule for brevity. In fact, as indicated on the income statement (see Exhibit 4), Fixed Charges are reported separately before the other expenses on this schedule. Exhibit 12 shows the recommended *USFRS* schedule template for collecting and reporting fixed charges, depreciation and amortization, interest expense, and gains/losses on the disposal of property.

Payroll Taxes and Employee Benefits

Earlier in this chapter, we identified payroll taxes and employee benefits as an important component of direct labor costs. As we have seen on a number of the

Exhibit 11 ***USFRS* Facilities Maintenance and Utilities Schedule**

Any Spa
Facilities Maintenance and Utilities Schedule
For the Month Ending March 31, 20XX

Facility Maintenance Expenses	
Building	$ 1,500
Contract Services	300
Equipment Rental	42
Equipment Repair	833
Grounds and Landscaping	267
Heating, Ventilating, and Air Conditioning	175
Locks and Keys	233
Operating Supplies	667
Sauna, Steam, and Pool Supplies and Repairs	542
Trash Removal	150
Other Repairs and Maintenance	41
Total Facility Maintenance Expenses	4,750
Utility Expenses	
Electric	3,833
Gas	1,167
Water	917
Total Utility Expenses	5,917
Total Facility Maintenance and Utilities Expenses	$ 10,667

sample schedules shown in the chapter, often a separate line item has been provided for payroll taxes and employee benefits. There are, however, a number of components that comprise payroll taxes and employee benefits well beyond this one-line provision. Also, in practical terms, when source deductions are reported and paid, it is important to have the appropriate information consolidated in one place without the need to search through *USFRS* schedules to get it all. To this end, a separate *USFRS* schedule was created to collect and report on payroll taxes and employee benefits separately. In fact, under the *USFRS*, this schedule feeds the various other spa schedules' line items that report payroll taxes and employee benefits. The total of each column represents the total amount to transfer to the appropriate line in the corresponding departmental schedule, while the totals of each line are used for regulatory reporting purposes. Exhibit 13 shows the recommended *USFRS* schedule template for payroll taxes and employee benefits. Exhibit 13 carries no particular values, as it is presented to provide a sense of format only. As with all other *USFRS* schedules, each spa would use only those lines and columns that apply to its operation. Additional columns and rows can be added or substituted to reflect the appropriate categories for each spa operation.

As we have noted, this information is required on a frequent basis for internal performance evaluation purposes. The actual payment dates of the tax liabilities

Exhibit 12 *USFRS* Fixed Charges Schedule

Any Spa Fixed Charges Schedule For the Month Ending March 31, 20XX	
Rent—Other Equipment	$ 833
Taxes Other Than Income and Payroll	
Real Estate Taxes	4,167
Personal Property Taxes	417
Total Taxes Other Than Income and Payroll	4,584
Insurance	
Building and Improvements	1,667
Liability	333
Total Insurance	2,000
Total Fixed Charges	$ 7,417
Depreciation and Amortization	
Building and Improvements	$ 2,500
Furnishings and Equipment	4,167
Total Depreciation and Amortization	6,667
Interest Expense—Mortgages	$ 2,500
(Gain) Loss on Sale of Property	$ (4,167)

will follow a separate cycle, perhaps quarterly, but the schedule provided simplifies that process as well.

Summary

The income statement, complete with all supporting departmental schedules, is the most useful financial statement for operational management. Managers use financial results to gauge performance, identify specific areas that need attention, and help them identify appropriate actions to effect change. The income statement reports sales and expenses that ideally result in net income, but sometimes in a net loss, for the period. Perhaps more important to the users than the isolated current period numbers are comparative results showing current actual performance versus budgeted/expected performance for the period, and versus prior results for the same period.

The income statement has different uses for different groups of people. External users such as inactive owners, creditors, and potential investors need general information about profitability, sales, and some expenses. Their primary interest is usually in the spa's ability to repay debt and/or earn an acceptable return on investment. Internal users such as the spa's operational managers need detailed

Exhibit 13 *USFRS* Payroll Taxes and Employee Benefits Schedule

Any Spa
Payroll Taxes and Employee Benefits—Schedule 19S-19L
For the (Period) Ending MO/DY/YR

	Sched 1L Massage	Sched 2L Skin Care	Sched 3L Hair	Sched 4L Nail	Sched 5L Fitness	Sched 6L Food & Beverage	Sched 7L Health & Wellness	Sched 9L Retail	Sched 10L Other Operating Departments	Sched 12L Support Labor	Sched 14L Admin & General	Sched 15L Marketing	Sched 16L Facility Maintenance and Utilities	Total
Payroll Taxes														
Federal Retirement (FICA)														–
Federal Unemployment (FUTA)														–
Medicare (FICA)														–
State Disability														–
State Unemployment (SUTA)														–
Total Payroll Taxes	–	–	–	–	–	–	–	–	–	–	–	–	–	–
Employee Benefits														
Auto Allowance														–
Childcare														–
Contributory Savings Plan (401k)														–
Dental Insurance														–
Disability Pay														–
Group Life Insurance														–
Health Insurance														–
Meals														–
Profit Sharing														–
Stock Benefits														–
Workers' Compensation														–
Other														–
Total Employee Benefits	–	–	–	–	–	–	–	–	–	–	–	–	–	–
Total Payroll Taxes and Employee Benefits	–	–	–	–	–	–	–	–	–	–	–	–	–	–

information as quickly as possible. If the financial results are not provided on a timely basis, it may be too late for the manager to identify the problems and opportunities and take effective action. For example, managers finding out from recently received financial results that there was a serious problem with inventory shrinkage or labor percentages four months ago may be limited in their ability to take any meaningful corrective action.

The income statement shows four major elements: revenues, expenses, gains, and losses. Revenues (increases in assets or decreases in liability accounts) and expenses (decreases in assets or increases in liability accounts) are directly related to operations, while gains and losses result from transactions incidental to the property's major operations.

The original *Uniform System of Accounts for Hotels,* on which the key principles of the *USFRS* are based, was published in 1926 to standardize income statements within the hospitality industry. Many changes and revisions have been made since then, the most recent being the Tenth Revised Edition of the *Uniform System of Accounts for the Lodging Industry,* published in 2006.

The *USFRS* also serves as an excellent responsibility-accounting model. Separate departmental schedules produce departmental performance results, which facilitates holding each department manager accountable for the results and various line items on his or her department's schedule. Department managers are also accountable for taking corrective actions where required. Consistent production of these schedules gives a clear picture of the effectiveness of a department manager's ability to take appropriate corrective actions.

Endnote

1. For the interested reader, inventory management is covered in more detail in the ISPA Foundation book *Retail Management for Spas: The Art & Science of Retail.*

Key Terms

cost of goods sold—The cost of the products that are sold in the operation of the business.

departmental contribution (income)—The difference between an operating department's revenue and direct expenses.

departmental schedules—Supplements to the income statement that provide management with detailed financial information by operating department and service center; also referred to as departmental statements.

direct operating expense—Expenses related directly to the department incurring them and consisting of cost of sales, direct payroll and related expenses, and other direct expenses.

earnings per share (EPS)—A mathematical ratio, generally used in large corporate structures that issue common stock shares, that provides a general indicator of the profitability of the spa by comparing net income to the average common shares outstanding. If preferred stock has also been issued, preferred dividends are subtracted from the net income before calculating earnings per share.

extraordinary items—Items (usually a loss) reported at the end of the income statement that are both highly unusual and infrequent in occurrence.

fixed charges—A category of expenses reported on the income statement that relates to decisions outside the area of control of operational management and consists of rent, property taxes, insurance, interest, depreciation, and amortization.

generally accepted accounting principles (GAAP)—Accounting methodologies that have been approved by all recognized professional accounting associations; GAAP covers transactions, presentation, and all other treatments of financial data.

gains—Increases in assets, reductions in liabilities, or a combination of both, resulting from a spa's incidental transactions and from all other transactions and events affecting the operation during the period, except those that count as revenues or investments by owners.

income statement—A report on the profitability of operations, including revenues earned and expenses incurred in generating the revenues for the period of time covered by the statement.

losses—Decreases in assets, increases in liabilities, or a combination of both, resulting from a spa's incidental transactions and from the other transactions and events affecting the operation during the period, except those that count as expenses or distributions to the owners.

management fees—The cost of using an independent management company to manage the spa operation. In some corporate structures, management fees might also refer to fees charged to the spa operations by the corporate head office for management advice and the direction they provide to the spa operations.

profit center—An operating department within the spa operation that generates revenues and incurs expenses.

responsibility accounting—The organization of accounting information (as on an income statement) that focuses attention on departmental results such as the massage, skin care, hair, and nail departments.

service center—A department within the spa operation that is not directly involved in generating revenue but that provides supporting services to revenue-generating departments within the operation.

undistributed operating expenses—Expenses not directly related to income generating departments, consisting of administrative and general expenses, marketing expenses, and facilities maintenance and utilities expenses.

Uniform System of Financial Reporting for Spas (USFRS)—A standardized accounting system prepared specifically for the spa industry offering detailed information about account classifications; formats; the different kinds, contents, and uses of financial statements; supporting departmental schedules and reports; and other useful information. The *USFRS* is an accounting system that, if commonly adhered to by a group of spas, would make the financial results of the spas comparable.

Review Questions

1. What are the major sections of the summary income statement?
2. Why are managers more interested in a summary income statement than outside investors?
3. What are the major differences between a revenue and a gain?
4. What are three examples of direct operating expenses for the massage department?
5. What is the difference between a loss and an expense?
6. How is the Cost of Goods Sold determined for the retail department?
7. What are the advantages of using the *Uniform System of Financial Reporting for Spas*?
8. What detailed expenses are included in the property operation, maintenance, and energy costs of the income statement?
9. Why are supplemental schedules valuable to management?
10. What two major criteria are required for an item to be reported as extraordinary?

Chapter 5 Outline

Competencies

1. Discuss ratio analysis, including the purposes of ratio analysis, what ratios express, and classes of ratios. (pp. 133–137)
2. List and describe operating ratios commonly used in the spa industry. (pp. 137–152)
3. List and describe liquidity and solvency ratios commonly used in the spa industry. (pp. 152–158)
4. List and describe activity and profitability ratios commonly used in the spa industry. (pp. 158–163)
5. Explain the limitations of ratio analysis. (pp. 163–164)

5

Ratio Analysis

It is 9:45 a.m. and Erica is at her desk preparing for the weekly resort staff meeting, which is every Thursday at 10:00 a.m. Normally the spa director attends the staff meeting, but she has a doctor's appointment this morning, so she asked Erica to attend the meeting in her place.

After the general manager makes his opening remarks and the routine weekly reports are delivered by the various department heads, it is the practice to go around the table and for each person to give a brief report on matters of interest to the entire group. When it is Erica's turn to report on the spa, the general manager welcomes her to the meeting and decides to challenge her by saying, "Erica, I noticed that your laundry expense last month was a little high. Have you looked into that?"

Erica immediately responded, "Sir, while the laundry expense was a few hundred dollars higher than had been budgeted, remember that the spa's treatment revenues ended the month 8 percent over budget. The additional treatments resulted in additional laundry expense. Laundry expense did, however, end the month right on budget at 1.8 percent of treatment revenues and is right on target year to date."

The general manager nodded and Erica went on to give her remarks. As she walked back to the spa, Erica smiled to herself, knowing that she nailed the answer. It brought back memories of pop quizzes she would be given by her father when she first assumed a spa management position. When Erica was a rookie spa junior manager, her father would call and pepper her with questions like: "Erica, what was your direct labor cost percentage in the skin care department last month?" Or, "What were your professional products cost per treatment last month?" Or, "What were your retail sales revenues per treatment last month?" At first, this grilling annoyed her, but as usual her father was trying to share some advice. When he ran a large resort that had several golf courses, a large tennis program, several restaurants, a membership program, and of course a spa, the monthly income statement could be 50–80 pages long, with thousands and thousands of numbers. It would be simply impossible to memorize all of the actual and budget numbers for the current month and for the same month prior year, plus all of the year-to-date numbers—and yet managers are expected to have at their command immediate answers to financial questions. Even if you were able to memorize all of the numbers for the month, you would have to do it all over again when the financial statements for the next month were published. When her father was the

CEO of the resort, he would say that the next call you picked up might be the owners' representative or someone from the corporate offices of the management company asking questions on small financial details such as, "Why were your chemical and fertilizer expenses for the golf course high last month?" or "Your payroll cost for housekeeping was over budget. Why is that?"

Her father learned over time that the best way to track all of the numbers was to master operational ratios. He would always use the example that it wasn't important to memorize that the cleaning supplies expense for housekeeping was $1,023 last month, but if you knew that cleaning supplies ran 28 cents per occupied room for a period of time and suddenly it went to 37 cents one month, you would be alerted to a potential problem and could analyze why that happened. Likewise, if you knew that the banquet kitchen food production payroll was budgeted at 12 percent of catering food sales, you could compare the actual results against that benchmark. Or, if the golf pro shop averaged a 48 percent cost of goods sold for retail merchandise revenues and suddenly one month it ran 55 percent, you could dig into the mix of sales and find out that there had been a special promotion on Callaway golf clubs that month that was very successful in generating retail sales, but, since the gross margin on "hard goods" is much smaller than with, say, golf shirts, you could understand the change in ratio.

Once, out of curiosity, Erica had counted the total number of line items on the spa department schedule and sub-schedules and had exclaimed, "Wow, we have 226 line items on the spa schedule!" If you add in the budget for the month, prior year, and variance, then add year-to-date actual results, budget year-to-date, and prior year's actual and variance, the spa had just under 2,000 numbers. Erica thought about Monica, whose Day Spa had another 79 line items for undistributed overhead and fixed expenses—she would have an additional 600 numbers to keep at her fingertips!

As the years went by and Erica gained more managerial experience, she understood why her father had administered his pop quizzes at the beginning of her management career, and she made it a point of studying the relationship between the many numbers that the spa kept track of. Now Erica considers herself very competent in ratio and statistical analysis.

The purpose of this chapter is to identify key operating and other ratios and statistics to assist in successful spa management. After reading this chapter, you should be able to answer the following questions:

1. What benchmarks are available for comparison?
2. What are the five common classes of ratios?
3. What class of ratios will managers use the most to manage the operations of a spa?
4. What operating ratios are widely used and useful in the spa industry?
5. How does the focus of liquidity and solvency ratios differ?

6. How do solvency ratios based on the income statement differ from those based on the balance sheet?
7. What is an excellent ratio for measuring management's ability to generate revenue and control expenses?
8. What are the limitations of ratio analysis?

One of the spa industry's leaders and the owner of many spas distills the economics of spas into a simple, basic truth: the only ways to build revenues for a spa are either to attract new clients or increase the amount current clients spend at the spa. It must also be acknowledged that, given the very nature of the spa industry, where each treatment requires a dedicated employee to deliver the service, it is extremely difficult to make a profit and still deliver a quality spa experience.

That is why management attention to the bottom line is so important, and that means gathering and analyzing all sorts of financial and other data. Like all businesses, spas have become increasingly data-driven. Most spas calculate and monitor a large number of ratios and statistics. In today's technological world, business decisions are no longer made based on just intuition or an impulse. Rather, they are driven by an increasing body of data that measures the successes and failures of the spa's current processes and practices and supports changes to the spa's operations and initiatives.

Ratio Analysis: An Overview

Spa financial statements contain a lot of financial information. A thorough analysis of this information requires more than simply reading the reported facts. Users of financial statements need to be able to interpret the reported facts to discover aspects of the spa's financial situation that could otherwise go unnoticed. This is accomplished through ratio analysis. A ratio gives mathematical expression to a relationship between two figures and is computed by dividing one figure by the other. By bringing the two figures into relation with each other, ratios generate new information. In this way, ratio analysis goes beyond the figures reported in a financial statement and makes them more meaningful, informative, and useful. In particular, ratio analysis generates indicators for evaluating different aspects of a spa's financial condition.

Ratio analysis is used to evaluate the favorableness or unfavorableness of various financial conditions. However, the computed ratios alone do not say anything about what is good or bad, acceptable or unacceptable, reasonable or unreasonable. While ratios are critical to any financial analysis, by themselves, ratios are neutral and simply express the numerical relationship between two figures. They are only indicators, and, as indicators, they are meaningful only when compared with useful criteria known as **benchmarks.** Benchmarks with which to compare the financial results of ratio analysis include:

- The spa's historical results (such as comparing this month's results to results from the same month last year)
- The spa's ratios compared against industry averages or ratio results from other spas

- The spa's ratio goals set by management

Let's take a closer look at these benchmarks. Many ratios can be compared with corresponding ratios calculated for the prior period in order to discover any significant changes. For example, the direct labor cost percentage (discussed later in the chapter) for the current month may be compared with the direct labor cost percentage of the same month in the prior year in order to determine whether the spa is succeeding in controlling these costs compared to the prior year.

Industry averages provide another useful standard against which to compare ratios. Spa managers may want to compare the direct labor cost percentage for their own operation with industry averages in order to evaluate their abilities to compete with other spas. An increasing number of industry financial studies are being published that include valuable benchmark ratios against which an individual spa can compare its performance. However, it is important to note that, when reviewing published benchmark studies, readers should make sure that the report carefully describes the spa types used in the study, as ratios can vary significantly between small strip-center day spas and major resort spas.

While ratios can be compared against results of a prior period and against industry averages, ratios are best compared against planned ratio goals. For example, in order to more effectively control the cost of direct labor, management may project a goal for the current month's direct labor cost percentage that is slightly lower than that for the same month of the previous year. The expectation of a lower labor cost percentage may reflect management's efforts to improve scheduling procedures and other factors related to the cost of direct labor. By comparing the actual labor cost percentage with the planned goal, management is able to assess the success of its efforts to control labor cost.

Different evaluations may result from comparing ratios against these different standards. For example, a direct labor cost of 40 percent for the current period may compare favorably with the prior year's ratio of 42 percent and with an industry average of 41 percent, but may be judged unfavorably when compared with the operation's planned goal of 38 percent. Therefore, care must be taken when evaluating the results of operations using ratio analysis. It is necessary to keep in mind not only which standards are being used to evaluate the ratios, but the purpose of the ratio analysis as well.

Purposes of Ratio Analysis

Spa managers, creditors, and owners often have different purposes in using ratio analysis to evaluate the information reported in financial statements.

Ratios help managers monitor operating performance and evaluate their success in meeting a variety of goals. By tracking a limited number of ratios, spa managers are able to maintain a fairly accurate perception of the effectiveness and efficiency of their operations. Most spa managers compute the direct labor cost percentage in order to monitor the largest expense of their operations, for example. Management often uses ratios to express operational goals as well. For example, management may establish such ratio goals as the following:

- Maintain a 1.5 to 1 current ratio.

- Do not exceed a debt-equity ratio of 1 to 1.
- Maintain a pre-tax profit margin of 10 percent.
- Do not exceed a direct labor cost of 40 percent.

Ratios are particularly useful to managers as indicators of how well goals are being achieved. When actual results fall short of goals, ratios help indicate where the problem or problems may be. In the direct labor cost percentage example presented earlier, in which an actual ratio of 40 percent compared unfavorably against the planned 38 percent, additional research is required to determine the cause(s) of the variation. This difference may be due to cost differences, sales mix differences, or a combination of the two. Only additional analysis will determine the actual cause(s). Ratio analysis can contribute significant information to such an investigation.

A spa's creditors use ratio analysis to evaluate the solvency of the spa and assess the riskiness of future loans. For example, the relationship of current assets to current liabilities, referred to as the current ratio, may indicate a spa's ability to pay its upcoming bills. In addition, lenders sometimes use ratios to express requirements for spa operations as part of the conditions set forth for certain financial arrangements. For example, as a condition of a loan, a lender may require a spa to maintain a current ratio of 2 to 1.

Individual spa owners, partners, and corporate officials of branded spas are also interested in ratios. Though the overall financial objectives of spas may differ, all these parties desire a financially strong business and will view ratios as a tool to measure the financial health of their spas.

Ratios are used to communicate financial performance. Different ratios communicate different results. Individually, ratios reveal only part of the overall financial condition of a spa. Collectively, however, ratios are able to communicate a great deal of information that may not be immediately apparent from simply reading the figures reported in financial statements. Ratios are of little value by themselves, but when viewed on a comparative basis against a benchmark, they can represent a very valuable performance measurement tool.

What Ratios Express

In order to understand the information communicated by the different kinds of ratios used in ratio analysis, it is necessary to understand the various ways in which ratios express financial information. Different ratios are read in different ways. For example, many ratios are expressed as percentages. An illustration is the direct labor cost percentage, which expresses the cost of direct labor in terms of a percentage of total sales of the department. If total massage sales for a given month are $100,000, while the cost of direct labor is $40,000, then the result of dividing the direct labor cost by the total massage department sales is .40. Because the direct labor cost percentage is a ratio expressed as a percentage, this figure is multiplied by 100 to yield a 40 percent direct labor cost.

Other ratios are expressed on a per-unit basis. For example, the massage revenue per treatment is a ratio expressed as a certain amount per massage served. It is calculated by dividing the total massage sales by the number of treatments.

Thus, in a given month, if 1,200 clients were given massage treatments and the total revenue during the month amounted to $120,000, then the average massage revenue per treatment would be $120,000 ÷ 1,200, or $100.

The proper way to express some ratios is as a turnover of so many times. Retail inventory turnover is one such ratio, determined by dividing, for example, the spa's annual retail revenues by the average retail inventory value, which yields the number of times the inventory has turned during the year. If a spa does $300,000 in retail sales and the sum of its average inventory (at retail) is $100,000, its turnover is three. A successful turnover rate is between three and four.

Finally, some ratios are expressed as a coverage of so many times. The denominator of such a ratio is always set at 1. The current ratio, determined by dividing current assets by current liabilities, is one of the ratios expressed as a coverage of so many times. For example, if a spa reported current assets of $200,000 and current liabilities of $100,000 for a given period, then the operation's current ratio at the balance sheet date would be 2 to 1 ($200,000 ÷ $100,000). This means that the spa possesses sufficient current assets to cover its current liabilities two times. Put another way, for every $1 of current liabilities, the spa has $2 of current assets.

The proper way to express the various ratios used in ratio analysis depends entirely on the particular ratio and the nature of the relationship it expresses between the two figures it relates. The ways in which different ratios are expressed are a function of how we use the information that they provide. As we discuss the ratios commonly used in the spa industry, you should be careful to note how each is expressed.

Classes of Ratios

Ratios are generally classified by the type of information they provide. Five common ratio classes or groupings are as follows:

1. Operating
2. Liquidity
3. Solvency
4. Activity
5. Profitability

Operating ratios assist in the analysis of a spa's operations. Liquidity ratios reveal the ability of a spa to meet its short-term obligations. Solvency ratios, on the other hand, measure the extent to which the spa has been financed by debt and is able to meet its long-term obligations. Activity ratios reflect management's ability to use the spa's assets, while several profitability ratios show management's overall effectiveness as measured by returns on sales, owners' equity, and investments.

The classification of certain ratios may vary. For example, some books classify the inventory turnover ratio as a liquidity ratio, but we consider it to be an activity ratio. Also, profit margin could be classified as an operating ratio, but it is generally included with the profitability ratios. Knowing the meaning of a ratio and how it is used is always more important than knowing its classification.

We will now turn to an in-depth discussion of individual ratios, with most of our attention focused on operating ratios. For each ratio discussed, we will consider its purpose, the formula by which it is calculated, and the sources of data needed for the ratio's calculation.

Operating Ratios

Spas find many operating ratios useful. These ratios can be sub-classified into a number of groups. In the following sections, we will discuss these operating ratio groups:

- Revenue ratios
- Treatment room utilization ratios
- Market segmentation ratios
- Labor cost ratios
- Expense ratios
- Retail ratios
- Undistributed operating expense ratios

Revenue Ratios

In this section, we will cover revenue ratios commonly used in the spa industry.

Revenue per Treatment. This is the most fundamental ratio for spas. The **revenue per treatment ratio** simply identifies the average selling price. For example, spas can add up the number of massages provided to clients over a given period, total the massage revenue for the same period, and determine the revenue per treatment for its massages by dividing the total massage revenue by the total number of massages. Revenue per treatment can also be calculated for all of a spa's treatments combined, as shown below:

	# of treatments	Revenue	Revenue per treatment
Massage	500	$50,000	$100.00
Skin Care	300	$36,000	$120.00
Hair	300	$18,000	$60.00
Nail	400	$18,000	$45.00
Total	1,400	$74,000	$52.86

The overall revenue per treatment for this spa is $52.86 (rounded), determined by dividing total spa revenue for the period by the number of treatments for the same period. This ratio is also known as *average treatment rate* or *ATR,* and is sometimes calculated separately for spa services and salon services, with the same ratio for salons being called the *average salon service rate* or *ASSR*. It is calculated in the same manner, by dividing salon services revenue by the total number of salon services.

Revenue per Customer/Guest. Also known as revenue per ticket, **revenue per customer/guest** measures the average spending by each spa guest. In the beginning of the chapter, we said that the only ways for a spa to build revenues are to attract new customers or have its current customers spend more. This ratio helps spa managers keep track of the rate of guest spending. The formula for revenue per customer/guest is as follows:

$$\text{Revenue per Customer/Guest} = \frac{\text{Total treatment and retail revenues in a period}}{\text{Total number of customers/guests in the same period}}$$

A spa would obviously want to trend this ratio over time and would strive to have the amount spent by each customer/guest increase over time.

Number of Treatments per Customer/Guest. This ratio is a variation of the revenue per customer/guest ratio and measures the average number of treatments that spa customers are booking. The formula for determining the **number of treatments per customer/guest** is as follows:

$$\frac{\text{Number of Treatments}}{\text{Per Customer/Guest}} = \frac{\text{Number of total treatments}}{\text{Total number of customers/guests in the same period}}$$

For a simple example, let's say that a spa does 120 total treatments on a given day and that the spa had 100 customers/guests. That would equate to 1.2 treatments per guest, based on 120 treatments divided by 100 guests. If the spa were to train its reservationists to always suggest a complementary service to guests as they called for their treatment appointments and this effort resulted in those same 100 guests booking 140 services (1.4 treatments per customer/guest), the spa would experience a 16.66 percent growth in the number of treatments per guest. Bear in mind that the additional treatments sold to the guests would likely be lower-priced services that will have a downward effect on the average treatment revenue; in this case, however, this would not bes not a bad thing, since more revenue is coming in. This demonstrates why spa leaders need to understand how each ratio influences other ratios and that, ultimately, revenues are the most important measure of a spa's financial success.

RevPAR. RevPAR or revenue per available *lodging* room applies to spas within a hotel or resort. For hotels, this is the basic hotel statistic that measures the total hotel revenues divided by the number of hotel room nights. A hotel with 250 hotel rooms that does $5 million in room revenues for the year would have a RevPAR of $5 million ÷ (250 × 365), or $54.79. A hotel or resort spa may interested in measuring its contribution to RevPAR. The RevPAR formula for a spa within a hotel/resort is as follows:

$$\text{RevPAR} = \frac{\text{Treatment revenues in a period}}{\text{Available room nights during the same period}}$$

Consider a spa that achieves $1.2 million in annual revenues and is located within a hotel with 150 rooms. The RevPAR contribution would be $21.92 (rounded), based on the following:

$$\text{RevPAR} = \frac{\$1{,}200{,}000}{150 \times 365}$$

RevPOR. RevPOR or revenue per occupied room is a variation of the RevPAR statistic. RevPOR measures total hotel revenues against the number of occupied rooms, which is generally tracked by month and year. Thus, for the hotel just mentioned with 150 rooms, let's say that it achieves 70 percent occupancy for the year. Occupied rooms would total 150 × 365 × .7, or 38,325 for the year. Thus, the spa with $1.2 million in revenues would generate $31.31 (rounded) per occupied hotel room ($1.2 million ÷ 38,325).

RevPATR. RevPATR or revenue per available treatment room is a spa measurement similar to a hotel's RevPAR measurement. RevPATR is based on the number of treatment areas within the spa. The formula to determine RevPATR is as follows:

$$\text{RevPATR} = \frac{\text{Total treatment revenues}}{\text{Number of total treatment rooms or stations}}$$

For example, a spa that has ten treatment rooms, three hair stations, two manicure stations, and three pedicure stations would have 18 available treatment stations. If the spa achieved $1.2 million in treatment revenues, spa managers would calculate the spa's RevPATR by dividing $1.2 million by 18 to arrive at $66,667 (rounded) in revenue per available treatment room/station.

This approach is also used by developers when constructing hotels. The developer will take the total development and construction cost of a hotel project and divide that by the number of hotel rooms the property will have to determine what the cost per room will be. Then, if the developer knows how much revenue the project will generate per guestroom, he or she can take the cost of capital and the cost to service the debt and predict the likelihood of the revenues per room's ability to service the debt and provide an adequate return on investment from the project. The same thing holds true for a spa project, where the developer/owner will total the construction cost of the spa itself and divide that by the number of treatment rooms/spaces. By determining the anticipated revenues per treatment room/space over the course of a year, the developer can demonstrate to potential lenders or partners that the spa revenues will service the debt and provide a reasonable return for the investors.

RevPATH. From an operational and revenue management perspective, there is a movement within the spa industry to focus principally on **RevPATH** or revenues per available treatment hour as a measurement of how effective the spa is at maximizing revenues. Smith Travel Research has launched a spa industry trends report monitoring changes in revenue per available treatment hour that promises to be the cornerstone metric to quantify spa industry revenue trends. Continuing with our example of the spa with 18 revenue stations, let's assume that the first appointment time is 9 A.M. each day and the last appointment hour is 8 P.M., with the spa closing at 9 P.M. The spa thus has 12 available hours each day to book appointments; multiplying 12 available hours by the 18 treatment stations equals 216 available treatment hours. If the spa achieves $8,000 in treatment revenues for a given day, it has achieved $37.04 (rounded) per available treatment hour for that day ($8,000 ÷ 216). Taken in isolation, this statistic is relatively meaningless, but if RevPATH is maintained by day, week, month, and year, over time the trends and prior-period comparatives will provide spa leadership with meaningful benchmarks by which they can measure the productivity of the spa.

The other positive aspect to this statistic is that it eliminates from analysis the fact that spa treatments will vary in length from a ten-minute brow wax to a one-and-a-half-hour massage treatment. By measuring revenues against hourly productivity, it doesn't matter if a treatment room is booked for a single one-hour treatment or if an esthetician performs a mini-facial and two waxing treatments in one hour in a single treatment room; RevPATH focuses only on the revenues generated by each treatment space during a fixed amount of time.

It should be noted that a spa can increase its RevPATH without increasing revenues at all by simply reducing its operating hours. For example, if spa leadership determines that revenues in the 8 P.M. appointment hour are significantly lower than the overall average, it might be appropriate to reduce the spa's hours of operation by eliminating that last treatment hour and closing the spa at 8 P.M. instead of 9 P.M.

RevPASH. RevPASH or revenue per available salon hour is a salon variation of the RevPATH calculation used by spas. RevPASH is calculated by dividing total salon treatment revenues for a time period by the total number of salon-station available hours for the same period.

Treatment Room Utilization Ratios

This section discusses common treatment room utilization ratios used in the spa industry.

Treatment Room Occupancy Percentage. This ratio is similar to the occupancy percentage hotel executives use to measure usage of hotel guestrooms, only it is for the spa's treatment rooms and stations. The formula for calculating **treatment room occupancy percentage** is as follows:

$$\text{Treatment room occupancy percentage} = \frac{\text{Number of treatment hours}}{\text{Total available treatment hours}} \times 100$$

Let's continue with the spa in our example that has 18 treatment rooms and is open 12 hours each day, which means it has 216 available treatment hours each day. If this spa delivers 100 hours of treatments on a given day, it would achieve a 46.3 (rounded) percent utilization rate or occupancy for that day (100 treatment hours ÷ 216 available treatment hours).

Looking at the industry as a whole, the average spa typically achieves a 30-45 percent utilization rate; this is explained in part by the fact that it is obviously more difficult to attract customers to book a 9 A.M. massage than it is to book customers for the 5 P.M. treatment hour. This 30-45 percentage range is especially challenging for managers of spas that are located within a hotel or resort, because hotel executives view a hotel guestroom occupancy of 60 percent or less as an indication that a hotel is underperforming. Hotel managers view an acceptable occupancy percentage for hotels as somewhere between 60 and 75 percent, and it is not uncommon for hotels to sometimes enjoy occupancies of above 75 percent, which is considered an outstanding result. Some unknowledgeable hotel executives tend to apply these same benchmarks to spa operations, and so a spa with a utilization percentage of 38 percent might be erroneously judged as drastically underperforming.

Number of Treatments per Treatment Room. This ratio is a variation of the treatment room occupancy percentage without factoring in the number of operating hours. It simply measures the number of treatments per treatment room during a given time period.

The formula for determining the **number of treatments per treatment room** is as follows:

$$\text{Number of treatments per treatment room} = \frac{\text{Total number of treatments}}{\text{Number of treatment rooms}}$$

Continuing with our spa that has 18 treatment rooms/stations and delivered 100 services in a day, the treatments per treatment room ratio for that day is simply 100 treatments divided by the spa's 18 treatment rooms/stations, which equals, 5.56 (rounded) treatments per treatment room/station.

The number of treatments per treatment room ratio is much easier to calculate than the treatment room occupancy percentage, but it does not provide an actual occupancy percentage for each treatment area. To calculate the percentage of occupancy using the number of treatments per treatment room ratio, you would simply divide the number of treatments per treatment room (in this case, 5.56) by the number of available treatment hours (for this spa, 12) and the result—46.3 (rounded)—is exactly the same as the result calculated using the treatment room occupancy percentage ratio.

Distribution of Revenues Percentages. Spa leaders will want to know the composition of revenues on at least a monthly and annual basis. A spa director will want to know two basic things. First, how were the spa's treatment revenues composed as a percentage of total treatment revenues? For example:

Treatment Department	Revenues	% of Sales
Massage Department	$120,500	60.1
Skin Care Department	43,583	22.0
Hair Department	17,167	9.5
Nail Department	16,650	8.4
Total	$197,900	100.0%

In addition to the overall mix of business percentages, it is very common for a spa to set targets within each service department for more detailed information. For example, a day spa may establish a goal of having 50 percent of total hair revenues be for color and chemical services.

Second, spa leadership will want to know the percentage contribution of all revenue departments to total revenues. For example:

Department	Revenues	% of Sales
Massage Department	$120,500	42.2%
Skin Care Department	43,583	15.3
Hair Department	17,167	6.0
Nail Department	16,650	5.8
Membership	14,500	5.1
Fitness Department	16,567	5.8
Food and Beverage	8,250	2.9
Retail Department	42,967	15.0
Rentals and Other	4,875	1.9
Total	$285,059	100.0%

Market Segmentation Ratios

Every spa uses market segmentation ratios to determine which market segments are using spa services and facilities. Once this information is known, management can adjust marketing strategies to generate additional sales to the market segment(s) they most want to reach. A resort/hotel spa will typically track at least these three markets:

- Hotel guest, leisure
- Hotel guest, group
- Local market

A day spa would likely track numerous market segmentation ratios and customer demographic composition. At a minimum, day spas will typically track these markets:

- New client
- Repeat client
- Promotion/discount/gift certificate client

Resort Capture Rate Ratios. It is critical for a resort/hotel spa to measure the percentage of guests purchasing spa services and those using the spa and fitness facilities. Spa leadership uses resort capture rate ratios such as the **resort capture rate ratio** and the **resort service capture ratio** to determine the percentage of hotel guests that are using spa services and whether additional measures are required to generate spa sales. The resort capture rate is calculated as follows:

$$\text{Resort capture ratio} = \frac{\text{Spa services used by resort guests + fitness facilities used by resort guests}}{\text{Total number of resort guests}}$$

The resort service capture rate is calculated as follows:

$$\text{Resort service capture ratio} = \frac{\text{Number of spa service resort guests}}{\text{Total number of resort guests}}$$

This ratio provides an overall picture, but many resort/hotels will break down the capture rate into group guests and leisure guests by using the following calculations:

- Group guest spa services divided by the total number of group guests staying at the property
- Leisure guest spa services divided by the total number of leisure guests staying at the hotel/resort

To illustrate the use of capture rate ratios, assume that on a given day, a spa within a resort sold 100 treatments, with 20 of those treatments sold to clients from the local market. Thus, 80 of the spa services for that day were sold to resort guests. Let's also assume that the 250-room resort ran at 70 percent occupancy that day, with 40 percent double occupancy. This equates to 250 rooms at 70 percent occupancy, equaling 175 occupied rooms, 40 percent of which were occupied by a second guest for a total of 70 additional guests, leaving a grand total of 245 guests. The guest mix for the day was 100 group guests and 145 leisure guests. Of the 80 treatments sold to resort guests that day, group guests accounted for 25 services and leisure guests accounted for 55 services. Thus, the capture rate for group guests was 25 services divided by 100 group guests, or 25 percent. The capture rate for leisure guest was 55 services divided by 145 leisure guests, or 38 percent (rounded). Finally, if we assume that 60 resort guests used the fitness facilities, the number of spa service guests (80 guests) plus the number of fitness facility guests (60 guests) totals 140; 140 divided by the 245 total resort guests would result in an overall resort capture rate of 57 percent (rounded).

Labor Cost Ratios

Labor is the largest expense in a spa operation. Labor cost ratios reveal spa leadership's ability to control costs in relation to departmental revenues. The *Uniform System of Financial Reporting for Spas (USFRS)* reports labor in two categories: direct labor, which is the actual cost of performing the spa services, and support labor, which cannot be assigned to a specific treatment but is required for the overall spa operation (support labor includes personnel such as spa reservationists, guest reception agents, and locker room attendants). There are only two common expressions of labor costs used in spa financial analysis—first, as a percentage of revenues, and second, as a labor cost per treatment. A third common labor ratio used in many other industries measures revenue per labor hour, but with the majority of spa therapists being compensated by a percentage commission on the revenue they produce or as a flat fee per service provided, this measurement is seldom used in spa metrics.

Direct Labor Cost Percentage. The **direct labor cost percentage** is determined as follows:

$$\text{Direct labor cost percentage} = \frac{\text{Departmental direct labor costs}}{\text{Departmental revenues}} \times 100$$

Suppose that revenues for a spa's massage department for a month were $120,500 and the direct payroll and related expenses were $69,083. Dividing the direct labor costs by the massage revenues results in a direct labor cost ratio of 57.3 percent (rounded).

It is important to track direct labor costs for each of a spa's four treatment departments (massage, skin care, hair, and nails) to identify the relationship between direct labor costs and revenues for each department. A spa would also track overall treatment direct labor cost. Total direct labor costs of $112,692 divided by total treatment department revenues of $197,900 results in a direct labor cost percentage for the combined departments of 56.9 percent (rounded).

We can also look at a related ratio known as the **direct labor cost per treatment ratio**. Using the same example above and an average massage department revenue per treatment of $100 and $45 for the average revenue per treatment for the nail department, the direct labor cost per treatment would be as follows:

$120,500 (massage revenues) ÷ $100 = 1,205 treatments
$69,083 (direct labor costs) ÷ 1,205 treatments = $57.33 per treatment

For those spas compensating their therapists on a commission only or fee-per-service basis, the direct labor cost percentages and dollars in direct labor cost per service will remain relatively constant unless the spa changes its commission structure or raises prices under the current compensation program. Thus, significant variances should trigger management to analyze the cost to determine if there are irregularities in reporting. For those spas that compensate service providers with a base wage plus commission, variances in direct labor costs can easily be affected by poor scheduling, in which therapists are on the clock collecting their base wage while not performing services. The direct payroll expense of the base wage for hours that the therapist is not providing services will increase the direct labor costs.

Therapist Productivity. In addition to the direct labor cost percentage, many spas will also measure therapist productivity to monitor scheduling efficiency. If a massage therapist works six hours on any given day and delivers five hours of services, his/her productivity for that day would be five divided by six, or a productivity of 83.3 percent (rounded). While this example is for an individual therapist, spas can monitor the overall productivity for all therapists scheduled in each of the four treatment departments by dividing the total number of treatment hours by the total number of hours worked by all therapists. The goal is obvious—the spa will want to have its therapists delivering services while on the clock and not just sitting in a break area waiting for a walk-in customer. This is especially critical for those spas that compensate their therapists with a combination of a base wage and commission, as the spa will incur direct payroll costs for the idle hours in which a therapist is on the clock but not generating revenues. Spas who use this type of compensation structure might want to consider having their accounting records set up to track the total cost of "idle time" within the direct labor cost category. This number in itself can be a very enlightening tool in clearly showing the total cost of "idle time" in a period; it may act as a powerful motivator for spa managers to find ways to minimize it. In general, a spa should strive to maintain a productivity level of 80 to 85 percent. (Treatment staff productivity of higher than 85 percent generally means that there is not sufficient staff availability to meet demand.) Even if there is no base wage and the therapists are compensated only by commission, it is undesirable to have therapists sitting around without appointments. Since they make money only when they are performing services, idle time can have a detrimental effect on morale.

Support Labor Cost Percentage. The support labor sub-schedule includes such positions as guest receptionist, host(ess), attendants, housekeepers, reservationists, and supervisors. These employees are not directly involved in the delivery of a spa service, but do support the massage, skin care, hair, and nail departments as well as retail sales in those spas that do not have a dedicated retail shop. In some cases, these individuals also provide support within the fitness and health and wellness departments. The payroll and related expenses for the support employees is not measured against treatment revenues alone, but rather against total spa revenues, and is monitored as a percentage of revenues. The formula for calculating the **support labor cost percentage** is as follows:

$$\text{Support labor cost percentage} = \frac{\text{Cost of support labor}}{\text{Total spa revenues}} \times 100$$

Suppose that a spa's total support labor for the month was $22,700, and total spa revenues for the month were $285,058. This would mean a support labor cost percentage of 7.96 percent (rounded) for the month ($22,700 ÷ $285,058). This percentage as a stand-alone number for any given period of time is relatively meaningless, but when compared with the labor cost percentages in previous months, on a year-to-date basis, and/or against budget and prior years, it is a valuable comparison of this month's operating performance relative to historical and benchmark standards the spa has achieved or set.

Other Spa Operated Departments Labor. For "Other Spa Operated Departments" such as retail, fitness, and other departments that might appear on the spa's income statement (such as Adventure Experiences, Pool and Beach Services, Children's Camp, etc.), the payroll for that specific department would be included on the spa sub-schedule for that department, and the labor costs would be measured against the revenues generated by that activity. For example, let's assume that a spa has a dedicated spa retail shop that is staffed by retail clerks and a retail manager. If the spa does $42,967 in retail sales for the month and its labor cost is $9,050, you would simply divide the labor cost by the retail revenues for a labor cost percentage of 21.06 percent (rounded).

Expense Ratios

In this section, we will discuss direct expenses, contribution margin, and indirect expenses.

Direct Expense Ratios. The *USFRS* was designed in such a way that treatment products and supplies used in the performance of the spa's treatments are charged as a direct expense on the schedule for the department using the products/supplies.

Two direct expense ratios—**direct cost percentage** and **direct cost per treatment**—may be easily determined as follows:

$$\text{Direct cost percentage} = \frac{\text{Direct costs}}{\text{Related revenue}} \times 100$$

$$\text{Direct cost per treatment} = \frac{\text{Direct costs}}{\text{Number of treatments}}$$

Suppose that a spa's skin care department had revenues of $43,583 for the month and the direct expenses for facial skin care products and supplies such as extraction utensils used only by the estheticians totaled $3,417 for the month. In order to keep our example simple, assume that the average revenue per skin care department treatment was $100, so that dividing the monthly revenues of $43,583 by $100 equals 436 (rounded) treatments performed during that month. The spa will maintain two ratios for this expense. To calculate the direct cost percentage of revenues for the skin care department for the month, we take the Professional Products and Supplies expense for the skin care department ($3,417) and divide it by the department's revenues ($43,583); this reveals a direct cost percentage for the month of 7.8 percent (rounded) of revenues. The spa would also monitor the cost of the professional products and supplies as a cost per treatment. Thus, $3,417 divided by 436 treatments reveals a direct expense of $7.84 (rounded) per treatment.

Contribution Margin. By charging each of the treatment departments with its direct therapist labor and the cost of the professional products and supplies used to perform the services within that department, the spa is able to determine the **contribution margin** for each department. Continuing with our skin care department example, assume that direct labor for the department was $24,958 for the month. By totaling the labor expense and the cost of professional products and supplies of $3,417, the direct expenses for the department totaled $28,375. Subtract that amount from the department's revenues of $43,583 to determine the total contribution margin of $15,208. The contribution margin percentage would be the $15,208 margin divided by $43,583 in revenues, or 34.9 percent (rounded). If we divide the contribution margin ($15,208) by the number of treatments (436), we learn that the contribution margin from each skin care treatment was $34.88 that month. The formula for determining contribution margin per treatment is as follows:

$$\text{Contribution margin per treatment} = \frac{\text{Revenue} - \text{Total direct costs}}{\text{Number of treatments}}$$

Spa management would perform this ratio analysis for each of its treatment departments to determine the contribution margin from each, and would also calculate the contribution margin ratio for their total revenues, labor, and professional products/supplies.

Indirect Operating Expenses. Indirect operating expenses are not specifically identifiable to an individual spa service department. Guests receiving services from one or more of the massage, skin care, hair, or nail departments also receive

Exhibit 1 Indirect Expense Ratios

Expense	Amount	% of revenue	Cost/treatment
Ambience	$ 592	.30%	$0.26
Contract Services	2,933	1.48%	1.27
Dues & Suscriptions	175	.09%	0.08
Equipment Rental	117	.06%	0.05
Guest Clothing	625	.32%	0.27
Guest Supplies	2,542	1.28%	1.11
Hospitality	783	.40%	0.34
Laundry	3,560	1.8%	1.55
Licenses and Fees	100	.05%	0.04
Linen	1,633	.83%	0.71
Operating Supplies	1,658	.84%	0.72
Professional Development	516	.26%	0.22
Telecommunications	183	.09%	0.08
Uniforms	225	.11%	0.10
Other	166	.08%	0.07

indirect benefit from the items listed on the Indirect Operating Expenses schedule such as "ambience," "equipment rental," "hospitality," etc. Accounting for these indirect costs can be done in one of two ways. Either an artificial allocation of the costs could be assigned to each of the treatment departments or—as was ultimately decided by the developers of the *USFRS*—spa managers can isolate these expenses and charge them against the total contribution of the four spa treatment departments.

Spa management monitors the relationship of the indirect expense amount to the various departments in two ways: as a percentage of total treatment revenues and as a cost per treatment. To illustrate this concept, see the indirect expense ratio numbers for a given month shown in Exhibit 1. (Assume that this spa's total treatment revenues for the month were $197,900, and that 2,300 spa treatments were performed during the month.) The indirect operating expenses shown in this exhibit are taken from the *USFRS*; individual spas may include or exclude specific line items to meet their own needs.

It is easier for spa managers to remember that the spa's laundry expense was 1.8 percent of treatment revenues than to remember the exact dollar amount of $3,560. It is easier to remember that the hospitality expense ran 34 cents per service than to recall that the expense was $783 for the month. Taken alone, a single ratio is somewhat meaningless, but over months and years, spa management will find that there are patterns to the ratios that enable management to quickly pick out expenses that appear to be out of line compared with historical results. Finally, a spa will want to monitor the total of direct professional products and supplies plus the indirect operating expenses, as the total relates to the revenues generated. In general, the total operating expense percentage should fall into the range of 8–12 percent. The *USFRS* provides a detailed expense dictionary to ensure that expense items are charged consistently to the correct expense account. Without consistent expense classification, comparative ratios can be misleading.

Retail Ratios

Experienced spa professionals understand the importance of retail revenues to the spa's financial success. Because treatment revenues require an individual therapist for each service performed, treatment contribution margins are relatively low in comparison with the margins for retail products. Retail operations in a spa can vary in size from a simple shelving unit in the guest reception area to full spa merchandise specialty shops with a retail manager and sales clerks. It will come as no surprise that there are many ratios that spa management tracks to ensure that the retail department is maximizing profitability. The most frequently used retail ratios are covered in this section.

Retail Revenues as a Percentage of Treatment and Overall Revenues. The formula for the **retail revenues as a percentage of treatment and overall revenues ratio** is as follows:

$$\text{Retail revenues as a percentage of total revenue} = \frac{\text{Retail revenues}}{\text{Total revenues}} \times 100$$

Let's continue with our earlier spa example in which retail revenue was just under $43,000 and total revenues were just over $285,000. Using these round numbers, retail revenues represented 15 percent of total spa revenues. As a ratio to spa treatment revenues of $197,900, the $43,000 in retail sales is 21.7 percent (rounded) of total treatment revenue.

Retail Revenues per Treatment. Another commonly used retail ratio is **retail revenues per treatment**. The formula for this ratio is as follows:

$$\text{Retail revenues per treatment} = \frac{\text{Total retail revenues}}{\text{Number of treatments}}$$

As you will recall, the monthly number of treatments for the spa we are using as an example was 2,300. To calculate the retail revenues per treatment, simply divide the retail revenues of $43,000 by 2,300 to get $18.70 of retail revenue per treatment (rounded). Again, just looking at one number for one month has little meaning, but tracking the historical ratio performance will establish trends. Comparing this ratio to published industry trends will provide managers with additional benchmarks by which they can measure their retail department revenue strength.

Mix of Retail Sales. While individual spas will establish their own merchandise categories to meet their specific needs, the *USFRS* has adopted the categories that apply to spa merchandise used by the major traditional retailers, as shown in Exhibit 2.

In a survey of spas with a dedicated retail shop, the mix of sales for the four merchandise classifications averaged as follows:

Exhibit 2 *USFRS* Merchandise Categories

Revenue
- Apparel
  - Footwear
  - Men's/Unisex
  - Robes and Terry
  - Women's
    - Total Apparel
- Gifts and Accessories
  - Books and Media
  - Fashion Accessories
  - Home
    - Total Gifts and Accessories
- Products
  - Bath and Body products
  - Hair Products
  - Make-up Products
  - Nail Products
  - Private Label Products
  - Skin Care Products
    - Total Products
- Other Retail
  - Snacks and Beverages
  - Sundries
  - Other
    - Total Other Retail

Total Revenue

• Products	51%
• Apparel	27%
• Gifts and Accessories	15%
• Other	7%

The relevance of tracking the mix of retail sales percentage is to guide management in establishing inventory levels. For example, it would be imprudent for a spa to have 40 percent of its retail inventory dollar value in Gifts and Accessories when that category of revenues contributes only 15 percent of revenues to the spa.

Cost-of-Goods-Sold Percentage. Many businesses, including spas, must know the cost of goods sold as they relate to sales. The **cost-of-goods-sold percentage** is determined as follows:

$$\text{Cost-of-goods-sold percentage} = \frac{\text{Cost of goods sold}}{\text{Total retail sales}} \times 100$$

Assume the cost of goods sold for January was $30,000 and the total retail sales were $60,000. The cost-of-goods-sold percentage would be 50 percent.

Management typically would compare this result to both the budgeted cost of goods sold percent for January and the historical cost-of-goods-sold percentage.

Average Retail Discount Percentage. Spas routinely offer retail promotions to stimulate additional retail sales. The **average retail discount percentage** allows managers to monitor the impact of discounts on retail revenues and the cost-of-goods-sold percentage. Most retail point-of-sales systems are capable of tracking the retail price for each item and the dollar value of discounts given. The average retail discount percentage is calculated as follows:

$$\text{Average retail discount percentage} = \frac{\text{Retail discounts' dollar value}}{\text{Total retail revenues}} \times 100$$

Retail Revenue per Service Department Treatment and by Individual Therapist. Clearly, guests receiving a facial are much more inclined to purchase at-home-care skin care products than clients simply having their nails done. Most spas will monitor not only overall retail revenues per treatment, but will separate the four service departments and calculate the retail sales per service by each department. Additionally, many spas will provide service providers a commission on the retail products they personally sell as an incentive to generate additional retail revenues. Thus, while the retail sales per skin care treatment might be in the $25–$35 range, the hair department might average $12 in retail sales per service. Spa software systems are designed to track retail revenues by individual service provider; management can monitor the retail sales level of each service provider to reward those who are doing very well and to coach those who are generating lower-than-desired retail revenues. Remember, however, that tying a retail sale to a specific therapist is often not a simple issue. For example, a guest having a full day at the spa may see several therapists, each with similar retail product recommendations, or a client having a manicure might, at checkout, purchase a night cream even though this was not recommended by anyone. It is important to establish fair and consistent guidelines regarding who gets credit for the sale, as it potentially affects therapists' wages. If poorly managed, it can be a source of friction among spa employees.

Revenue per Square Foot and Discounts

Two other useful ratios are essentially individual categories in themselves. These are **revenue per square foot** and the **average service discount ratio**.

Revenue per Square Foot. The revenue per square foot ratio is determined as follows:

$$\text{Revenue per square foot} = \frac{\text{Total spa revenues}}{\text{Square footage of the spa facilities}}$$

It is sometimes difficult to determine a spa's square footage, as many spas will include outside relaxation areas, outdoor pools, and treatment cabanas in the spa's marketing materials in order to portray an image of an expansive spa with significant square footage. The standard used by most industry studies is to include only "air-conditioned" or "under-a-roof" square footage for this ratio. A spa may state that it has 15,000 square feet in its marketing brochure, but if 5,000 square feet of that total includes an outside pool and deck, plus a landscaped spa garden where guests can sit and relax, the revenue per square foot ratio would use only the 10,000 square feet of air-conditioned area in the ratio calculation. If a spa with 10,000 square feet does \$3.4 million in total spa revenues, \$3.4 million divided by 10,000 equals \$340 in revenue per square foot.

This ratio can also be calculated as profit per square foot. If the spa with 10,000 square feet has a net income of \$167,200, its profit per square foot is \$16.72 (\$167,200 divided by 10,000). Both of these ratios are most frequently used by investors and lenders as a measurement of the spa's ability to cover the development and construction cost of building the spa facility. Of course, it is unfair to simply use only spa revenues to measure the spa's ability to pay debt service for a hotel/resort spa, as the incentive to include a spa in a resort development project is to generate additional room revenues, RevPAR, and net income. For a day spa development, however, the revenue and net income per square foot is an important statistic in determining the relationship between the spa's net income and the costs for facility lease and build-out costs.

Average Service Discount Ratio. The typical day spa will routinely use discounts and coupons to attract new clientele and stimulate service revenues. Without careful analysis and frequent monitoring of revenue, discounts and coupons can skew profitability comparisons from one period to another. The average service discount ratio provides managers and owners the opportunity to monitor how revenues are affected by discount and coupon promotions. The average service discount ratio is calculated as follows:

$$\text{Average service discount ratio} = \frac{\text{Total service discounts}}{\text{Total number of services}}$$

Undistributed Operating Expense Ratios

To refresh your memory, undistributed operating expenses are unique to day spas. These expenses are grouped into three expense categories:

- Administrative and general
- Marketing
- Facilities maintenance and utilities

In a hotel/resort spa, these expenses are commonly charged against the total property revenues. A day spa, as an individual business unit, must charge these expenses against spa revenues.

Among these three major categories of expenses there are 50 separate line item expenses listed in the *USFRS*. While it would be unnecessary to maintain ratios for all 50 line items—for example, to track what the spa's postage expense is per treatment, or track trash removal as a percentage of total spa revenues—a spa should at a minimum track what the total expenses for each of these three categories of expenses are as a percentage of total spa revenues.

Exhibit 3 Non-Operating Ratios

Ratio	Formula
1. Current ratio	Current assets/current liabilities
2. Operating cash flows to current liabilities ratio	Operating cash flows/average current liabilities
3. Solvency ratio	Total assets/total liabilities
4. Debt-equity ratio	Total liabilities/total owners' equity
5. Long-term debt to total capitalization ratio	Long-term debt/long-term debt and net assets
6. Number of times interest earned ratio	Net income + income taxes + interest expense/interest expense
7. Inventory turnover ratio	Cost of goods used/average retail inventory
8. Property and equipment turnover ratio	Total net revenue/average net book value of property and equipment
9. Asset turnover ratio	Total net revenue/average total assets
10. Profit margin ratio	Net income/total net revenue
11. Operating efficiency ratio	Income before fixed charges/total net revenue
12. Return on assets ratio	Net income/average total assets
13. Return on owners' equity ratio	Net income/average owners' equity

Of course, there may be individual line item expenses that management would be interested in monitoring, such as the spa water expense per treatment or the percentage of credit card commissions to total spa revenues. Each spa operation must identify those individual line items that management wishes to track. On the other hand, it would be critical for spa leadership to know what it is spending in total for marketing as a percentage of total spa revenue, as marketing expenses should be measured against the additional revenues that the marketing generates.

Other Ratio Classes

We now turn our attention to liquidity, solvency, activity, and profitability ratios. As mentioned earlier, **liquidity ratios** reveal the ability of a spa to meet its short-term obligations; **solvency ratios** measure the extent to which the spa has been financed by debt and is able to meet its long-term obligations; **activity ratios** reflect management's ability to use the spa's assets; and **profitability ratios** show management's overall effectiveness as measured by returns on sales and investments. The remainder of the chapter will be devoted to an in-depth discussion of individual ratios within these four ratio classes (see Exhibit 3 for a list of the non-operating ratios that will be presented). For each ratio discussed, we will consider its purpose, the formula by which it is calculated, and the sources of data needed for the ratio's calculation. It should be noted that these ratios are best understood and developed by spa management with the assistance of an accounting professional. Exhibits 4 through 6, the financial statements of our hypothetical spa, will be used throughout our discussion.

Liquidity Ratios

The ability of a spa to meet its current obligations is important in evaluating its financial position. For example, referring to the numbers in Exhibits 4–6, can The Spa meet its current debt of $160,300 at the end of 20X2 as it becomes due? Several liquidity ratios can be computed that suggest answers to this question.

Current Ratio. The commonest liquidity ratio is the **current ratio**, which is the ratio of total current assets to total current liabilities. It is expressed as a coverage of so many times. Using figures from Exhibit 4, the 20X2 current ratio for The Spa can be calculated as follows:

$$\text{Current} = \frac{\text{Current assets}}{\text{Current liabilities}}$$

$$= \frac{\$281{,}800}{\$160{,}300}$$

$$= \underline{\underline{1.76}}$$

This result shows that for every $1 of current liabilities, The Spa has $1.76 of current assets. Thus, there is a cushion of $.76 for every dollar of current debt. Considerable shrinkage of inventory could occur before The Spa would be unable to pay its current obligations.

Operating Cash Flows to Current Liabilities Ratio. A recent ratio made possible by the statement of cash flows is operating cash flows to current liabilities. The operating cash flows are taken from the statement of cash flows for a period, while current liabilities come from the balance sheets at the start and end of that period. This measure of liquidity compares the cash flow from a spa's operating activities to its obligations at the balance sheet date that must be paid within 12 months. Using the relevant figures from Exhibits 4 and 6, the 20X2 **operating cash flows to current liabilities ratio** for The Spa is computed as follows:

$$\begin{array}{c}\text{Operating cash flows to} \\ \text{current liabilities ratio}\end{array} = \frac{\text{Operating cash flows}}{\text{Average current liabilities}}$$

$$= \frac{\$289{,}900}{\$155{,}850}$$

$$= \underline{\underline{1.86}}$$

The average current liabilities is the sum of the total current liabilities at the end of each year divided by two. For The Spa, average current liabilities was calculated as follows: ($151,400 + $160,300) ÷ 2 = $155,850.

The 20X2 ratio of 1.86 shows that $1.86 of cash flow from operations was provided by The Spa during 20X2 for each $1 of average current debt.

Exhibit 4 Balance Sheet

The Spa
Balance Sheet
December 31, 20X1 and 20X2

Assets

	December 31, 20X1	December 31, 20X2
Current Assets		
Cash in Bank	$ 42,400	$ 45,600
Accounts Receivable	98,100	100,200
Inventories:		
Retail	47,000	55,000
Professional	21,500	22,000
Food and Beverage	12,500	13,000
Total Inventory	81,000	90,000
Prepaid Expenses	40,000	45,000
Other Current Assets	900	1,000
Total Current Assets	262,400	281,800
Property and Equipment		
Land	200,000	200,000
Buildings	2,200,000	2,200,000
Furniture, Fixtures and Equipment	1,457,000	1,546,000
Automobiles	42,000	42,000
Total Property and Equipment	3,899,000	3,988,000
Less: Accumulated Depreciation	(1,204,800)	(1,254,800)
Net Property and Equipment	2,694,200	2,733,200
Other Assets		
Security and Lease Deposits	35,000	35,000
Other Assets	18,800	20,000
Total Other Assets	53,800	55,000
Total Assets	$3,010,400	$3,070,000

Liabilities and Owners' Equity

	December 31, 20X1	December 31, 20X2
Current Liabilities		
Accounts Payable	$ 24,750	$ 25,600
Sales Tax Payable	1,050	1,100
Gratuities Payable	3,000	2,900
Current Portion of Long-Term Debt	25,000	25,000
Income Taxes Payable	18,000	20,000
Accrued Expenses	14,000	15,000
Deferred Revenue—Gift Certificates	57,500	62,000
Customer Deposits	5,600	5,700
Other Current Liabilities	2,500	3,000
Total Current Liabilities	151,400	160,300
Long-Term Liabilities		
Notes Payable	525,000	500,000
Total Long-Term Liabilities	525,000	500,000
Owners' Equity		
Common Stock	1,000,000	1,000,000
Retained Earnings	1,334,000	1,409,700
Total Owners' Equity	2,334,000	2,409,700
Total Liabilities and Owners' Equity	$3,010,400	$3,070,000

Exhibit 5 Summary Statement of Income

The Spa
Summary Statement of Income
For the year ended December 31, 20X2

	Net Revenues	Cost of Sales	Payroll and Related Expenses	Other Expenses	Income (Loss)
Spa Departments					
Massage	$1,446,000	$	$ 829,000	$ 45,000	$ 572,000
Skin Care	523,000		299,500	41,000	182,500
Nail	199,800		108,400	6,600	84,800
Hair	206,000		115,400	10,500	80,100
Total Spa Contributions	2,374,800		1,352,300	103,100	919,400
Indirect Expenses					
Indirect Support Labor			272,400		272,400
Indirect Operating Expenses				190,000	190,000
Total Indirect Expenses			272,400	190,000	462,400
Spa After Indirect Expenses	2,374,800		1,624,700	293,100	457,000
Memberships	174,000				174,000
Other Operated Departments					
Fitness	198,800		200,900	22,900	(25,000)
Food and Beverage	99,000	32,100	44,800	18,000	4,100
Retail	515,600	268,000	108,600	22,700	116,300
Rentals and Other Income	58,500				58,500
Total Operated Departmental Contributions	871,900	300,100	354,300	63,600	153,900
Income Before Undistributed Expenses	3,420,700	300,100	1,979,000	356,700	784,900
Undistributed Operating Expenses					
Administrative and General			101,300	65,300	166,600
Marketing			34,200	64,900	99,100
Facilities Maintenance and Utilities				128,000	128,000
Total Undistributed Operating Expenses			135,500	258,200	393,700
Income Before Fixed Charges	$3,420,700	$ 300,100	$2,114,500	$ 614,900	391,200
Fixed Charges					89,000
Income Before Depreciation, Amortization, Interest and Income Taxes					302,200
Depreciation and Amortization					80,000
Interest Expense					30,000
Loss on Sale of Property					(50,000)
Income Before Income Taxes					242,200
Income Taxes					75,000
Net Income					$ 167,200

Exhibit 6 Statement of Cash Flows

The Spa
Statement of Cash Flows
For the year ended December 31, 20X2

Net Cash Flows from Operating Activities:		
Net income		$ 167,200
Adjustments to reconcile net income to net cash flows from operating activities:		
Depreciation	$ 80,000	
Loss on sale of equipment	50,000	
Increase in accounts receivable	–2,100	
Increase in inventory	–9,000	
Increase in prepaid expenses	–5,000	
Increase in other current assets	–100	
Increase in current liabilities	8,900	122,700
Net cash flow from operating activities		289,900
Net Cash Flows from Investing Activities:		
Sale of equipment	20,000	
Purchase of equipment	–189,000	
Purchase of other assets	–1,200	
Net cash flows from investing activities		–170,200
Net Cash Flows from Financing Activities:		
Payment of long-term debt	–25,000	
Payment of dividends	–91,500	
Net cash flows from financing activities		–116,500
Net Increase in Cash During 20X2		3,200
Cash at the beginning of 20X2		42,400
Cash at the end of 20X2		$ 45,600

All users of ratios would prefer to see a high operating cash flow to current liabilities, as this suggests spa operations are providing sufficient cash to pay the spa's current liabilities.

Solvency Ratios

Solvency ratios measure a spa's degree of debt financing and are partial indicators of the spa's ability to meet its long-term debt obligations. These ratios reveal the equity cushion that is available to absorb any operating losses. Primary users of these ratios are outsiders, especially lenders, who generally prefer less risk to more risk. This may seem to illustrate the old adage that if you want to borrow money, first you have to prove you don't need it. High solvency ratios generally suggest that a spa has the ability to weather financial storms.

This class of ratios includes two major groups—those based on balance sheet information and those based on income statement information.

Solvency Ratio. A spa is solvent when its assets exceed its liabilities. Therefore, the **solvency ratio** is simply total assets divided by total liabilities. Using figures from Exhibit 4, the solvency ratio in 20X2 for The Spa is determined as follows:

$$\text{Solvency ratio} = \frac{\text{Total assets}}{\text{Total liabilities}}$$

$$= \frac{\$3{,}070{,}000}{\$660{,}300}$$

$$= \underline{\underline{4.65}} \text{ times}$$

The total liabilities of $660,300 is the sum of the current liabilities and long-term liabilities. This result means that The Spa has $4.65 of assets for each dollar of liabilities. The higher this ratio, the less the financial risk.

Owners, investors, and corporate officials of branded spas desire to minimize their investment by using leverage. The greater the leverage, the lower the solvency ratio. Creditors generally would favor a higher solvency ratio because their risk is reduced as net assets increase relative to debt. Spa managers seek a middle position between creditors and owners or partners.

Debt-Equity Ratio. Another solvency ratio from a balance sheet perspective is to compare a spa's total liabilities to its total owners' equity. Using figures from Exhibit 4, the **debt-equity ratio** for 20X2 for The Spa is as follows:

$$\text{Debt-equity ratio} = \frac{\text{Total liabilities}}{\text{Total owners' equity}} \times 100$$

$$= \frac{\$660{,}300}{\$2{,}409{,}700} \times 100$$

$$= \underline{\underline{27.40\%}}$$

The Spa's debt-equity ratio at the end of 20X2 indicates that for each $1 of owners' net worth, The Spa owed creditors $.27.

Owners, investors, and corporate officials of branded spas view this ratio similarly to the way they view the solvency ratio. That is, they desire to minimize their investment by using leverage. The greater the leverage, the higher the debt-equity ratio. Creditors generally would favor a lower debt-equity ratio because their risk is reduced as net assets increase relative to debt. Spa managers, as with the solvency ratio, seek a middle position between creditors and owners or partners.

Long-Term Debt to Total Capitalization Ratio. Still another solvency ratio is the calculation of long-term debt as a percentage of the sum of long-term debt and net assets, commonly called total capitalization. Figures from Exhibit 4 can be used to calculate the 20X2 **long-term debt to total capitalization ratio** for The Spa:

$$\text{Long-term debt to total capitalization ratio} = \frac{\text{Long-term debt}}{\text{Long-term debt and owners' equity}} \times 100$$

$$= \frac{\$500{,}000}{\$2{,}909{,}700} \times 100$$

$$= \underline{\underline{17.18\%}}$$

Long-term debt of The Spa at the end of 20X2 is 17.18 percent of its total capitalization. Creditors prefer a low percentage because it indicates a reduced risk on their part; spa owners, on the other hand, prefer a high percentage because of their desire to minimize their investments.

Times Interest Earned Ratio. The **times interest earned ratio** is based on financial figures from the income statement and expresses the number of times interest expense can be covered. The greater the number of times interest is earned, the greater the safety afforded to a spa's creditors. Since interest is subtracted to determine the bottom line of the income statement for a day spa, it is added to Net Income plus Income Taxes to form the numerator of the ratio, while interest expense is the denominator. Figures from Exhibit 5 can be used to calculate the 20X2 number of times interest earned ratio for The Spa:

$$\text{Times interest earned ratio} = \frac{\text{Net income + Income taxes + Interest expense}}{\text{Total liabilities}}$$

$$= \frac{\$272{,}200}{\$30{,}000}$$

$$= \underline{\underline{9.07}} \text{ times}$$

The result indicates that earnings prior to interest expense cover interest expense 9.07 times. A spa's owners, partners, creditors, and managers all view a high ratio as better. However, since a very high ratio may indicate a lack of financial leverage, owners, partners, and managers may prefer a lower ratio than creditors.

Activity Ratios

Activity ratios measure management's effectiveness in using its resources. Management is entrusted with the spa's property, inventory, equipment, and other resources to provide services for spa guests. Since the property and equipment of most spas constitute a large percentage of the spa's total assets, it is essential to use these resources effectively. Although inventory is generally not a significant portion of total assets, management must adequately control it in order to minimize the cost of sales and as a security measure to minimize shrinkage.

Retail Inventory Turnover Ratio. The **inventory turnover ratio** shows how quickly the retail inventory is being used. Generally speaking, the quicker the inventory turnover, the better, because inventory can be expensive to maintain and, in some cases, must be removed from retail shelves and cannot be sold because of expiration dates. For example, some natural skin care products without preservatives have short expiration dates. Maintenance costs include storage space, insurance, personnel expense (including the time required to complete physical inventories, record keeping, and, of course, the opportunity cost of the funds tied up in inventory. Spa inventories are also highly susceptible to pilferage and must be carefully controlled. The larger the inventory, the more difficult it is to keep track of all the inventoried items, and the greater the temptation may become for staff to pilfer items.

The 20X2 retail inventory turnover ratio for The Spa is calculated as follows:

$$\text{Retail inventory turnover} = \frac{\text{Cost of sales}}{\text{Average retail inventory}}$$

$$= \frac{\$268{,}000}{\$51{,}000}$$

$$= \underline{\underline{5.25}} \text{ times}$$

The average retail inventory is determined by summing the beginning and ending retail inventory and dividing by two. Thus, for The Spa, (\$47,000 + \$55,000) ÷ 2 = \$51,000.

The retail inventory turned 5.25 times during 20X2, or approximately once every 70 days. The speed of retail inventory turnover generally reflects how the inventory is managed. Although a high retail inventory turnover is desired because it means that the spa is able to operate with a relatively small investment in inventory, a turnover that is *too* high may indicate possible stockout problems. Failure to provide desired retail items to spa guests may result not only in immediately disappointed guests, but also in negative goodwill if this problem persists. Too low an inventory turnover suggests that retail items are overstocked.

All interested parties (spa owners, partners, creditors, and managers) prefer relatively high inventory turnovers to low ones, as long as stockouts are avoided. Ideally, as the last inventory item is sold, the shelves are being restocked.

Property and Equipment Turnover Ratio. The **property and equipment turnover ratio** (sometimes called *the fixed asset turnover ratio*) is determined by dividing total revenue by average total net book value of property and equipment (cost less accumulated depreciation) for the period.

This ratio measures management's effectiveness in using property and equipment to generate revenue. A high turnover suggests the spa is using its property and equipment effectively to generate revenues, while a low turnover suggests the spa is not making effective use of its property and equipment and should consider disposing of part of them.

A limitation of this ratio is that it places a premium on using older (depreciated) property and equipment, since their book value is low. Furthermore, this ratio is affected by the depreciation method employed by the spa. A spa using an accelerated method of depreciation will show a higher turnover than a spa using the straight-line depreciation method, all other factors being the same.

Using figures from Exhibits 4 and 5, The Spa's property and equipment turnover ratio for 20X2 is determined as follows:

$$\text{Property and equipment turnover} = \frac{\text{Total revenue}}{\text{Average net book value of property and equipment}}$$

$$= \frac{\$3{,}420{,}700}{\$2{,}713{,}700}$$

$$= \underline{\underline{1.26}} \text{ times}$$

Average NBV of property and equipment is the average of beginning and ending property and equipment: ($2,694,200 + $2,733,200) ÷ 2. The turnover of 1.26 times reveals that total net revenues were 1.26 times the average total net book value of property and equipment.

All interested parties (owners, partners, corporate officials of branded spas, creditors, and managers) prefer a high property and equipment turnover ratio. Spa managers, however, should resist retaining old and possibly inefficient property and equipment with high upkeep costs, even though they result in a high property and equipment turnover.

Asset Turnover Ratio. Another ratio that measures the efficiency of management's use of spa assets is **asset turnover**. It is calculated by dividing total revenue by average total assets. The two previous turnover ratios presented, retail merchandise inventory turnover and especially property and equipment turnover, concern a large percentage of the total assets. The asset turnover ratio examines the use of total assets in relation to total income. Limitations of the property and equipment turnover ratio are also inherent in this ratio to the extent that property and equipment make up total assets.

Using figures from Exhibits 4 and 5, The Spa's 20X2 asset turnover ratio is calculated as follows:

$$\text{Asset turnover ratio} = \frac{\text{Total revenue}}{\text{Average total assets}}$$

$$= \frac{\$3{,}420{,}700}{\$3{,}040{,}200}$$

$$= \underline{\underline{1.13}}$$

The average total assets is determined in the same way as average property and equipment, discussed earlier. The asset turnover indicates that each $1 of assets generated $1.13 of net revenue in 20X2.

As with the property and equipment turnover ratio, all concerned parties (spa owners, partners, corporate officials of branded spas, creditors, and managers) prefer this ratio to be high, because a high ratio means effective use of assets by management, unless management is hanging on to old (depreciated) assets, as discussed previously.

Both the property and equipment turnover ratio and the asset turnover ratio are relatively low for most hospitality segments, especially spas and lodging.

Profitability Ratios

Profitability ratios reflect the results of all areas of management's responsibilities. The profitability ratios we are about to consider measure management's overall effectiveness, as shown by returns on sales (profit margin and operating efficiency ratio), return on assets, and return on owners' equity.

Profit Margin Ratio. Spas are often evaluated in terms of their ability to generate profits on sales. **Profit margin**, a key ratio, is determined by dividing net income for a day spa facility, or spa departmental profit for a hotel/resort spa, by total revenue (these figures are taken from the income statement). Profit margin is an overall measurement of management's ability to generate revenue and control expenses, thus yielding the bottom line. In this ratio, the net income or spa departmental profit is the income remaining after all spa expenses have been deducted, both those controllable by front line spa supervisors and those directly related to decisions made by the spa's management team.

Using figures from Exhibit 5, the 20X2 profit margin of The Spa can be determined as follows:

$$\text{Profit margin ratio} = \frac{\text{Net income}}{\text{Total revenue}} \times 100$$

$$= \frac{\$167{,}200}{\$3{,}420{,}700} \times 100$$

$$= \underline{\underline{4.89\%}}$$

If the profit margin is lower than expected, then expenses and other areas should be reviewed. Poor pricing and low sales volume could be contributing to the low margin. To identify the problem area, management should analyze both the spa's overall profit margin and the profit margins for each spa department that generates revenue. If the spa's departmental margins are satisfactory, the problem would appear to be with the spa's overhead expense.

Operating Efficiency Ratio. The **operating efficiency ratio** is a better measure of management's performance for a day spa operation than the profit margin because it tends to better reflect the outcome of factors over which management has greatest control. This ratio is the result of dividing income before fixed charges by total revenue. Income before fixed charges is the result of subtracting expenses generally controllable by management from total revenue. Non-operating expenses include fixed charges that are directly related to decisions made by a spa's owners, partners, or corporate officials for a branded operation, not management. Fixed charges are expenses relating to the capacity of the spa, including rent, real estate taxes, insurance, depreciation, and interest expense. Although these expenses are generally the result of owners' decisions and thus beyond the direct control of active management, management can and should review tax assessments, insurance policies, and quotations and then make recommendations to the ownership that can affect the spa's total profitability.

Using figures from Exhibit 5, the 20X2 operating efficiency ratio of The Spa can be calculated as follows:

$$\text{Operating efficiency ratio} = \frac{\text{Income before fixed charges}}{\text{Total revenue}} \times 100$$

$$= \frac{\$391{,}200}{\$3{,}420{,}700} \times 100$$

$$= \underline{\underline{11.44\%}}$$

The operating efficiency ratio shows that just over $.11 of each $1 of income is available for fixed charges and bottom-line profits.

The next two profitability ratios compare profits to either assets or owners' equity. The result in each case is a percentage and is commonly called a *return*.

Return on Assets Ratio. The **return on assets (ROA) ratio** is a general indicator of the profitability of a spa in relation to its assets. Unlike the two preceding profitability ratios drawn only from income statement data, this ratio compares bottom-line profits to the total investment—that is, to the total assets. It is calculated by dividing net income by average total assets.

Using figures from Exhibits 4 and 5, The Spa's 20X2 return on assets is calculated as follows:

$$\text{Return on assets} = \frac{\text{Net income}}{\text{Average total assets}}$$

$$= \frac{\$167{,}200}{\$3{,}040{,}200}$$

$$= \underline{\underline{5.5\%}}$$

The Spa's 20X2 ROA means there was 5.5 cents of profit for every dollar of average total assets.

A very low ROA may result from inadequate profits or excessive assets. A very high ROA may suggest that older assets require replacement in the near future or that additional assets need to be added to support growth in revenues. The determination of low and high is usually based on industry averages and a spa's own ROA profile, developed over time.

ROA may also be calculated by multiplying the asset turnover ratio (an activity ratio) by the profit margin. For 20X2, the ROA for The Spa can be calculated as follows:

$$\text{ROA} = \text{Asset turnover ratio} \times \text{Profit margin}$$

$$= 1.13 \times .0489 \times 100$$

$$= 5.5\%$$

Return on Owners' Equity Ratio. A key profitability ratio for spas is the **return on owners' equity (ROE) ratio**. The ROE ratio compares the profits of the spa to the ownership's investment. It is calculated by dividing net income by the average owners' equity.

Using relevant figures from Exhibits 4 and 5, the 20X2 ROE for The Spa is calculated as follows:

$$\text{Return on owners' equity} = \frac{\text{Net income}}{\text{Average owners' equity}} \times 100$$

$$= \frac{\$167{,}200}{\$2{,}371{,}850} \times 100$$

$$= \underline{\underline{7.05\%}}$$

Average owners' equity is the average of owners' equity at the start and end of the year. In 20X2, for every one dollar of owners' equity, 7.05 cents was earned. To spa's ownership, this ratio represents the financial results of all of management's efforts. The ROE reflects management's ability to produce financial results for the owners.

Individual Spa Performance Indexing. A number of spa industry financial surveys will include an Index number in its report. This number enables a participating spa to compare its results with the other participants in the survey. If the industry segment or competitive set performance for RevPATH is reported to be $36 and a spa's performance for RevPATH is $25, the index is determined by dividing the individual spa's performance of $25 by the industry segment or competitive set performance of $36 and multiplying the result by 100. In this case, $25 divided by $36 yields .694 times 100, resulting in an Index of 69.4, which means that the individual spa is performing at 69.4 percent of the reported industry average.

Limitations of Ratio Analysis

Ratios are extremely useful to owners, creditors, and managers in evaluating the financial condition and operations of a spa. However, ratios are only indicators. Ratios do not resolve a problem or even reveal exactly what the problem is. At best, when they vary significantly from past periods, budgeted standards, or industry averages, ratios only indicate that there *may* be a problem. Much more investigation and analysis are required.

Ratios are meaningful when they result from comparing two *related* numbers. Retail cost of sales percentage is meaningful because of the direct relationship between retail cost of sales and retail sales. A goodwill to cash ratio is meaningless due to the lack of any direct relationship between goodwill and cash.

Ratios are most useful when compared with a standard. A retail cost of sales percentage of 55 percent has little usefulness or meaning until it is compared with a standard or benchmark such as past performance, industry averages, or the spa's budgeted percentages.

Ratios may be used to compare spas. However, many ratios, especially operating ratios, will not result in meaningful comparisons if the two spas are in completely different segments of the spa industry. For example, comparing ratios for a destination spa to ratios for a day spa would probably not serve any meaningful purpose.

In addition, if the accounting procedures used by two separate spas differ in any of several areas, then a comparison of their ratios will likely show differences related to accounting procedures as well as to financial positions or operations, which makes the comparison not only meaningless but misleading. Standardization and consistency of accounting procedures are two of the main advantages provided by the *USFRS*.

No single ratio tells the entire story. Often, many ratios must be used to understand the financial picture of a spa. Generally, the same ratios should be viewed over a series of time periods.

Finally, financial ratios are generally computed from figures in the financial statements. These figures are based on historical costs. Over time, the effects of inflation render some of these figures less useful. For example, an average retail sales check of $15 in 20X9 for a given spa is not necessarily a better performance than $12 in 20X3; if the inflation rate was greater than 25 percent for the 20X3–20X9 time period, $15 in 20X9 is worth less than $12 in 20X3. Ratios that are most affected by inflation include those that contain property, equipment, or owners' equity in either the numerator or denominator. In addition, depreciation, since it relates to the historical cost of property and equipment, is often understated, so income figures involving depreciation expense are often overstated.

Accountants have used some fairly sophisticated techniques, such as restating the financial statements in constant dollars of equal purchasing power, to overcome this limitation in ratio analysis. However, as desirable as this correction is, it is often not used because of the major effort and time required to use it. An alternative approach is to apply an inflation correction factor to ratios that are affected by inflation. For example, using the just-mentioned retail sales example, assume that inflation for the 20X3–20X9 period was 50 percent. The comparison of retail sales for 20X3 and 20X9 would be as follows:

20X3 (historical)	$12
20X3 (adjusted to current dollar equivalent)	$18*
20X9 (current dollars)	$15

*$12 × 150% = $18

Thus, it is clear that the 20X3 retail sales check was higher than the 20X9 retail sales check when inflation is considered.

Even though these limitations are present, a careful use of ratios that acknowledges their shortcomings will result in an enhanced understanding of a spa's operations and overall financial position.

Summary

Ratio analysis permits investors, creditors, and operators to receive more valuable information from the financial statements than they could receive from reviewing the absolute numbers reported in the documents. Vital relationships can be monitored to determine operating performance in comparison with other periods and the budget. A combination of ratios can be used to efficiently and effectively communicate more information than that provided by the statements from which they are calculated.

There are five major classifications of ratios: operating, liquidity, solvency, activity, and profitability. Although there is some overlap among these categories, each has a special area of concern. It is important to be familiar with the types of ratios in each category, to know what each ratio measures, and to be aware of the targets or standards against which they are compared. For example, a couple of liquidity ratios focus on the spa's ability to cover its short-term debts. However, each person examining the spa's financial position will have a desired performance in mind. Creditors desire high liquidity ratios, which indicate that loans will probably be repaid. Investors, on the other hand, like lower liquidity ratios, since current assets are not as profitable as long-term assets. Management reacts to these pressures by trying to please both groups.

Many ratios covered in this chapter focus on operations. Not every operating ratio discussed in the chapter will be used by every spa manager, and some will be used more frequently than others. The purpose of presenting them all is to show how they are computed and what they mean. A few years ago, a uniform system of accounts for the spa industry was developed. In the near future, consulting firms most likely will be issuing industry operating reports that will convey the results of operations using the standardized approaches set forth in the uniform system. These reports will allow managers to make meaningful comparisons of their spa's operating results to spa industry financial averages.

A number of the operating ratios focus on revenue, since generating revenue is a major challenge in such a competitive industry. Common revenue ratios are revenue per treatment, revenue per customer/guest, RevPAR, RevPATH, and treatment room utilization. A number of ratios cover operating costs such as direct labor cost percentage, therapist productivity, support labor percentage, cost of goods sold percentage, and indirect expense percentages.

It is important to realize that a ratio by itself is not meaningful. It is only useful when it is compared with a standard: an industry average, a ratio from a past period, or a budgeted ratio. The comparison against budget ratios is the most useful for management. Any significant difference should be analyzed to determine its probable cause(s). Once management has fully investigated areas of concern revealed by the ratios, then corrective action can be taken to rectify any problems.

Key Terms

activity ratios—A group of ratios that reflect management's ability to use the spa's assets and resources.

asset turnover—An activity ratio for measuring the efficiency of management's use of spa assets; it is calculated by dividing total revenues by average total assets.

average retail discount percentage—A ratio that allows spa managers to monitor the impact of discounts on spa revenue; it is calculated by dividing the dollar value of retail discounts for a time period by the spa's total retail revenues for the same period.

average service discount ratio—Helps spa managers monitor the use of discounts and coupons to attract business. It is calculated by dividing total service discounts for a time period by the total number of services for the same period.

benchmark—Something that serves as a standard by which something else can be measured; benchmarks for current spa ratios may be the spa's historical data or industry averages.

contribution margin—Sales less cost of sales for a spa product or department; represents the amount of sales revenue that is contributed toward a spa's fixed costs and/or profits.

cost of goods sold percentage—A ratio calculated by dividing cost of goods sold for a time period by total retail sales for the same period.

current ratio—Ratio of total current assets to total current liabilities expressed as a coverage of so many times; calculated by dividing current assets by current liabilities.

debt-equity ratio—Compares the debt of a spa to its net worth (owners' equity) and indicates the spa's ability to withstand adversity and meet its long-term obligations; it is calculated by dividing total liabilities by total owners' equity.

direct cost percent—A direct expense ratio used by spa managers to monitor and control direct expenses; it is calculated by dividing direct costs for a time period by related revenue for the same period.

direct cost per treatment—A direct expense ratio used by spa managers to monitor and control direct expenses; it is calculated by dividing direct costs for a time period by the number of treatments for the same period.

direct labor cost percentage—Helps managers monitor and control labor costs; it is calculated by dividing departmental direct labor costs by departmental revenues.

inventory turnover ratio—A ratio showing how quickly a spa's inventory is moving from storage to productive use; it is calculated by dividing the cost of sales by the average retail inventory.

liquidity ratios—A group of ratios that reveal the ability of a spa to meet its short-term obligations.

long-term debt to total capitalization ratio—A solvency ratio showing long-term debt as a percentage of the sum of long-term debt and owners' equity; it is calculated by dividing long-term debt by long-term debt and owners' equity.

number of treatments per customer/guest—Measures the average number of treatments that spa customers are booking; calculated by dividing the total number of treatments for a period of time by the total number of customers/guests for the same period.

number of treatments per treatment room—This ratio is a variation of the treatment room occupancy percentage without factoring in the number of operating hours; it simply measures the number of treatments per treatment room during a given time period. It is calculated by dividing total number of treatments for a time period by the number of treatment rooms.

operating cash flows to current liabilities ratio—A liquidity ratio that compares the cash flow from the spa's operating activities to its obligations at the balance sheet date that must be paid within twelve months; it is calculated by dividing operating cash flows by average current liabilities.

operating efficiency ratio—A measure of management's ability to generate sales and control expenses; calculated by dividing income before fixed charges by total revenue.

operating ratios—A group of ratios that assist in the analysis of a spa's operations.

profit margin—An overall measure of management's ability to generate sales and control expenses; calculated by dividing net income by total revenue.

profitability ratios—A group of ratios that measure management's overall effectiveness as measured by returns on sales and investments.

property and equipment turnover ratio—A ratio measuring management's effectiveness in using a spa's property and equipment to generate revenue; calculated by dividing average total property and equipment into total revenue generated for the period.

ratio analysis—The comparison of related facts and figures.

resort capture rate ratio—Measures the percentage of guests purchasing spa services; it is calculated by adding the spa services used by resort guests plus the fitness facilities used by resort guests divided by the total number of resort guests.

resort service capture ratio—Measures the percentage of guests purchasing spa services; it is calculated by dividing the number of spa service resort guests by the total number of resort guests.

retail revenues as a percentage of treatment and overall revenues—A ratio spa managers use to determine the contribution of retail revenues to the spa's total revenues; it is calculated by dividing retail revenues for a time period by total spa revenues for the same period.

retail revenues per treatment—A ratio spa managers use to determine the average retail revenue collected per spa treatment; it is calculated by dividing total retail revenues for a time period by the number of spa treatments for the same period.

return on assets (ROA)—A ratio providing a general indicator of the profitability of a spa by comparing net income to total investment; calculated by dividing net income by average total assets.

return on owners' equity (ROE)—A ratio providing a general indicator of the profitability of a spa by comparing net income to the owners' investment; calculated by dividing net income by average owners' equity.

revenue per customer/guest—Measures the average spending by each spa guest; it is calculated by dividing a spa's total treatment and retail revenues for a time period by the total number of customers/guests for the same period.

revenue per square foot ratio—A spa usage ratio calculated by dividing total spa revenues by the square footage of the spa facilities. A spa's square footage is that footage that is air conditioned or under a roof; outside relaxation areas, pools, and treatment cabanas are excluded.

revenue per treatment—A way for the spa to identify the average selling price for a treatment or product; for example, for massages, the calculation for determining revenue per treatment is to divide the total massage revenue for a time period by the total number of massages for the same period.

RevPAR—For hotels, measures revenue per available guestroom; for spas located within hotels or resorts, RevPAR measures treatment revenue per available guestroom; it is calculated by dividing treatment revenues for a time period by available room nights for the same period.

RevPASH—Revenue per available salon hour; calculated by dividing total salon treatment revenue for a period by the total number of salon station available hours for the same period. It is similar to RevPATH calculation used by spas.

RevPATH—Revenue per available treatment hour; it is calculated by dividing total treatment revenue for a time period by the total available treatment hours for the same period.

RevPATR—Revenue per available treatment room. RevPATR is a spa measurement similar to a hotel's RevPAR measurement; it is based on the number of treatment areas within the spa and is calculated by dividing total treatment revenues for a time period by the number of total treatment rooms/stations for the same period.

RevPOR—Revenue per occupied room. For hotels, measures revenue per occupied guestroom; for spas located within hotels or resorts, RevPOR measures treatment revenue per occupied guestroom; it is calculated by dividing treatment revenues for a time period by occupied guestrooms for the same period.

solvency ratio—A measure of the extent to which a spa is financed by debt and is able to meet its long-term obligations; calculated by dividing total assets by total liabilities.

solvency ratios—A group of ratios that measure the extent to which a spa has been financed by debt and is able to meet its long-term obligations.

support labor cost percentage—A ratio to help spa managers monitor and control support labor costs; it is calculated by dividing the cost of support labor for a time period by total spa revenues for the same period.

times interest earned ratio—A ratio based on financial figures from a spa's income statement that expresses the number of times interest expense can be covered; it is calculated by adding a spa's net income plus income taxes plus interest expense, and dividing this sum by the spa's interest expense.

treatment room occupancy percentage—Calculated by dividing the number of treatment hours for a time period by the total number of treatment hours available for the same period.

Review Questions

1. What is the major difference between liquidity and solvency ratios?
2. What are ratios best compared to?
3. How do ratios express financial information?

4. If you are investing in a hotel, which ratios would be most useful? Why?
5. What do activity ratios highlight and what are two examples of activity ratios?
6. How is the treatment room occupancy percentage calculated? How is it used?
7. Of what value is the massage department revenue/total revenue to the manager of a spa?
8. How is the average service discount calculated and how is it useful to the spa's manager?
9. What is the purpose of determining the direct labor cost percentage and for what departments should it be determined?
10. What are the limitations of ratio analysis?

Chapter 6 Outline

The Importance of Pricing
Relationship of Price and Demand
Informal Pricing Approaches
Cost Approaches to Pricing: Three Modifying Factors
Markup Approaches to Pricing
Bottom-Up Approach to Pricing
Menu Engineering
- Contribution Margin
- Guest Demand
- Menu Mix

Using Menu Engineering
Retail Pricing
- Initial Markup
- Markdowns
- Maintained Markup
- Pilferage
- Transfers
- Discounts
- Discount Promotions
- Incorrect Inventory
- Delays in Record Keeping
- Uncounted Inventory

Competencies

1. Discuss the importance of pricing and explain how the concept of price elasticity of demand applies to spa operations. (pp. 173–176)
2. Describe informal approaches to pricing and identify factors that modify cost approaches to pricing. (pp. 176–178)
3. Use markup and bottom-up approaches to pricing spa services and products. (pp. 178–181)
4. Explain the menu engineering approach to pricing spa services. (pp. 181–186)
5. Discuss retail pricing issues for spas. (pp. 186–192)

6

Pricing and Menu Engineering

ERICA PICKED UP THE PHONE and answered, "Good afternoon, The Spa at the Luxury Resort, this is Erica at your service."

"Hey Erica," said Monica. "Have you been invited over to see the new Any Day Spa opening in a few weeks in Dana Point?"

"Yes," Erica answered, "I have a message from the spa director there, inviting me to come over for a tour. Why do you ask?"

"Well, I went over this afternoon. While there's still quite a bit of work left to do, it is going to be a fabulous spa," said Monica, "The owner has selected really nice finishes and the equipment is all top rate. I was especially impressed with the relaxation lounge. It's just beautiful, with a great hospitality station and iPods that the guests can use to select their favorite music theme while relaxing."

"That sounds great," replied Erica. "I'll have to make a point of calling the spa director back and driving up to see it."

"That's not the big news," Monica added. "I asked if she had her service menu ready. While she did not have the final brochures back from the printer yet, she showed me the proof. I was shocked—she's going to open with an hour massage at only $90. That's $25 less than I charge, and $40 less than you get for a 50-minute massage."

"When I asked why her prices were so low, she told me that the owner saw the economy was sluggish for the past few months and that they had better open with the best prices in the area. I know that I have price-conscious customers who will drive an extra 15 minutes to save $25.

"Erica, I'm nervous. I'll ask my spa's owner if she would approve lowering our prices when the new spa opens."

"Monica, you can't run scared just because someone in the area has lower prices," said Erica. "I mean, if you drop your price for an hour massage by $25, that's a reduction of more than 20 percent. I know that your profit percentage is about 13 percent. If you reduce prices by that much, you will be giving up all your profit dollars. You know business is always cyclical. Revenues will grow for several years, like they have recently, and then there will be downturns like after 9/11 and back in the early 80s. But business always cycles back up. If you just slash prices now, it will be a lot harder to increase prices in the future.

"Remember how easy pricing was in the early 1990s during the years of explosive growth of spas?" asked Erica. "A new resort would open in southern

California and its management would think, 'We are the newest, biggest, and best spa,' and they'd open with prices much higher than ours. And what did we do? We all raised our prices based only on our assumptions about the market and where we thought our quality was, compared to the other nearby spas. Well, now that the economy is soft, we don't want to get into a price war by assuming that lower prices will build business. Heck, if price was all that mattered, the cheapest cars would always be the best sellers—but that just isn't the case. Customers are measuring value, not just price."

Erica then shared with Monica advice her father had given her years earlier:

"It's easy to calculate the selling price of a 'widget' by taking the materials cost plus the manufacturing cost, then adding the desired margin—and that becomes the price. It's much harder to set the price for a service.

"He dealt with that for his entire career, trying to set room rates for the hotels he ran," said Erica. "He said that hotel guests have so many more options today and have experienced so many resorts than they did in the 60s and 70s. He described the process of 'moments of truth' this way: The first-time guest looks around the lobby and thinks 'This lobby is much nicer than resort A, but not as nice as resort B'. Then the guest judges the check-in process, compared with other resorts he had stayed at. Throughout his stay, he subconsciously tallies up how the guestroom, restaurant, golf course and spa stack up against other resort experiences. He compares the resort staff with the staff at other properties. Finally, the ultimate moment of truth happens at checkout. The guest looks at the cost and mentally totals the pluses and minuses. He determined whether his resort stay was a better value or worse than that of another resort.

"The same thing happens with each of our spa guests every day," Erica continued. "The average spa guest today will have experienced more than three spas in the past year. It's the quality of overall experience and value that will determine if they are going to come back."

Monica felt some relief with these thoughts: "The new spa has all new therapists, is spending very little time in pre-opening training and is using a very inexpensive software package. They'll probably have a lot of bugs to work out during their first few months, so I am not going to over react. I'll focus on all components of our service experience, the spa's marketing program and will complete a full menu engineering analysis to determine what pricing adjustment might make sense."

Erica thanked Monica for the heads up and said she was going to tour the new spa very soon; it would be important to update her competitive set data now that the new spa was closer to opening.

Pricing is one of the most important and difficult decisions spa managers make. If prices are set too high, lower demand may result in reduced sales. When prices are set too low, demand may be high, but lowered sales revenue is likely to result in costs not being covered. Either way, the spa's profitability may be placed in jeopardy. How can a manager ensure that prices are appropriate?

Establishing prices that maximize revenues is difficult. Some managers would suggest that the process of setting effective prices involves a bit of trial and error. Yet, while no method guarantees maximum profits, good managers will seek to establish a rational basis for their pricing decisions. General approaches to the pricing challenge provide ways of using relevant information and the manager's knowledge of the relationship among sales, costs, and profits to establish a reasonable basis for effective pricing.

Our discussion of cost approaches to pricing in this chapter will answer many of the most important questions about the pricing process, such as the following:

1. Which costs are relevant in the pricing decision?
2. What are informal pricing methods?
3. What is the common weakness of informal pricing methods?
4. What is meant by elastic and inelastic demand?
5. What are the common cost methods of pricing various spa treatments?
6. How may popularity and profitability be considered in setting treatment prices?
7. What is the real focus of menu engineering?
8. What is meant by the term initial markup in retail pricing?
9. What are several of the retail realities that will affect cost of goods sold?

We will begin this chapter by discussing the importance of pricing and the need to maximize profits. Next, we will explain and illustrate the concept of price elasticity of demand. We will then consider a variety of approaches to pricing, including spa treatment menu engineering. Finally, we will discuss the basic principles of retail pricing and maintained markup, and the factors that affect the costs of retail sales.

The Importance of Pricing

A major determinant of a spa's success is pricing. Whether prices are set too low or too high, the result is the same: a failure to maximize profits. When prices are below what the market is willing to pay, the spa will earn less revenue than it could have. Alternatively, prices set too high will reduce demand and thereby fail to achieve the operation's potential for profit. Management's goal is to set prices that result in profit maximization.

Another factor to consider when setting prices is the positioning of the spa's offerings within the marketplace. Prices set too low may tend to degrade the perceived quality of products, whereas inflated prices may tend to reduce the perceived value from the guest's perspective.

Profits should not result simply because revenues happen by chance to exceed expenses. Profits should occur because revenues generated have been carefully calculated to exceed expenses. The emphasis should not be defensive; that is,

Exhibit 1 Price Elasticity of Demand Formula

$$\text{Price Elasticity of Demand} = \frac{\dfrac{\Delta Q}{Q_o}}{\dfrac{\Delta P}{P_o}}$$

where:

ΔQ = Change in quantity demanded
Q_o = Base quantity demanded
ΔP = Change in price
P_o = Base price

on keeping costs down to make a profit. Aggressive management should set out to generate sufficient revenues to cover costs. Cost containment is a respectable secondary objective after marketing efforts are undertaken to achieve the spa's revenue goals.

In this chapter, prices will be approached from a cost perspective. However, this is not meant to suggest that other factors, such as market demand and competition, are irrelevant. In most situations, they are an important component of the pricing decision.

Relationship of Price and Demand

The concept of **price elasticity of demand** provides a means for measuring how sensitive demand is to changes in price. In general, the relationship between price and demand is as follows: as the selling price of a product or service decreases, all else being equal, more will be sold. When the price of a product is increased, only rarely is more of the product sold, everything else being equal.

The demand for a product or service may be characterized as elastic or inelastic. **Elastic demand** is sensitive to price changes, whereas **inelastic demand** is not. In general, when demand is elastic, a price increase will decrease total sales. Up to a point, price decreases will increase total units or services sold. Inelastic demand, on the other hand, states that a percentage change in price results in a smaller percentage change in quantity demanded. When prices are increased, the percentage reduction in quantity demanded is less than the percentage of the price increase. Therefore, revenues will often—but not always—increase despite some decrease in the quantity demanded.

Exhibit 1 illustrates the price elasticity of demand formula for mathematically determining whether the demand is elastic or inelastic. The base quantity demanded (Q_o) is the number of units sold during a given period before changing prices. The change in quantity demanded (ΔQ) is the change in the number of units sold during the period the prices were changed in comparison to the prior period. The base price (P_o) is the price of the product and/or service for the period prior to the price change. The change in price (ΔP) is the change in price from the base price. Strictly speaking, this equation will virtually always yield a negative number, since it is the result of dividing a negative change in quantity demanded by a positive price change or vice versa. (In other words, as price goes up, quantity demanded goes down and vice versa.) By convention, however, the negative sign is ignored.

If the elasticity of demand exceeds 1, the demand is said to be elastic. That is, demand is sensitive to price changes. With an elastic demand, the percentage change in quantity demanded exceeds the percentage change in price. In other words, additional revenues generated by the higher price are likely to be more than offset by the decrease in demand. When demand is elastic, a price increase will decrease total revenues. Up to a point, price decreases may increase total revenues.

If elasticity of demand is less than 1, demand is said to be inelastic. That is, a percentage change in price results in a smaller percentage change in quantity demanded. Every operation desires an inelastic demand for its products and/or services. When prices are increased, the percentage reduction in quantity demanded is less than the percentage of the price increase. Therefore, revenues will customarily—but not always—increase despite some decrease in the quantity demanded.[1]

Let's look at an example illustrating the calculation of price elasticity of demand. A day spa sold 500 massages during a recent 30-day period at $70 per massage. For the next 30-day period, the price was increased to $80, and 450 massages were sold. The demand for massages over this period is considered to be inelastic, since the calculated price elasticity of demand is less than 1. The calculation of price elasticity of demand is as follows:

$$
\begin{aligned}
\text{Price Elasticity of Demand} &= \frac{50}{500} \div \frac{10}{80} \\
&= .1 \div .125 \\
&= \underline{\underline{.8}}
\end{aligned}
$$

To further illustrate this example, in the first period the spa sold 500 massages for $70 each, yielding revenues of $35,000. When the price is increased to $80, the number of massage treatments sold drops to 450 but the revenues at the higher price yield revenues of $36,000, an increase of $1,000. If, on the other hand, the number of massages sold decrease to 425 when the price is increased by $10, the price elasticity of demand equation would result in 1.25. This would make the price change elastic, and revenues would have declined by $1,000 to $34,000.

In general, the demand for products and services in the spa industry is considered to be elastic. Generally, demand will be elastic where competition is high due to the presence of many operations and where the products and/or services offered are fairly standardized. On the other hand, where competition is low or nonexistent or where an operation has greatly differentiated its products and/or services, then demand may be inelastic. At the extreme, some resorts, clubs, destination spas, and luxury hotel spas are known to have an inelastic demand for their products and services. However, these are generalizations, and there are exceptions.

Informal Pricing Approaches

There are several informal approaches to setting prices for spa services. Since each of these approaches ignores the cost of providing the service, they are only briefly presented here as a point of departure for our discussion of more scientific and useful approaches to setting prices.

The most popular informal pricing approach is that which sets prices based on competition. If the competition charges $95 for a 60-minute massage, or an average of $35 for a manicure, then managers using competitive pricing set those prices as well. When the competition changes its prices, managers using this pricing approach follow suit. As the number of spas has increased significantly over the past ten years, novice owners and managers have tended to set their prices based on this informal pricing approach.

For example, assume the Any Spa is trying to set its prices. The managers decide to review what the area competition charges for the same services they plan to offer and discover the following:

	One-hour massage	Basic facial	Manicure	Hair cut
Spa 1	85	95	25	45
Spa 2	105	125	45	75
Spa 3	95	110	30	55

Based on the above information, the managers ask themselves the following questions:

- Should we aim to be the best spa in the area and be the price leader?
- Do we want to set our prices mid-range in the hopes of stealing market share from the higher-priced spa?
- Do we set our prices with below market pricing with the expectation of capturing existing market share and possibly expanding the size of the market?

Although this approach may seem reasonable when there is significant competition in a market, it ignores the many differences that exist among spa operations, such as location, product quality, atmosphere, customer goodwill, and so forth. Further, it ignores the cost of producing the goods and services sold. Spa operations must consider their own cost structures when establishing prices. Trying to match a dominant operation with a low cost structure may cause a spa to go out of business if it ignores its own costs and prices its products strictly following the competitive approach.

Another informal pricing approach used by some managers is intuition. Intuitive pricing is based on what the manager feels the guest is willing to pay. Generally, managers using this approach rely on their experience regarding guests' reactions to prices. However, as with competitive pricing, intuition ignores costs and may result in a failure not only to generate a reasonable profit, but even to recover costs.

A third approach is psychological pricing. Here, prices are established on the basis of what the guest "expects" to pay. This approach is primarily used by relatively exclusive locations (such as destination and luxury resort spas) and by operators who think that their guests believe "the more paid, the better the product." Although psychological pricing does possess a certain merit, it fails to consider costs and, therefore, may not result in profit maximization.

Finally, the trial-and-error pricing approach first sets a price, monitors guests' reactions, and then adjusts the price based on these reactions. Although this approach appears to consider the guests, there are problems with this method, including:

- Monitoring guests' reactions may take longer than the manager can allow.
- Frequent changes in prices based on guests' reactions may result in price confusion among guests.
- There are many outside, uncontrollable factors that affect guests' purchase decisions. An example illustrates this problem: a 10 percent price increase in services may appear to be too high if appointments are down by more than 10 percent over the next 30 days. However, other factors that may be part of the consumer decision include competition, economic climate changes, and so on.
- The trial-and-error approach fails to consider costs.
- The informal price approaches do have some merit, but they are most useful only when coupled with cost approaches.

Cost Approaches to Pricing: Three Modifying Factors

Before looking at specific cost approaches to pricing, we need to set the stage. When pricing is based on a cost approach, three modifying factors to consider are historical prices, perceived price/value relationships, and competition. These price modifiers relate to the pricing of nearly all products and services.

First, prices that have been charged in the past must be considered when pricing the spa's services. A dramatic change dictated by a cost approach may seem unrealistic to the consumer. For example, if a 30-minute manicure with a realistic price of $35 was mistakenly priced at $25 for two years, the spa manager may need to move slowly from $25 to $35 by implementing several price increases over a period of time.

Second, the guests must perceive that the products and/or services are reasonably priced in order to feel that they are receiving a good value. Many guests today appear to be more value–conscious than ever. Most are willing to pay prices much higher than a few years ago, but they also demand value for the price paid. The perceived value of a manicure includes not only the actual manicure, but also the atmosphere, location, quality of service, and many other often-intangible factors.

Third, the competition cannot be ignored. If an operation's product is viewed as substantially the same as a competitor's, then everything else being equal, the prices would have to be similar. For example, assume that an spa's price calculations for a 60-minute massage may suggest a $120 selling price; however, if a strong nearby competitor is charging $85 for a 60-minute massage, everything else being the same, then competition would dictate a lower price. However, remember that it is extremely difficult for everything else to be the same: the location is at least slightly different, one spa is likely to have a better ambience than another, one may use superior products, one may offer a more highly trained staff, and so on.

Markup Approaches to Pricing

A frequently used approach to pricing spa services and spa retail pricing is marking up the cost of the goods sold. The **markup** is designed to cover all direct and indirect costs of spa services, such as rent, utilities, indirect labor, supplies, interest expense, and taxes; it also contributes to the desired profit.

Under the markup approach to pricing, the first step is to determine the direct cost of the service. For example, a spa's direct cost of performing a 60-minute premier facial includes direct labor cost (service technician payroll and matching taxes), direct product cost (products used to perform the service, including makeup remover; cleanser; toner; exfoliant; mask; oil/serums; and eye, lip, and face creams), and direct supply cost (four cotton swabs, eight 2×2 cotton pads, disposable hair net, and so on). Once the actual cost to perform the service is known, the desired markup can be added. The markup must help cover indirect spa expenses and contribute to the desired profit.

To illustrate, let us assume that a 60-minute premier facial is a new service that spa management is going to add to the menu of services. The spa director decides to use historical data to complete the markup calculation. To start the process, the spa director will determine the exact direct costs of the treatment, based on the spa's compensation plan and the actual costs of the products and supplies that will be used for the new facial. We will use the figures in Exhibit 2, where Total Direct Expenses equal 63.5 percent of Total Net Revenue. Total Indirect Expenses and Total Undistributed Operating Expenses combine to equal 24.5 percent of revenues. The spa in the exhibit achieves an income before fixed charges of 12 percent. Assume the spa is satisfied with these results. Thus, if the direct costs of the new service (including wages, benefits, and direct product and supply costs) totaled $88.90 and the spa director wants to maintain the same percentage relationships between costs and price, the pricing calculation would be:

$88.90 (total direct costs) ÷ 63.5% (desired cost percentage) = $140.00

The spa director might want to increase the profit before fixed charges for this treatment to 14 percent. In that case, he or she would simply change the desired cost percentage from 63.5 percent to 61.5 percent in the above equation, generating a price of $88.90 ÷ 61.5 percent, or $144.55 (likely rounded up to $145). However, if the therapists are compensated on a straight commission percentage basis, the labor cost percentage would remain constant and the only area in which the spa could reduce its cost percentage would be the costs of professional products and supplies used in the treatment. If, on the other hand, the therapists are paid on a set fee-per-service basis, the compensation would remain constant after the price

Exhibit 2 ***USFRS* Statement of Income—Short Version**

Any Spa
Statement of Income (Short Version)
For the Month Ending March 31, 20XX

Net Revenue	$ 285,058
Total Direct Expenses	181,116
Gross Margin	103,942
Total Indirect and Undistributed Expenses	69,908
Income Before Fixed Charges	34,034
Fixed Charges	7,417
Income Before Depreciation, Amortization, Interest Expense & Income Taxes	26,617
Depreciation and Amortization	6,667
Interest Expense	2,500
(Gain) and Loss on Disposal of Property	(4,167)
Income Before Income Taxes	21,617
Income Taxes	6,250
Net Income	$ 15,367

increase, so the direct cost percentage might be reduced by the desired 2 percent on that factor alone.

This method has some shortcomings: First, it fails to take into consideration the unique nature of the market or competition, or both. Second, it is based on costs rather than market conditions. Third, it assumes that the competition uses the same approach and that customers are willing to buy services at those prices.

Bottom-Up Approach to Pricing

A more recently developed cost approach is the bottom-up approach to pricing. In determining the average price per treatment, this approach considers costs, desired profits, and expected number of treatments sold. In other words, this approach starts with desired profit, adds income taxes, then adds fixed charges, followed by undistributed operating expenses, indirect expenses, and direct operating expenses. It is called bottom–up because the first item, net income (profit), is at the bottom of the statement of income. The second item, income taxes, is the next item from the bottom of the income statement, and so on. The approach involves the following seven steps:

1. Calculate the desired profit by multiplying the desired rate of return on investment (ROI) by the owners' investment.
2. Calculate pretax profits by dividing desired profit (Step 1) by 1 minus the tax rate.
3. Calculate fixed charges. This calculation includes estimating depreciation, interest expense, property taxes, insurance, amortization, rent, and any management fees.
4. Calculate undistributed operating expenses. This calculation includes estimating costs in the following areas: administrative and general; sales and marketing; property operation and maintenance; and energy.
5. Calculate the required service department income. The sum of pretax profits (Step 2), fixed charges and management fees (Step 3), and undistributed operating expense (Step 4) equals the required service department income.
6. Determine the service department revenue. The required service department income (Step 5) plus service department direct expenses of payroll and related expenses plus other direct expenses equals service department revenue.
7. Calculate the average price of the service by dividing service department revenue (Step 6) by the number of services expected to be sold.

Exhibit 3 illustrates the bottom–up approach to pricing. The owner plans to invest $590,542 in the development of this prospective spa. Funds borrowed from financial lenders total $1,560,000, and the annual interest rate is 8 percent. The average tax rate for this newly developed spa is forecasted to be 35 percent.

The required return (net income) of $59,054 is determined by multiplying the owners' investment of $590,542 by 10 percent (the required ROI). The earnings before taxes of $90,853 is determined by dividing the net income of $59,054 by 65 percent (one minus the assumed average tax rate.)

The fixed charges are determined as follows:

Interest expense of $124,800:	$1,560,000 × 8%
Depreciation of $180,000:	Estimate of the depreciation on all depreciable assets including the building, furniture, fixtures and equipment
Property taxes:	Estimate based on the millage rate and assumed assessed valuation
Insurance:	Estimate based on insurance coverage for the property and contents

The major operating expense categories of administrative and general; sales and marketing; and facility maintenance and utilities, are estimated based on the use of industry averages for these areas.

Exhibit 3 Sample Bottom-Up Pricing

Total Capital Invested	$590,542
Required Rate of Return on Investment	10%
Required Return	$ 59,054
Add:	
Earnings Before Taxes (at 35 percent)	$ 90,853
Fixed Charges	
Interest Expense	$124,800
Depreciation	180,000
Property Taxes	23,500
Insurance	10,250
Undistributed Operating Expenses	
Administrative and General	$ 71,300
Sales and Marketing	42,500
Facility Maintenance & Utilities	54,750
Required Department Income	$597,953
Direct Expenses (direct payroll and expenses)	
Payroll (including benefits)	$109,200
Other Direct Costs	81,300
Total Service Department Revenue	$788,453
Unitary Services Anticipated	6,572
Price per Service (rounded)	$ 120

The sum of earnings before taxes, fixed charges, and undistributed operating expenses equals $597,953, which is the required department income. The number of services anticipated to be provided equal 6,572. The related payroll and other direct costs to provide these services equal $190,500. Therefore, the total service department revenue equals $788,453, which results from summing the required department income of $597,953 and the direct expenses of $190,500. Dividing the total service department revenues of $788,453 by 6,572 services results in an average price per service of $120.[2]

The potential flaw with this method is in estimating operating expenses. If operating expenses are underestimated, this formula will not deliver the expected result.

Menu Engineering

Thus far, our pricing discussions have revolved around the process for developing pricing for a new spa operation creating its first menu of services or for a spa that is adding a new treatment to the treatment menu. However, the most critical pricing discipline is to periodically dissect the menu of services to critically examine both pricing and demand or service popularity.

Traditionally, spas have focused principally on the direct cost percentage for each service. This emphasis resulted in many managers evaluating the profitability of their spa only by reviewing the direct treatment cost percentage. However, this percentage is not the best guide for evaluating treatment sales.

Menu engineering is a process developed in the 1970s for restaurants to evaluate menu profitability. This method has been modified to become a valuable tool for spas to evaluate the sales demand and contribution margin of each treatment on their services menus.

This sophisticated approach considers both the profitability and popularity of competing menu items. The emphasis is on **gross margin** in dollars, defined as the cost of goods sold subtracted from revenues.[3] For all practical purposes, treatment cost *percentages* are ignored. The emphasis on gross margin dollars rather than treatment cost percentage is based on the fact that managers bank dollars, not percentages.

Menu engineering requires the manager to know each menu item's direct costs, selling price, and quantity sold over a specific period of time. The menu item's gross margin for all individual menu treatments sold (selling price minus direct cost) is characterized as either high or low in relation to the average gross margin for all competing menu items sold.

One key to this process is to compare only similar competing menu items. For example, a 50-minute body treatment should be compared to a 50-minute massage, not a 30-minute haircut and style. However, while keeping those like/like comparisons in mind, it is good practice to step back and make an overview assessment in order to understand the menu and how those treatments work together to generate profitability.

Menu engineering depends on three key elements: contribution margin, guest demand, and menu mix.

Contribution Margin

To produce the most profit-oriented spa menu of services, the spa must first calculate the direct cost of each treatment listed on the menu. This will establish each treatment's profitability based on its *contribution margin* (also known as gross margin). A treatment's contribution margin reveals how many dollars each individual treatment sale contributes to the indirect and undistributed operating expenses and profits of the spa operation. Contribution margin is the mathematical difference between a treatment's price and its direct cost. The higher the contribution margin, the more desirable the treatment is to sell.

Contribution margin is important because it gives a factual picture of each treatment's role in the overall revenue mix and is more revealing than treatment cost percentages. Let's look at an example that demonstrates this. Treatment cost percentage is determined by dividing the treatment's cost to the spa (including product, payroll and supply costs) by its price on the menu. Consider a $200 specialty massage with a total direct expense of $87.41 (product cost + payroll cost + supply cost), which has a treatment cost percentage of 44 percent, while a $140 facial that costs the spa $49.25 has a treatment cost percentage of 35 percent. Based on this comparison, you might believe the facial to be more profitable than the massage because its cost percentage is lower. However, each $200 massage generates $112.59 after direct expenses for the spa, while each $140 facial generates $90.75 after direct expenses. If a client has a free hour to spend at the spa, would you want the client to book a massage or a facial?

Even though the facial has a lower treatment cost percentage, the massage generates more dollars after paying the treatment's direct costs to the spa. Contribution margin enables spa management to look beyond the treatment cost percentage in order to accurately see the value of each treatment's role in the menu mix and overall revenues.

Guest Demand

In reviewing a treatment's contribution margin, operators must also take into account the treatment's popularity in order to determine its total dollar contribution to overall spa revenues. A treatment's popularity is determined by **guest demand**, defined by the number of clients receiving that service over a certain period. If the $200 massage has a higher contribution margin than a $140 facial, but is booked significantly less often, then the $140 facial is a better performer on the menu—and should possibly be promoted more heavily.

Menu mix

Menu mix (MM) is the relative popularity of treatments, based on analysis of guest preferences in treatment selection. MM looks at the number of treatments sold in proportion to all treatments sold on the menu. This analysis reveals guest preference patterns. Menu mix percentage is the count for each menu item sold, expressed as a percentage of total menu items sold.

Using Menu Engineering

Before developing a menu engineering strategy, a manager needs four key items:

- A list of the treatments offered, organized according to treatment department (massage, skin care, hair, and nails) in order to specify competing items
- A periodic (monthly or quarterly) total of the number of each individual treatment sold
- The total direct cost of each treatment (direct payroll + professional product cost + treatment supply costs)
- A list of the menu selling prices for each treatment being evaluated

With the revenue and sales history data in hand, the menu engineering spreadsheet can be used to quickly assess each treatment's performance on the spa's menu. Once the contribution margin and menu mix are calculated, they can be compared to each other to determine an overall ranking for each treatment on the menu. From this analysis, management can clearly see which treatments they should promote more highly. Exhibit 4 is an expanded illustration of a menu engineering spreadsheet for a typical small spa.

Exhibit 4 Menu Engineering Example

A	B	C	D	E	F	G	H	I	J	K	L	M	N	O	P
	Trtmnt. Duration	Price	Payroll %	Payroll	Supply Cost	Per Trtmnt. Cost	Treatment Contrib. Margin	Number of Trtmnts.	Menu Mix	Total Treatment Revenue	Total Treatment Cost	Total Treatment CM	CM Category	MM Category	Classification
Massage															
Swedish	50 min	$120	40%	$48.00	$4.00	$52.00	$68.00	761	13.78%	$91,320.00	$39,572.00	$51,748.00	High	High	Star
Swedish	80 min	$160	40%	$64.00	$4.00	$68.00	$92.00	212	3.84%	$33,920.00	$14,416.00	$19,504.00	High	High	Star
Deep Tissue	50 min	$145	40%	$58.00	$6.00	$64.00	$81.00	365	6.61%	$52,925.00	$23,360.00	$29,565.00	High	High	Star
Deep Tissue	80 min	$195	40%	$78.00	$6.00	$84.00	$111.00	125	2.26%	$24,375.00	$10,500.00	$13,875.00	High	Low	Puzzle
Shiatsu	50 min	$135	40%	$54.00	$0.00	$54.00	$81.00	96	1.74%	$12,960.00	$5,184.00	$7,776.00	High	Low	Puzzle
Shiatsu	80 min	$195	40%	$78.00	$0.00	$78.00	$117.00	58	1.05%	$11,310.00	$4,524.00	$6,786.00	High	Low	Puzzle
Reiki	50 min	$130	40%	$52.00	$0.00	$52.00	$78.00	109	1.97%	$14,170.00	$5,668.00	$8,502.00	High	Low	Puzzle
Reflexology	25 min	$90	40%	$36.00	$0.00	$36.00	$54.00	192	3.48%	$17,280.00	$6,912.00	$10,368.00	High	High	Star
Skin Care															
Deep Cleansing Facial	50 min	$130	40%	$52.00	$20.00	$72.00	$58.00	398	7.21%	$51,740.00	$28,656.00	$23,084.00	High	High	Star
Hydrating Facial	50 min	$155	40%	$62.00	$26.25	$88.25	$66.75	285	5.16%	$44,175.00	$25,151.25	$19,023.75	High	High	Star
Ultra Lift	80 min	$175	40%	$70.00	$30.00	$100.00	$75.00	120	2.17%	$21,000.00	$12,000.00	$9,000.00	High	Low	Puzzle
Toning/Firming Facial	80 min	$175	40%	$70.00	$31.60	$101.60	$73.40	94	1.70%	$16,450.00	$9,550.40	$6,899.60	High	Low	Puzzle
Nails															
Manicure	25	$35	45%	$15.75	$6.00	$21.75	$13.25	400	7.24%	$14,000.00	$8,700.00	$5,300.00	Low	High	Plowhorse
Deluxe Manicure	45	$50	45%	$22.50	$9.75	$32.25	$17.75	88	1.59%	$4,400.00	$2,838.00	$1,562.00	Low	Low	Dog
Pedicure	45	$50	45%	$22.50	$8.50	$31.00	$19.00	420	7.60%	$21,000.00	$13,020.00	$7,980.00	Low	High	Plowhorse
Deluxe Pedicure	60	$80	45%	$36.00	$14.00	$50.00	$30.00	93	1.68%	$7,440.00	$4,650.00	$2,790.00	Low	Low	Dog
Hair															
Haircut/style	50	$55	45%	$24.75	$3.50	$28.25	$26.75	225	4.07%	$12,375.00	$6,356.25	$6,018.75	Low	High	Plowhorse
Shampoo/style	30	$45	45%	$20.25	$3.50	$23.75	$21.25	350	6.34%	$15,750.00	$8,312.50	$7,437.50	Low	High	Plowhorse
Single process	50	$55	45%	$24.75	$11.00	$35.75	$19.25	190	3.44%	$10,450.00	$6,792.50	$3,657.50	Low	High	Plowhorse
Foil Highlights	75	$90	45%	$40.50	$9.00	$49.50	$40.50	240	4.35%	$21,600.00	$11,880.00	$9,720.00	Low	High	Plowhorse
Body															
Brow Shaping	20	$30	45%	$13.50	$3.00	$16.50	$13.50	310	5.61%	$9,300.00	$5,115.00	$4,185.00	Low	High	Plowhorse
Bikini Wax	25	$50	45%	$22.50	$6.00	$28.50	$21.50	241	4.36%	$12,050.00	$6,868.50	$5,181.50	Low	High	Plowhorse
Restore Fango Wrap	50	$115	45%	$51.75	$21.00	$72.75	$42.25	87	1.58%	$10,005.00	$6,329.25	$3,675.75	Low	Low	Dog
Hydro Tub Soak	25	$60	45%	$27.00	$6.00	$33.00	$27.00	64	1.16%	$3,840.00	$2,112.00	$1,728.00	Low	Low	Dog
TOTALS									5523	$533,835.00	$268,467.65	$265,367.35			
							Avg. Cost/Trtmnt		50.29%						
							Avg. CM/Trtmnt		$48.05						
							Hurdle		2.92%						

Exhibit 4 *(continued)*

Notes on certain columns and calculations

B: Treatment Duration includes clean-up time.

D: Payroll Percentage is calculated based on average payroll for each treatment department plus benefits.

E: Payroll equals Price × Payroll Percentage (column C × column D)

F: Supply Cost includes professional products used for the delivery of each individual service, as well as actual supplies used in the treatment (e.g., cotton rounds, brushes, waxing strips or eye pads used specifically for the individual service)

G: Total Cost per Treatment sums Payroll and Supply Cost (columns E and F).

H: Treatment Contribution Margin equals Price minus Total Cost per Treatment minus (column C − column G).

I: Total Number of Treatments is the number of treatments sold during the time period analyzed.

J: Menu Mix is the number of times each given treatment was used, expressed as a percentage of the total of all treatments. To calculate, divide Total Number of Treatments for each treatment by overall treatment total (column I by the Total Number of Treatments—5,523 in this case) sold during the specified time frame.

K: Total Treatment Revenue equals Price × Number of Treatments (column C × column I).

L: Total Treatment Cost equals Total Cost per Treatment × Number of Treatments (column G × column I).

M: Total Treatment Contribution Margin equals Total Treatment Revenue minus Total Treatment Cost (column K − column L).

N: Contribution Margin Category will either be high or low based on whether it exceeds or falls below the average contribution per treatment. To calculate this average, take the overall total for Total Treatment Contribution Margin and divide it by the overall total for Number of Treatments (column M total ÷ column I total).

O: Menu Mix Category will either be high or low based on whether it exceeds or falls below what is known as the **hurdle rate**. To calculate, use this formula: (100% ÷ actual number of treatments offered) × 70%. Example: (100% ÷ 9) × 70% = 7.78%

P: Classification: Each treatment is classified as a star, plow horse, puzzle, or dog based on the contribution margin and menu mix.

While a spa service's contribution margin tells us how many dollars each item adds to revenues, you need to know how popular the service is to determine the total dollar amount it contributes. Menu engineering therefore takes each items contribution margin and its popularity into account to determine into which four categories it falls: star, plow horse, puzzle or dog. Exhibit 5 defines these categories.

It is obviously advantageous to keep the stars and lose the dogs, but what should be done about the plow horses and puzzles? Let's start with the puzzles, which are profitable but relatively unpopular. The challenge is to make them

Exhibit 5 Menu Engineering Categories

Type	Contribution Margin Category	Menu Mix Category	Explanation
Stars	High	High	Stars are popular and provide a high contribution margin.
Plow Horses	Low	High	Plow Horses are popular but low in contribution margin.
Puzzles	High	Low	Puzzles are not popular but provide a high contribution margin.
Dogs	Low	Low	Dogs are not popular and have a low contribution margin.

popular. There are many ways to accomplish this, including renaming the service, changing its description, and changing the service duration to make it sound different or more appealing. For example, changing a "Seaweed Wrap" to a "Detoxification Body Cocoon," "Soothing Sea Bath" or "Ocean Refresher Wrap" may boost its appeal to guests.

Plow horses are popular items with less than ideal contribution margins. The challenge with the plow horse is to reduce the cost of the treatment without sacrificing popularity. An expensive product in the treatment can be replaced with something just as effective but not as costly. As an example, let's examine a Ginseng Body wrap. The wrap starts off with a gommage, a product that lightly and gently exfoliates the skin before the ginseng is applied. Instead of using the gommage, therapists could body brush the client and achieve very similar results while eliminating the product cost. Or the manager might consider a price increase as a way to improve the service's contribution margin.

The key to successful menu engineering is to conduct the analysis on a regular basis. Over time, the analysis will highlight demand trends and changes in contribution margins that result from changes in therapist compensation programs or product price changes. Clearly, this is a better mechanism for changing prices to increase spa profitability, compared with practices like simply raising all treatment prices across the board.

Retail Pricing

To this point, the content of this chapter has dealt with the strategies for setting prices for spa treatments and ways to evaluate how much each service on the treatment menu contributes to profitability. Spa leaders must also master retail pricing. Retail revenues are vital to overall spa profitability. A discussion of retail pricing requires a different vocabulary and profitability measurements from the terms we have used to discuss the pricing of services.

The spa industry has relied on experts from traditional retailing to identify the areas of retail sales a spa professional must become familiar with to operate a successful retail program. The International SPA Association Foundation has created a text and course titled *Retail Management for Spas: The Art & Science of Retail,* that covers in significant detail all of the competencies a spa professional must master to maximize retail revenues and profitability. For the purposes of this chapter, we will cover the basic principles of establishing retail prices using **maintained markup** and identify factors that affect the costs of retail sales.

In traditional retail operations, managers do not use the term *pricing;* instead, the establishment of prices is called the *initial markup.* In the evaluation of spa treatments, we focus on the contribution margin; in retail, the most critical measurement of retail success is **cost of goods sold**. In the menu engineering section, we discussed menu mix; in a retail operation, the focus is on retail merchandise classifications and revenues by category. In setting prices for spa services, direct labor, professional products, and supplies determine the treatments' contribution to profitability; by contrast, the most important factor in retail is the cost of the merchandise purchased and its relationship to the revenues generated. A retail operation determines its gross margin when the overall cost of goods sold is subtracted from revenues.

Just a decade or two ago, spa retailers simply used the relatively primitive **keystone method** to set retail prices at double the price the spa paid for it. For example, if a spa purchased a bottle of facial cleanser for $9, it would set the retail price at $18; a spa logo sweatshirt that cost $22.50 was sold for $45.

In the past, a typical spa almost never marked down the price of the merchandise sitting on its retail shelves unless it discontinued a treatment product line. Merchandise could sit on the shelves for weeks, months, or perhaps even years. **Inventory turnover** was not monitored, so the total value of retail merchandise recorded on the spa's balance sheet would simply grow and grow until the owner or resort general manager told the spa director that the spa could not buy any additional merchandise until the number of dollars tied up in retail inventory had decreased.

Today, spa professionals are expected to thoroughly understand retail management and the nuances of maximizing the retail contribution to spa profits. In every spa retail survey taken over the past ten years or so, spa skin care and body product sales have been the number one category of retail sales, generally accounting for more than half of total retail revenues. But the history of spa products reveals that they were generally available only at spas ten years ago. Today, almost every traditional retailer carries a line of spa products, and spa beauty products are readily available via the Internet. The competition is fierce, so effective pricing and inventory control are critical for success.

Let's examine some of the key attributes of retail pricing in a spa.

Initial Markup

The starting point for establishing retail prices and cost-of-goods-sold percentage is initial markup. Setting and achieving **markup** goals is a key factor in achieving the desired gross margin percentage. Markup goals are determined by the type of merchandise carried and the perceived retail worth of those products. The markup percentage is calculated as follows:

$$\text{Markup percentage} = \frac{\text{Retail price} - \text{Item cost}}{\text{Retail price}} \times 100$$

For example, an item that sells for \$10 with a cost of \$4 would have a 60 percent markup.

A quick way to establish the suitable retail price is to divide the cost of the merchandise (from the invoice) by the cost complement of the markup goal—for example, assume a spa wants the above \$4 item to have a 60 percent markup; this means that 40 percent of the retail price is the item's cost, so \$4 ÷ 40 percent = \$10. If the result is an unusual amount for a price, round off the answer to a price point suitable for the spa's pricing policy. As an example requiring rounding, assume that Any Spa has received a case of body moisturizers from the vendor at a cost of \$16.50 each, including freight, and that the spa's markup goal for that type of product is 58 percent. The cost complement of 58 percent is 42 percent. Divide the cost of \$16.50 by the cost complement of the markup goal, 42 percent. The result is \$39.29. Since \$39.29 would be a strange price for the merchandise, and Any Spa's policy is to price merchandise at the even dollar, the retail price would be set at \$40.

The two methods for achieving higher markup are raising the retail price (which may decrease an item's salability) and lowering the cost through vendor negotiation. Factors to consider in establishing markup include:

- Manufacturer's suggested retail price
- Competition and availability of merchandise in the local market
- Exclusivity, such as items with the spa's private label logo
- Operating expenses
- Expected inventory turnover
- Sales history
- Customer requests

The initial markup and cost-of-goods-sold budget are what spa professionals must determine in order to set a retail department profit goal. Spa professionals can determine their initial markup goal based on their overall profit goal for the retail department. It is critical, however, to remember that merely setting an initial markup goal by merchandise category does not ensure that the spa will achieve the desired overall cost-of-goods objective as there are several factors that can increase the cost-of-goods percentage through the normal course of retail activity. Several of the retail realities that influence the cost-of-goods-sold percentage that must be anticipated when establishing the selling prices include markdowns, maintained markup, pilferage, transfers, discounts, discount promotions, incorrect physical inventory counts, delays in recordkeeping, and uncounted inventory. Let's look at each of these.

Markdowns

Markdowns are any reduction in retail price after merchandise has been received in stock. Discounts to employees may be recorded separately from markdowns of merchandise in stock, but the effect of those discounts is the same as that of markdowns.

While markdowns should typically be avoided—and one of the goals of planning is to minimize the need for markdowns—spa professionals must mark down products in the following instances:

- Overbuying or incorrect buying
- Product does not match customer needs or buying habits
- Recession or downturn in local economy affects sales unexpectedly and overstocks result
- Increased competition that it feels it must meet
- Damaged merchandise (flood, tornado, hurricane, or just shopworn)
- Late deliveries with inadequate selling time remaining in season (e.g., sun products or summer apparel collection received too late)
- Products getting close to expiration date
- Repackaging or discontinued items

Markdowns are expressed as a percentage of net sales, just like any other expense. This provides a measurement of the profitability of sales activity and is an essential part of the planning process. Note: Many traditional apparel, gift, and accessories stores run with a 20 percent markdown rate and still remain successful as a result of careful initial markup planning. Thus, it is critical for a spa retail operation to collect data on the percentage of markdowns to guide spa leadership in adjusting the initial markup goals.

Assume a group of suntan lotions were initially priced at $20. These lotions are not selling well and a markdown is necessary to accelerate sales and clear those products from stock before the winter moisturizing products arrive. The lotions are sold for 20 percent off the retail price. In determining the effect of the markdown on profit, this is *not* referred to as a 20 percent markdown in the merchandising records. It is a 25 percent markdown, determined as follows. The original retail price was $20, so the price at 20 percent off is $16. This $4 markdown is measured against the net sale of $16 ($4 ÷ $16).

If total sales for the month in suntan lotions was $2,500, and those sales included both regular-price merchandise and the marked-down lotion, and the total dollar markdown on the merchandise marked down was $250, the total markdown percentage for the merchandise group would be 10 percent (that is, $250 ÷ $2,500).

Maintained Markup

The amount above cost at which goods are sold establishes the maintained markup, which is the actual gross margin (before freight or other adjustments are included). Let's look at an example using the following information:

Total Buy:	100 body moisturizers
Unit Cost	$16.50
Retail:	$40.00
Sell-through:	90 body moisturizers at $40.00
	10 body moisturizers at $30.00 (deleted)

Initial Markup:

Retail	−	Cost	=	Initial Markup
$40.00	−	$16.50	=	$23.50
Initial Markup	÷	Retail Price	=	Initial Markup Percentage
$23.50	÷	$40.00	=	58.8%

Maintained Markup:

	Units		Dollars		Extension	Markup
Sales at Retail	90	×	$40	=	$3,600	58.8%
Markdown Sales	10	×	$30	=	$ 300	45.0%
Total Net Sales					$3,900	
Total Cost	100	×	$16.50	=	$1,650	

Gross Margin

Net Sales	−	Cost	=	Gross Margin
$3,900	−	$1,650	=	$2,250

Maintained Markup

Gross Margin	÷	Net Sales	=	Maintained Markup
$2,250	÷	$3,900	=	57.7%

Pilferage

Loss of inventory can be due to internal or external theft. The cost of retail merchandise stolen will reduce the total value of the spa's ending physical inventory and will increase the cost-of-goods-sold percentage and thus reduce the retail department's gross margin. The retail industry benchmark on inventory loss is approximately 2 percent of retail sales revenue.

Transfers

On occasion, a spa runs out of a specific treatment product. When this happens, the therapists often take a retail package of the product to use for treatments as a professional product. Any time this is done, the transfer of merchandise from retail inventory to product expense must be recorded as a product transfer. Retail products transferred from retail to professional products that were not recorded will have two outcomes. First, the retail cost of goods sold will be increased, as the retail product is not accounted for in the ending physical retail inventory. Second, the cost of the treatment's professional products expense will be understated, as the cost of the product has not been recorded as an addition to professional products expense.

Discounts

It is customary to offer spa employees a discount, and sometimes spa members will have a standard discount on retail merchandise included as a membership benefit. If a significant amount of merchandise is sold at a discount, it will increase the cost of goods sold. Note: Typical membership discounts are 20 percent and staff discounts usually range between 20 and 30 percent.

Discount Promotions

Some discount promotions may be so successful that they increase the overall cost of goods sold. For example, a candle that is a "gift with purchase" offer has a real cost associated with it, and will be included in the cost of goods sold. Special promotions like this must each be evaluated for the profit contribution from the promotion. Did the promotion increase not only revenue, but also dollars put into the bank?

Incorrect Inventory

For example, the purchase price of a night cream is $100 and there are 10 units counted in the inventory. The value of the inventory is recorded as $1,000. However, if the cost is mistakenly recorded as $10 per unit, the value of the inventory would be $100, making the total value of the retail ending physical inventory understated and the reported cost of sales too high.

Delays in Record Keeping

Sometimes merchandise has been received by the spa, but the invoice has not been given to the accountant. When this happens, it is not recorded in the general ledger as an addition to inventory, causing the cost of goods to be understated one month and overstated in the month when it is given to the accountant.

Uncounted Inventory

In this case, merchandise has been received and the accounting staff has processed the invoice, but the merchandise is sitting in a retail storage room or in the manager's office and not counted. This will understate the inventory and increase the cost of sales.

To believe that none of the factors discussed above are going to happen at Any Spa would be naïve and unrealistic. The lesson to be learned is that there are factors that will increase the retail cost of goods sold that must be factored into the setting of retail prices. Most spas will track markdowns and discounts, then establish a markdown percentage factor to consider when establishing retail prices. As a general practice, a spa should strive to keep the markdown percentage less than 5 percent. As an example, a logo sweatshirt is purchased for $22.50 including freight. With a cost-of-goods-sold goal of 52 percent for apparel, the selling price is calculated as follows:

Merchandise cost including freight: $22.50

Cost of Goods Sold goal for apparel: 52%
$\$22.50 \div .52 = \$43.26$

Add 5 percent for anticipated markdowns:
$\$43.26 \times 1.05 = \$45.42$

Rounded Selling Price = $46.00

We strongly suggest that spa professionals take the retail management course, which covers many more specific retail management skills, including retail planning, purchasing retail merchandise, inventory management, sales and service, visual merchandising, retail marketing and opening a spa retail operation.[4]

Summary

An optimal pricing structure can play a large role in the profitability of a spa. If treatments are underpriced, profits are lost, and if treatments are overpriced, demand may decrease, causing a decrease in profits. Management needs to be aware of these effects and set prices accordingly.

The relationship between the percentage change in price and the resulting percentage change in demand is called elasticity. In order to determine the price elasticity of demand for a product, the manager utilizes this formula:

$$\frac{\text{Change in Quantity Demanded}}{\text{Base Quantity}} \div \frac{\text{Change in Price}}{\text{Base Price}}$$

If the result (ignoring the negative sign) is greater than 1, the demand for the product is said to be elastic. In other words, a change in price results in a larger percentage change (drop) in the quantity demanded, so raising prices results in reduced revenues. Inelastic demand exists when the percentage change in price is greater than the percentage change in demand, and the formula results in an answer of less than 1. Every spa professional would prefer to have services and merchandise with inelastic demand. When this is the case, raising prices results in increased revenues because the percentage decrease in demand is less than the percentage increase in prices.

There are a number of informal pricing methods. Some managers base prices on what the competition charges. Other managers assume that they intuitively know the price the public will accept. Still another method is psychological pricing, by which managers determine what they think customers expect to pay.

These methods, although frequently used, fail to examine costs. More technical methods, such as the markup and the bottom–up approaches, start with costs to determine prices that result in adequate net income.

The markup approach multiplies cost by a markup based on the desired product cost percentage. There are significant shortcomings to this method as well.

The bottom-up approach to pricing determines the average price per treatment, and considers costs, desired profits, and expected treatments sold.

The cost approaches appear rigorous and objective; however, they generally are based on estimates. Further, when the proposed price is computed on the basis of one of the cost approaches presented, careful consideration must be given to prices being charged by the competition before implementing any price changes. Differences in price must be supported by a different offering, such as a better location, more amenities, and so on.

Spa menu engineering is a sophisticated approach to analyze both the profitability and popularity of competing spa services. The process allows management to evaluate the individual treatments on its menu of services in terms of sales demand and contribution margin. Menu engineering requires the spa manager to know each menu item's direct costs, selling price, and quantity sold over a specific period of time. The result of the process is to classify each treatment as a star, plow horse, puzzle, or dog based on its contribution margin and menu mix.

Pricing retail merchandise is accomplished by marking up the products' cost. Other factors in establishing the selling price are the manufacturers suggested retail price, exclusivity, expected inventory turnover, sales history, customer requests and so on. Other considerations for establishing the retail markup goal and resulting gross margin would include markdowns, maintained markup, pilferage, transfers, discounts and the need to properly count and cost physical inventory at the end of each accounting period.

Endnotes

1. A third situation occurs when the elasticity of demand is exactly 1. In this case, demand is said to be unit elastic, meaning that any percentage change in price is accompanied by the same percentage change in quantity demanded.
2. Percentages and dollar amounts in this section are rounded off for ease of calculation.
3. Gross margin can also be presented as a percentage, calculated as the cost of goods sold divided by revenues. Also known as profit percentage.
4. The course and text are available from the American Hotel & Lodging Educational Institute at 1-800-344-4381 or online at www.ahlei.org.

Key Terms

cost of goods sold—The total of all costs involved in purchasing merchandise for resale. The most critical measurement of retail success in relationship to revenues generated.

elastic demand—A situation in which the percentage change in quantity demanded exceeds the percentage change in price.

gross margin—The difference between the sales and the production costs excluding overhead, payroll, taxation, and interest payments. Gross margin can be defined as the amount of contribution to the business enterprise, after paying for direct-fixed and direct-variable unit costs, required to cover overheads (fixed commitments) and provide a buffer for unknown items.

guest demand—The number of customers who receive goods or services over a certain period.

hurdle rate—The minimum rate of return a business will accept before investing in a project or enterprise.

inelastic demand—A situation in which a percentage change in price results in a smaller percentage change in quantity demanded.

inventory turnover—A ratio showing how quickly a spa operation's inventory is moving from storage to productive use. Calculated by dividing the cost of products used by the average product inventory.

keystone method—A way to set retail prices that simply doubles the price paid for the merchandise to be sold.

maintained markup—Actual gross margin; the amount above cost at which goods are sold.

markdown—A reduction in the selling price of an item from its initial markup.

markup—An approach to pricing goods and services that determines retail prices by adding a certain percentage to the cost of goods sold. The markup is designed to cover all non-product costs (for example, labor, utilities, supplies, interest expense, taxes and so forth) as well as desired profit.

menu engineering—A method of menu analysis and pricing that considers both the profitability and popularity of competing menu items.

menu mix—The relative popularity of treatment menu items in proportion to all items sold on the menu.

price elasticity of demand—An expression of the relationship between a change in price and the resulting change in demand.

Review Questions

1. What are the four informal pricing methods?
2. What is the major disadvantage inherent with informal pricing?
3. What is price elasticity of demand?
4. What is the philosophy behind bottom-up pricing?
5. What is the major focus of menu engineering?
6. What are the four labels for treatments using menu engineering?
7. What is the markup approach for pricing retail items?
8. How does the overstatement of retail inventory at the end of this month impact profits this month?
9. How are pretax profits calculated when the bottom-up pricing approach is used?
10. How is a markdown percentage determined?

Chapter 7 Outline

Competencies

1. Identify types of budgets and budget horizons, describe the purposes of budgeting for operations, and identify the roles and responsibilities of those involved in the budgeting process. (pp. 200–203)
2. Explain the process of preparing an operations budget. (pp. 203–217)
3. Describe the budgeting control process and explain how variances and significant variances are determined. (pp. 217–224)
4. Use information from budget reports to calculate and analyze several kinds of variances related to revenue, cost of goods sold, and labor. (pp. 224–232)
5. Describe the proper management response to the results of variance analysis, explain reforecasting, and discuss budgeting at spa chain brands. (pp. 232–234)

7
Operations Budgeting

IT IS EARLY SEPTEMBER and Erica is just returning to the spa from a meeting of all department heads with the general manager and controller to discuss next year's budget. In August, Erica was promoted to spa director when the previous director, Ann, took a job in Chicago to be closer to her family. Work on the budget really begins in August as the marketing plan is written and the resort's occupancy, average rate, and resulting rooms revenue is signed off on by the corporate office and resort ownership. In a hotel, the number of occupied rooms and the average rate are the cornerstones of the entire budget process. Erica actually enjoys being part of the budget process, because it provides her with that one time of the year when she can take time to examine the historical data in significant detail, define objectives for the following year, and help develop a plan for achieving the spa's financial objectives. She can also carefully review changes in the local spa market, study the hotel guest capture in detail, and carefully review the contribution margin of each spa service to consider adjustments in pricing and changes to the spa menu of services. Finally, it is also a time to reflect on the success of last year's programs and create new initiatives in order to build revenues or reduce expenses.

The general manager and corporate controller provided Erica with what they are projecting for the economic environment, and she must determine how these conditions are likely to affect spa operations. She is a little nervous, as this will be the first time she will be ultimately responsible for the spa's budget. She takes pride in the fact that developing the annual budget for the spa is a lot more complicated than for other hotel areas such as the housekeeping department or bell stand operations. It seems to her that all that most of the department heads in the hotel need to do is divide the number of budgeted room nights by some productivity standard, such as a housekeeper cleaning 15 rooms per day, and multiply that times an average rate of pay for the next year to budget labor costs, and use some historical expense metric such as nine cents per occupied room to calculate cleaning product expenses. No, hers is much more like the challenge facing the food and beverage manager, as they both have a number of revenue areas within their departments—she deals with a massage and body work department, a skin care area, and a fitness operation; the food and beverage director has the restaurant, the catering operation, and the room service operation to budget. It is that very challenge that gets Erica's creative juices flowing. She understands that whatever she sets for herself, it will be something she will have to live with for twelve long months. The decisions she makes during the next 30 days will affect her professional life for the entire next year. However, she finds some relief in knowing that every month she will have the opportunity to prepare revised forecasts, explain differences between actual results and the budget, and propose appropriate new actions based on current and expected future conditions.

Erica has always thought of herself as an optimist, but this has been tempered over the years by the spa directors for whom she has worked. Often they would remind her that she can't make a spa financially successful simply by optimism. Then she read the book *Good to Great* by Jim Collins, and the chapter "Confront the Brutal Facts" had a significant impact on how she approached the budget process. She learned how to start with a careful examination of the "brutal facts" as a frame of reference for all budget decisions. Then, armed with an honest and diligent effort to determine the truth of the situation, she sought to make the right budget decisions as they became more self-evident. She also recalled her father, a vice president of operations for a small hotel management company, saying that he included in every budget package an instruction letter to his general managers which featured the following warning: "I want no sand-baggers or dreamers—I will ferret you out in the budget review process!"

Erica learned early on to keep excellent historical data from which she could make defensible budget projections. She also recalled one of the keynote speakers at a recent ISPA conference who was billed as a "futurist" and talked about how one should go about predicting the future. Based on what the speaker said, Erica knew that it was not a process by which you simply pulled estimates out of the air. Just because a spa does 38 manicures on April 9 this year does not mean you should simply add, say, 5 percent for April 9 of next year. If April 9 was a Wednesday this year, it may well be the Thursday before Easter next year. A better comparison would be the Thursday before Easter of this year, on which the spa did 56 nail services because a number of women wanted to have their nails done just before the holiday. Therefore, due to the anticipated 5 percent increase in overall business, Erica has the data to make a good prediction that April 9 next year could generate 60 nail services.

Erica also knows that having the spa's supervisors participate in the budgeting process is essential to having the entire spa team accept the budget for next year. Supervisor involvement in creating the budget also helps develop future spa directors, so when she returns to her office, Erica sends each of the supervisors an e-mail announcing that the first spa budget meeting will occur in two days. She ends the day by putting her historical data in her briefcase so she can spend some time over the next two nights refreshing her memory of the previous two years. This data includes the monthly financial statements for the spa so far this year; her daily summary of spa revenue reports, on which she has written notes concerning special influences on the business each day; her number-of-treatments-by-day-of-the-week spreadsheets for the past two years; and her monthly manager's letter and variance reports.

That evening, Erica met her friend Monica and the conversation ultimately turned to budgeting. When Erica said how much more complicated the spa budget was than for hotel departments like front desk and housekeeping, Monica said, "Are you kidding me? Your budget is a piece of cake! You have many advantages in a hotel spa than I do not with my day spa." Monica rattled off all of the things Erica does not have to budget, such as energy expenses, maintenance and administrative expenses, general expenses like credit card commissions and accounting services, and marketing expenses—all of which are charged to the entire property as part of undistributed overhead expenses. A day spa income statement is charged for all of these expenses, Monica pointed out, and one must budget each line item. "Plus," Monica added, "you do not have to think about fixed charges like rent or depreciation, or interest expense and taxes. Heck, you resort spa directors all tout your 25 percent spa departmental profit and I have to struggle to make 7 to 10 percent net income at my spa."

This chapter explores the process a spa goes through to develop a realistic operations budget. The chapter will give you the tools to collect the critical information that will assist you in making good decisions and assumptions during the budget process. The budget process includes monitoring actual performance against the budget as the year progresses, identifying significant variances, analyzing variances to determine their causes, and planning appropriate actions to keep things on track.

Every spa director or spa owner plans for the future. Some plans are formal and others are informal. Budgets are formal plans reduced to dollars. Budgets provide answers to many questions, including the following:

1. What are the forecasted revenues for the following budget year (broken down by month or by accounting period)?
2. What is the budgeted labor cost for the year?
3. How many treatments are expected to be sold during any given month, and what is the expected average treatment revenue?
4. What are the projected retail revenues per treatment expected to be?
5. What will the indirect support labor and indirect operating expenses be for the year?
6. What changes have taken place within the local market? Is any new competition expected to open during the following year?
7. What changes will the spa make to its menu of treatments and pricing for the following year?
8. Will the spa introduce a new membership program, or what modifications may it make to any existing membership programs?

9. If there is a residential component to a hotel/spa project, what can the spa expect in revenues from new unit owners?
10. How close were the spa's actual results for the current year compared to budget?
11. What is the projected net income for the year for day spas? What will the income before undistributed overhead expenses be for a hotel/resort spa?

This chapter is divided into two major sections. The first section investigates types of budgets, budgeting horizons, the reasons for budgeting, and the process of preparing the operations budget, including an explanation of who is responsible for budget preparation. The second major section focuses on budgetary control and variance analysis, and on how spa operations use budget reports in the budgetary control process.

Types of Budgets

Spa operations may prepare several types of budgets. The **operations budget,** the topic of this chapter, is also referred to as the revenue and expense budget, because it includes management's plans for generating revenues and incurring expenses for a given period. The operations budget includes not only the spa's revenue departments (massage and bodyworks department, skin care department, hair department, and nail department, along with a fitness department in many cases and possibly a membership department), but also indirect operating and support departments. It is also important to remember that the *Uniform System of Financial Reporting for Spas (USFRS)* was designed to comply with the 80-year history within hotels to create undistributed overhead expenses of "administrative and general," "marketing," "energy," and "property maintenance" off the individual revenue department schedules, whereas for a day spa facility, the annual budget must include planned expenses for service centers such as accounting and human resources, plus depreciation, interest expense, and other fixed charges. Simply stated, a budget includes all revenues and all expenses that appear on the income statement and related subsidiary schedules. Annual operating budgets are normally subdivided into monthly periods. It is strongly advised that for revenues, the budget not simply be divided into months but actually be built on a day-by-day basis for the entire year, thus allowing management to monitor actual results throughout the year against the planned revenue on a month-to-date and year-to-date basis.

Two other types of budgets are the cash budget and the capital budget. The cash budget is management's plan for cash receipts and disbursements. Capital budgeting pertains to planning for the acquisition of new or replacement equipment or major renovations to the spa facility.

Budget Horizons

The annual operations budget must be subdivided into monthly plans in order for management to use it effectively as an aid in monitoring operating performance. The monthly plans allow management to measure the operation's overall performance several times throughout the year. Certain elements of the monthly plan are then reduced to weekly and daily bases. For example, many spas operations have daily revenue plans that differ by property type, day of the week, and season. The daily revenue is compared to these daily revenue goals on the daily report of operations. Any significant differences or **variances** require analysis, determination of causes, and, if necessary, corrective action. (Variance analysis will be discussed later in the chapter.) In addition, every month all revenue and expense amounts are compared to the budgeted amounts, and all significant variances are analyzed and explained.

Many hospitality organizations and some larger day spa organizations also prepare operations budgets on a long-range basis. A common long-range period is five years. A five-year plan consists of five annual plans. The annual plans for the second through fifth years are much less detailed than the current year's annual plan. When long-range budgets are used, the next year's budget serves as a starting point for preparing the operations budget. The long-range budget procedure is used to review and update the next four years and add the fifth year to the plan.

Strategic planning, also referred to as long-range planning, is recognized as essential to the controlled growth of major hospitality brands and the role spas will play in future hotel/resort developments. Successful day spas engage in strategic planning as well, as they look into the future and strategically plan for things like adding medical services or attempt to determine the point where the spa will reach capacity and need more space. Strategic planning not only considers revenues and expenses (as do annual operating plans), but also evaluates and selects from among major alternatives those that provide long-range direction to the operation. Major directional considerations may include the following:

- Evaluating whether a proposed acquisition should include the addition of a spa; will a spa have a positive effect on the hotel/resort operation or be deemed unfeasible?
- Determining whether the hospitality brand with its expansion into foreign markets should include a spa component.
- Determining whether a spa should be operated by the property or leased to a third-party operator.
- Considering whether a single-property operation should add a spa facility or possibly expand the existing spa facility.

Many hospitality brands in the United States prepare long-range operating budgets.

Reasons for Budgeting

Many small spas have not formalized their operations budgets. Often, the overall goals, sales objectives, expense projections, and desired bottom line remain "in the head" of the owner/manager. An ISPA survey conducted in preparation for the development of this text revealed that 27 percent of the responding spas said they do not prepare operating budgets. However, there are many reasons every spa should use formalized budgeting. Several of them are briefly described below:

1. Budgeting requires spa management to examine alternatives before selecting a particular course of action. For example, there are pricing alternatives for each spa service sold. Also, there are many different marketing decisions that must be made, such as where to advertise, how much to advertise, how to promote, when to promote, and so on. There are also several approaches to staffing and compensation, each of which will affect the quality and cost for services provided. In nearly every revenue and expense area, several courses of action are available to spa operations. Budgeting provides management with an effective and disciplined means of evaluating these alternatives.

2. Budgeting provides a standard of comparison. At the end of the accounting period, spa leadership is able to compare actual operating results to a formal plan. Significant variances may be analyzed to suggest the probable cause(s) that require additional investigation and possibly corrective action. While the preparation of budgets is independent of budgetary control, it is inefficient not to use budgets for control purposes.

3. Budgeting enables management to look forward, especially when strategic planning is concerned. Too often, spa leadership is either solving current problems or reviewing the past. Budgeting requires management to anticipate the future. Future considerations may be both external and internal. External considerations include the economy, inflation, and major competition. Internal considerations are primarily issues such as staff openings and, for spas in hotels, variances in hotel occupancy and the mix of business for the following year. Spa operations should aggressively attempt to shape their environment rather than merely react to it.

4. When participative budgeting is practiced, the budget process involves all levels of spa supervision. This involvement motivates the lower-level supervisors because they have real input in the process rather than being forced to adhere to budget numbers that are imposed upon them. Too often, autocratic budgeting approaches result in unsuccessful spa teamwork, as lower-level supervisors blame the budget preparers (higher-level managers) instead of accepting responsibility for poor operating results.

5. The budget process provides a channel of communication whereby the operation's objectives are communicated to the lowest supervisory levels and in some cases to the entire spa staff. Lower-level supervisors are able to react to the spa's objectives and suggest operational goals such as treatments sold, pricing schemes, labor expense, and so on. We should never forget that it is the people who provide service every day who will have the most practical insights into how to improve it. When the budget is used as a standard of comparison, the operating results are also communicated to lower-level supervisors. This allows for ongoing dialogue with the entire spa management team. The budget is a great tool to clarify areas of responsibility and identify some of the benchmarks that will be used to measure individual performance and the performance of the spa team as a whole. Furthermore, lower-level spa supervisors can be required to explain significant variances—why they exist, what the causes are, and what action is to be taken.

6. Finally, to the degree that prices are a function of costs, the budget process (which provides estimates of future expenses) enables spa leadership to review treatment and retail product prices in relation to their contribution margins. Price changes can be the result of planning, thereby allowing such changes to be properly implemented. Price changes made on the spur of the moment often result in unprofessional price execution.

For most spa directors, the most important benefit of an operations budget is that it provides a standard of comparison.

Personnel Responsible for Budget Preparation

The complete budget process includes both budget preparation and **budgetary control.** The major purpose of budgeting is to allow the spa leadership team to work together to accomplish three of its management functions: planning, execution, and control.

In most large branded hospitality organizations, the corporate office under the direction of the organization's senior corporate officers will outline the budget process and forward a budget package to the individual property general manager and property controller. The general manager will likely conduct a series of budget meetings with key department heads, including the spa director, who will be responsible for preparing their individual department budgets in coordination with the property controller. For day spas, unless it is part of a large multi-unit organization, it will be the owner or general manager who will take the lead in assembling the data and preparing the budget revenue forecast and corresponding expenses.

The final budget should ideally be the result of an overall team effort rather than a decree from above by the CEO or owner. A participative management approach to budgeting should result in maximizing the motivation of department managers to see that budget goals are met.

The Budget Preparation Process

The major elements in the budget preparation process are as follows:

- Financial objectives
- Revenue forecasts
- Expense forecasts
- Spa departmental income/net income forecasts

The operations budget process begins with the corporate officers of a major hospitality brand, the principals of an independent hotel/resort, or the owner(s) of a day spa establishing financial and other objectives. A major financial objective set by many spas and business firms in general is long-term profit maximization. Long-term profit maximization may mean that the operation does not maximize its profits for the next year. For example, in the next year, profits could be increased by postponing major maintenance projects or making the decision to eliminate locker room attendants; however, in the long run, cuts in these programs may damage the long-term financial well-being of the spa. Another objective may be to provide high-quality service even if it means incurring higher labor costs than allowable to maximize profits. Other objectives set by hospitality brands have been to have the most highly regarded spa operations in the luxury segment of the hospitality industry, or to have all of their spas rated as four-star spa operations by Mobil Travel Services, or to be recognized as the spa operation with the best reputation by major travel publications in their readers' surveys. Many more examples of objectives could be listed. The critical point is that the major objectives be established. They are then communicated to the spa leadership and are the basis for formulating the operations budget.

When a management company operates a hotel spa for independent owners, the owners' long- and short-term expectations for the spa must be fully considered. Generally, the owners reserve the right to approve the operations budget. Therefore, failure to consider their views will most likely result in their rejection of the plan, as well as damaged relationships and the need to redo the budget. Several of the major hotel chains, such as Hilton, Hyatt, and Marriott, manage many more hotels than they own. Thus, their management teams at the managed properties must work closely with the owners of each hotel.

Forecasting Revenue

Forecasting revenue is the next step in preparing the operations budget. Revenue is the product of volume and price, so forecasting revenue is about forecasting volume and price. In order to forecast revenue, spa leadership must gather information regarding the economic environment, marketing plans, capital budget, and detailed historical financial operating results of each of the revenue departments within the spa operation.

Information regarding the economic environment includes such items as:

- Expected inflation for the next year.
- Ability of the spa to pass on cost increases to guests.
- Changes in competitive conditions—for example, the emergence of new competitors or the closing of former competitors.
- Historical trends, including hotel guest capture rates, average treatment revenues by service department, local market contribution by day and month and by day of the week (which is the most critical metric for a day spa operation), and retail sales per treatment or guest.
- Increased residential housing within the local market or new retail traffic generators within the area.
- Business travel trends.
- Tourist travel trends.
- For international operations, other factors such as expected wage/price controls and the political environment may need to be considered.

In order for this information to be useful, it must be expressed in usable numbers. For example, regarding inflation and the ability of the spa to increase pricing, the estimates for the following year might suggest that inflation is expected to be 3 percent for the next year. Management might decide to adjust prices for all services and retail products by an average of 2–4 percent, with the spa services menu to be reprinted in March of the budget year.

Marketing plans include, but are not limited to, advertising and promotion plans. What advertising is planned for the upcoming year? How did the advertising, special offers, and promotions such as trunk shows affect revenues in the current year? Which promotions, such as a Valentine's Day or Mother's Day special offer, will be repeated in the following year? Are there new promotions that will be introduced? Most importantly, what revenue outcomes are expected from the various advertising campaigns? Which promotions will be used, and when will they be used during the budget year? What results can be expected? Are reduced treatment prices being offered during non-peak demand times of the day or on traditionally slow days? Are special-gift-with-purchase programs or couples' promotions being introduced? Answers to these questions and many others must be provided in order for spa leadership to be able to prepare their budgets.

Capital budgeting information includes the time of renovations or the addition of equipment. For an existing spa, day construction begins and completion date of renovations must be projected in order to effectively estimate spa sales.

The most effective way to begin the revenue forecasting process is to begin with what you know from historical financial data, which should be detailed by spa revenue department. The data should be on at least a monthly basis, and, in many cases, on a daily basis. The types of historical data a spa director must maintain and be able to easily access would include information such as the following:

- In a hotel/resort, are there meeting or incentive groups that met at the property last year, that have rebooked for the budget year? If so, the spa director can review the group history report and accurately forecast revenue for the days that the group will again be at the property.
- Again for hotels/resorts, are there new meeting groups booked for the budget year that have included in their contract a commitment to a block of spa services?
- One of the most basic data points for both day spa and resort spa operations is the number of treatments sold by day of the week by spa revenue department.
- Is the spa's business seasonal? Are there high-demand months, shoulder months, and off-season months during which business is slow, and what are the variances in treatments sold by month, week, and day of the week during peak months and off-season months?
- There is a "truism" in the day spa world that the only way a spa can increase revenues is by attracting more customers or inducing the existing number of customers to spend more (which is measured by average revenue per ticket). Thus, for day spas, knowing the average number of clients by day of the week is an essential piece of historical data. Very few hotel/resort spas limit their access to just guests of the hotel and must compete as day spas, building local day spa business, and thus it is equally important for them to track this local guest and revenue-per-ticket data.

- For hotel spas, the capture rate of hotel guests is an essential budgeting metric. Some hotels will use a capture rate based on occupied rooms; others may base it on the number of guests expressed as a percentage of guests that use the spa. For example, if a hotel has 100 occupied rooms and runs a 20-percent double occupancy percentage, the spa will use either a 25-percent capture rate of 100 occupied rooms or 25 spa clients, or a 20-percent capture rate percentage of the 120 hotel guests or 24 spa guests. Either metric is satisfactory, providing it is consistently used and that the percentage of double occupancy remains relatively consistent. In a day spa environment, an equivalent sort of metric is called client retention. Out of the client database, how many clients had return visits or how many visits should be planned for in the coming year from the current client database and how many new customers should be expected? This is critical information when considering how much marketing should be directed at retaining clients and how much should be geared toward attracting new clients.
- The spa will track the sources of treatment revenues, which can be quite different for different types of spas, as illustrated below:

  Treatment Revenues, Full Resort/Hotel Spa with Hair and Nail Departments:

  - Massage: 55 percent
  - Skin Care: 20 percent
  - Hair: 10 percent
  - Nails: 15 percent

  Treatment Revenues, Salon/Day Spa

  - Massage: 18 percent
  - Skin Care: 20 percent
  - Hair: 50 percent
  - Nails: 12 percent

  Treatment Revenues, Day Spa, No Hair/Nail Departments

  - Message: 45 percent
  - Skin Care: 55 percent

  The key is that all spas must track their treatment mix to accurately budget.
- All spas will track the retail revenues per treatment or per guest, which is essential for forecasting retail revenues.
- If the spa has a membership program, leadership will know the historical trend of how many new memberships have been sold each year for the past several years and what the retention rate for members is.
- Clearly, some days of the week are busier than others, and it is simple to examine each month of the current year and the budget year to determine if, for example, they contain the same number of Saturdays, or if a month with

five Saturdays this year slips to four Saturdays next year, which can move revenues from one month to the next.

- In a hotel, the spa director will know if the hotel marketing department is introducing a new "room and spa" package or modifying an existing package, and how many are forecasted to be sold during the following budget year.
- The spa's daily revenue summary will give the spa director the revenue trends for holiday weeks throughout the year, which can be used to forecast the following budget year.
- Often, revenues are affected simply by therapist staffing, particularly for a new spa, which may be able to recruit only a limited number of nail technicians or hair stylists because they may be reluctant to move to a new spa due to uncertainty with regard to the quality of the spa, the number of customers it will have during its early existence, and of course the possibly be losing a regular client base that they have established over time because of location. Additionally, a new spa may decide to open with minimum staffing until revenue volume builds. The point is that revenues may increase as staffing levels increase. Therapist attrition is much more difficult to anticipate, but the staff retention rate may be important factor in forecasting revenues.

There are, of course many other financial metrics that spa professionals will draw from when developing revenue forecast budgets. Consider the analogy of putting together a jigsaw puzzle, in which you typically start with the border because of the straight edges on the border pieces; similarly, for spa revenue budgeting, the spa leadership team should begin the process by gathering the solid, easily identifiable historical data from which they can start to get a handle on the bigger picture and move forward.

Historical financial trends data can serve as a validation of budget revenue forecasting. When the initial revenues are projected by each spa revenue department, they should be compared with historical trends. For example, Exhibit 1 shows the massage department's historical revenue trends over the past four years. In this example, there would have to be a strongly defensible argument explaining why the spa is not forecasting massage revenues to continue the historical pattern (10 percent growth) over the past four years. The same would be true if the historical trends showed an average annual growth in massage department revenues of 5 percent during the prior four years and the budgeted revenues were suddenly jumped to 11 or 12 percent. In this case, the massage department manager(s) putting together the spa budget would need to provide a compelling justification for the dramatic growth in their revenue expectations. Building a budget based on historical trends is known as **incremental budgeting.**

A more accurate alternative approach to validating budgeted revenue is to compare the revenue projection on the number of treatments and the average treatment revenue. This approach considers the two variables—numbers sold and prices—separately. For example, an analysis of the past financial information in Exhibit 2 shows that the number of massage and body treatments increased 3.5 percent from 20X1 to 20X2, increased only 1.2 percent between 20X2 and 20X3,

Exhibit 1 Massage Department Revenue Trends

Year	Revenue	Increase over prior year	
		Amount	%
20X1	$ 960,000	—	—
20X2	$1,055,000	$ 95,000	10%
20X3	$1,160,000	$105,000	10%
Current Year	$1,275,000	$115,000	10%
Budget	$1,400,000	$125,000	9.8%

actually went down 2 percent the following year, and is now budgeted to increase significantly with a 5.1 percent growth. Meanwhile, the average revenue per treatment increased 6 percent in the first year, 9 percent during the second year, and a significant 12 percent between the actual/estimate for the current year as compared with the previous year. So, while massage department revenues have grown at a rate of about 10 percent, when you analyze the revenues as a product of the number of treatments sold and the average dollars per treatment, there are now two variables upon which to estimate the revenues for the budget year. In this example, spa leadership has made the forecasting decision that the significant price increases during the current year have adversely affected the number of treatments sold. For the budget year, the strategy will be to be less aggressive in overall price increases and perhaps to offer discounted services during periods of low customer demand to build the number of treatments sold.

The simple analysis of revenue growth percentage from the spa's historical experience becomes more complicated when the two components of revenue are dissected in the historical trends. It is important to bear in mind that the best way to project revenues is to begin with the number of services expected to be sold multiplied by the anticipated price per treatment, but the resulting forecast must always be validated against historical trends (barring any unique current conditions not relating to historical trends) to assure their defensibility. It is also very common in a hotel/resort spa that there will be a corporate or ownership revenue and profit expectation as part of the budget instructions for all department heads. If the hotel is budgeting a growth in room revenue of 9 percent, it is unlikely that the property general manager or the management company would approve a 2 percent growth in spa revenues. In the most recent PKF Consulting survey, the total departmental revenue for the spas in the survey grew 5.0 percent from 2006 to 2007, slightly less than the 5.5 percent growth in total hotel revenue. There is not a direct correlation between a hotel's room revenue and spa revenue, because a spa, like the food and beverage department, must rely on significant local customer support to be successful. It is also very likely in a day spa that the owners would simply mandate that they want the budget for the following year to reflect a 10 percent growth in overall revenues and 10 percent growth in net income.

Clearly, forecasting and budgeting are not simple, straight-line processes that start at A and end at Z. In almost all cases, revenue projections are done on a

Exhibit 2 Massage Department Revenue Trends: Two Factors

Year	Revenue	# of treatments sold	% change	Av. Treatment $	% change
20X1	$ 960,000	11,300	—	$ 85.00	—
20X2	$1,055,000	11,700	3.5%	$ 90.00	6%
20X3	$1,160,000	11,840	1.2%	$ 98.00	9%
Current year	$1,275,000	11,600	(2.0%)	$110.00	12%
Budget	$1,400,000	12,200	5.1%	$115.00	4.5%

first-draft basis and then managers must go back repeatedly to test other assumptions and marketing initiatives in order to reach the final budget forecast. Today, most budgeting is done on budget spreadsheets with formulas to build revenues and establish expenses. The best spreadsheet programs will include each of the spa's department sub-schedules that will flow forward to a consolidated statement of income. They will include two to three years of historical data along with year-over-year percentages of change, ending with a budget column and percentage change over the current year actual/estimate numbers. With a spreadsheet program, it is simple to make a forecasting change or investigate alternative budget assumptions, such as what effect would a $2.00 increase in average dollars per treatment in any given treatment department have on the overall spa statement. The program will calculate all of the resulting changes based on the formulas set in the budget program.

There are several forecasting techniques that are typically used by personnel preparing a spa budget (see Exhibit 3).

Estimating Expenses

The next step in the budget formulation process is estimating expenses. Expenses are categorized both in relation to the spa's revenue departments (massage, skin care, hair, nails, fitness, retail, rentals, and other direct expenses) and as indirect expenses for support labor (including spa guest reception, reservations, host/hostess/attendant, housekeeping, and supervision). Additionally, indirect operating expenses and how they react to changes in volume (fixed/variable) will affect the budgeting of expenses. The forecasting of expenses is similar to the approach used in forecasting revenue. A variety of metrics are used to budget expenses.

Budgeting for Labor Costs. There are two approaches to budgeting labor expenses for a spa: using a historical average percentage of revenue to establish the labor expense, or building a fixed and variable staffing budget. Budgeting labor costs is easiest in spas that use fully commissioned therapists. The direct labor cost for each of the treatment department's sub-schedules records the therapist's commission expense against the revenue for that treatment area. Thus, if the YTD or previous year-end commissions payroll expense is 32 percent of revenues, it will remain the same even if the spa increases prices, unless of course the spa has different percentages of commissions for different services. For those spas that compensate

Exhibit 3 Revenue Forecasting Techniques

Technique	Example
1. Expected number of treatments to be sold in each treatment department multiplied by the expected average revenue per treatment amount.	The spa forecasts 6,000 skin care treatments during the budget year multiplied by an average revenue per treatment of $80, which equals $480,000.
2. Expected number of spa customers multiplied by their average number of treatments, which is then multiplied by the average revenue per treatment.	If the day spa is projecting 100,000 guests for the budget year and 1.2 treatments per guest at a revenue per treatment of $80, the spa would forecast 100,000 × 1.2 × 80 for a total treatment revenue of $9,600,000.
3. Average of several past years' revenues multiplied by 1 plus *x* percent.	If a spa's nail department achieved $38,000 in April of 20X1, $41,000 in April of 20X2 and $36,000 in April of 20X3, the average would be $38,300; adding a 10 percent growth, as projected by management, would equal a budget of $42,130.
4. When forecasting the remainder of the current year, assume that spa treatment revenues are running 105 percent of budget. The spa could then reasonably project that the same performance will continue for the remaining months of the year and forecast each of the remaining monthly revenues at budget times 1.05 percent.	The spa's hair department revenues through August of the year are at $480,000 YTD compared to a budget of $460,000, or 4.3 percent ahead of the current year's budget. If the budget for October is $55,000, it would be reasonable to project that the estimated actual revenues for October of the current year would be $55,000 times 1.043 or $57,365 for the month.
5. If retail revenues average $18 per treatment, for all treatments the total retail revenue could be budgeted by multiplying the total number of treatments times $18 plus *x* percentage of growth. A spa should maintain historical data of retail sales by revenue department, as the retail sales of skin care products per facial will be significantly higher than retail sales per manicure, but the principal is the same in all cases.	If the retail sales for skin care treatments is $30 and the spa is forecasting 800 skin care services for April in the budget year, 800 × $30 plus *x* percent would equal the projected retail revenues expected to be generated by the skin care department. The same process would be used for each of the other revenue departments.
6. Changes in a hotel's advance bookings from the previous year.	If the spa were in a city that had been awarded the Super Bowl for the budgeted year and the hotel is projecting to be completely sold out with a minimum five-night stay, it would be reasonable to increase spa revenues over those dates based on increased occupancy.

Exhibit 3 *(continued)*

7. Last year's actual revenues are adjusted subjectively.	In February of this year, there was a tremendous ice storm in a southern location that essentially closed down the city for several days, resulting in almost no local customers at the spa. Leadership may use the previous year's revenue history or the budget amount, or subjectively assign an increased number of local clients for the budget year forecast.
8. The spa is offering something new for the budget year.	The spa will be adding treatment cabanas around the pool in the budget year or has purchased two additional manicure tables. Management would assign some logical increase in revenues for the new service offering.

their therapists on a fee-for-service basis, the labor percentage may actually go down a bit if prices are raised. Likewise, the distribution of service charges will remain constant unless there is a change in the distribution among spa employees. It is somewhat more complicated for spas that pay a base wage plus commission, as there may be hours that the therapist is on the clock but not performing a service. Generally, these hours are not significant and there are no substantial variances from one year to the next unless the compensation program has been altered.

The cost of providing employee benefits has been increasing dramatically over the past few years, as evidenced by the most recent PKF Consulting study of changes between 2006 and 2007, which found that spa departmental labor costs for the hotels in the survey increased by 6.6 percent. The increase in labor costs was driven in part by the mounting burden of benefits, which is reflected in the 8.7 percent growth in payroll and related expenses. Because of the rapidly growing costs of benefits, there has been a recent trend in the spa industry to move away from a large full-time therapist base to more on-call, part-time therapists who are not eligible for benefits.

The fixed and variable staffing process is generally used for support spa labor such as spa guest receptionists, attendants, and supervisors. Whether a spa's activities are very busy or very slow, at least one guest receptionist is required. When the spa is very busy, one or more attendants must also be scheduled. For example, assume a guest receptionist can handle a maximum of 70 treatments per day. When more than 70 treatments are forecast in a day, a second attendant is required. Assume that a second attendant can handle 6 treatments per hour. Furthermore, assume that the guest receptionist and the attendant are paid $12 and $10 per hourly, respectively. The forecasted number of treatments and hourly pay for these two positions for a week in June are shown in Exhibit 4.

Budgeting Operating Expenses. There are four possible metrics that can be used to forecast operating expenses:

Exhibit 4 Support Labor Illustration

	Sunday	Monday	Tuesday	Wednesday	Thursday	Friday	Saturday
Forecasted Treatments	80	40	45	50	45	90	100
Labor Hours:							
Receptionist	8	8	8	8	8	8	8
Attendant	2	0	0	0	0	4	5
Total Daily Wages:	$116	$96	$96	$96	$96	$136	$146

- A percentage of revenue
- A set dollar amount per treatment
- A fixed dollar amount per accounting period/month
- A fixed amount on specific accounting periods during the budget year

A percentage of revenue. The classic percentage of revenue example would be the retail cost of goods sold percentage. For example, historically the spa retail department may have incurred a cost of goods sold percentage of 51.5 percent of retail sales; therefore, the spa director may decide to budget 50 percent. In this case, multiplying the projected retail revenues by 50 percent would result in the projected cost of goods sold. There are other variable expenses that would be budgeted in the same way, such as administrative and general expense for credit card commissions; if they have historically been 1.5 percent of total spa revenues, spa leadership would likely use the same percentage unless a new rate had been negotiated with the credit card companies. Laundry is another expense that could similarly be projected as 1.5 percent of total spa revenues, but the spa may elect to track its laundry expense as a percentage of treatment revenues, understanding that revenues such as retail sales or fitness use insignificant amounts of laundry. The expense might therefore be budgeted at 1.8 percent of treatment revenues. Expenses such as operating supplies and uniforms would also typically lend themselves to the use of a percentage-of-revenue metric for budgeting purposes.

A set dollar amount per treatment. Professional products and supplies used in the delivery of services lend themselves to the set-dollar-amount-per-treatment approach to budgeting. The *Uniform System of Financial Reporting for Spas* is designed in such a manner that the specific treatment product expenses for each treatment revenue department is expensed as a direct expense against the revenue for that treatment department. Thus, spa leadership would know, for example, that the cost of professional products and supplies for the skin care department runs $7.25 per skin care service as an average for the past year or more and would thus budget accordingly, making adjustments for any changes in product line and the cost for that line, or even simply adjusting for price increases on existing lines announced by the supplier. Another example that lends itself to this budgeting approach would be the hospitality expense, which includes things like complimentary fresh fruit, teas, and water in the spa's relaxation lounge. The historical data dividing the total annual expense for the previous year(s) by the total number of treatments might yield an expense of $1.10 per treatment and so, again, the spa's managers could use the historical data to project the following year's budget number for this expense. Another example would be Guest Supplies, which is the account that includes the cost of the spa locker room area's supplies and amenities that are provided on a complimentary basis to spa guests such as shampoo, body lotion, razors and shaving cream, Q-tips and cotton balls, and so on. The consumption of these items is dictated by the number of treatments during any given period, and thus using the metric of dollars-per-treatment seems most logical.

A fixed dollar amount per accounting period/month. Examples of a routine monthly expense would be for things such as a monthly window washing contract for $250 per month, or a software maintenance contract that is billed monthly, or an equipment rental agreement with a set monthly expense, adjusting of course for any inflationary price increases included in the agreement.

A fixed amount on specific accounting periods during the budget year. Several easy examples of these expenses would include things like ISPA membership renewal, which is done each year in July; or attendance at the ISPA conference at a cost of $2,000 for registration and travel, which is held each October or November; or the annual renewal of a county business license that happens each March. A spa would not want to take the $2,000 ISPA conference expense and divide it by 12 and record $166 in expense and budget that amount each month with no actual expense for 11 of the 12 months. Therefore, the entire amount should be budgeted for the month in which the expense will occur.

There are no set rules with respect to which budget metric should be used for all spas, as any individual spa can establish its own metrics depending on the level of sophistication of its record keeping, but the better the historical data, the better the metrics and thus the more accurate the budgeting for expenses will be.

Budgeting for Undistributed Overhead Expenses. With budgeting for undistributed overhead expenses, we have reached a point of clear distinction in the budgeting process for hotel/resort spas and day spas. For hotel/resort and destination spas, the expenses for administrative and general, marketing, and facility maintenance and utilities will appear for the entire property and not be included as a schedule for the spa operations, in accordance with the *Uniform System of Accounts for the Lodging Industry*. The lodging uniform system uses the principal of responsibility accounting, where departmental income of revenue departments, including spas, is computed by charging against revenues only a limited number of expenses that are traceable to the specific department. It has been recommended that day spas use the format of undistributed operating expenses to record these expenses, which are applicable to the entire spa operation. The format and line items will vary according to the needs of individual spas, which would modify the schedules to meet their own needs and requirements. Exhibits 5 through 7, from *USFRS*, are the recommended expense schedules for the Administrative and General, Marketing, and Facility Maintenance and Utilities expense categories, respectively.

Spa managers, in conjunction with ownership and perhaps an outside accounting professional, will estimate their undistributed overhead expenses

Exhibit 5 Administrative and General Schedule

	Current Period
PAYROLL AND RELATED EXPENSES	
Management Salaries	$
Administrative Salaries and Wages	______
Total Salaries and Wages	
Payroll Taxes and Employee Benefits	______
Total Payroll and Related Expenses	
ACCOUNTING EXPENSES	
Audit and Other External Expenses	
Payroll Processing Expenses	
Other Accounting Expenses	______
Total Accounting Expenses	______
OTHER EXPENSES	
Bank Charges	
Cash Over/Short	
Contract Services	
Corporate Office Charges	
Credit and Collection	
Credit Card Commissions	
Donations	
Dues and Subscriptions	
Human Resources	
Information Systems	
Legal and Professional	
Licenses and Fees	
Loss and Damage	
Meals and Entertainment	
Operating Supplies	
Postage	
Professional Development	
Provision for Doubtful Accounts	
Security	
Telecommunications	
Travel	
Other	______
Total Other Expenses	______
TOTAL ADMINISTRATIVE AND GENERAL EXPENSES	$ ______

based on experience and expected changes. Generally, the historical amounts are adjusted to reflect higher costs. For example, assume that the spa engages an outside accounting firm to file taxes, process payroll, and produce monthly financial statements on a retainer basis of $1,200 per month. During budget preparation, management determines that the monthly fee will be increased to $1,350 per month for the budget year; the historical amount would be adjusted to reflect the higher costs. In general, each line item within the overhead expense schedules would be forecasted using one of the four forecasting approaches for spa expenses described earlier in the chapter, which are known as incremental expense budgeting.

Exhibit 6 Marketing Schedule

	Current Period
PAYROLL AND RELATED EXPENSES	
Salaries and Wages	$
Payroll Taxes and Employee Benefits	______
Total Payroll and Related Expenses	______
OTHER EXPENSES	
Advertising Broadcast	
Advertising Print	
Agency Fees	
Collateral Materials	
Complimentary Guests	
Contract Services	
Direct Mail	
Dues and Subscriptions	
In-House Promotions	
Meals and Entertainment	
Postage	
Professional Development	
Special Events	
Telecommunications	
Trade Shows	
Travel	
Other	______
Total Other Expenses	______
TOTAL MARKETING EXPENSES	$ ______

A different budgeting approach, which is often used for areas such as marketing, is **zero-base budgeting.** Zero-base budgeting unlike the incremental approach, requires all expenses to be justified. In other words, the assumption is that the overhead department starts with zero dollars (zero base) and must justify all budgeted amounts. Let's look at an example that illustrates the differences between the incremental budgeting and zero-base budgeting approaches.

Assume that the marketing expenses for a spa had a total budget of $20,000 in 20X1. In 20X2, cost increases are expected to average 5 percent, and new advertising in the monthly city magazine is expected to cost $500 per month. Under the incremental approach, the marketing budget might be set at $27,000, determined as follows:

$$(\$20{,}000 \times 1.05) + (\$500 \times 12) = \$27{,}000$$

Under zero-base budgeting, the marketing department would have to justify every dollar budgeted. That is, documentation would be required showing that all budgeted amounts are cost-justified. This means all brochures, flyers, advertising, creative design and ad insertions, and so forth would have to be shown to yield greater benefits than their cost.

Exhibit 7 Facility Maintenance and Utilities Schedule

	Current Period
PAYROLL AND RELATED EXPENSES	
Salaries and Wages	$
Payroll Taxes and Employee Benefits	
Total Payroll and Related Expenses	
OTHER EXPENSES	
Facility Maintenance Expenses	
Building	
Contract Services	
Dues and Subscriptions	
Equipment Rental	
Equipment Repair	
Grounds and Landscaping	
Heating, Ventilating, and Air Conditioning	
Licenses and Fees	
Locks and Keys	
Operating Supplies	
Sauna, Steam, and Pool Supplies and Repairs	
Trash Removal	
Uniforms	
Other Repairs and Maintenance	
Total Facility Maintenance Expenses	
Utility Expenses	
Electric	
Gas	
Water	
Other Fuels	
Total Utility Expenses	
TOTAL OTHER EXPENSES	
TOTAL FACILITY MAINTENANCE AND UTILITIES EXPENSES	$

Projecting Fixed Charges

The next step in the budget formulation process for day spas is projecting fixed charges. Fixed charges include depreciation, insurance expense, property taxes, rent expense, and similar expenses. These expenses are fixed and are projected on the basis of experience and expected changes for the next year.

Exhibit 8 illustrates how the interest expense budget for the following year is determined by estimating interest expense based on current and projected borrowings. This hypothetical spa is expected to owe $2 million on a first mortgage note for the entire year and plans to borrow $200,000 at the middle of the budget year. The total projected interest expense for 20X2 is $167,000.

Even though fixed charges are by their nature considered to be fixed, management and/or spa ownership may be able to affect the fixed amounts for the year. For example, property taxes are generally based on assessed valuation and a property tax rate. A reduction in the assessed valuation will result in a reduction in the spa's property taxes. Thus, if the property is over-assessed, management should pursue a reduction that, if successful, will lower the property tax expense.

Exhibit 8 Interest Expense Budget for 20X2

Debt	Principal	Interest Rate	Time	Amount
First Mortgage	$2,000,000	8%	Year	$160,000
Second Mortgage	200,000	7%	6 mo.	7,000
			Total	$167,000

Some spas have been successful in obtaining reductions in their assessments, thus reducing this "fixed" expense for the year.

The final step of the budget formulation process is for the preparer to calculate the forecasted net income or income before undistributed expenses for the hotel/resort spa. If this bottom line is acceptable to the property general manager, top corporate officers, and/or the owners, then the budget formulation is complete. If the bottom line is not acceptable, then spa managers will be required to rework their budgets to provide a budget acceptable to senior management and/or owners. Many changes may be proposed in this rework process, such as price changes, marketing changes, and cost reductions, to mention just a few. Often, the corporate office or the owner will provide a targeted bottom line number before the budget is prepared. More often than not, budgets must be reworked several times before an acceptable budget is produced.

Budgetary Control

In order for budgets to be used effectively for control purposes, budget reports must be prepared periodically (generally on a monthly basis) for each level of financial responsibility. In a spa, this would normally require budget reports for revenues, expenses, and service centers' profits.

Budget reports may take many forms. Exhibit 9 is a sample summary income statement that is consistent with the structure recommended in *USFRS*. It is prepared monthly and covers all of the spa's operations. It is used by the spa's top management and, depending on the spa's size and corporate structure, it is also made available to corporate executives and financial analysts. In addition to variances from budget, variances from last year's actual are also shown in order to put the budget and actual results in perspective and to provide management with trend information. Depending on the needs and desire of management, this budget report can be expanded to include columns for the year-to-date (YTD) cumulative actual results, plus YTD budget and YTD prior year. This is helpful in assessing if the current month variances might be the result of a single anomaly to prior month results or if they are representative of a continuing trend that needs serious attention lest it derail the entire year.

Exhibit 10 is a monthly budget report for the skin care department in a format that is consistent with *USFRS*. It provides a more detailed breakdown of just two lines from the income statement: (1) Net Revenue Skin Care and (2) Direct Expenses Skin Care. The departmental report (sub-schedule) shows the elements

Exhibit 9 Monthly Summary Income Statement

ANY SPA

STATEMENT OF INCOME (Expanded)
FOR THE {period} ENDING MO/DY/YR

	Monthly Actual	Monthly Budget	Monthly Prior Year	Budget Variance	Prior Year Variance
Net Revenue					
Massage	$120,500	$125,000	$120,192	$ (4,500)	$ 308
Skin Care	43,583	40,000	38,462	3,583	5,121
Hair	17,166	15,000	14,423	2,166	2,743
Nail	16,650	20,000	19,231	(3,350)	(2,581)
Fitness	16,567	14,000	13,462	2,567	3,105
Food and Beverage	8,250	8,000	7,692	250	558
Health and Wellness	-	-	-	-	-
Memberships	14,500	15,000	14,423	(500)	77
Retail	42,967	45,000	43,269	(2,033)	(302)
Rental and Other	4,875	5,000	4,808	(125)	67
Other Operating Activities	-	-	-	-	-
Total Net Revenue	285,058	287,000	275,962	(1,942)	9,096
Cost of Goods and Direct Expenses					
Massage	72,833	77,000	74,757	(4,167)	(1,924)
Skin Care	28,375	26,000	25,243	2,375	3,132
Hair	10,492	9,000	8,738	1,492	1,754
Nail	9,583	11,000	10,680	(1,417)	(1,097)
Fitness	18,650	15,000	14,563	3,650	4,087
Food and Beverage	7,908	8,000	7,767	(92)	141
Health and Wellness	-	-	-	-	-
Retail	33,275	35,000	33,981	(1,725)	(706)
Other Operating Activities	-	-	-	-	-
Total Direct Expenses	181,116	181,000	175,729	116	5,387
Gross Margin	103,942	106,000	100,233	(2,058)	3,709
Indirect Expenses					
Indirect Operating Expenses	15,833	17,000	16,505	(1,167)	(672)
Indirect Support Labor	21,267	23,000	2,330	(1,733)	(1,063)
Total Indirect Expenses	37,100	40,000	38,835	(2,900)	(1,735)
Undistributed Operating Expenses					
General and Administrative	13,883	13,000	12,621	883	1,262
Marketing	8,258	5,000	4,854	3,258	3,404
Facility Maintenance and Utilities	10,667	11,000	10,680	(333)	(13)
Total Undistributed Operating Expenses	32,808	29,000	28,155	3,808	4,653
Income Before Fixed Charges	34,034	37,000	33,243	(2,966)	791
Fixed Charges					
Insurance	2,000	2,000	1,942	-	58
Management Fees	-	-	-	-	-
Rent	834	900	874	(66)	(40)
Real Estate/Personal Property Taxes	4,583	5,000	4,854	(417)	(271)
Total Fixed Charges	7,417	7,900	7,670	(483)	(253)

Exhibit 9 *(continued)*

Income Before Depreciation, Amortization, Interest Expense & Income Taxes	26,617	29,100	25,573	(2,483)	1,044
Depreciation and Amortization	6,667	7,000	6,996	(333)	(329)
Interest Expense	2,500	3,000	2,885	(500)	(385)
(Gain) and Loss on Disposal of Property	(4,167)	-	-	(4,167)	(4,167)
Total	5,000	10,000	9,881	(5,000)	(4,881)
Income Before Income Taxes	21,617	19,100	15,692	2,517	5,925
Income Taxes	6,250	5,500	4,537	750	1,713
Net Income	$ 15,367	$ 13,600	$ 11,155	$ 1,767	$ 4,212

that make up revenues, wages, benefits, and other direct departmental expenses. This report will be of importance to recipients of the broader operational budget report in Exhibit 9, since there was a material variance (positive in this case) in revenues and, as one would expect, direct departmental expenses in the skin care department. The greater detail of the departmental report in Exhibit 10 will help the reader identify what functional areas within the department were responsible for the positive variance. In instances when a variance is deemed to be out of character yet material, that information might then lead to a more detailed targeted investigation to ensure that all transactions were properly recorded, inventories and usage were properly calculated, and so on. Managers can use positive results as opportunities to recognize and thank those responsible or to challenge and motivate others. Typically, negative or **unfavorable variances** get nearly all of management's attention, but it is important for managers to understand the potential power of positive or **favorable variances** and pay attention to them as well.

In order for budget reports to be useful, they must be timely and relevant. Budget reports issued weeks after the end of the accounting period are too late to allow managers to investigate variances, determine causes, and take timely action. Relevant financial information includes only the revenues and expenses for which the individual department head is held responsible. For example, including allocated overhead expenses such as administrative and general salaries on a skin care department budget report is rather meaningless from a control viewpoint, because the skin care department manager is unable to affect these costs. Furthermore, they detract attention from the expenses that the skin care department manager can take action to control.

Relevant reporting also requires sufficient detail to allow reasonable judgments regarding **budget variances** and enhance management's ability to take corrective action. Of course, information overload (which generally results in management's failure to act properly) should be avoided. Some report versions may contain percentage variances as well as dollar variances. (Percentage budget variances are determined by dividing the dollar variance by the budgeted dollar amount.) This can be helpful information if used properly, but it can also be

Exhibit 10 Monthly Skin Care Department Budget Report

ANY SPA

Skin Care Department Contribution Schedule
FOR THE {period} ENDING MO/DY/YR

	Monthly Actual	Monthly Budget	Monthly Prior Year	Budget Variance	Prior Year Variance
Revenue					
Facial Treatments					
Standard Facials	$21,250	$19,500	$18,538	$ 1,750	$ 2,712
Specialty Facials	14,167	13,500	12,656	667	1,511
Total Facial Treatments	35,417	33,000	31,194	2,417	4,223
Waxing Services					
Body Hair Removal	833	1,000	922	(167)	(89)
Face Hair Removal	1,250	1,000	1,031	250	219
Total Waxing Services	2,083	2,000	1,953	83	130
Other					
Breakage	167	-	265	167	(98)
Service Charges	5,583	5,000	4,885	583	698
Other Revenue	833	500	621	333	212
Total Other	6,583	5,500	5,771	1,083	812
Total Revenue	44,083	40,500	38,918	3,583	5,165
Allowances	500	500	456	-	44
Net Revenue	43,583	40,000	38,462	3,583	5,121
Direct Expenses					
Payroll and Related Expenses					
Salaries and Wages	2,625	2,500	2,332	125	293
Commissions	12,333	12,000	11,865	333	468
Contract	1,125	1,000	1,098	125	27
Distributed Service Charges	4,458	4,000	3,856	458	602
Payroll Taxes and Employee Benefits	4,417	4,000	3,772	417	645
Total Payroll and Related Expenses	24,958	23,500	22,923	1,458	2,035
Other—Professional Products and Supplies	3,417	2,500	2,320	917	1,097
Total Direct Expenses	28,375	26,000	25,243	2,375	3,132
Departmental Contribution	$15,208	$14,000	$13,219	$ 1,208	$ 1,989

a distraction if used in isolation. For example, in the budget variance column in Exhibit 10, Face Hair Removal revenue was 25 percent higher than budget but only brought in $250 additional dollars, while Standard Facials revenue was only 9 percent higher than budget but brought in $1,750 more. So, do you spend your time trying to repeat what went right based on percentage variance or dollar variance? The answer depends on the circumstances; you can't assume that you should always land on the percentage side or the dollar side.

There are five steps in the budgetary control process:

1. Determination of variances

2. Determination of significant variances
3. Variance analysis
4. Determination of problems
5. Management actions to correct problems

We will take a look at each of these steps in the following sections.

Determination of Variances

Variances are determined by using the budget report to compare actual results to the expected budget results. As mentioned earlier, the budget report form used often discloses both monthly variances and year-to-date (YTD) variances. There is substantial value in reporting the YTD amounts. Variance analysis generally focuses on monthly variances, because the year-to-date variances are essentially the sum of monthly variances. However, the YTD amounts help put the current month's variances into perspective. YTD information is helpful in assessing if the current month variances might represent corrective blips to prior month results or if they are representative of a continuing trend.

Exhibit 11 shows what the budget report in Exhibit 10 might look like at the end of the 4th month of the fiscal year with YTD information added. Variances on this report are only shown in dollars. Showing the variances in percentage terms would further enhance this report. The budget variances result from subtracting the budget dollar figures from the actual dollar results. Similarly, the **prior year variances** result from subtracting the prior year's results for this accounting period from results for the current period. Using budget variances as an example, dollar variances are considered either favorable or unfavorable based on the following:

	Situation	Variance
Revenues	Actual exceeds budget	Favorable
	Budget exceeds actual	Unfavorable
Expenses	Budget exceeds actual	Favorable
	Actual exceeds budget	Unfavorable

These same principals are true when evaluating variances between the current month's actual numbers and the actual numbers for the same month last year, or when comparing YTD actual to YTD budget.

Variances should be determined for all line items on budget reports along with an indication of whether the variance is favorable or unfavorable. The kind of variance can be indicated by marking it "F" for favorable or "U" for unfavorable, or by placing parentheses around unfavorable variances and showing favorable variances without parentheses. Some enterprises simply asterisk unfavorable variances.

Although it is important to identify the root causes of unfavorable variances and take appropriate timely action to correct them, it is also important to give consideration to favorable variances as well. Finding out what went right and how to repeat it can be as productive as chasing down what went wrong and stopping it.

Exhibit 11 Monthly Skin Care Department Budget Report with YTD Results

ANY SPA

Skin Care Department Contribution Schedule
FOR THE {period} ENDING MO/DY/YR

	Monthly Actual	Monthly Budget	Monthly Prior Year	Budget Variance	Prior Year Variance	YTD Actual	YTD Budget	YTD Budget Variance
Revenue								
Facial Treatments								
Standard Facials	$ 21,250	$ 19,500	$ 18,538	$ 1,750	$ 2,712	$ 85,000	$ 78,000	$ 19,500
Specialty Facials	14,167	13,500	12,656	667	1,511	56,668	54,000	13,500
Total Facial Treatments	35,417	33,000	31,194	2,417	4,223	141,668	132,000	33,000
Waxing Services								
Body Hair Removal	833	1,000	922	(167)	(89)	3,332	4,000	1,000
Face Hair Removal	1,250	1,000	1,031	250	219	5,000	4,000	1,000
Total Waxing Services	2,083	2,000	1,953	83	130	8,332	8,000	2,000
Other								
Breakage	167	-	265	167	(98)	668	-	-
Service Charges	5,583	5,000	4,885	583	698	22,332	20,000	5,000
Other Revenue	833	500	621	333	212	3,332	2,000	500
Total Other	6,583	5,500	5,771	1,083	812	26,332	22,000	5,500
Total Revenue	44,083	40,500	38,918	3,583	5,165	176,332	162,000	40,500
Allowances	500	500	456	-	44	2,000	2,000	500
Net Revenue	43,583	40,000	38,462	3,583	5,121	174,332	160,000	40,000
Direct Expenses								
Payroll and Related Expenses								
Salaries and Wages	2,625	2,500	2,332	125	293	10,500	10,000	2,500
Commissions	12,333	12,000	11,865	333	468	49,332	48,000	12,000
Contract	1,125	1,000	1,098	125	27	4,500	4,000	1,000
Distributed Service Charges	4,458	4,000	3,856	458	602	17,832	16,000	4,000
Payroll Taxes and Employee Benefits	4,417	4,000	3,772	417	645	17,668	16,000	4,000
Total Payroll and Related Expenses	24,958	23,500	22,923	1,458	2,035	99,832	94,000	23,500
Other—Professional Products and Supplies	3,417	2,500	2,320	917	1,097	13,668	10,000	2,500
Total Direct Expenses	28,375	26,000	25,243	2,375	3,132	113,500	104,000	26,000
Departmental Contribution	$ 15,208	$ 14,000	$ 13,219	$ 1,208	$ 1,989	$ 60,832	$ 56,000	$ 14,000

Determination of Significant Variances

Virtually all budgeted revenue and expense items on a budget report will differ from the actual amounts, with the possible exception of fixed expenses. This is only to be expected, because no budgeting process, however sophisticated, is perfect. Therefore, simply because a variance exists does not mean that management should analyze the variance and follow through with corrective action. Only significant variances require this kind of management analysis and action.

Criteria used to determine which variances are significant are called **significance criteria.** They are generally expressed in terms of both dollar and percentage differences. Dollar and percentage differences should be used jointly, due to the weakness of each when used separately. Dollar differences fail to recognize the magnitude of the base. For example, a large spa may have a $1,000 difference in monthly massage department revenue from the monthly budgeted amount, yet the $1,000 difference based on a monthly budget of $100,000 results in a percentage difference of only 1 percent. Most managers would agree this is insignificant. However, if the massage revenue budget for the month was $10,000, a $1,000 difference would result in a percentage difference of 10 percent, which most managers would consider significant. This seems to suggest that variances should always be considered significant based on the percentage difference. However, the percentage difference also fails at times. For example, assume that the budget for a particular expense is $100. A dollar difference of $20 results in a 20 percent difference. The percentage difference appears very significant, but little (if any) managerial time should be spent analyzing and investigating a $20 difference.

Therefore, the dollar and percentage differences should be used jointly in determining which variances are significant enough to warrant further analysis and research as to cause. The size of the significance criteria will differ among spa properties in relation to the size of the operation and the controllability of certain revenue or expense items. In general, the larger the operation, the larger the dollar difference criteria before it is considered significant. Also, the greater the control exercised over the item, the smaller the criteria.

For example, a large spa operation may set monthly significance criteria as follows:

Revenue	$1,000 and 5 percent
Direct expense	$500 and 2 percent
Fixed expense	$50 and 1 percent

A smaller spa operation may set significance criteria as follows:

Revenue	$200 and 5 percent
Direct expense	$100 and 2 percent
Fixed expense	$50 and 1 percent

Notice that the change in criteria, based on size of operation, is generally the dollar difference. The significance criteria for both large and small operations decrease as the item becomes more controllable. Being clear about the time frame applied to the criteria is also critical. For example, while for a smaller spa $200 may be the trigger point for monthly revenue variance, it would almost certainly not be that low for an annual revenue variance.

To illustrate the determination of significant variances, the significance criteria listed above for a large spa operation will be applied to the monthly budget report for the skin care department of Any Spa shown in Exhibit 10. As we examine the monthly budget report, we see that:

1. The variance for Face Hair Removal revenue was $250, or 25 percent more than budgeted. While the percentage variance exceeds the 5 percent criteria threshold, the dollar amount falls well short of the $1,000 threshold. This item would not be considered a significant variance.
2. The variance for Standard Facials revenue was $1,750, or 8.97 percent. It exceeds the dollar criteria of $1,000 and it also exceeds the percentage criteria of 5 percent. Therefore, this item would be considered a significant variance.
3. The variance for Contract payroll under the Direct Expenses category was $125, or 12.5 percent more than budgeted. While the percentage variance exceeds the 2 percent criteria threshold, the dollar amount falls well short of the $500 threshold. This item would not be considered a significant variance.
4. The variance for Other—Professional Products and Supplies was $917, or 36.7 percent more than budgeted. It easily exceeds the dollar criteria of $500 and it also easily exceeds the percentage criteria of 2 percent. Therefore, this item would be considered a significant variance.

It is also worth noting that the simplicity with which a variance can be explained has no role in determining its significance. For instance, a significant increase in direct labor might readily be explained by a similar increase in service revenue. But because the amount of the variance is significant, it should be investigated—even if only to confirm the assumption that it relates to similar changes in revenue.

Variance Analysis

Variance analysis is the process of investigating variances in order to give management more information, particularly information about possible or probable causes. With this additional information, management is better prepared to confirm the causes of any variances and take appropriate actions.

We will look at variance analysis for three general areas—revenue, cost of goods sold, and variable labor. The basic models presented in these areas can be applied to other similar areas such as direct expenses and indirect expenses. For each area, we will start with an information template and create some simple formulae.

Revenue Variance Analysis. Revenue is the product of price and volume. Therefore, revenue variances occur because of price and/or volume differences and are referred to as *price variances* (PVs) or *volume variances* (VVs).

Let's use the numbers shown in Exhibit 12 to help us with our discussion of revenue variance analysis. Exhibit 12 tells us that there was a $1,750 favorable variance with respect to standard facial revenues for the month. It also tells us that $1,575, or 90 percent, of this favorable variance was due to achieving greater volume than was budgeted, and the other $175 (10 percent) of the variance was due

Exhibit 12 Skin Care Department Revenue, Standard Facial: Budget vs. Actual

	No. of Standard Facials	Average Price	Total Revenue	
Budget	260	$ 75.00	$19,500	
Actual	281	$ 75.62	$21,250	
Difference	21	$0.62277	$ 1,750	(F)

to a combination of achieving a higher average unit price than was budgeted and the interrelationship between the volume variance and the price variance. Here is the rationale behind these statements and calculations, followed by the formulae:

- Volume was 21 facials greater than expected/budgeted. At the expected/budgeted price per facial of $75.00, this equals $1,575 more revenue (21 × $75) due to volume alone.
- Price was $0.62 (rounded) higher per facial than was expected/budgeted. At the budgeted volume of 260 facials, this equals $162 of additional revenue (260 × $0.62277) due to price alone.
- So far we have identified the portions of the total revenue variance that are due strictly to volume variance and to price variance. There is also a third factor contributing to the revenue variance, and that is the interrelationship of the volume and price variances themselves. The favorable price variance of $0.62 times the favorable volume variance of 21 additional facials equals $13 (rounded).
- Add these three variance components together ($1,575 + $162 + $13) and we account for the total variance of $1,750.

In the example used here, all the variances were favorable. The same principles and calculations would apply if they were all unfavorable or if they were mixed.

If we want to put this into a fairly simple formula, let's start with a formula legend as follows:

- PV = Price Variance
- VV = Volume Variance
- P-VV = Price-Volume Variance
- BV = Budgeted Volume
- AV = Actual Volume
- BP = Budgeted Price

- AP = Actual Price
- (F) = Favorable, (U) = Unfavorable

The price variance formula would be:

$$\begin{aligned} PV &= (AP - BP) \times BV \\ &= (\$75.62277 - \$75.00) \times 260 \\ &= \$0.62277 \times 260 \\ &= \$162 \text{ (rounded) (F)} \end{aligned}$$

(favorable because actual price was higher than budgeted)

The volume variance formula would be:

$$\begin{aligned} VV &= (AV - BV) \times BP \\ &= (281 - 260) \times \$75.00 \\ &= 21 \times \$75.00 \\ &= \$1{,}575 \text{ (F)} \end{aligned}$$

(favorable because actual volume was higher than budgeted)

The cost-volume variance would be:

$$\begin{aligned} P\text{-}VV &= (AP - BP) \times (AV - BV) \\ &= (\$75.62277 - \$75.00) \times (281 - 260) \\ &= \$0.62277 \times 21 \\ &= \$13 \text{ (rounded) (F)} \end{aligned}$$

(favorable because both actual price and actual volume were favorable)

If any of the individual components ended up with a negative value, that component would be an unfavorable variance component.

In the case of the price-volume variance (P-VV) formula, it should be noted that due to the marvels of mathematics, its contribution to the overall variance will be unfavorable when the price and volume variances are different—that is, when one is favorable and the other is unfavorable. When the price and volume variances are the same—that is, either both are favorable or both are unfavorable—then the price-volume variance (P-VV) will be favorable.

Cost of Goods Sold Variance Analysis. The **cost of goods sold variance** occurs because of differences between actual costs and budgeted costs due to cost and volume. Beyond some different terminology, the principles applied here are similar to those in the previous section. That is, a variance arises when the amount paid for the goods sold differs from the budget, and the total amount sold differs from the budgeted sales. The variances related to the cost of goods are called the *cost variance* (CV), the *volume variance* (VV), and the *cost-volume variance* (C-VV).

For example, let's look at the cost of goods sold component of a hypothetical spa's retail department as it relates to Baby's Bum Night Cream, the most popular product sold at this spa under the retail skin care category. The information in Exhibit 13 tells us that there was a favorable variance of $62.50 with respect to the cost of goods sold for Baby's Bum Night Cream for the month. We know it is a favorable variance because the total cost was lower than budgeted. Let's analyze the information and establish the appropriate formulae:

Exhibit 13 Cost of Goods Sold Data

	No. of Jars Sold	Average Cost per Jar Sold	Total Cost Of Goods	
Budget	80	$50.00	$4,000.00	
Actual	75	$52.50	$3,937.50	
Difference	(5)	$ 2.50	$ 62.50	(F)

- Volume (number of jars) was five jars short of what was expected/budgeted. At the expected/budgeted average cost per jar of $50.00, this means that $250 (5 × $50.00) of the total variance was due to volume. It is important to shift gears and remember that because we are analyzing a cost, this is actually a favorable variance component because the lower number of covers contributes to a reduced cost.
- Average cost per jar was $2.50 higher than was expected/budgeted. At the budgeted volume of 80 jars, this equals $200 more in costs (80 × $2.50) Since this component contributes to higher cost, it is an unfavorable variance component.
- At this point we have identified the portions of the total cost of goods sold variance that are due strictly to volume variance and to price variance. As with the previous example on revenue, there is also a third factor contributing here, and it is the interrelationship of the volume and price variances themselves. The unfavorable average cost variance of $2.50 times the favorable volume variance of five units equals $12.50. This is a favorable variance component, since the five fewer jars sold pulled the overall cost of goods down below what it would have otherwise been.
- Add these three variance components together ($250.00 (F) – $200.00 (U) + $12.50 (F)) and we account for the total favorable variance of $62.50.

Remember that when we are dealing with cost variances, components that reduce costs are favorable and those that increase costs are unfavorable.

If we want to put this into a fairly simple formula, let's start with a formula legend as follows:

- CV = Cost Variance
- VV = Volume Variance
- C-VV = Cost-Volume Variance
- BV = Budgeted Volume
- AV = Actual Volume

- BC = Budgeted Cost
- AC = Actual Cost
- (F) = Favorable, (U) = Unfavorable

The cost variance formula would be:

$$
\begin{aligned}
CV &= (AC - BC) \times BV \\
&= (\$52.50 - \$50.00) \times 80 \\
&= \$2.50 \times 80 \\
&= \$200.00\ (U)
\end{aligned}
$$

(unfavorable because actual cost was higher than budgeted)

The volume variance formula would be:

$$
\begin{aligned}
VV &= (AV - BV) \times BC \\
&= (75 - 80) \times \$50.00 \\
&= -5 \times \$50.00 \\
&= -\$250.00\ (F)
\end{aligned}
$$

(favorable because actual volume was lower than budgeted and this lower volume reduced the cost)

The cost-volume variance would be:

$$
\begin{aligned}
C\text{-}VV &= (AC - BC) \times (AV - BV) \\
&= (\$52.50 - \$50.00) \times (75 - 80) \\
&= \$2.50 \times -5 \\
&= -\$12.50\ (F)
\end{aligned}
$$

(favorable because if the number of jars had not been reduced as they were (by five jars), then the impact of the negative unit cost variance would have multiplied by these additional units and increased the overall unfavorable variance)

Variable Labor Variance Analysis. Variable labor expense is labor expense that varies directly with activity. Variable labor increases as sales increase and decreases as sales decrease. In a spa operation, the use of estheticians to provide facial services and the use of massage therapists to provide massage services are good examples of variable labor, particularly when they are remunerated on a fee-per-service basis. Everything else being the same, the more facials and/or massages provided, the higher the payroll costs for the estheticians and massage therapists who provide those services.

As a quick very simplified example, let's say you pay a massage therapist $50.00 to provide a one-hour massage priced at $120.00. In this case:

1 massage = $120 revenue = $50 labor
2 massages = $240 revenue = $100 labor
3 massages = $360 revenue = $150 labor

As the number of massages and related revenue double, the labor cost doubles; as the number of massages and related revenue triple, the labor cost triples; and so on. This is a true variable cost.

To further clarify what variable labor is, let's look at the opposite of variable labor, fixed labor. In the extremely unlikely event that estheticians and massage therapists were paid a set annual salary, then this would be regarded as a fixed labor expense, since no matter how many services the estheticians or massage therapists delivered, their remuneration would stay the same. In many cases, depending on the exact compensation structure and its components, expenses will have both a variable and a fixed component.

It is important to know and understand that there are different wage structures and each of them determines the variability of the labor costs. However, the remainder of the discussion on labor in this section will only pertain to variable labor, which we will simply call labor expense. That is, any reference to "labor expense" will be a reference to only "variable labor expense."

In a variable labor expense environment, variances result from three general causes—volume, rate, and efficiency. All budget variances for labor expense may be divided among these three areas. *Volume variances* (VV) result when there is a different volume of work than forecasted. *Rate variances* (RV) result when the average wage rate is different than planned. *Efficiency variances* (EV) result when the amount of work performed by the labor force on an hourly basis differs from the forecast. Of course, as with revenue variance analysis and with cost of goods sold variance analysis, there is a variance (called the *rate-time variance*) due to the interrelationship of the major elements of the labor budget variance. The formulae for these **variable labor variances** are:

$$\text{VV} = \text{Volume Variance} = \text{BR}\,(\text{BT} - \text{ATAO})$$
$$\text{RV} = \text{Rate Variance} = \text{BT}\,(\text{BR} - \text{AR})$$
$$\text{EV} = \text{Efficiency Variance} = \text{BR}\,(\text{ATAO} - \text{AT})$$
$$\text{R-TV} = \text{Rate-Time Variance} = (\text{BT} - \text{AT})\,(\text{BR} - \text{AR})$$

Where:

BR (Budgeted Rate): The average wage rates budgeted per hour for labor services.

BT (Budgeted Time): Hours required to perform work according to the budget. For example, if the work standard for a standard facial is one per hour (60 minutes) per esthetician, then estheticians would require 260 hours to provide 260 standard facials (260 facials × 1 per hour = 260 hrs).

ATAO (Allowable Time for Actual Output): Hours allowable to perform work based on the actual output. This is determined in the same way as budgeted time, except that the work is actual versus budget. For example, if 281 standard facials were actually provided, the allowable time given a work standard of 1 standard facial per hour would be 281 hours (281 facials × 1 per hour = 281).

AR (Actual Rate): The actual average wage rate paid per hour for labor services.

AT (Actual Time): The number of hours actually worked.

Exhibit 14 Labor Expense, Budget and Actual—Skin Care Department Standard Facials

Skin Care—Standard Facials

	No. of Standard Facials	Time per Facial		Total Time		Wage per Hour	Total Wages	
Budget	260	60.00	min	260.00	hrs	$32.00	$8,320	
Actual	281	60.00	min	281.00	hrs	$31.00	$8,711	
Difference	21	-	min	21.00	hrs	$(1.00)	$ 391	(U)

In summary, based on the labor expense data in Exhibit 14 and these definitions:

BR = $32.00
BT = 260
ATAO = 281
AR = $31.00
AT = 281

If we apply these results to the formulae, the volume variance is determined as follows:

VV = BR(BT − ATAO)
= $32(260 − 281)
= $32(−21)
= −$672 U

(unfavorable because actual volume was higher than budgeted and as a result drove up the actual total cost.)

The rate variance formula would be:

RV = BT(BR − AR)
= 260($32.00 − $31.00)
= 260($1.00)
= $260 (F)

(favorable because the actual rate was lower than budgeted and as a result contributed to making the actual total cost lower than it would have been)

The efficiency variance formula would be:

EV = BR(ATAO − AT)
= $32(281 − 281)
= $32(0)
= $0

(neither favorable nor unfavorable—efficiency was exactly as budgeted)

The rate-time variance would be:

$$\begin{aligned} \text{R-TV} &= (\text{BT} - \text{AT})(\text{BR} - \text{AR}) \\ &= (260 - 281)(\$32 - \$31) \\ &= -21 \times \$1 \\ &= -\$21.00 \text{ (F)} \end{aligned}$$

(favorable because if the rate had not been reduced it would have served to combine with the higher volume to push the total dollar cost higher)

In summary:

Volume Variance	=	$672 (U)
Rate Variance	=	−$260 (F)
Efficiency Variance	=	$ 0
Rate-Time Variance	=	−$ 21 (F)
Total Variance	=	$391 (U)

Variance Analysis of Significant Variances. Once significant variances have been identified, based on the criteria that the spa has set to help it separate significant from insignificant variances, the appropriate managers need to investigate those significant variance components over which they have some control. For example, volume variances may be beyond the control of the operating manager if demand fell short of budget expectations due to ineffective marketing/advertising or generally poor economic conditions. However, if volume fell short because the operating manager did not staff the spa to accommodate demand and business was turned away because there was not enough staff scheduled, then there is accountability on the part of the operating manager. The operating manager would also be accountable when customer comment cards (or similar communication) indicated that customers would not come back due to inferior service, sub-standard cleanliness, etc. Spa managers need to look closely at and understand each significant variance and investigate all of its causes.

The key issue here is in identifying cause *in a timely manner,* with a view to taking whatever actions are reasonably achievable to quickly stop the recurrence of negative variances. Do not forget about favorable variances—they need to be looked at, too. Is a large favorable variance showing up as the result of an error in misclassifying revenue or expenses to the wrong department? Is it due to an inaccurate inventory count or valuation that will reverse itself next month and bring with it an offsetting negative variance? Can we repeat the positive causes so we might have similar favorable variances in each future month? Who warrants recognition?

Just because a particular variance does not meet the spa's "significant" threshold does not mean you should ignore it. Setting the "significant" criteria provides some valuable minimum guidelines, but there may be times when we choose to disregard the guidelines. For example, if the guideline is "more than $500 and more than 2 percent," we might be tempted to ignore a 1 percent variance in a $1,000,000 line item. However, a 1 percent variance in the $1,000,000 line item is twice the amount that a 100 percent variance would be for $5,000 line item, which would certainly warrant attention. There may also be a situation where a large negative error is offset by a large positive error, causing the net variance to fall outside the "significant" guidelines. The point is that major revenue and expense line items should periodically be reviewed to ensure their accuracy and reliability.

Determination of Problems

The analysis of a revenue variance will reveal differences due to price and/or volume, but not *why* the price and/or volume variances exist. Similarly, the analysis of variable labor expense will reveal differences due to rate, efficiency, and volume but, again, not the exact cause(s) of the variances. Additional investigation by management is required.

For example, assume that the analysis of the estheticians' labor variance relating to standard facials revealed that a significant portion of an unfavorable variance was due to a higher-than-budgeted average pay rate. Management must investigate this rate variance to determine why the average pay rate was higher than budgeted. The unfavorable labor rate variance may be due to staffing problems, excessive overtime pay, or a combination of these two factors. It may be due to the scheduling of more senior, higher-paid estheticians for more hours than originally planned, with lower paid junior estheticians being scheduled for fewer hours. There may be other reasons. Each significant variance requires further management investigation to determine the cause(s).

Management Actions to Correct Problems

The final step to complete the budgetary control process is taking action to correct a problem. For example, if a major cause of the average pay rate variance for estheticians doing standard facials is excessive overtime being paid, this may be controlled by requiring all overtime to be approved in advance, with a predetermined minimum number of hours' notice being given to the next-highest management level. Without sufficient notice, the manager will likely not have a reasonable opportunity to find less expensive suitable alternatives. If senior estheticians are being scheduled for more hours/services than budgeted, this may warrant a policy whereby junior, lower-paid estheticians are scheduled to do standard facials and the senior, more highly paid estheticians are scheduled to do specialty facials and other specialized or signature treatments.

If spa managers don't identify the real (as opposed to assumed) cause(s) of variances, they won't be able to take appropriate, effective action.

Reforecasting

No matter how you look at it, budgeting and forecasting are attempts at predicting the future. Obviously, this is very difficult, and the future often has a way of unfolding in unexpected ways. Therefore, regardless of the extensive efforts and the sophisticated systems and methods used in formulating operations budgets, many spas reforecast their expected operations as they progress through the budget year and as previous expectations are met or unmet. Some spa managers think that reforecasting is necessary only when actual results begin to vary significantly from the budget; others might decide to reforecast at predetermined periods (quarterly, semi-annually, etc.). Some spas might even start reforecasting at the beginning of the budget year and continue to reforecast every month for the entire year.

The catastrophic global economic events of 2008–2009 and the conditions in the United States immediately following 9/11 are prime examples of both the uncertainty of the future and why it is frequently necessary to reforecast. It doesn't take such drastic events for managers to reforecast, however. At any point during the year when it becomes obvious, for any reason, that the budget you set or accepted at the beginning of the period is now an unrealistic expectation for the period, it makes sense to reforecast.

There is no one right answer for every spa or every manager in terms of when you should reforecast or to what extent. However, if you reforecast on a monthly or quarterly basis, you can provide more realistic expectations in a timelier manner than if you wait until there is a huge divide between actual and budget results. For example, at say the half-year mark, you might be doing very well in achieving budgeted expectations, which would normally not give you cause to reforecast. But you now know that there are conditions in place today that suggest there is going to be a much larger growth in demand in the third and fourth quarters than you had originally expected at the beginning of the year. You don't have enough staff to accommodate that level of volume and it takes time to secure great people for your team. So if you don't start planning now for these near-future growth opportunities, you won't be able to take advantage of them when they come. And, of course, the opposite could be true, when it is essential to start establishing your battle plans now for what looks like poor conditions coming your way in the near future.

Even if you do reforecast, some would argue there is merit in keeping the original budget column intact and just adding a new reforecast column. One of the reasons for this is that it is not always just external factors that can render original budget numbers meaningless. The original budget may become meaningless because it was poorly constructed in the first place or because managers "negotiated" the lowest performance levels they could so that their monthly performance would always be positive and not draw investigative attention. Poor performance by a manager who is full of excuses that sound good may be the reason for negative variances. So, the risk is that if the original budget gets removed from the picture, it is like giving everyone a fresh start when some may not deserve it.

Budgeting at Spa Chain Brands

This chapter has been oriented toward operations budgeting at a single spa property, which represents a huge majority of spa operations. However, spa chain brands also have a growing presence within the spa industry and represent a major portion of spa industry revenue. Because of the size and complexity of these often international chains, and the fact that many are associated with international hotel and resort chains, they are likely to have their own large corporate accounting and financial analysis staff departments with well-established accounting policies and practices, including those policies and practices that provide direction to budget reporting and variance analysis. These spa chains face a number of budgeting challenges that the single operation spa does not, including such factors as multi-currency conversion. Such complexities are outside the scope and purpose of this chapter.

Summary

The budgeting process is valuable to the operation of a spa. In order to formulate a meaningful budget, the overall financial objectives of the spa must be stated, and each department must look ahead and estimate how its future performance will contribute to those objectives. In other words, if we don't know where we want to go, it is almost impossible to figure out how to get there and just as difficult to know how we are doing. With a realistic, well-constructed budget, managers can compare actual operating results to budget expectations. Significant variances between budgeted and actual results can be identified and studied. Where appropriate, timely corrective action can be taken to get back on track. The budget process forces managers to set goals and strive to see that they are met—or, if you have a truly great management team, strive to see by how much they can be surpassed!

In order to achieve budget objectives, revenues and expenses must be reviewed frequently (typically monthly), because proper variance identification and timely appropriate action will be necessary in order to stay on course. Where one exists, a spa's marketing and sales department will usually have played the lead role in setting the revenue targets and then be accountable for achieving them. So they, rather than the operating department managers, would need to act on revenue variance. Everyone's role in budget setting, variance follow-up, and reforecasting will involve observing past trends, carefully analyzing key business and economic conditions that exist today, and projecting these variables forward. Managers must go well beyond just extending a trend line on a graph; they must also take into account forces in the economy, new developments within their markets, and other significant events and trends that will affect the spa's operation. After all, graph lines extended forward have the inherent assumption behind them that whatever happened in the past is going to continue into the future. Budget projections need to be monitored and analyzed. All of the key assumptions used in preparing the original budget should be reassessed on a regular basis to reaffirm their validity. If actual results are falling behind the spa's goals, then solutions need to be found and implemented until those goals are met. If actual results are moving ahead of the spa's goals, then ways to sustain the causes of these positive results need to be found and implemented. Significant variances should be broken down into components, such as price and volume for revenues, and rate, volume, and efficiency for labor. Management can then address any deficiencies and take corrective action to keep operations heading toward budgeted goals.

In the chapter we addressed the subject of variance in terms of a series of interrelated spreadsheets that show comparisons, both in terms of dollars and percentages, among a variety of accounting periods. However, it is important to note that the written report that will accompany these spreadsheets is as important as the spreadsheets themselves. The written report will summarize key variance findings and what they mean, and will explain the analysis and the rationale behind recommended actions. It will also identify and explain all the key assumptions inherent in the budget objectives and outline all of the significant factors that have gone into related decisions. This type of explanation is essential to the owner or spa director for assessing overall operations and understanding why department managers have made changes they feel are appropriate.

Key Terms

budget variance—A variance between an actual outcome and a budgeted outcome.

budgetary control—The use of budgets as baseline yardsticks against which actual performance results are measured.

cost of goods sold variances—A group of variances used to examine differences between budgeted and actual amounts paid for goods sold and the total amount sold.

favorable variance—A variance that has an overall positive impact on net departmental contribution and/or overall net income when compared to the budgeted amount. Also called a positive variance.

incremental budgeting—Forecasting budgets based on historical financial information.

operations budget—Management's detailed plans for generating revenue and incurring expenses for each department within the operation; also referred to as the revenue and expense budget.

prior year variance—A variance between an actual outcome and the outcome for the same period in a prior year.

revenue variances—A group of variances used to examine differences between budgeted and actual prices and volumes.

significance criteria—Criteria used to determine which variances are significant; generally expressed in terms of both dollar and percentage differences.

strategic planning—Budgetary planning that not only considers revenues and expenses, but also evaluates and selects from among major alternatives those that provide long-range direction to the operation. Also called long-range planning.

unfavorable variance—A variance that has an overall negative impact on net departmental contribution and/or overall net income when compared to the budgeted amount. Also called a negative variance.

variable labor expense—Expense for labor that varies in direct proportion to changes in the level of activity and/or sales volume.

variable labor variances—A group of variances used to examine differences between budgeted and actual variable labor expense.

variance—The difference, positive or negative, between an actual outcome and a benchmark outcome. The benchmark most commonly will be the budgeted outcome but it could also be a prior-year outcome.

variance analysis—The process of identifying and investigating causes of significant differences (variances) between budgeted plans and actual results.

zero-base budgeting—An approach to preparing budgets that requires the justification of all expenses; assumes that each department starts with zero dollars and must justify all budgeted amounts.

Review Questions

1. How does a budget help an establishment to realize its operating goals?
2. How is the budget formulated?
3. Why should budgets be prepared at various levels of sales?
4. What constitutes a "significant" variance?
5. What do volume variances highlight for management?
6. Why is an increase in volume favorable in revenue analysis and unfavorable in cost analysis?

Chapter 8 Outline

Competencies

1. Define revenue management and outline its history. (pp. 241–242)
2. Identify the business attributes needed for the effective use of revenue management. (pp. 242–244)
3. Describe various ways to measure revenue management results. (pp. 244–246)
4. Identify and describe several key elements in implementing revenue management and analyzing its results. (pp. 246–252)
5. Define and use controlled availability, controlled discounting, premium pricing, and sales leverage. (pp. 252–257)

8

Revenue Management

MONICA WAS OUT OF TOWN for a few days attending an International Spa Association Knowledge Network seminar on revenue management. When she got back to work, she called Erica to get together for lunch and share what she had learned during the seminar. When they arrived for lunch and placed their order, Erica said, "How was the revenue management seminar? Did you learn anything new?"

"It was great!" Monica responded. "Sometimes you think that revenue management is only useful during periods of high demand, but I learned many new strategies to implement whether we're facing high or low demand." Monica went on to say that the presenter opened the seminar by telling a story of what happened in 2001–2002, when most hotels simply cut prices in reaction to the downturn in business following the terrorist attacks of September 11. Research conducted by Eye for Travel reported that the deep price cuts following 9/11 did long-term damage to the hospitality industry. Many hotels lowered rates to stimulate demand and increase occupancy, but the competition quickly copied that strategy, rendering it ineffective. The presenter went on to explain that simply cutting prices will affect spa profitability for years to come and will delay the opportunity to capitalize when business picks up. It also can do irreparable damage to a spa's brand reputation.

"I'm eager to hear about alternatives to discounting," Erica responded. "The process of revenue management has come a long way recently." She went on to share a story her father used to tell her about the days before yield management, which is what the process was called before it became known as revenue management. "Dad used to say how frustrating it was when the hotel would be sold out on many nights and yet 20 to 30 percent of the rooms were sold at significant discounts. Back in the '70s and early '80s, it was as if the hotel accepted reservations simply on a first-come, first-served basis. Not only that, but back then, a typical hotel would have dozens of room rates—the rack rate and a commercial rate, of course, and also a AAA rate and government rate, a special rate for AARP members, airline rates, and special contracted rates for high-volume local commercial accounts, plus all of the many group rates that the sales staff would negotiate for meetings. In those days, no one

This chapter was produced in collaboration between Paul Schmidt, Owner, Living Energy Design; Jeremy McCarthy, Director of Global Spa Development and Operation, Starwood Hotels & Resorts Worldwide; and Frank Pitsikalis, Founder and CEO, ResortSuite.

really tracked booking pace very well, as everything was done manually. I can't imagine what it was like before computers! We've come a long way since those primitive beginnings," Erica said. "So, what new things did you learn at the seminar?"

"The most important thing I learned," Monica said, "was to be smarter with discounting. More than ever, we need to work closely with our marketing staff to create innovative and profitable promotions and discounts. You really have to understand your customer segments—whether regular repeat customers, discount buyers, or new clients—and gauge the likely effect discounting will have on their current and future purchases. For example, I know that I have a core number of loyal clients who love the experience at our spa. They're not likely to go somewhere else just to save a few dollars, so why slash prices for *all* my customers? The key is to find new ways to add value rather than just assume that I need to drop all my prices. Most customers are more interested in value than price, so we need to offer value-added components to our spa experience so that our customers feel they are getting more value for their money. The add-ons will help differentiate our spa experience. Of course, the presenter covered how important it is to keep on top of the contribution margin for each of our spa services, to figure out which treatments bring us more profits. He also discussed strategies for tweaking our compensation plan to help keep us from losing profit to labor costs when we discount treatments. We didn't talk just about discounting, as there are always times that we know the spa will be fully booked. The presenter outlined pricing strategies for peak-usage times as well and showed us ways to avoid filling our appointment schedule with reduced-rate treatments, so we save room for full-price customers."

This chapter discusses how revenue management practices can assist in maximizing profitability during periods of high and low demand. After reading this chapter, you should be able to answer the following questions:

1. What is revenue management?
2. What does perishability mean with regard to spa services?
3. What are three types of variable demand?
4. How is the potential average hourly treatment rate determined when there is a range of rates for services at each station type?
5. What happens when treatment staff productivity is only 60 percent?
6. What is the ultimate goal of revenue management?
7. From a revenue management perspective, what is the preferred therapist compensation plan?
8. In general, when is the best time to discount rates?
9. Which is more important in revenue management, prices charged or gross margins?

Revenue Management Basics

Revenue management is commonly described as making available the right product to the right customer at the right price and at the right time. This description establishes the idea of variability and control with each of these factors and the inherent motivation to strive for situations that bring the most revenue to the business and the most value to the customer.

Revenue management has proven successful in the airline, lodging, car rental, cruise line, railroad, and tourism industries—basically, in situations where reservations are taken for a perishable commodity like they are in spas. There are various approaches to revenue management. Often, each approach is modeled to meet the needs of a specific industry or individual operation. Because the spa industry has a much higher degree of direct customer contact than most industries, more importance must be placed on delivering value than is necessary in many other industries.

As an activity, revenue management is about making predictions and decisions—predictions about how much and what type of business to expect, and the subsequent decisions a spa leader makes to get the most revenue from that business. Keys to successful implementation are the abilities to monitor demand, develop reliable forecasts, and establish strategies to respond to changes in anticipated demand.

This chapter presents the common elements and basic assumptions used in revenue management analysis. Although a certain amount of revenue management analysis can be performed manually, as it was done just 10 to 15 years ago, the data capture and calculations involved are highly repetitive and are therefore more efficiently handled using computers and specialty application software.

The Origins of Revenue Management

Anyone who has booked a flight in recent decades has encountered revenue management. Known as yield management in its early years, revenue management was originally conceived by American Airlines in the late 1970s after the deregulation of the airline industry. American Airlines saved an estimated $1.4 billion and earned a profit of $893 million during a four-year period by using techniques designed to yield more revenue from the same available inventory. By analyzing past trends and the competitive landscape, airlines today strive to keep their planes as fully occupied as possible by increasing or reducing fares depending on the day of the week, time of day, and seasonal fluctuations in demand. The goal is not only to maximize revenue during periods of high demand, but also to ensure that the greatest amount of revenue is realized during non-peak times, thereby greatly increasing overall profit. By enlisting strategies to drive business toward off-peak times, revenue management can actually alter the behavior of consumers. For example, the airlines learned that many vacation travelers, who are not as bound to set schedules as business travelers, will alter their travel plans to fly on days of the week that are less expensive.

When hotels first started using revenue management, they focused strictly on guestroom rates and the basic economic principles of supply and demand. If demand for room nights was projected to be low, the revenue management strategy would dictate keeping room rates low in an attempt to attract as much business as possible. As demand increased for a given time frame, the hotel would open or close room rate categories in an attempt to maximize revenue. In addition, hotels tended to align rate strategies with market segments by offering select discounts to featured groups, such as members of the American Automobile Association or AARP. Further technical developments of sophisticated forecasting techniques and booking technologies have enabled the hotel industry to respond to real-time changes in supply and demand with optimal room rates.

The application of revenue management in the spa industry borrows from all of the strategies just mentioned, and new avenues will likely be developed that champion the value that guests receive while achieving the most advantageous revenue mix for the spa.

Revenue Management Criteria

Revenue management is not an appropriate or useful tool in many industries. A clear set of attributes determines how well revenue management will work in any particular industry. Revenue management is most appropriate and helpful to industries that have:

- Perishable inventory.
- Variable demand.
- Fixed capacity.
- Sales via reservations.
- Multi-pricing capability.
- Low variable costs.
- Price-conscious markets.

Perishable Inventory. An important criterion for implementing revenue management is that the inventory of the item being sold or service being performed is perishable. This is very true of the spa industry. An unused treatment cannot be saved or inventoried for later use; every hour a treatment room, manicure table, or hair station goes unused is lost potential revenue that cannot be recovered.

Variable Demand. Revenue management is effective in industries with products or services that have variable demand (alternating periods of high and low demand). Nearly all spas face the challenges of demand that varies daily, weekly, and seasonally.

Fixed Capacity. Another important trait is limited capacity in relation to supply and demand. The number of seats on an airline flight or rooms in a hotel is fixed. If an airline flight has more demand for seats than it has seats available, it can't add seats to the plane. Neither can a hotel add rooms (in the short-term) to meet excess demand. Revenue managers must use price to help smooth out the peaks and valleys of demand. While some spas may have limited opportunities to expand treatment availability by using in-room services or poolside cabanas in a hotel or even by extending the spa's treatment hours, the number of treatment rooms is basically fixed. (On the other hand, the number of salable treatment hours can vary depending on how staff is scheduled. Therefore, one revenue management challenge of the spa industry is maintaining an adequate supply of scheduled therapists to meet demand, while not adding unnecessary labor costs by being overstaffed for the existing business.)

Sales via Reservations. Revenue management strategies are extremely effective in industries that conduct the majority of their business through advanced reservations. The spa industry is no exception. While some day spas have a relatively high percentage of walk-ins, the vast majority of spas do most of their business through reservations that are booked days, weeks, or even (in the case of resort spas) months in advance.

Multi-Pricing Capacity. A spa's ability to segment its customer base also lends itself to revenue management. Different categories of spa guests can be offered different prices at different times. For example, a resort hotel spa may offer preferential pricing to entice bookings from market segments like local residents, employees, conference guests, senior citizens, and so on.

Low Variable Costs. Industries with products or services that have low variable costs provide revenue management leverage. When the added cost of one more customer is low, discounted prices can still generate acceptable profits. For example, the total added cost to an airline when it adds one more customer to a flight is quite small; in this case, it is easy to see how the revenue from that one more ticket can be profitable even if it is heavily discounted.

In spas, while the variable costs associated with a treatment (such as supplies, laundry, and product) typically come in at less than 10 percent of the treatment's price, special attention must be given to the cost of labor associated with the treatment. Depending on how therapists are compensated, this expense tracks not just with the volume of appointments, but is also influenced by the relative distribution of the appointments on the schedule. Another way to view this is that for spas, some empty treatment hours represent a higher potential revenue loss than others. This fact adds a layer of complexity to evaluating the profitability of a discounted treatment.

Price-Conscious Markets. The last attribute to evaluate is the degree to which price will influence purchasing behavior. We have already established that the airlines' revenue management strategy recognizes that a significant segment of their customers place more value on the price they can get than the time or even the day that they fly. In the spa industry, changes in price can also have a profound impact on a guest's purchase decision. Whether delineated by time (time of day, day of week, season, etc.) or by market segment, offering multiple price points for the same service can drive more bookings from more customers.

Spa customers are used to paying a premium for a high-touch experience, and they expect personal attention and excellent service. Since sales of high-end services may be incongruous with the idea of discounting, introducing variability in prices for spa treatments must be done in the context of a well-thought-out strategy. The presentation to customers must avoid diminishing the perceived value of the services and risking a devaluation of the spa's brand.

Measuring Revenue Management Results

Spa managers measure their spa's success in various ways: number of customers served; average amount spent per guest; utilization of therapists and treatment rooms; percentage of retail revenue; revenue per square foot; revenue per treatment; and, in the case of hotel and resort spas, hotel guest capture rate or spa revenue per occupied guestroom. While such measures are valuable for many purposes, they do not explicitly reflect the spa's revenue-production performance. **Revenue per available treatment hour** (or **RevPATH**), on the other hand, combines information from the average customer expenditure and treatment room use (or occupancy) to provide a measure of the flow of revenue through the spa and an indication of how effectively a spa is using its productive capacity. Because it embraces capacity use and average expenditures, RevPATH is a much better indicator of the revenue-generating performance of a spa than are the commonly used measures just mentioned. RevPATH indicates the rate at which revenue is generated and captures the trade-off between average expenditure and facility use.

While observing the relative change in RevPATH is productive, it is also useful to establish a point of reference or standard against which we can compare RevPATH to understand the ultimate degree of success being achieved. **Potential revenue** is the calculation that establishes this standard. The potential revenue equation is as follows:

Potential Average Hourly Treatment Rate × Number of Stations × Available Hours = Potential Revenue

Approaches to determining potential revenue are described below. Since different methods affect the comparison, once a method has been determined to be appropriate for your spa, it is important to use that method consistently.

When determining the potential hourly treatment rate, the first challenge is assigning different weight values to the range of price points on the standard spa menu. If a basic massage costs $100 and a deluxe treatment costs $140, how do you calculate realistic potential revenue?

The second factor to consider is whether there are different rates attached to specific treatment station types. A pedicure station is limited to services that likely have a different price range than a massage room or a skin care room; hair stations present their own unique challenge, because a good color artist can work on several clients at the same time, and the nature of coloring services and associated upgrades dictates a much different pricing model.

The third factor is determining how to best average the range of rates for services in each station type. Since the goal is to arrive at a realistic potential revenue, a suggested method is to analyze historical data from a representative period to determine the overall percentage of each treatment type booked at your spa and then use these percentages to help determine your potential average rate. For example, if your massage rooms are typically booked with basic massages 50 percent of the time, deep-pressure massages 30 percent of the time, and specialty

Exhibit 1 Treatment and Turnaround Time's Effect on Spa Scheduling

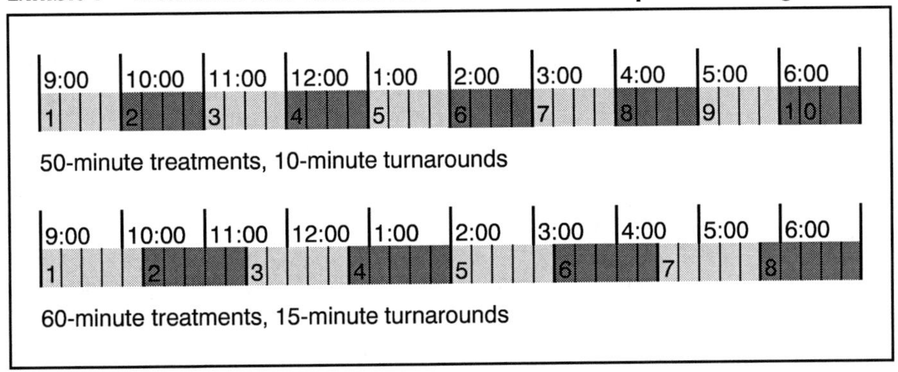

body treatments 20 percent of the time, the potential average revenue for massage rooms might be determined as follows:

Treatment Type	Price per Hour		% of Mix		Potential Average Rate per Hour
Basic Massage	$100	×	50%	=	$ 50
Deep Pressure	$120	×	30%	=	$ 36
Specialty	$140	×	20%	=	$ 28
			Total		$114

Determining the number of treatment stations and number of available time slots is a simple process of counting the possible stations per hour and hours per day. Be sure to be clear about the actual duration of your spa's treatments, including the standard allotted turnaround time, before calculating the number of possible treatments per day. Exhibit 1 shows the difference between a spa that schedules 50-minute treatments with a 10-minute turn and a spa that schedules 60-minute treatments with a 15-minute turn.

When all the data is added to the potential revenue formula, it looks like this:

Station Type	Number of Stations	×	Potential Average Treatment Rate	×	Available Hours *(per day in this case)*	=	Potential Revenue
Massage	15	×	$114	×	12	=	$20,520
Pedicure	4	×	60	×	10	=	2,400
Manicure	4	×	50	×	10	=	2,000
Hair	2	×	35	×	8	=	560
			Total Potential (Daily) Revenue				$25,480

Two simpler but less scientific approaches to determining potential revenue are as follows:

1. Use the price of the basic treatment for that station (standard massage or no-frills facial, etc.) as the average treatment rate in the calculation. This method provides a lower result that leaves out the additional revenue generated from booking specialty treatments with higher rates. While this method does provide a valid baseline for measuring performance, management must keep in

mind that it is reasonable to set a higher goal for true potential RevPATH achievement.

2. Use a round number based on a quick historical analysis—for example, consider total treatment revenue divided by total number of treatments for a representative sample of three months from the previous year to determine the average treatment rate in the calculation.

The **yield statistic** is another way to express RevPATH. It provides a simple description of revenue performance in a format that is useful when comparing performance with other spas or groups of spas, because it doesn't reveal dollar volume and is unaffected by scale. The yield statistic is calculated as follows:

$$\text{Yield} = \frac{\text{Actual revenue}}{\text{Potential revenue}}$$

Treatment room utilization (TRU) is a critical measurement of demand against a spa's maximum available inventory. Where RevPATH measures efficiency, TRU completes the picture by adding an indication of volume as a percentage of maximum potential. The formula for calculating TRU is as follows:

$$\text{TRU} = \frac{\text{Number of occupied treatment rooms}}{\text{Total available treatment rooms}}$$

Treatment staff productivity is also an important measure in revenue management, because it helps with the challenge of scheduling enough available capacity while not being overstaffed for the demand. Productivity is measured by dividing the number of treatment hours delivered by the number of hours worked. Generally, it is not done on a daily basis, but to illustrate, consider a one-day snapshot for an individual therapist. If a therapist works eight hours on a given day and provides six one-hour treatments and two 30-minute treatments, we would divide seven treatment hours produced by eight hours worked for a productivity percentage of 87.5 percent. Spa leadership in practice measures productivity for each treatment revenue center by dividing the total number of service hours generated by the total therapist hours in that treatment discipline. The treatment length of time is totaled as .25 for a quarter hour, .50 for half-hour services, and 1.0 for all 50–60 minute treatments. A 90-minute period would be recorded as 1.5.

Be careful not to assume that higher treatment staff productivity is always better. In general, treatment staff productivity below 70 percent is a sign of overstaffing and leads to labor costs that significantly cut into profits. However, treatment staff productivity higher than 85 percent generally means that there is not sufficient staff available to meet demand. Since as little as one additional treatment can justify the hourly payroll for a single staff member's entire shift, the accurate forecasting of demand is paramount to maximizing revenue potential.

Applying Revenue Management

There is no magic equation for choosing the best mix of revenue management strategies for any given spa. The key to any successful revenue management strategy is careful and ongoing analysis of the current demand patterns, market segments, spa capacity, resource mix, booking pace, and contribution margins on services. Additionally, the spa's current overall profit performance needs to be well understood to establish a baseline for measuring the success of added revenue management techniques. Remember, the ultimate goal of revenue management is to increase the spa's RevPATH and overall profitability while not adversely affecting the guest experience.

Keys to Successful Implementation

While most revenue management concepts are not that complex, successful implementation of revenue management techniques involves detailed analysis and careful decision-making. Because of this, revenue management is more easily applied in a mature, stable spa that has a historical baseline and is managed within a framework of clear and effective policies and procedures. New spas will lack historical data to accurately inform initial revenue management strategies for at least the first year. With new spas, it is important to establish a revenue management mindset and to employ those revenue management strategies that don't depend on historical data. It is also critical to collect the right data from day one.

Management Support. The time and care involved in implementing revenue management demands that you have full support from all managers at the spa as well as support from executive management or corporate directors. The accounting department also needs to be on board and included in relevant aspects of the initial analysis and set up.

Data Integrity. It should be clear by now that good revenue management decisions follow from good information. It is critical to be data-driven as much as possible when analyzing and monitoring your operation using revenue management goals. Be clear when you are making assumptions or educated guesses about demand, your market, and so on, and find objective data to back up your assumptions whenever possible.

When working with large amounts of data, it is always useful to be highly systematic in how the data is extracted, processed, and interpreted. Begin with determining who will be looking at the information and what they will need to do to make it useful. Make sure this person has the data interpretation and spreadsheet skills to perform the task. Avoid a "paralysis by analysis" situation in which nothing useful is actually produced. Then decide what data should be extracted. At a minimum, the number of treatments sold to date and the staffed capacity for each day or other specified time range will be required. If the spa management software is sophisticated enough, you will be able to pull additional detail for each treatment, including when the treatment was booked, whether it was changed or canceled, and whether it was upgraded at the time of service.

Historical data is vital for making forecasts. However, the following points are worth noting when using historical data:

1. Is future performance likely to resemble past performance? As market and business conditions change, so does the validity of using historical data in the forecasting process. An expanding or contracting economy may affect the usefulness of historical data drawn from a dissimilar economic period. That

being said, patterns such as distribution of treatments by day-of-week, time-of-day, seasonality, and booking pace are all essential elements of forecasting, even if the overall volumes of business have changed.

2. When looking at historical data, it is important to identify and in some cases isolate special events that may have influenced performance and patterns. Special events such as Christmas will repeat predictably in the future; however, other special occurrences such as weather-related peaks or troughs might not occur in any predictable fashion.
3. Business practices can significantly affect the way that historical data should be interpreted. For example, assume changes to an existing booking were in the past made by canceling the original appointment and generating a new booking at the new time; this practice inflates both the level of demand and true frequency of cancelations. If this or any operating practice has been changed, then the implications on data interpretation need to be understood.
4. The addition of new competition within the market can alter historical trend data.
5. For a hotel/resort spa, there may be a large group meeting during the period being forecasted that may create significant additional demand; however, the group may be tied up in meetings all day and provide little to no business for the spa, which would require a change in capture-rate assumptions.
6. For urban hotel and day spas, the city may be hosting a large citywide convention or major sporting event that will create additional demand.
7. The spa may be marketing a special coupon or discount promotion that will be expected to generate additional demand.
8. The spa may have just increased pricing that may reduce bookings.
9. The spa may have historically had a difficult time recruiting nail technicians, but now has more technicians, which will increase bookings. Or the reverse may be true—the spa may have lost some therapists and is now unable to fully staff all days and time periods.

Even considering these points, it is still likely that historical data will yield valuable information for the production of future forecasts, especially from the perspective of day-of-week patterns and seasonality.

Next, determine whether the historical data will be accessed by using and manipulating an existing report or by creating a new report that contains just the detail required. Then a decision must be made about where the data will be stored and used once it has been extracted. Typically, a spreadsheet program will allow for data import and for additional inputs and calculations to be built in to fully use the information. Lastly, determine how often the task of extracting and processing the data will be repeated. While hourly review is prudent in some cases, most spas will benefit from extracting data for daily or weekly measurements. Whatever frequency is appropriate, it is important to maintain the cycle in a consistent fashion.

Therapist Compensation. A spa's compensation practices will affect its revenue management practices. If the spa pays its therapists a straight commission based on the revenue each therapist generates, the labor cost will remain a constant percentage of revenue and the contribution margin will be static. One strategy to improve the contribution from treatments is to treat added charges for premium services as added fees instead of part of the treatment revenue, removing the implied obligation to pay a commission on it. In contrast, with a fixed-fee-per-service compensation program, the spa would achieve a higher contribution margin when it is able to charge a higher price for a treatment, but when the spa is discounting services, the therapist cost would remain constant and the spa would have a lower contribution. Finally, the implications of hourly pay of any kind for therapists must be thought through carefully, because this will affect your revenue management strategies as well. An hourly wage increases the costs involved with having therapists on the schedule during low-demand periods and places a priority on using techniques that reduce the number of gaps between treatments on the schedule. When an hourly wage is used, it also becomes important to have policies and procedures that allow the spa manager flexibility in bringing staff in or sending them home in response to demand, thus avoiding idle labor costs by dynamically managing available capacity and therapist productivity.

In general, revenue management is more manageable and effective with fixed-fee-for-service compensation, which allows for fluctuations in treatment pricing without having automatic changes in compensation. This approach also encourages a structured upgrade compensation program that rewards employees for selling and furthers the revenue manager's goal at the same time by driving RevPATH up.

Job-Specific Training. Careful staff training is an important part of implementing revenue management successfully. Reservationists and front desk agents need to be trained and perhaps even provided with scripts that can guide their responses during price-related conversations with guests. Therapists need to understand the revenue management system and how to maximize the value the customer is receiving without emphasizing price. For example, suppose a guest confronts a therapist, saying "All I wanted was a basic pedicure, but your front desk person said that wasn't available now. Why not? You can do that, right?" How do you want your therapists to answer that question?

Constant Review. Once revenue management strategies are put in place, it immediately becomes more challenging to analyze demand because demand is now being influenced by your pricing and availability adjustments. There will often be special circumstances that will cause a manager to override the base assumptions that your revenue management strategy was built on. This is why it is important to have regular revenue management meetings with key decision-makers to review and update performance, predictions, and special circumstances. These meetings should occur weekly and be systematic and consistent in what they review.

Analysis and Preparation

Understanding your spa's normal demand cycles is the foundation of your revenue management strategy. Most spa software will allow you to pull demand data and compare it to previous days, weeks, months, and years. Use this data to determine the following:

- Are there specific times when you consistently turn away appointments?
- Are there specific times when you consistently have less than half your treatment rooms full?
- Are these occurrences recurring, and what determines the schedule and frequency (time of day, day of week, event or holiday, weather, season, etc.)?

Studying the primary factors that drive variability in demand can reveal the most effective ways to maximize demand and revenue at your spa.

Building on the insights gained in looking at demand, you should analyze your customers and your market in detailed and specific ways. Here is an outline for a general inquiry that will help identify which revenue management strategies will work for your business:

- Where do your customers come from geographically?
- How often do they visit?
- For a hotel/resort spa, how long do they stay?
- Are your customers associated with specific industries, professions, clubs, or other definable groups?
- What are the primary reasons they visit your property?
- Do they come in groups, or alone, or both?
- Do they look more for special offers, or do they tend to come at a specific time or on a specific day?
- Do they come just for treatment(s)? Or will they also be using other spa facilities?
- How far in advance do they book appointments?
- What are the individual preferences of your top customers? Do they request a specific therapist or personal trainer? What treatments do they book? What is their retail purchase history? Do they have lunch or a snack while visiting the spa? Do they have any special needs (such as an oversized robe or slippers)?
- Are your customers receptive to giving the spa their e-mail address to receive notices of special spa offers?

As you begin to see your customers in groups with definable characteristics, put on your marketing hat and consider whether there are specific channels through which you can communicate directly with each specific group. For example, hotel guests can be targeted through direct appeals by front desk staff, customized guestroom key card sleeves, or in-room marketing. Spa members can be targeted through direct mail, e-mail, or perhaps a member newsletter. Conference participants can be reached via conference materials, web-based information, and "name badge privileges."

Analyzing Margin. Establish a clear view of the contribution margin for each service, package, and add-on on your menu by subtracting inclusive service charges, direct therapist compensation, and professional products and supplies from your advertised price. Then carefully look at how any current discounting programs affect the margin. Also be aware of the relative percentage of volume booked for each treatment type and what the constraining factors are—the amount of trained staff, the need for special rooms or equipment, lack of demand, minimum booking lead time for prep, and so forth.

A clear view of the margin range available from your services and associated pricing policies is important in revenue management because it allows the revenue manager increased leverage during both high-demand and low-demand periods. When demand is forecasted to be high, controlling availability can be used to favor high-margin services; when demand is forecasted to be low, margin awareness can inform controlled discounting strategies to avoid sacrificing too much profit while motivating price-conscious customers to book off-peak appointments.

Establishing a Forecasting System. Since revenue management decisions should stem from the most accurate prediction of future business available, forecasting demand can be seen as the starting point for the revenue management cycle. Numerous approaches can be taken for producing forecast numbers, ranging from "gut feelings" or the old-fashioned pad-and-pencil approach to highly sophisticated algorithm-based computer systems. Whatever approach is used, one common requirement is access to the right data.

The raw data required to produce forecasts for spas will likely come from the spa's scheduling software system, along with any historical data spreadsheets that the spa director has developed and the director's journal of factors that have affected revenues in the past. In some cases, useful data can be extracted from the spa's point-of-sale reports or the system that records daily accounting entries, but there is often little ability to analyze time frames shorter than one day, and virtually no way to support booking pace analysis with these sources.

Long-range forecasting is most commonly applied during the annual budgeting process and sometimes revisited once or twice during a budget cycle, especially in response to a major unanticipated event (a large shift in the economy, for example). The cornerstones of accurate long-range forecasting are established history, a clear understanding of operating ratios, and a thorough grasp of the business, economic, and social factors that shape the spa's market.

Short-range forecasting allows a spa leader to predict business levels and plan ahead for staffing, product, and other resource needs. The operational value of short-range forecasting depends on the leader's ability to take a detailed snapshot of current conditions, compare it with a similar snapshot from the past (last year or last month, for example), and focus the projection on a specific time period, like the next two weeks or the last ten days of the month. Quick access to current data about when appointments are being booked is best supported when your scheduling software allows you to extract detailed booking reports. Often, the data in these reports must be manipulated to reveal the key indicators for an accurate forecast.

Setting Up a Pace Reporting System. Beyond the static view offered by simple forecasts, another aspect of predicting upcoming business levels involves measuring *pace*, or the rate at which appointments are being booked for a specific date or time period. It is even better to look at the current pace and compare it with the pace of a similar time frame in the past. In order to analyze pace, an operator needs to compare volume booked per day for each day across the time frame of interest.

Volume can be measured in terms of revenue, number of treatment hours, or both. Sometimes the only data readily available is even less specific—like a simple number of bookings, regardless of the duration of each treatment, for example. Whatever data is available can provide a worthwhile comparison as long as it is applied consistently. Once a valid basis for comparison is established, a report can be generated that compares the volume of bookings on a given day or other time period with the same time periods from the previous year. A comparison of current bookings with the number of bookings required to meet budget is often useful as well. Such a pace report can tell the spa leader how quickly appointments are being booked for a particular day or time frame, whether this rate is higher or lower than the same time last year, and whether it is sufficient to meet or exceed budget.

When comparing current and past data, especially when comparing one year with another, you may want to compare similar days of the week rather than simply the same date. The straight comparison of calendar dates from one year to the next can result in large variations. In spas that have very different business patterns on Fridays and Saturdays, for example, it may not make sense to use data from Friday, February 23 of the previous year to forecast demand on Saturday, February 23 of the current year. Of course, the revenue manager can choose to adjust the data to compare relative days of the week or not. As usual, consistency is the key.

On a practical level, a regular weekly or monthly review of the pace report will alert spa managers—sometimes days or weeks before they would notice otherwise—to potential spikes or dips in business levels. Staffing needs can be anticipated so the spa can better avoid either being short-staffed and forced to turn business away when rooms are available, or being over-staffed and burdened with excessive payroll costs. An accurate and consistent pace report also helps spa managers understand trends and be more proactive in discussing with a general manager, senior financial officer, or owner how anticipated booking patterns might affect the spa's revenue, labor, or profit.

Revenue Management in Action

Most spas already present a varied range of prices to their customers. Almost every spa has a menu with a variety of treatments from basic to deluxe that represent a range of prices. In addition, many spas already offer preferential pricing, usually anywhere from 5 to 20 percent off for specific categories of customers such as locals, conference guests, or employees. Revenue management begins by leveraging this initial dynamic range to encourage the booking of higher-priced treatments more often and to drive discounts to typically slower times.

The two variables that a spa revenue manager can manipulate to smooth out demand and increase volume are the availability and the price of treatments. These variables can be manipulated in different ways, depending on whether demand is forecast to be high or low. When demand is predicted to be high, treatments with a lower margin can be restricted to ensure that the spa's capacity for higher-margin treatments is filled. Discounted treatments and treatments with lower margins can be favored at low-demand times to cater to more price-conscious customers.

Controlled Availability

Restricting the availability of low-margin treatments or enhancements at busy times can protect a spa from having to turn away high-margin bookings because the time slots are already booked with low-margin treatments. Controlling availability in this way can also serve to increase bookings during low-demand hours. For example, consider a busy Saturday where there are only four more appointments available after 1 P.M., but plenty of availability in the morning. A revenue management decision could be made to allow regular massages at $100 to be booked only in the morning and limit at least a portion of the highly requested afternoon appointments to just higher-priced services. The same concept can be applied with some treatment enhancements, like 15 minutes of rest or recovery in the treatment room following a service; this adds value to the guest but adds little or no cost per treatment for the spa as long as time is available that will not otherwise be booked. If a spa makes these enhancements available only when the spa is typically slow, the guests who want that added value will choose to book at the slower time, leaving time slots open for sale during the busier periods that might otherwise have been blocked.

Controlled Discounting

While blanket discounting can create problems in the high-value world of spas, controlled discounting can help drive demand to typically low-demand times and fill gaps in the schedule without compromising the customer's perceived value. The first task is controlling *when* already discounted treatments (like specials for locals or other customer groups) are booked. Instead of offering all locals 10 percent off at any time, for example, a spa can choose to limit the offer to weekdays only or for any appointment before 2 P.M. to avoid giving the discount when another customer is likely willing to pay full price for the same time slot. Beyond this, any subset or segment of a spa's customer base that can be targeted with a focused marketing message can be leveraged by price to increase use during predictable low-demand periods. A midweek summer special for school teachers, for example, can attract new business from a market that may not be able to afford standard prices, without the spa losing out on full-price business during peak times.

Another form of controlled discounting uses coupons to target a specific market while limiting the spa's exposure by controlling the number of coupons put into circulation. For example, hotel guests can be offered a one-time 15 percent discount on any two treatments booked before 2 P.M. via a coupon delivered at check-in that is valid for their stay only. Or, to encourage more business from existing customers, a "bounce back" coupon could be given to spa guests who spend over $300, inviting them to come back any morning within the next two weeks and enjoy a discount or free upgrade on an additional treatment.

Combining controlled availability with controlled discounting can help a spa reach more guests with lower price points on slower days or weekends without lowering the price of regular treatments. For example, a spa can create special treatments or packages with value pricing built in that are only available during slow times. Such packages might include "daybreak" packages offering bundled services at the start of the day, mid-week "bring a friend" specials, or an "early bird" lunch hour special at 10:30 A.M.

There are obviously many ways to employ controlled availability and discounting to influence customer behavior. The key is to carefully design the right mix of offers that works for your spa market and make sure your staff is trained in how to sell them.

Premium Pricing

At we have discussed, a basic principle of revenue management is that changing the price can influence the customer's behavior and give the revenue manager leverage in shifting some of the inherent demand from busy times to slower times. Within the airline and hotel industries, there is enough sophisticated forecasting capability and consumer acceptance to allow managers to change prices in a fully dynamic fashion in an effort to maximize both utilization and revenue per transaction. Within the spa industry, however, employing fully dynamic pricing strategies is highly challenging and risks customer alienation and dissatisfaction.

Variable pricing in spas is most successful when the prices are attached to fixed time-based variations that are offered to all customers. Spas that have very high demand periods at set times daily or weekly can, in effect, charge customers a premium for the privilege of booking at the most desirable times. When applied in the right situation, this peak-pricing model can improve RevPATH *and* overall guest satisfaction at the same time. The key is for spas to create and communicate variable pricing strategies in a logical way that will be understood and accepted by their customers.

For example, a spa at a ski resort is likely to experience excessive demand for treatments between the time the ski lifts close and the dinner hour each day. The demand might be so high that these treatment times get booked weeks in advance, leaving many customers frustrated at not being able to get in to the spa when they most want to. To capitalize on this high demand and at the same time provide a customer service, the spa might implement peak-hour pricing whereby a $20 surcharge is added to any treatment provided at 4, 5, or 6 P.M. The probable result is that some of the customers who were booking in advance will decide that they prefer the value pricing of non-peak hours and choose to schedule at a different time, leaving more of the most popular times open for other guests who are happy to pay more to get the time they want. In addition to booking more appointments and generating more revenue, another benefit for a spa pursuing this strategy is that many of the therapists who before were coming in to work during the busy 4–6 P.M. period and then going home may find themselves booked more often at

3 and 8 P.M. as well, making their shifts more productive and improving the spa's labor percentage at the same time.

Sales Leverage

Booking agents are in a position to influence reservations sales and, with specific training, can manage the flow of walk-ins and same-day bookings to serve both the customer and the spa at the same time. It is important to establish specific sales scripts tailored to customer motivation (like price-sensitivity or time-sensitivity) that lead customers to bookings that satisfy their requests and optimize spa revenue.

Last-minute specials or "one-time" offers can be employed to fill a one- or two-hour schedule gap or open availability at a high-demand time. Last-minute specials/offers can drive valuable walk-in business and help fill gaps in the schedule that would otherwise lead to idle labor costs. Appointment requests that are sitting on a waiting list can be leveraged against existing appointments if the booking agent can use a free upgrade, value coupon for a future booking, or small discount to encourage a customer with an existing booking to move to a different time. Sometimes, it can be as simple as waiving a change fee for a guest who is calling to move his or her peak-hour appointment inside the changes/cancellations window. In this case, the spa still receives the full revenue and a peak-hour time slot is opened up.

There are obviously many ways to use controlled availability, discounting, and pricing to influence customer behavior. The effectiveness of these actions depends on ensuring they are activated only at the times when they will be most effective. Careful monitoring is required to make sure these strategies are ultimately resulting in increased volume in general and not reducing revenue from business that would have occurred anyway.

Revenue Management in Action: An Example

In Exhibit 2, there are 100 available treatment hours shown for a given day. There are 46 hours booked with basic treatments (BTs) at $100 each, 13 hours booked with premium treatments (PTs) at $120 each, and 41 blank hours with no treatments scheduled. If no revenue management strategies are applied, total revenue for the day would be $6,160, RevPATH would be $61.60, and TRU would come in at 59 percent.

If we apply premium pricing of +$20 at the high-demand hours of 4, 5, and 6 P.M., six BTs and three PTs shift to off-peak times, opening up more peak hours that get filled due to the high demand. RevPATH goes up by $15.60, and nearly $1,600 in additional business is booked (see Exhibit 3).

Controlled discounting offering 15 percent off two-hour packages before 2 P.M. adds eight more booked hours to the schedule at the discounted rate. RevPATH improves again by $6.80, with $680 in additional gross revenue (see Exhibit 4).

Finally, last-minute offers at 30 percent off are made, filling six more hours that would have otherwise generated labor costs for idle therapists bringing in no revenue. This brings in $5 in added RevPATH and $504 more in gross revenue (see Exhibit 5).

Exhibit 2 No Revenue Management Applied (Natural Demand)

Room	10 AM	11 AM	12 PM	1 PM	2 PM	3 PM	4 PM	5 PM	6 PM	7 PM
1	BT	BT	BT	BT	BT	BT	BT	BT	BT	BT
2		BT	BT	BT	BT	BT	BT	BT	BT	BT
3			BT	BT	BT	BT	BT	BT	BT	BT
4				BT	BT	BT	BT	BT	BT	
5						BT	BT	BT	BT	
6							BT	BT	BT	
7							BT	BT	BT	
8							BT	BT	BT	
9							PT	PT	PT	
10	PT	PT	PT	PT	PT	PT	PT	PT	PT	PT

Total Rev	$ 6,160.00
RevPATH	$ 61.60
TRU	59%

Exhibit 3 Peak-Hour Premium Added

Room	10 AM	11 AM	12 PM	1 PM	2 PM	3 PM	4 PM	5 PM	6 PM	7 PM
1	BT	BT	BT	BT	BT	BT	BT+	BT+	BT+	BT
2		BT	BT	BT	BT	BT	BT+	BT+	BT+	BT
3			BT	BT	BT	BT	BT+	BT+	BT+	BT
4				BT	BT	BT	BT+	BT+	BT+	BT
5					BT	BT	BT+	BT+	BT+	BT
6					BT	BT	BT+	BT+	BT+	
7						BT	BT+	BT+	BT+	
8							BT+	BT+	BT+	
9					PT	PT	PT+	PT+	PT+	PT
10	PT	PT	PT	PT	PT	PT	PT+	PT+	PT+	PT

Total Rev	$ 7,720.00
RevPATH	$ 77.20
TRU	68%

Looking at Exhibits 2–5, we see that through applying three basic revenue management strategies, the spa's treatment room utilization rate (TRU) increases from 59 percent to 82 percent and gross revenue increases by 45 percent (see Exhibit 6)!

Exhibit 4 Controlled Discounting Added

Room	10 AM	11 AM	12 PM	1 PM	2 PM	3 PM	4 PM	5 PM	6 PM	7 PM
1	BT	BT	BT	BT	BT	BT	BT+	BT+	BT+	BT
2		BT	BT	BT	BT	BT	BT+	BT+	BT+	BT
3			BT	BT	BT	BT	BT+	BT+	BT+	BT
4				BT	BT	BT	BT+	BT+	BT+	BT
5		VT-	VT-		BT	BT	BT+	BT+	BT+	BT
6		VT-	VT-		BT	BT	BT+	BT+	BT+	
7			VT-	VT-		BT	BT+	BT+	BT+	
8			VT-	VT-			BT+	BT+	BT+	
9					PT	PT	PT+	PT+	PT+	PT
10	PT	PT	PT	PT	PT	PT	PT+	PT+	PT+	PT

Total Rev	$ 8,400.00
RevPATH	$ 84.00
TRU	76%

Exhibit 5 Last-Minute Specials Added

Room	10 AM	11 AM	12 PM	1 PM	2 PM	3 PM	4 PM	5 PM	6 PM	7 PM
1	BT	BT	BT	BT	BT	BT	BT+	BT+	BT+	BT
2		BT	BT	BT	BT	BT	BT+	BT+	BT+	BT
3			BT	BT	BT	BT	BT+	BT+	BT+	BT
4				BT	BT	BT	BT+	BT+	BT+	BT
5		VT-	VT-	GT-	BT	BT	BT+	BT+	BT+	BT
6		VT-	VT-	GT-	BT	BT	BT+	BT+	BT+	
7			VT-	VT-	GT-	BT	BT+	BT+	BT+	
8			VT-	VT-	GT-	GT-	BT+	BT+	BT+	
9				GT-	PT	PT	PT+	PT+	PT+	PT
10	PT	PT	PT	PT	PT	PT	PT+	PT+	PT+	PT

Total Rev	$ 8,904.00
RevPATH	$ 89.00
TRU	82%

Summary

Revenue management in spas can be very effective in improving a spa's financial picture. The practice of revenue management needs to be tempered by the awareness that, especially in spas, it puts factors into play that may influence the little,

Exhibit 6 Results of Applying Three Basic Revenue Management Strategies

	Natural Demand	+ Peak-Hour Premium	+ Controlled Discounting	+ Last-Minute Specials
Total Rev	$ 6,160.00	$ 7,720.00	$ 8,400.00	$ 8,904.00
RevPATH	$ 61.60	$ 77.20	$ 84.00	$ 89.04
TRU	59%	68%	76%	82%

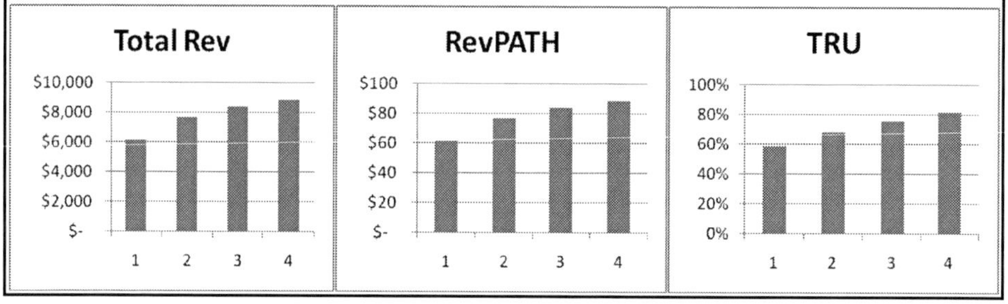

difficult-to-quantify things that make the guest experience special and are integral to a spa business's success. Higher revenue and bigger contributions are great, but a good spa leader can never lose track of guest satisfaction and employee morale in such a high-touch industry.

Since sophisticated revenue management is relatively new in spas, the spa customer needs to be approached with care when introducing prices that can change in a way that we have all come to accept and expect when booking plane tickets or hotel rooms. Spa managers should be aware that variable pricing is not the only revenue management strategy. They should consider other methods for driving spa revenue as well. It is likely that, over time, spa-specific strategies will be developed that succeed in accomplishing the goals of improving revenue and profit while also improving the overall experience of customers before, during, and after their visits.

As the industry develops commonly accepted revenue management strategies for maximizing both profit and customer satisfaction, spa-goers will begin to respond to the techniques that serve their needs consistently and comfortably. This will likely drive the development of industry-accepted standards involving differential pricing and demand-driven booking systems.

One thing is certain: revenue management is a powerful tool that will inevitably find a place in the spa industry and play a major role in supporting the spas that grow and flourish over time.

Key Terms

potential revenue—A calculation that establishes a standard against which actual spa performance can be measured; equals potential average hourly treatment rate × the number of treatment stations × available hours.

revenue management—Commonly described as making available the right product to the right customer at the right price and at the right time.

revenue per available treatment hour (RevPATH)—Combines information from the average spa customer expenditure and treatment room use (or occupancy) to provide a measure of the flow of revenue through the spa and an indication of how effectively a spa is using its productive capacity.

treatment room utilization (TRU)—A critical measurement of demand against a spa's maximum available inventory; treatment room utilization is calculated by dividing the number of occupied treatment rooms by the total available treatment rooms.

yield statistic—A simple description of spa revenue performance in a format that is useful for comparing performance to other spas or groups of spas. Equals actual revenue divided by potential revenue.

Review Questions

1. What is the fixed capacity element of a spa?
2. What is the best measure of a spa's revenue production performance?
3. What is the purpose of calculating potential revenue?
4. How is treatment room utilization calculated?
5. How is treatment staff productivity determined?
6. What makes implementing revenue management so difficult in a new spa?
7. How does therapist compensation impact revenue management practices?
8. When should a spa use premium pricing?

Chapter 9 Outline

Competencies

1. Define cash management and explain the importance of bank selection. (pp. 263–266)
2. Describe the cash conversion cycle and explain how to calculate an effective interest rate. (p. 266)
3. Distinguish between income and cash flows. (pp. 267–268)
4. Outline general procedures in internal cash control, and discuss control issues in terms of purchase order systems and petty cash funds. (pp. 268–276)
5. Explain how to prepare a bank reconciliation. (pp. 277–280)
6. Discuss how the following factors affect cash management: accounts receivable, inventory, current liabilities, gift card sales, cash budgeting, and float. (pp. 280–294)
7. Explain the format and function of the statement of cash flows and describe the issues involved in preparing one. (pp. 294–307)

9

Cash Management

MONICA WAITED NERVOUSLY for the owner's cell phone voice mail recording to finish so she could leave a message. "Mrs. Rittermum? This is Monica. I need you to call me at the spa as soon as you get this message. We have an emergency and I need to know what you want me to do about it."

Monica hung up. Mrs. Rittermum had left early that day to fly out and visit her family for the long holiday weekend. She was probably still on the flight, or she wouldn't have her cell phone off. Monica waited nervously at her desk at The Day Spa for the owner's return call, and once again reviewed the cash disbursement journal to figure out just what went wrong.

An hour ago, she'd checked the bank balance for the operating account and made an alarming discovery. There wasn't enough money in the account to cover the payroll checks that would be distributed the next day. She immediately began to panic—nothing like this had ever happened before.

Employees were paid every other Friday. She knew that all of her employees would deposit their checks on Friday—especially since the bank would be closed on Monday because of the holiday. She could only imagine what would happen if some of the checks came back to the employees marked "insufficient funds." Monica could think of nothing worse than having employees tell other staff members that their paycheck had bounced. That would greatly compromise the trust that employees had in the spa and in Monica.

Monica, completely flustered, looked through the paperwork again. She'd been keeping a close eye on the income statements and couldn't understand why this had happened. The spa had always done well financially and the income statement was always positive. Monica had never paid much attention to cash management because there had never been a problem before. It had been a soft month, as school was out and a lot of the spa's regular customers were on vacation. In her review of disbursements, she saw that some large checks had been written to pay quarterly taxes and the spa's insurance bill. The bottom line was that the bank balance was about $10,000 short of covering tomorrow's payroll.

It was 9 P.M. before the spa's owner called back, wondering whether a water line had broken or a customer had been injured in the spa. Monica quickly reassured her and then told her about the payroll problem.

"How in the world could you let that happen?" demanded Mrs. Rittermum. "Didn't you check the bank balance before you submitted the payroll?" Monica explained that she hadn't because they'd managed to keep their expenses down and were showing a healthy profit for the month.

"Now what do you expect me to do?" Mrs. Rittermum asked. "I don't have $10,000 just sitting in my personal checking account." "I don't know," Monica replied miserably. With exasperation, the owner said, "I'll call the bank in the morning and make a draw on our line of credit. Nice way to start my weekend vacation."

Monica left the spa that night knowing that the owner was angry with her—and had every right to be, since no one likes unpleasant surprises, especially when it comes to money. After a mostly sleepless night, she returned to the spa and found a message that all had been resolved and she was to distribute the paychecks at noon.

When the owner returned the following week, she again vented her disappointment in Monica and warned her that something like this had better never happen again. About a month later, Mrs. Rittermum took Monica to meet with an accountant she had retained to help with the more sophisticated spa accounting matters. One of the things he discussed with her was how income and cash are often not the same thing. Monica nodded—that was a lesson she would never forget. Since that awful Thursday, she'd become much more conscious of the operating budget, the statement of income, and cash management. The accountant explained the importance of the statement of cash flows and cash flow forecasting.

Monica continued to meet with the accountant monthly—often on her days off—to maintain the statement of cash flows and the cash flow forecast. It was immediately after one of these meetings that she and Erica had a yoga class together. As they changed in the locker room, Monica talked to Erica about the challenges of cash forecasting.

"I've never had to do that," Erica said. "Sounds like I'm pretty lucky. The resort controller and general manager take care of cash flow projections." "Trust me, you're lucky!" Monica replied.

Erica continued. "Sometimes we'll be told during department head meetings that we have to watch our payrolls for the next month, or we're told not to purchase anything unless we absolutely need it, but it's not the same as for you in the day spa. You have to manage your cash far more closely than I ever do."

Cash management refers to the management of a spa's cash balances (currency and demand deposits), cash flow (cash receipts and disbursements), and short-term investments in securities. Cash management is critical to both large and small spa operations. Insufficient cash can quickly lead to insolvency and bankruptcy. This chapter will address many questions regarding cash management, including the following:

1. What is the difference between income and cash flows?
2. What is contained in a cash budget?
3. How are cash receipts forecasted?
4. How do short-term and long-term cash budgeting approaches differ?

5. What are the relevant factors to consider when investing working capital funds?
6. What are compensating balances?
7. How does a lockbox system speed up cash flow?
8. Why is depreciation expense irrelevant in cash flow considerations?
9. Why are investors interested in cash flow?
10. How are noncash current assets related to cash flow?
11. What are the three major activities shown on the Statement of Cash Flows (SCF)?
12. How does a spa account for gift card sales?
13. How do the direct and indirect methods of preparing the SCF differ?

Our discussion of cash management will identify the uses and importance of cash in a spa. We will consider the distinction between income and cash flows and explain what is meant by negative cash flow. We will discuss basic approaches to using cash budgets for planning purposes. We will also address the major areas of spa operations affecting the process of cash budgeting, such as management of working capital, including accounts receivable, inventory, and current liabilities. Gift certificate sales accounting will also be illustrated. Finally, we will discuss the Statement of Cash Flows.

Cash and Its Importance

In a spa, cash consists of petty cash funds, cash on hand (cash banks) for operational purposes, and cash in the bank. Cash on hand includes cash in the front desk cash drawer for making change and undeposited cash receipts. Cash in the bank includes operating accounts (demand deposits), savings accounts, sweep accounts, overnight investments, and money market funds. Some spas also consider time deposits and certificates of deposit as cash. In our discussion, all of these elements will be considered cash equivalents.

Petty cash funds are established for making minor cash purchases. These funds are normally maintained on an **imprest basis**—that is, they are replenished by the amount of disbursements since the previous replenishment.

House banks are maintained in order to facilitate cash transactions with guests. Each cash drawer should hold only as much as is needed to transact daily business. Since house banks do not generate earnings, these cash balances should be minimized. Small spas may maintain only a single house bank for drawer cash, while larger spas may have individual drawer cash banks for each guest reception employee, as well as a house bank used to make change for the individual cash drawers.

Ideally, the spa's cash balance in a demand deposit bank account should be zero. That is, daily deposits should equal disbursements from the account. However, cash received and cash disbursed are generally not uniform because the cash receipts for a day seldom equal the cash disbursements for the same day. Therefore, most operations maintain minimum balances in their checking accounts to cover checks drawn. The reason for keeping these cash balances is commonly referred to as a **transaction motive**. Sophisticated cash management systems often use a sweep account where funds in excess of a predetermined amount are swept out of the operating account daily and invested in "overnight investments" or money market funds.

The size of the checking account balance is also influenced by banks. Some banks demand that depositors maintain substantial amounts in their accounts to cover bank services and to serve as compensating balances for bank loans. For example, an operation receiving a loan for $100,000 may be required to maintain a 10-percent compensating balance. This means $10,000 must be maintained in the checking account. Since no interest is earned on the compensating balance, the **effective cost** of the loan is higher than its stated interest rate. The effective cost is determined by taking all elements into account. For example, assume that a spa receives a one-year loan of $100,000 at 10-percent interest with a compensating balance requirement of $10,000. The effective interest rate is 11.1 percent, as illustrated below:

$$\frac{\text{Effective}}{\text{Interest Rate}} = \frac{\text{Annual Interest on Loan}}{\text{Loan} - \text{Compensating Balance Requirement}}$$

Loan	=	$100,000
Less compensating balance	=	($10,000)
Effective loan amount	=	$90,000

Interest = $100,000 × 10% = $10,000
Effective Interest Rate = $10,000 ÷ $90,000 = 11.1%

Aggressive financial managers attempt to keep cash balances as low as possible given in-house cash needs and banking requirements. The cost of maintaining excessive in-spa cash or checking accounts is the opportunity cost. The opportunity cost equals the earnings available if the cash were invested. For example, if a spa has an average annual checking account balance of $40,000 when the bank requires only $25,000, the opportunity cost is the interest that could be earned on $15,000. At an interest rate of 5 percent, the opportunity cost is $750 annually ($15,000 × .05).

Investors/owners also have a keen interest in an operation's cash position. Investors and owners make money in two ways: they receive cash dividends/bonus payments and their wealth increases as the stock price or value of the spa increases. However, corporations are able to pay cash dividends only as cash is available. Therefore, those investing in corporations for dividends will review financial statements, especially the statement of cash flows, to determine whether the operation has sufficient cash to pay dividends and whether it will be operated in a manner that will allow dividend payments in the future.

Bank Selection

One of the most critical elements of cash management and overall financial management is choosing a commercial bank. A variety of banking institutions exist,

Income from Operations and Cash Flows

Income from operations results from spa operations generating revenues and incurring expenses. An operation's income statement is prepared on an accrual basis in order to appropriately match revenue in a financial reporting period with the corresponding expenses in the same period. When revenues exceed expenses, there is income or profit. When expenses exceed revenues, there is loss. In contrast, **cash flows** result from the receipt and disbursement of cash. It is possible for an operation to generate profit, yet have a negative cash flow (cash disbursements exceeding cash receipts). This was the situation presented in the chapter's opening story, where Monica confused accrual-based profits with the availability of sufficient cash. It is also possible to generate a substantial operating loss, yet have positive cash flow.

Cash flow over any period of time, whether a week, month, quarter, or year, is strictly a measure of cash receipts into the spa and cash disbursements out of the spa. The simplest method of understanding the difference between cash flow and profit/loss is to think of cash flow as simply a checkbook.

Many cash receipts in a spa do not directly affect the income statement. These include, but are not limited to:

- Sale of gift certificates.
- Guest prepayments for services to be performed in the future.
- Loans from banks.
- Loans from shareholders or partners.
- Investments by shareholders or partners.
- Proceeds from the sale of capital equipment or other assets.
- Collection of accounts receivable.

Cash disbursements in a spa that do not directly affect the income statement include, but are not limited to:

- Payment for the purchase of capital equipment.
- The principle portion of payment of loans to banks or shareholders (interest expense is deducted on the income statement).
- Payment of dividends to shareholders or partner distributions.
- Payment for the purchase of prepaid items, e.g., prepaid insurance, prepaid rent, etc.
- Payment of accounts payable or other accrued expenses.

A spa may withstand negative cash flows for short periods of time if cash reserves are adequate to cover the deficits. However, over long periods, negative cash flows will most likely result in failure, even if **income flows** are positive. Many profitable businesses have gone under because of cash flow problems.

Most businesses, including spas, have peaks and valleys in their operations. Generally, more cash is required during peak periods because cash is tied up in higher-than-usual inventories, accounts receivable, and labor. Therefore, cash planning is important to ensure sufficient cash at all times. Cash planning is achieved by preparing cash budgets for several months into the future, but it should be noted that this can only be done when profit and loss budgets/forecasts are available for several months into the future.

Internal Control of Cash

Cash is the most vulnerable of all assets. It is therefore essential to have an effective system of internal control over cash in all phases of the spa operation. The theft of cash is always possible. The following is a list of general procedures that help ensure that cash is adequately controlled:

- Cash-handling duties should be segregated.
- Bookkeeping and cash-handling duties should be separated.
- All expenditures should be paid by check or **electronic funds transfer** (EFT).
- Mechanical devices should be used to help safeguard cash.
- Technicians and front desk personnel should use pre-numbered sales tickets.
- Cash, checks, and payment card receipts should be deposited intact or processed daily.
- Employees should be bonded, and pre-hiring credit checks and background checks should be performed.
- Rigid detailed policies and procedures covering every aspect of cash handling need to be developed, explained, and readily available to all employees, and strictly enforced. Internal and external cash audits should be performed periodically.
- A voucher system/purchase order for disbursements should be implemented.

The following sections discuss each of these procedures.

Segregate Cash-Handling Duties. The responsibility for handling cash should be divided among two or more individuals. The segregation of cash-handling duties does not guarantee that fraud will not occur, but it makes fraud more difficult because it makes collusion necessary.

For example, a spa that divides cash-handling duties might have the employee who opens mail record any cash or checks mailed to the spa. This employee should forward the cash and checks to another employee, who will prepare the bank deposit. The employee opening the mail should also prepare a list of the day's receipts and send a copy of it to the accountant. The person preparing the bank deposit should forward a duplicate deposit ticket to the accountant. The accountant can then compare the list of cash receipts with the day's deposit ticket to look for any discrepancies.

Separate Bookkeeping and Cash-Handling Duties. Employees who have access to cash should not have access to accounting records such as the cash receipts or cash disbursements journals. Similarly, employees who have access to the accounting records should not have access to cash. Separating the bookkeeping and cash-handling duties can be a very challenging chore in a small spa with limited personnel available. Nonetheless, this is a very important control, as it helps prevent employees from taking cash and hiding the fact by making inaccurate bookkeeping entries.

Pay for All Expenditures by Check or EFT. All disbursements should be made by check or by EFT after proper authorization procedures are completed. Checks written for more than a certain amount should require two signatures. The only exception to paying by check or EFT should be the small business transactions that invariably occur, such as small freight charges. Such small expenditures should be paid out of a petty cash fund for which one person only is responsible. (Petty cash procedures will be discussed in more detail later in the chapter.) As the name indicates, EFT is a method of distributing cash electronically, without sending a hard copy of a check through the banking system's check-clearing process. Due to its convenience and lower cost, EFT is growing more popular. EFT is commonly used to pay for rent, mortgage, utility, insurance, and payroll costs.

Use Mechanical Devices to Help Safeguard Cash. Whenever feasible, mechanical devices should be integrated into the spa accounting systems to assist in safeguarding cash. Point-of-sale (POS) systems, cash registers, time clocks, and check protectors are examples of such devices. The cash register, for example, should record all transactions on a two-ply tape that is locked inside the register and inaccessible to the employee operating the machine. At the end of a shift, the employee operating the cash register should count the cash and transfer it to the accountant's office, where the cash receipts will be listed on a deposit slip. A third employee from the accounting department should remove the tape from the machine, compare the total to the cash amount listed by the cashier, and record the cash sales in the appropriate journal. POS systems allow the same controls as the cash register system.

Use Pre-Numbered Sales Tickets. Where practical in a spa operation, pre-numbered sales tickets or POS pre-numbered control numbers should be used to check in and check out guests. Any guest control numbers or pre-numbered sales tickets that are not accounted for at the end of the day must be investigated immediately by the appropriate manager, as it may represent a guest who left without paying or some other irregular or prohibited activity.

Deposit Cash Daily. All the spa's cash receipts should be deposited daily and intact in the bank. All checks received from guests should immediately be restrictively endorsed with the words "for deposit only." Daily deposits:

- Limit the availability of cash receipts for employee theft.
- Facilitate reconciliation of deposits to the general ledger cash account.
- Allow for funds to be available for use immediately in the case of cash and upon clearing through the banking system in the case of checks.

Miscellaneous small expenditures should never be paid for out of the day's receipts; instead, they should be paid for through the petty cash fund. Payment of small items out of the day's receipts complicates the daily reporting reconciliation.

Process Credit Cards Daily. All credit cards should be processed daily through the credit card processing company in order to prevent theft and maximize cash flow. Credit card payments are generally processed by a third-party processing company that charges a fee to the spa in exchange for processing. In some cases, the fee is deducted from the credit card charge amount and the spa is paid a net amount. In other cases, the charge is assessed as a separate charge. The funds from the credit cards usually are deposited into the spa's bank account within a few days after processing, so it is vital to process credit card payments daily to make funds available sooner. Some processors batch several credit charges and deposit a lump sum consisting of several charges to the spa bank account. Credit card deposits add an additional layer of complexity to the reconciliation of the spa bank account due to the processing fees involved; this complexity adds to the necessity to process the credit card charges daily.

Employee Bonding. Employees who handle cash or the accounting of cash should be bonded by an insurance company. Bonds of this type are commonly referred to as fidelity bonds. In the event of a defalcation of funds, the spa will be reimbursed for the loss minus the deductible. Prior to accepting the risk and issuing the bond, the insurance company will often assess the internal control of the spa and suggest improvements.

Audit Procedures. Periodic reviews of the internal control system policies and procedures that safeguard cash should be performed internally by the company's auditors and externally by independent certified public accountants.

In recent history there have been serious abuses in the area of financial reporting by companies. The abuses involving WorldCom and Enron led to the demise of once-prestigious Arthur Andersen, LLP, which had issued clean opinions on the financial statements for both companies. One of the results of these abuses is the Sarbanes-Oxley Act of 2002. This act created the Public Company Accounting Oversight Board to oversee the work done by auditors on public companies. The act requires the financial offices of publicly traded companies to file quarterly statements swearing that their company's financial statements are complete and accurate. In addition, public companies must file annual internal control reports and auditors must evaluate the internal controls of their clients.

Purchasing and Cash Disbursements. A purchase order system should be implemented to control cash disbursements. The next section of this chapter discusses the workings of a purchase order system and its coordination with an accounts payable/cash disbursement system.

Purchase Order System

All spas, regardless of size, should develop a purchase order system to facilitate proper management and internal control of cash expenditures. A rule of thumb is to mandate that every cash disbursement other than payroll must be initiated with a purchase order. From that mandate, exceptions can be developed along with an alternative approval process. The usual exceptions will include:

- Utility bills, including phone, cable, DSL, and electricity.
- Contractually agreed-upon items such as rent, mortgage loan payments, insurance premium payments, etc.
- Credit card payments used to purchase travel, meals, entertainment, etc.
- Some petty cash items like certain small employee reimbursements.

Purchase orders should be issued to all other vendors. The purchase order at a minimum should state the description of the item purchased, the number of items purchased, the purchase price per unit, expected delivery date, and shipping and payment terms. It should also be signed and dated by the person issuing it and initialed where required by the person authorizing the transaction.

In a small day spa, the spa director or the owner may prepare purchase orders manually in numeric sequence and maintain them in a manual filing system. POS systems usually generate purchase orders automatically in numeric sequence for inventory replacement items. POS systems can be integrated with both the receiving system and the customer invoice/cash disbursements functions. To gain a better understanding of the internal control features, consider the functions of a manual system that a spa should use.

The purchase order usually begins with a requisition from a spa supervisor for needed items. The requisition is approved at the appropriate authority level and a purchase order is completed for the purchase. At least four copies of the purchase order should be made; the original for the vendor, a copy to be retained in an "open order" file, a copy for the receiving function, and a copy for the accounting department. Purchase orders should be printed in pre-numbered numerical sequence in order to maintain adequate internal control.

From a cash management perspective, the purchase orders in the open order file represent future commitments of cash and are very useful in forecasting cash flow. Obviously, manual systems are hard to manage; POS systems provide this information in order by date.

Receiving. When a spa receives merchandise, the receiving copy of the purchase order is matched with the transportation company's shipping documents, bill of lading, etc. Discrepancies are noted, shipping documents are attached to the receiving copy of the purchase order, and the receiving documents are forwarded to the accounting department after being dated and signed as correct (or as amended) by the receiver.

Accounts Payable/Cash Disbursements. The accountant will generally receive three separate documents: the vendor invoice, the accounting copy of the purchase order, and the receiving documents. The purchase order and the receiving documents should be matched to the vendor invoice; discrepancies should be noted and communicated to the purchasing department. The accountant reviews the purchase order for appropriate approvals by the buyer.

At this point, it is important to understand that the high-level approval process of the purchase should have already been completed. The purchase requisition, receiving documents, and purchase order should be approved by the spa director or appropriate department head before the purchase and before reaching the accounting department. Good internal control dictates that the accounting department is to compare the approval signatures on the documents to a facsimile signature list of approved signatures.

After the three documents are compared and all discrepancies resolved, the documents are considered a voucher. In older accounting systems, an additional document (voucher) was attached to the vendor invoice, receiving document, and purchase order document. Information already present on the three documents was written on the voucher, including invoice number, purchase order, invoice date, receiving date, payment amounts, vendor name and address, etc. The voucher was then used to enter the data into an automatic data-processing system. An inherent problem with this process was the failure of clerical staff to accurately transcribe the information from the original documents to the voucher.

Modern systems have virtually eliminated the extra document. Generally, data is entered directly from the source document and control totals are used to verify accuracy. With POS systems, much repetitive entry is eliminated. Simultaneous entries are made to expense accounts or balance sheet accounts such as Retail Inventory and to the accounts payable account. Additionally, subsidiary ledgers such as Inventory, Accounts Payable, etc., are automatically updated and posted.

After entry and verification, the voucher package is filed in an open or unpaid accounts payable file in either alphabetical or chronological order, according to the system in place. The open or unpaid accounts payable file in essence becomes the accounts payable subsidiary ledger. The sum of the open accounts payable vouchers in the file should be balanced to the accounts payable subsidiary ledger at least monthly.

All systems allow a due date for each invoice to be entered, designating the check preparation date. Bill payment varies from spa to spa, depending upon the size of the spa and the sophistication of the cash management system. Ideally, the spa should pay bills at least weekly in order to take advantage of vendor terms and discounts.

When the date of payment arrives, an employee in the accounting department prepares a cash requirements report listing the checks that should be paid based upon the date they are due. Payments should allow for check processing time and mail time, as well as processing time at the vendor level. The spa director or accountant reviews the cash requirements request for payment. The accountant removes the voucher package from the file and prepares the checks. The unsigned check, along with the voucher package, is given to the treasurer, controller, spa director, or owner (depending upon the organization) to sign. By having all the documents in front of him or her at time of signature, the higher authority who receives the check and voucher package can perform a final check to verify the accuracy and validity of the cash disbursement. As an additional control feature, many spas require two signatures on all checks, often from senior managers or executives who are not part of the routine purchase order or purchasing process. In an ideal system of internal control, no single person or department would prepare a check *and* sign it. After a signature on the check is obtained, the check and any attachments are mailed and the voucher package, along with a copy of the check or a stub, is filed in a paid vendor file in alphabetical order. Each vendor should have a separate file, and new files must be created for the beginning of each calendar or fiscal year.

An accounts payable voucher system, with its requirements for written approval, provides a trail of documentation that is referred to as an **audit trail**.

Cash Disbursements That Do Not Require Purchase Orders. At the beginning of this section, items were listed that generally do not require purchase orders, such as utility payments, contractual payments, etc. Invoices or payment coupons for these types of payments will generally be mailed directly to the spa without the need for a purchase order. In all cases, the accountant must be aware of the arrangements made by spa management for these types of payments.

Prior to entry into the accounts payable/accounting system, the accountant must scrutinize the invoice against established rates and obtain the appropriate approval signatures on the invoice. Once approved, invoices for these items are entered directly into the accounts payable system and, from that point forward, handled in the same manner as items purchased with the use of a purchase order.

Occasionally, items must be purchased within a shorter time frame than is available to generate a purchase order. In these cases, a **check request** form should be prepared and the appropriate approvals secured prior to the purchase or immediately afterward in cases of emergency. Once approved, check requests and the attendant documentation are entered directly into the accounts payable system and, from that point forward, handled in the same manner as items purchased with the use of a purchase order.

Credit cards. Credit cards can be very helpful in managing cash flow, and the use of these cards has increased dramatically. Often, the spa will pay for products and expenses on a credit card and, in effect, add 25 to 30 days of cash flow. Furthermore, by using one card to pay the balance on a second card, the cash flow can be increased an additional 25 to 30 days. However, spas must take care not to incur excessive credit card fees. Spas also must be careful not to let their cash flow system become completely dependent on such strategies.

Each charge made to the credit card must be entered into the accounting system as a separate line item, regardless of the size. For example, if a utility bill is paid on an American Express card issued to the spa, the utility bill must first be approved for payment and then entered into the accounting system as a debit to Utility Expense and a credit to the Accounts Payable—American Express account. The utility bill will be marked as paid by American Express and filed in the paid vendor file.

When the corporate credit card statement is received, the entries to the Accounts Payable—American Express account must be reconciled to the credit card statement, and the reconciliation must be approved by the controller, spa director, or other appropriate party. After approvals have been obtained, the statement is scheduled for payment in the same manner as other disbursements. Many modern software systems provide specific credit card processing modules that automatically capture the credit card charges and credits to the Accounts

Payable—Credit Card account and the offsetting expense or balance sheet accounts. Also, many systems allow for downloading the charges and credits made to credit cards directly from the bankcard's electronic data base. Care must be taken in the download process to verify the legitimacy of the charges and to allocate the charges and credits to the proper accounts.

Many small spa owners use a credit card for both personal and business charges. We strongly recommend that the spa select a card that is used only for business purposes. Comingling of personal and business expenses, even if properly recorded and reimbursed by the owner, can be used in a lawsuit or by taxing authorities to "pierce the corporate veil" of liability protection provided by the use of a corporate, partnership, or limited liability company entity.

Bank debit cards. Many banks will issue commercial cards using the cash in the spa commercial bank account as the collateral to make the purchase. The card can either be used as a credit card or as a debit card. If the card is used as a credit card, the spa will have some limited recourse to the vendor through the credit card company in the case of a return or a dispute regarding the purchase. If the card is used as a debit card, the bank or credit card company will not intervene on the spa's behalf in the event of a dispute with the vendor.

If the card is used as a debit card, a password must be entered at time of purchase or at the time the card is used to withdraw cash from an automated teller machine (ATM). In response to increasing fraudulent transactions that compromised credit cards, many stemming from Internet purchases, most major credit card issuers have introduced chip technology and require a password as well as a signature for credit card transactions.

Because of the difficulties in maintaining internal control and preventing theft of cash, it is strongly recommended that bank debit cards not be used for purchases in a spa operation. If such a card is used, usage should be limited to the owner or designated employee and the owner should electronically access the spa's commercial bank account to verify the usage. Card usage should be very limited, and when not in use the card must be in the owner's or other bonded employee's possession at all times. Dollar amount transaction limits and daily cash withdrawal limits can be established on most bank cards, which further reduces the inherent risk.

Regardless of whether the card is used as a debit card or a credit card, cash in the amount of the purchase is immediately withdrawn from the spa's commercial bank account.

Electronic payments. Most taxing entities and state agencies now require that payments be made electronically. In addition, many vendors, particularly international vendors, require electronic payments. Electronic payments are generally facilitated by providing the taxing authority or vendor the spa's bank account number and bank routing number. The vendor or taxing authority then processes an approved payment request through the Federal Reserve banking system that extracts the funds from the spa's bank account immediately.

Before processing the electronic payment request, the necessary approvals from the spa director, accountant, controller, owner, or other appropriate party must be obtained. All records of the transaction must be printed and saved in order to facilitate tracing and reconciliation of the bank account. The actual payment request should be made by the same party that is responsible for signing checks for the spa.

Vendor statements. Entries into the accounts payable system should only be made from an original vendor invoice, never from a copy or duplicate. Also, payments must never be made solely based on information from a vendor statement. When vendor statements are received, they should be reconciled to the vendor invoices on hand to ensure the balance shown as an account receivable by the vendor is the same amount shown as the spa's account payable. The vendor should be advised of any discrepancies immediately and the appropriate remedy agreed upon.

Employee expense reports. The spa should develop or purchase a standard expense report form that complies with tax guidelines as well as specific guidelines or rules of the spa. All employees should complete the form, attach the necessary documentation, and obtain the appropriate approvals before receiving reimbursement for their expenses incurred on behalf of the spa.

Cash balances. Excellent cash management requires the spa to know the amount of cash on hand on a fluid, up-to-the-minute basis using the accounting system and POS system. Additionally, electronic online bank account access allows a spa to manage cash and the investment of cash by easily keeping track of **cash float**. Cash float is the difference in the cash balance shown on the spa's general ledger cash account and that shown on the bank account. For example, the spa may have issued and mailed a check in the amount of $5,000 to its landlord on January 25. The landlord receives the check on January 28, deposits it on January 29, and the landlord's bank does not receive the funds from the spa's bank account until January 31. During the six-day period, the spa has $5,000 in cash float. The topic of float is discussed further later on in the chapter.

Petty Cash

Although a spa would prefer to have all purchases paid for by check using the purchase order system, it is not always possible to do so. For instance, a small collect-on-delivery (C.O.D.) package may arrive or a small purchase of postage stamps or office supplies may be necessary. Such miscellaneous expenditures are paid out of a small fund of cash called the **petty cash** fund.

A spa starts a petty cash fund by cashing a check for an amount that it considers adequate to cover small, miscellaneous transactions. A single person designated as the custodian of the fund keeps the cash under his or her control in an envelope, a cardboard box, or a drawer, preferably locked away for safekeeping.

Assume that a spa writes a check for $100 and cashes the check, receiving various denominations of bills and change. The total amount of cash held by the company has not changed as a result of this transaction; rather, the composition of cash has changed. There is now $100 more in actual cash in the firm and $100 less in demand deposits. Petty cash is listed separately in the general ledger accounts; however, on the balance sheet, it can be listed separately or included in the Cash account.

Disbursements from the petty cash fund must be supported by receipts such as cash register tapes, invoices, or other documents. At any given time, the total of the cash and receipt amounts should equal the amount of the fund; in this case, the cash and receipt amounts should total $100. When the cash in the fund is reduced to a level considered inadequate to cover likely expenditures, the fund is said to need reimbursing or replenishing. A check is drawn and cashed for an amount that will replenish the fund (that is, bring it back to its original level—in this case, back to a level of $100).

To illustrate the reimbursement of a petty cash fund, assume that an examination of the fund for a spa reveals $18 in cash and the following receipts: postage, $38; freight charges, $27; and office supplies, $17. Using the check request form, a check will be requested, approvals will be obtained, and a check will be written for $82 payable to the spa. The entries in the accounting system from the check form will be as follows:

	Debit	Credit
Postage Expense	$38	
Freight Expense—Inbound	27	
Office Supplies	17	
Cash—Spa Bank		$82

The most common entry involving the petty cash fund is the entry to reimburse the fund. This particular journal entry does not involve the Petty Cash account.

Occasionally an employee, when reimbursing the petty cash fund, will find that the receipts and remaining cash do not equal the amount of the fund. For example, a $100 fund may contain $12 and the following receipts, which total $86: spare parts, $23; spa operating supplies, $18; freight charges, $32; and postage, $13. If the credit to Cash was entered as simply the total of the debits to the expense accounts, the fund would not be properly replenished. Remember, replenishing the fund means bringing it back to its original balance of $100. In this case, there is a $2 shortage unaccounted for in the fund ($12 + $86 = $98). To avoid underfunding or overfunding the petty cash fund, businesses follow this three-step procedure:

1. Debit the expense accounts relating to the receipts in the fund ($86).
2. Subtract the amount of the remaining cash from the amount of the fund, and credit Cash for that amount. ($100 − $12 = $88).
3. If the credit entry does not equal the debit entries, use the Cash Short and Over account to balance the entry. ($88 − $86 = $2).

The Cash Short and Over account is a miscellaneous expense or revenue account, depending on its balance at the end of the year. As part of the control procedures, the activities in this account should be reviewed on a periodic basis for individual entries in excess of an agreed amount or repetitive shortages causing a growing debit balance, which should require explanation by the petty cash custodian. A debit balance indicates expense, while a credit balance indicates revenue. At the end of the fiscal period, the Cash Short and Over account is closed into the income summary account just as the other nominal accounts are.

Bank Reconciliation

A **bank reconciliation** is a monthly procedure that provides additional control over cash. The bank reconciliation explains any differences between the bank's cash balance and the cash balance (demand deposits) in the spa's books. The spa starts its bank reconciliation when it receives a statement from the bank or by accessing the online bank account if a mid-month reconciliation is desired or required. Most commercial banks offer the option of receiving electronic portable document format (PDF) versions of the bank statement in order to save postage, expedite delivery, and eliminate paper usage.

For internal control purposes, care must be taken that the bank statement is delivered unopened whether by mail or e-mail to the individual responsible for preparing the bank reconciliation. Unless it is the spa owner, the person reconciling the bank should not have check-signing authority, electronic payment authority, or transfer authority in any of the banks he or she is reconciling; this non-owner also should not have purchase authority or approval authority over expenditures.

The bank statement provides a list of the deposits made by the company, the company's checks that have cleared the bank during the month, electronic payments, and other miscellaneous debits and credits to the bank balance. Included with the bank statement are the company's canceled checks that have cleared the bank; however, to save money and go "green," many banks do not return cancelled checks.

Any differences in the bank and book balances of cash may be due to any of the following possible reasons:

- *Deposits in transit:* Deposits in transit are deposits made by the spa at the end of the month but not included on the bank statement. For example, a spa may drop a deposit in the bank's night depository on June 30. The bank would then record it as a July 1 deposit and include it on the July bank statement. Deposits in transit also include credit card payments made by spa guests that have not been processed by the credit card processing company and deposited to the spa bank account. In some cases, credit card transactions may take as much as a week from the date of acceptance to be deposited as cash into the spa bank account.
- *Outstanding checks:* Outstanding checks are checks written by the spa to third parties who have not yet presented them to the bank for collection. Any check that has been outstanding for more than 90 days should be considered lost, and, depending upon the amount of the check, a stop payment order to the commercial bank account should be made.
- *Not-sufficient-funds (NSF) checks:* NSF checks are checks that the bank returned to the spa because the customer writing the check did not have enough funds to cover it. NSF checks are often called *bounced checks*. Generally, banks will process a check presented with insufficient funds twice. After the second failed process attempt due to insufficient funds, banks usually charge the spa back for the check amount and the spa is responsible for collecting the check from the guest. Banks usually charge quite a high service charge for

NSF checks, and it is commonplace for the spa to charge that amount (or even add a punitive premium) to the client. To eliminate bounced checks, a spa may decide to contract with a check validation service that will preauthorize checks and guarantee payment for a fee.

- *Bank service charges:* Bank service charges are charges for services provided by the bank, such as fees for new checks or fees charged to the spa for deposits or checks written. Another common charge would be the monthly bank fee for processing bank credit card slips that the firm has deposited. Bank service charges are highly negotiable and vary in method of calculation and payment.
- *Credits for interest earned or receivables collected:* If the checking account earned interest on the average balance held in the account, a credit would appear on the bank statement for this amount.
- *Clerical errors:* Clerical errors are simply errors made by the bank, the spa, or both. For example, the spa may mistakenly record a check written for $97 as $79. The bank would pay the recipient $97 and the error of $18 would cause a difference between the bank and book balances.

Preparing a Bank Reconciliation

Although there are several ways to proceed when preparing a spa bank reconciliation, we recommend the following steps:

1. Compare the deposits listed on the bank statement with the deposits listed in the company's records. Any deposit not listed on the bank statement represents a deposit in transit and should be added to the balance listed on the bank statement. However, if there is a missing deposit on the bank statement that did not occur at the end of the month, follow up immediately with the bank, which may have credited the wrong account.
2. Put the returned canceled checks in numerical order or use the numeric listing provided on the statement. Compare the amounts on the bank statement with the amounts on the checks and investigate any discrepancies. Compile a list of checks that have been written but not returned with or listed on the bank statement. The sum of check amounts from this list, which is called an *outstanding check list,* should be subtracted from the *balance per bank* (that is, the balance listed on the bank statement). The outstanding check list from the previous month's bank reconciliation should be examined and any canceled checks received with the current statement should be checked off that list. Any checks still not returned should be included on the current month's outstanding check list.
3. Add any credit memoranda listed on the bank statement to the *balance per books* (that is, the balance listed in the company's books). These credit memoranda could include such items as interest earned or notes receivable collected.
4. Deduct from the balance per books any debit memoranda on the bank statement, such as bank service charges, credit card fees, and NSF checks.

5. Make any necessary corrections resulting from errors made by either the bank or the spa. For example, perhaps the company entered a $56 amount in the check register when the check was actually written for $65. This would necessitate a reduction of $9 in the balance per books.
6. After making all necessary adjustments to both the bank and book balances, verify that the adjusted balances are equal.
7. Make any necessary adjusting entries to the books. Note that items requiring adjusting entries will appear in the portion of the bank reconciliation dealing with the adjusted *book* balance.

Illustration of a Bank Reconciliation

Assume that the Any Spa received its bank statement and it showed an ending balance of cash in bank of $5,078.63. A check in the amount of $50 was returned as NSF, the account was credited with interest earned in the amount of $4.23, and the bank charged $8 for processing credit card fees. Furthermore, assume that the balance per books is currently $5,265.10. The following checks were written in June but not returned with the bank statement:

Check #	Amount
1194	$ 75.00
1198	23.82
1200	146.58
1202	12.90

An examination of the deposits on the bank statement reveals that a deposit the spa made on June 30 for $400.00 is not included on the statement. Suppose that check #1197 for $45.00 for office supplies was incorrectly recorded on the books as $54.00. Using this information along with the bank statement, Any Spa comes up with the following:

Any Spa
Bank Reconciliation
June 30, 20XX

Balance per bank statement, June 30, 20XX			$5,078.63
Add: Deposit in transit from June 30			400.00
Deduct: Outstanding checks:			
	#1194	$ 75.00	
	#1198	23.82	
	#1200	146.58	
	#1202	12.90	(258.30)
Adjusted bank balance:			$5,220.33
Balance per books, June 30, 20XX			5,265.10
Add: Interest earned during June			4.23
Error in recording check #1197			9.00
Deduct: NSF check		$ 50.00	
Bankcard draft processing fees		8.00	(58.00)
Adjusted book balance:			$5,220.33

The bank reconciliation for the Any Spa indicates that the correct cash balance at June 30 is $5,220.33. Remember, the books currently have a cash balance of $5,265.10. The important last step in the reconciliation process is to make the necessary journal entries to adjust the cash balance.

	Debit	Credit
Accounts Receivable—Any Spa Guest	$50.00	
Bank Service Charges	8.00	
Office Supplies		$ 9.00
Interest Income		4.23
Cash in Bank—Any Spa		44.77

The owner, spa director, controller, or other designated employee must approve the completed bank reconciliation in order to maintain internal control over cash.

Management of Working Capital

The management of working capital is closely related to the management of cash. **Working capital** (current assets less current liabilities) is directly related to cash. Changes in any components of working capital directly affect the balance of cash. These relationships assume that other activities (such as sales and expenses) remain constant. For example, if marketable securities decrease, cash increases, provided everything else remains the same. Therefore, it is imperative that spa managers understand the management of these elements of working capital.

Accounts Receivable

Accounts receivable arise from sales on account. Spas would prefer to transact only cash sales; however, in order to increase sales, credit is occasionally extended to individual spa guests or group bookings. Credit commences when the guest receives a service or purchases a product without paying at the time of receipt, and continues until the guest pays the bill.

The Accounts Receivable—Credit Card account for most spas is used when services or products are sold to a guest and the guest pays for their purchase with a bank debit card or a bank credit card such as a MasterCard, Visa, American Express, or Discover card.

Spas negotiate a contract with a credit card processor or with their commercial bank to provide credit card processing services. The processor will provide credit card processing terminals or will hook up electronically through the spa's POS system. Processing fees can be substantial, so care must be taken to negotiate with several different processors in order to receive the best rate and processing time. Think about this: if all of your spa's sales were paid for by credit card for which you paid a processing fee of 3 percent, and the spa operated with a bottom line of 9 percent, the spa would be paying the equivalent of *one-third* of its bottom line in processing fees.

When presented with a guest's credit card, spa staff initially process it to determine availability of credit amounts and to generate a transaction for the individual client. Generally, at the end of the day, all credit card transactions received during the day are batched and transmitted to the processor after reconciliation with the daily checkout report. At that point the credit cards received for the day are posted as a debit (increase) to the Accounts Receivable—Credit Cards account.

If the guest pays with a bank debit card, the cash is usually transferred from the guest's bank account within one banking day. Other bank cards such as Visa or MasterCard may take from two to five days to complete the processing cycle and transfer cash to the spa's bank account; American Express usually requires five to ten days.

Regardless of the time required, upon receipt of the cash the spa credits (decreases) the Accounts Receivable—Credit Card account and debits the Cash in Bank account for the deposit. Some processors deduct their service fee from each transaction and deposit a net amount, while others assess and deduct the fee at the end of the month. It is less costly and therefore advisable to negotiate the month-end method.

A Hotel Guest Accounts Receivable account is typically found in hotel/resort environments. The spa guests usually have a choice of paying by debit or credit card, charging the payment for spa services to their room, or (if they are part of a group with approved spa usage in the group's booking contract), charging the services to the group master account. When checking out from the hotel, the guest pays all charges incurred within the hotel by check or payment card. Until the guest checks out of the hotel, the guest charges are booked as a debit to Accounts Receivable—Room-XXX-Guest Name.

Member Accounts Receivable are used when spas sell memberships. Memberships are generally acquired by the payment of a fee designated as an initiation fee, which in fact is simply a form of revenue and/or deposit that may or may not be paid back to the member at some future uncertain date. The member may also be responsible for a predetermined amount of monthly dues that cover certain uses of the club, resort, or spa. If a member uses a spa service, his or her member account is charged for the service and the member is billed monthly for all purchased services and merchandise purchased. To remain in good standing, the member must pay the monthly billing within a designated period of time. In many cases, the member is required to keep a credit card on file to guarantee payment of the monthly amounts due for services, merchandise, and dues.

Accounts receivable statements to members should be mailed on a regular basis, usually monthly. A series of collection letters should be used to speed collection of delinquent accounts receivable. Delinquent accounts should be turned over to collection agencies only after the operation has made all reasonable collection efforts. Collection agency fees may range from 30 to 50 percent of the delinquent amount.

A **lockbox system** speeds the flow of cash from accounts receivable to the bank. This system consists of a post office box from which bank personnel collect all incoming mail and deposit any checks directly into the spa's bank account. This process may speed the cash flow from collection of accounts receivable by up to three days. In addition, it enhances internal control over mail cash receipts because company personnel do not have access to this cash. However, the bank does charge for this service, usually by the number of checks handled. If the operation receives many small payments, the cost of a lockbox system may exceed the benefits.

Accounts receivables are monitored by the use of ratio analysis and the preparation of an aging schedule of accounts receivable. Three useful ratios are accounts receivable to sales, accounts receivable turnover, and number of days of accounts receivable outstanding (the last being a variation of the accounts receivable turnover). These ratios are useful in detecting changes in the overall accounts receivable as they relate to sales.

An aging of accounts receivable is useful for monitoring delinquent accounts. Maximum efforts should be exerted to collect the oldest accounts. The aging schedule is also useful for estimating the uncollectible accounts at the end of the accounting period.

Inventory

Almost all spas offer retail products to their guests. The International Spa Association (ISPA) *2004 Spa Industry Study* found that spas get an average of 18 percent of their revenue from retail sales. More importantly, retail revenue can be an even greater percentage (commonly 22 to 26 percent) of the spa's profitability. In order to maximize the opportunities from retail sales, the spa must have adequate retail inventory on hand to supply the demand. The purchase and maintenance of retail inventory requires the use of cash and can have an enormous effect on cash needs.

As an example, assume that Any Spa's annual revenues are $4,000,000 and that 20 percent of the annual revenue ($800,000) is generated from the sale of retail products. Further, assume that retail inventory (valued at retail value) is $200,000, which provides Any Spa an ideal three-month stock-to-sales ratio. Lastly, assume that the actual cost of the inventory is 50 percent of the retail cost ($200,000 × 50% = $100,000). As a result of these assumptions, Any Spa has on average $100,000 of cash invested in retail inventory. During seasonal periods or periods immediately following purchases from "buying trips to market," cash needs may be substantially higher than $100,000, while cash needs during slow times of the year may be less than $100,000.

The important lesson is that the purchase of inventory held for retail sales is one of the primary drivers of the need for cash in a spa. Management of the inventory is vital in the management of cash. For additional help in inventory management, see ISPA's text *Retail Management for Spas: The Art & Science of Retail.*

Professional Products and Supplies

In addition to inventory held for retail, spas have a large investment in products used by technicians in providing services to clients. It is important from a cash flow perspective to control and monitor these products in the same way that retail product inventory is controlled.

The cost of the professional products and supplies used in the delivery of spa and salon treatments is generally in the range of 5 to 7 percent of total treatment revenues. Using the example of Any Spa, assume treatment revenues are $3,200,000. The cost of professional products and supplies used in a year would therefore range from \$160,000 to \$224,000. Because of the significant amount of cash invested in the professional products and supplies and their accessibility to many spa employees, spa leadership must manage this inventory in the same manner that they manage retail inventory. Furthermore, stock-outs on key professional products can affect treatment revenues (cash) and client retention (future cash).

Current Liabilities

A large portion of current assets is financed by current liabilities in spa operations. Assume that Any Spa has current assets equal to \$281,800 and current liabilities equal to \$160,300. The current ratio (current assets divided by current liabilities) is 1.76, meaning that for every \$1 of current liabilities, Any Spa has \$1.76 of current assets. Suppliers do not charge interest to hospitality operations for amounts owed in the normal course of business. This practice is called **trade credit.** Everything else being the same, the longer a spa can delay paying its bills, the greater its reliance on trade credit to finance its operations.

Current liabilities consist primarily of trade accounts payables, taxes payable, accrued wages, the current portion of long-term debt, and the current portion of gift cards payable. The remainder of this section focuses on trade payables, as the other payables must generally be paid on stipulated dates.

Trade payables resulting from purchases on account generally require payment in 30 days. Sometimes, suppliers offer cash discounts to spa operations to encourage their customers to pay their accounts early. For example, a supplier may provide a 2 percent cash discount if the invoice is paid within ten days of the invoice date. Thus, the terms of sale per the invoice are simply shown as 2/10, *n*/30. The *n*/30 means that if the discounted invoice is not paid within ten days of the invoice date, then the entire amount (net) is due within 30 days of the invoice date. Since a discount is available for early payment, the decision not to take advantage of the discount is a cost to the spa. Essentially, the spa is paying more than it could have paid. One measure of this cost is known as the effective interest rate.

The following example illustrates the calculation of the effective interest rate. Assume that a spa purchases a computer for \$8,000 and is offered terms of 3/10, *n*/30. The effective interest rate of 56.44 percent is the result of:

Interest calculated amount = \$8,000 purchase × 3% = \$240.00
Interest period = 30 days − 10 days = 20 days
Interest per day = \$240.00 ÷ 20 days = \$12.00 per day.
Annual interest amount = \$12.00 × 365 days = \$4,380.00.
Interest rate = \$4,380 ÷ (\$8,000 − \$240) = 56.44%

By not taking the discount within ten days, the spa will spend \$240 for the use of the \$8,000 owed to the supplier over an additional 20 days. Thus, the spa would be wise to pay the invoice within the cash discount period, even if it had to borrow funds to do so, as long as the annual interest rate on the loan is less than 56.44 percent.

In general, management should pay bills only when they are due except when cash discounts are available for early payments. The payment of invoices earlier than required results in a higher cost of doing business, since the cash expended could have been invested. However, management must consider the intangible factor of supplier relations as well as credit reporting. Keeping on favorable terms with suppliers is especially advantageous when the spa occasionally needs special favors—such as receiving inventory two days sooner than normally available.

Guest Deposits and Prepayments

Resort spas may require a deposit by check or credit card in order to reserve a block of time at the spa for a guest. These charges represent advanced deposits, which are liabilities to the spa until the guest arrives and uses the time reserved. At checkout, the advanced deposit amount is credited against the total charges and the guest either receives a refund of the balance or pays any additional amount.

Gift Card Sales

Gift card sales are a major source of cash for a spa. While gift card sales occur throughout the year, substantial peaks occur during the Christmas shopping season and before other holidays such as Valentine's Day and Mother's Day. Gift cards are also very popular gift items for birthdays, anniversaries, and other celebratory occasions.

Gift cards and certificates can be sold in various denominations or as payment for a particular spa service or package of services. More commonly, the cards are sold for a specific dollar amount, which can be redeemed by the person receiving the gift card at a later date for either spa services or retail products.

Regulations affecting the sale and redemption of gift cards vary from state to state in the United States. At the writing of this text, according to the Consumers Union, roughly one half of the states' regulations either do not allow expiration dates or set limits on the expiration dates that can be used. Regulations regarding "use fees" (fees that on a monthly or other stated time basis decrease the face value amount of the card) also vary, with approximately 30 states not permitting any fees or limiting the fees to a very small amount.

Before determining a gift card policy, the spa's attorney should take into account the regulations of the particular state or states in which the spa is doing business. And regardless of the individual state's regulations, the spa must take into account good business practices as promulgated by the Better Business Bureau as well as other consumer advocacy groups. Guest and consumer goodwill is valuable, and egregious gift card policies that unfairly benefit the spa at the consumers' expense have the potential to severely damage the spa in the event of a consumer investigation by the media. Even without the media, such poor policies will almost certainly have a negative impact on repeat gift card purchases.

From a marketing perspective, gift cards offer a two-fold opportunity, i.e., both the purchaser and the recipient may be new clients. The capture of information from both the buyer and the recipient allow significant future marketing opportunities. Furthermore, many recipients of gift cards will purchase additional services or merchandise over and above the amount of the gift card at the time of redemption.

From an accounting perspective, the sale of a gift card is not recorded as revenue, but as Deferred Revenue—Gift Cards, which is reflected as a liability on the balance sheet of the spa. Nothing has been done to earn the money paid for the gift card; it cannot properly be recorded on the income statement as revenue until the spa earns it by providing the bearer with services or merchandise. Until earned, the card represents a liability to the spa to provide services or merchandise to the bearer at a future date to be determined by the bearer. Revenue is recorded at the time the gift card is redeemed. The following entry would record the cash sale of a gift card in the amount of $250.00:

	Debit	Credit
Cash in Bank	$250.00	
Deferred Revenue—Gift Cards		$250.00

Various methods are used to record the sale of gift cards and certificates, ranging from the manual preparation of gift certificates to the use of outside gift card processors to the use of an in-house POS system. The sale of gift cards, the cash flow management issues involved, and the attendant accounting issues require adequate internal control and accurate recordkeeping, both for financial reporting and tax reporting purposes.

Ideally, a gift card sale should be created and recorded through the POS system, with the system issuing the card. Contact information for both the buyer and the recipient should be obtained if possible. It is imperative that the date of sale, amount of the sale, and card control number be recorded in the Deferred Revenue—Gift Card database. It is also imperative that the database be capable of maintaining remaining/outstanding card balances, year of issue, amount used by card, small balance card amounts (i.e., $5.00 or less), etc.

When the recipient uses the card to receive services or purchase products from the spa, revenue is at that point earned by the spa. Assume that the recipient (Amy) of the gift card sold for $250.00 used the card to pay for massage services of $100.00, a gratuity of $20.00, product sales of $75.00, and a sales tax of $7.50. The entry to record the revenue is as follows:

	Debit	Credit
Deferred Revenue—Gift Card	$202.50	
Massage Revenue		$100.00
Gratuity Payable		20.00
Revenue—Products		75.00
Sales Tax Payable		7.50

In this example, Amy has a balance remaining on the card of $47.50, which can be used at a later date. Cash should not ever be exchanged with a guest to redeem the balance of a card unless state regulations require that the bearer of the card may redeem the card for cash. Not only does giving cash back eliminate the opportunity to earn a profit on services and products provided, but it also creates an opportunity for fraud.

A material amount of gift card sales goes unused. At the time of writing, *Consumer Reports* estimated that 19 percent of the people in the retail community who received a gift card in 2005 never used it. The percentage in the spa industry may be higher overall, but it is likely much lower in a day spa environment. Cards are not used for a variety of reasons—the recipient may not be comfortable with visiting a spa, the card may be lost or forgotten, the bearer may move away, etc. Also, recipients often either forget about small balances or just do not feel the urge to use the small amounts that may be left.

This unused gift card issue is referred to as **gift card breakage**. While some states have laws (escheat) governing unclaimed property that regulate gift card breakage, in most cases gift cards have no expiration dates and, while they remain unredeemed, represent an indefinite obligation of the retailer.

As time passes, the likelihood of gift card redemption decreases until at some point deferred revenue from gift card breakage should be realized and recorded by the spa. As the spa measures historical patterns of redemption, it will be able to compute a weighted average gift card breakage estimate. It is recommended that at least four years of history be considered and that the gift card breakage remaining at the end of the fourth year be recorded as income to the spa.

Because of the nature of the redemption process, some of the gift card redemption takes place as Current Deferred Revenue—Gift Card and some takes place as Long-Term Deferred Revenue—Gift Card; in other words, a portion of the redemptions will occur in the next twelve months and another portion will take place after the next twelve months. The historical pattern of redemption and breakage will allow the calculation of an estimated current portion of the deferred revenue and a calculation of the long-term portion.

It is vital from the perspective of a spa financial statement to understand and report the deferred revenue correctly. Even in a small spa, the amount of outstanding gift card balances can quickly escalate. As a result, balance sheet financial ratios can quickly become unmanageable and the spa may have difficulty obtaining financing.

To understand the accounting and cash flow complexities of spa gift cards, assume the following multiple year examples for Any Spa:

- Gift card sales 20X6 = $425,000
- Gift card sales 20X7 = $450,000
- Gift card sales 20X8 = $475,000
- Gift card sales 20X9 = $500,000
- Gift card redemptions in year of sale—Year 1 30%
- Gift card redemptions—Year 2 30%
- Gift card redemptions—Year 3 15%
- Gift card redemptions—Year 4 5%
- Average gift card breakage 20%

The following table demonstrates the determination and calculation of historical patterns and gift card breakage:

Description	20X9	20X8	20X7	20X6	Total
Deferred Revenue from Sales of Gift Cards —Annual	$500,000	$475,000	$450,000	$425,000	$1,850,000
Gift card redemptions —20X6				(127,500)	(127,500)
Gift card redemptions —20X7			(135,000)	(127,500)	(262,500)
Gift card redemptions —20X8		(142,500)	(135,000)	(63,750)	(341,250)
Gift card redemptions —20X9	(150,000)	(142,500)	(67,500)	(21,250)	(381,250)
Deferred Revenue —Gift Cards—12-31-X9	$350,000	$190,000	$112,500	$85,000	$737,500
Write off of Gift Card Breakage—20X6				(85,000)	$652,500
Deferred Revenue —Gift Cards—12-31-X9	$350,000	$190,000	$112,500	$-0-	$652,500

Deferred Revenue—Gift Cards for the four-year period in the above table totals $1,850,000 for Any Spa. If Any Spa's start-up year was 20X6, sales of gift cards for the year totaled $425,000 and redemptions of $127,500 (30 percent) left a year-end balance in Deferred Revenue—Gift Cards of $297,500. From a cash flow viewpoint, the spa deposited into its bank account $297,500 in cash net of current year services rendered, with an obligation to provide services at a later time.

In 20X7, Any Spa sold an additional $450,000 in gift cards and redeemed 30 percent ($135,000) of the cards sold in 20X7. Additionally, 30 percent of the 2006 gift cards were redeemed ($127,500), leaving a Deferred Revenue—Gift Card balance at the end of 20X7 of $485,000:

20X6 Gift Card Sales	$425,000
20X7 Gift Card Sales	450,000
Less: 30% redemption of 20X6 gift cards in 20X6	(127,500)
30% redemption of 20X6 gift cards in 20X7	(127,500)
30% redemption of 20X7 gift cards in 20X7	(135,000)
Balance of Deferred Revenue—Gift Cards	$485,000

After two years of gift cards, Any Spa now has deposited $485,000 in cash from gift card sales for which it has not provided services.

In 20X8, Any Spa sold an additional $475,000 in gift cards and redeemed 30 percent ($142,500) of the cards sold in 20X8. Additionally, 30 percent of the 20X7 gift cards was redeemed ($135,000) and 15 percent of the 20X6 cards was redeemed $(63,750), leaving a Deferred Revenue—Gift Card balance of $618,750 at the end of 20X8:

20X6 Gift Card Sales	$425,000
20X7 Gift Card Sales	450,000
20X8 Gift Card Sales	475,000
Less: 30% redemption of 20X6 gift cards in 20X6	(127,500)
30% redemption of 20X6 gift cards in 20X7	(127,500)
15% redemption of 20X6 gift cards in 20X8	(63,750)
30% redemption of 20X7 gift cards in 20X7	(135,000)
30% redemption of 20X7 gift cards in 20X8	(135,000)
30% redemption of 20X8 gift cards in 20X8	(142,500)
Balance of Deferred Revenue—Gift Cards	$618,750

Three years after start-up, Any Spa has a liability/deferred revenue in the amount of $618,750 in unredeemed gift cards outstanding.

In 2009, Any Spa sold $500,000 in gift cards and redeemed $150,000 of the cards sold in 20X9. In addition, 30 percent of the 20X8 gift cards was redeemed ($142,500), 15 percent of the 20X7 cards ($67,500) was redeemed, and 5 percent of the 20X6 cards ($21,250) was redeemed, leaving a balance prior to adjustment of $737,500:

20X6 Gift Card Sales	$425,000
20X7 Gift Card Sales	450,00
20X8 Gift Card Sales	475,000
20X9 Gift Card Sales	500,000
Less: 30% redemption of 20X6 gift cards in 20X6	(127,500)
30% redemption of 20X6 gift cards in 20X7	(127,500)
15% redemption of 20X6 gift cards in 20X8	(63,750)
5% redemption of 20X6 gift cards in 20X9	(21,250)
30% redemption of 20X7 gift cards in 20X7	(135,000)
30% redemption of 20X7 gift cards in 20X8	(135,000)
15% redemption of 20X7 gift cards in 20X9	(67,500)
30% redemption of 20X8 gift cards in 20X8	(142,500)
30% redemption of 20X8 gift cards in 20X9	(142,500)
30% redemption of 20X9 gift cards in 20X9	(150,000)
Balance of Deferred Revenue—Gift Cards	$737,500

At the end of 20X9, Any Spa has $85,000 of the 20X6 gift card sales that are unredeemed and the redemption of the remaining cards is both unpredictable and unlikely. Although there is some chance that holders of the remaining outstanding cards issued in 20X6 will appear at the spa for redemption, it is more likely that the majority of the outstanding balance will not be redeemed. Therefore, in keeping with the four-year period of open redemption, the $85,000 is concluded to be breakage and removed from the Deferred Revenue—Gift Cards and reported as income to the spa in 20X9.

The entry to record the write off of the 20X6 gift card breakage is as follows:

	Debit	Credit
Deferred Revenue—Gift Cards	$85,000	
Other Income		$85,000

Other retail operations have chosen to write off gift card breakage to either sales or selling expenses or general and administrative expenses. It is our opinion that neither of those approaches is appropriate and could severely skew ratios and operating results. In financial statements prepared with disclosures, it is recommended that a footnote be included describing the year and accounting methodology used in the calculation of the Other Income. For those wise spas adhering to the *Uniform System of Financial Reporting for Spas*, a separate schedule is provided to record and detail rentals and other income.

Ideally, the individual gift cards making up the breakage total should be removed or segregated from the primary database. Doing so accomplishes two goals; it keeps the database total equal to the general ledger total and requires that any guest attempting to benefit from the breakage accounts receives additional scrutiny from management.

Although the breakage accounts have been written off and removed or segregated from the database, if a guest wishes to redeem a breakage gift card, he or she should be allowed to do so if that is in line with governing regulations and the spa's policy of redemption.

Assume that Amy from the previous example held the balance ($47.50) of the card previously used for five years. Further, assume that Amy then visited Any Spa and purchased merchandise in the amount of $60.00 plus tax of $6.00. Amy wishes to pay for the purchase with a combination of the breakage gift card and a credit card. Following are the entries to record the transaction:

	Debit	Credit
Other Income	$47.50	
Accounts Receivable—Credit Cards	18.50	
Revenue—Products Sales		$60.00
Sales Tax Payable		6.00

The logic in recording the breakage gift card transaction in Other Income is that the amount of $47.50 was credited to Other Income in a prior period and we are in effect simply reversing that entry. Secondly, when the spa establishes this policy of accounting for breakage, an annual entry to income will be posted each year. The annual posting of the income will offset any breakage gift card redemptions after write-off.

For federal income tax purposes, it is important for the spa to select the accrual method of accounting. If the spa should choose the cash method of accounting, the Internal Revenue Service will more than likely interpret the sales of gift cards to be revenue in the year the card is sold. The tax impact of that position has the potential to be very expensive due to the failure to defer the tax payment until redemption of the gift card.

Historical patterns of redemption will allow the accounting for Current Portion—Deferred Revenue—Gift Cards and Long-Term Portion—Deferred Revenue—Gift Cards, which is illustrated in the following table:

Description	20X9	20X8	20X7	20X6	Total
Deferred Revenue—Gift Card Balance as of December 31,20X9	$350,000	$190,000	$112,500	–0–	$652,500
20X7 Cards to be redeemed in 20Y0 (5% × $450,000)			(22,500)		(22,500)
20X8 cards to be redeemed in 20Y0 (15% × $475,000)		(71,250)			(71,250)
20X9 cards to be redeemed in 20Y0 (30% × $500,000	(150,000)				(150,000)
Long-Term Portion Deferred Revenue —Gift Cards	$200,000	$118,750	$90,000		$408,750
Current Portion Deferred Revenue—Gift Cards	$150,000	$71,250	$22,500		243,750

The Any Spa Balance Sheet for the year ending December 31, 20X9, will have a line item titled Current Portion Deferred Revenue—Gift Cards in the amount of $243,750 classified as a current liability. The line item Long-Term Portion Deferred Revenue—Gift Cards in the amount of $408,750 will be classified as a long-term liability.

Based on the above tables, the Any Spa manager/owner/accountant is able to draw the following conclusions regarding budgeting cash flow for 20Y0:

- Revenue of $243,750 will be generated by the redemption of prior year gift cards.
- Revenue from 20X9 gift card sales was $500,000 and the sales are trending up about 5 percent annually; $525,000 in gift card sales can be forecast for 20Y0.
- Any Spa will redeem $157,500 of the $525,000 gift card sales in 20Y0.
- Net cash flow from gift card sales is forecast to be a positive amount of $123,750. Sales ($525,000) less 20Y0 redemptions ($157,500) less 20Y0 redemptions of prior years' gift cards ($243,750) equals $123,750.

The condition of the economy can play a huge role in gift card cash flow planning. In times of recession, guests will slow down the purchase of the gift cards, while the recipients of cards are more likely to use them to conserve their cash. As a result, the cushion, or "gift card float" can disappear, and cash flow can be squeezed severely. In periods of economic growth, the opposite is prone to occur.

As shown in the above examples, sales of gift cards can result in large deferred revenue liabilities that can threaten the financial existence of a spa. A conservative risk management approach to limiting the risk involved is to maintain a "Trust" bank account where cash or cash equivalents are maintained in the same amount as the balance in the Deferred Revenue—Gift Card account. Balances in the Trust account can be invested in order to generate income.

Alternatively, the spa may choose to maintain a particular current ratio and debt-to-equity ratio by investing the cash that would otherwise be in the Trust bank account into other assets. The obvious danger to that approach is the risk of a "run" on the gift cards outstanding.

When the purchase of an existing spa business is under consideration, pay very close attention to the gift card situation. Often, the amount of gift cards outstanding is unknown. If the purchase includes liabilities, the buyer will be responsible for those outstanding gift card liabilities.

Monitoring the historical redemption patterns and adjusting the above calculations as needed are vital in the cash flow management planning process. The above example is presented on an annualized basis. In reality, the redemption patterns should be trended on a monthly basis to be used as a reliable predictor of cash flow. The management of cash from gift card sales is absolutely critical and emphasizes the need for forward cash planning. As already noted, a large part of annual gift card sales is right near year end. Assuming the spa has a calendar fiscal year end, this means that the spa will begin the year "cash rich" and seeing a big bank balance can be very tempting for all sorts of obvious reasons. But disciplined management of that cash must prevail, because it represents service that must be delivered with related wages, products, and overheads to pay.

Cash Budgeting

Cash budgets are prepared to reflect the estimated cash receipts and cash disbursements for a specific period. In certain situations, cash may be in short supply and a cash deficit may be projected. If the estimated cash receipts and beginning cash (estimated available cash) are not sufficient to cover projected cash disbursements, spa management must take action. Even if estimated available cash is greater than projected cash disbursements, the projected cash balance must be reviewed to determine if it is a sufficient buffer for any cash receipt shortfalls and/or unplanned cash disbursements. If the estimated cash balance is insufficient, the spa must plan to increase cash receipts, decrease cash disbursements, or do both. Management actions to cover temporary deficits may include obtaining short-term bank loans, obtaining loans from owners, deferring equipment purchases, deferring dividend payments, or a combination of such actions.

If the estimated cash balance at the end of the period appears excessive, then the excess cash should be temporarily invested. The six factors management should consider when investing excess cash are risk, return, liquidity, cost, size, and time:

1. *Risk* refers to the probability of losing the investment. Management should generally take a minimum risk when investing, especially when investing short-run funds. For example, investments in government securities such as Treasury bills are considered risk-free.

2. *Return* refers to the rate of return that can be received on the funds. Generally, the greater the risk and the longer the investment period, the greater the return.

3. *Liquidity* refers to the ability to convert the investment to cash. When cash is invested temporarily, it should generally be invested in fairly liquid investments so it can be quickly liquidated as required.
4. *Cost* refers to the brokerage cost of investing.
5. *Size* refers to the amount of funds available for investing. In general, the more money available for investing, the higher the return.
6. *Time* refers to the amount of time the excess funds are invested. Generally, the longer the investment time, the higher the return.

Because managers need to know in advance whether cash shortages or excesses are likely, they project cash flows when they prepare cash budgets. There are two basic approaches to cash budgeting: the cash receipts and disbursements approach and the adjusted net income approach. The method used depends primarily on the length of time for which the cash budget is prepared.

The **cash receipts and disbursements approach** is useful when forecasting cash receipts for periods of up to one to two months. It shows the direct sources of cash receipts, such as cash sales, collection of accounts receivable, bank loans, sale of capital stock, and so forth. It also reveals the direct uses of cash, such as payment of operating supply purchases, payroll, mortgage payments, and dividend payments. Because the cash receipts and disbursements method reflects the direct sources and uses of cash, it is easy to understand. However, it should generally not be used for periods exceeding six months. Projected figures beyond this point become increasingly unreliable, especially when actual operations differ significantly from the operations budget.

The cash receipts and disbursements format consists of two major sections: estimated cash receipts and estimated cash disbursements. Estimated cash receipts are added to the estimated beginning cash to project the estimated cash available for the period. Estimated cash disbursements are subtracted from estimated cash available to determine estimated ending cash. This figure is then compared with the minimum cash required in order to identify any shortage or excess. (The process of estimating cash receipts and cash disbursements will be presented later in this chapter.)

The **adjusted net income approach** is generally preferable for budgeting cash for periods longer than one to two months. It also reflects the estimated cash balance for spa management's evaluation. In addition to its usefulness for longer periods of time, it emphasizes external, as opposed to internal, sources of funds.

The adjusted net income method is an indirect approach to cash budgeting because the sources and uses related to operations are indirect rather than direct; for example, direct sources from operations such as cash sales are not shown, nor are direct uses for operations such as disbursements for payroll. This approach has two major sections: sources and uses. The sources section consists of internal and external sources. Internal sources are primarily cash from operations (chiefly reflected by net income plus income tax expense, depreciation, and other expenses that do not require cash). External sources of funds include proceeds from bank loans and the sale of capital stock. The sum of the beginning cash and the sources of cash is the estimated cash available.

The uses of cash are subtracted from cash at the beginning of the year plus sources of cash to find the estimated cash at the end of year. This figure is compared with the minimum cash requirement in order to determine any excess or shortage.

The adjusted net income approach, much like the statement of cash flows prepared on an indirect basis, focuses directly on changes in accounts receivable, inventories, and current liabilities, including Deferred Revenue—Gift Cards. This requires management to consider the amount of cash tied up in accounts receivable and inventory, and cash provided by current liabilities and Deferred Revenue—Gift Cards. Therefore, this approach encourages closer spa management review of these working capital accounts.

From a practical viewpoint, both cash budgeting approaches are useful. The cash receipts and disbursements approach should be used for short-term budgets prepared on a weekly or one- to two-month basis. The adjusted net income approach is useful for long-term cash budgets. A spa should prepare cash budgets for long-range periods corresponding to each annual operations budget prepared for several years into the future.

Information for Cash Budgeting

The operations budget is the major source of information for preparing a cash budget. For example, estimated cash sales for a period are based on total sales for the period and the estimated percentage of the sales that is paid for with cash.

In addition to the operations budget, the following information is necessary to prepare a cash budget:

- Estimated percentages of cash, credit sales, and sales of gift cards.
- Estimated amount of gift card redemptions.
- Estimated collection experience for credit sales—that is, when the credit sales will be collected. For example, the collection experience may be 90 percent during the month of sale, and 10 percent in the following month.
- Estimated other cash receipts, including bank loans, sale of capital stock, and proceeds from sale of fixed assets and investments.
- Estimated payments for inventory items. For example, 10 percent of purchases may be paid during the month of purchase and 90 percent paid in the following month.
- Estimated payroll payments. A monthly payroll where all employees are paid on the last day of the month for that month means simply using the payroll expense estimates from the operations budget. Payroll distributed in any other way requires many more calculations.
- The payment schedules for other operating periods. Some operating expenses, such as utilities, are generally paid the month after they are expensed. Operating supplies are often paid for before the recognition of the expense when spa operations carry them as Supplies—Inventory. Each type of expense must be reviewed to determine when the related cash expenditure is made.

- Certain expenses (such as property taxes and insurance) are paid only once or twice a year. In these cases, the payment date, not the expense from the operations budget, should be considered.
- A schedule of debt payments (not part of the operations budget) is required to determine total debt payments.
- Additional information including, but not necessarily limited to, forecasted dividend payments and forecasted fixed asset and investment purchase

Float

The use of **float** is another element of cash management. Float is time between the subtraction or addition of cash to the company's books and the actual subtraction or addition to the company's bank account. For example, assume that Any Spa pays a supplier $1,000 on account. When the check is written, the cash is subtracted from the company's cash (general ledger) account. Assume that the check is mailed to the supplier, who receives it three days later. The supplier deposits the check the following day in its own bank, which is different from Any Spa's bank, and two days later the funds are deducted from Any Spa's bank account. Any Spa actually had use of the $1,000 for six days—from the day the check was written and deducted from the books until the day its bank paid the $1,000. This type of float is called **payment** or **disbursement float**. Any Spa benefits from this float, and any reasonable steps to increase payment float are to Any Spa's advantage.

On the other hand, when Any Spa deposits a guest's check or credit card into its bank account, it increases its cash account on the books but must wait to use the funds until its bank has received the funds from the guest's bank. This difference is called **collection float**. The difference between payment float and collection float is **net float**. Since management prefers a positive net float, it should take whatever legal actions it can (referred to as "playing the float") to increase payment float and decrease collection float.

The use of online banking, which enables the spa to view daily transactions in its bank account, allows much better management of net float. Banks generally maintain demand deposit accounts online showing "available funds." Available funds differ from the spa's general ledger cash account balance by the amount of the net float. By reviewing the bank's available funds balance daily and forecasting the future posting by the bank of the components of net float, the spa is able to pinpoint cash flow and invest the excess funds.

Statement of Cash Flows

Traditionally, the principal financial statements used by spas have been the income statement and the balance sheet. The balance sheet shows the financial position of the business at the end of the accounting period. The income statement reflects the results of operations for the accounting period. Although these statements provide extensive financial information, they do not provide answers to such questions as:

- How much cash was generated by operations?

- What amount of property and equipment was purchased during the year?
- How much long-term debt was borrowed during the year?
- What amount of funds was raised through the sale of capital stock?
- What amount of dividends was paid during the year?
- How much was invested in long-term investments during the year?

The **statement of cash flows (SCF)** is designed to answer these questions and many more as it shows the sources and uses of cash for the accounting period. The SCF shows the effects on cash of a spa's operating, investing, and financing activities for a specific accounting period of time. It explains the change in Cash for the accounting period; that is, if Cash decreases by $3,000 from January 1, 20X1 (the beginning of the accounting period), to December 31, 20X1 (the end of the accounting period), the SCF will reflect the decrease in the sum of cash from the firm's various activities.

For purposes of this statement, *cash* is defined to include both cash and cash equivalents. **Cash equivalents** are short-term, highly liquid investments such as U.S. Treasury bills and money market accounts. Firms use cash equivalents for investing funds that are temporarily not needed for operating purposes. Generally, these short-term investments are made for 90 days or less. Since cash and cash equivalents are considered the same, transfers between cash and cash equivalents are not considered cash receipts or cash disbursements for SCF purposes.

The major purpose of the SCF is to provide information regarding the cash receipts and disbursements of a business that will help users (investors, creditors, managers, and others) to:

1. Assess the spa's ability to generate positive future net cash flows. Although users of financial statements are less interested in the past than in the future, many users, especially external users, must rely on historical financial information to assess a spa's future abilities. Thus, the investor interested in future cash dividends will review the SCF to determine past sources and uses of cash to evaluate the spa's ability to pay future dividends or bonuses.

2. Assess the spa's ability to meet its obligations. Users of financial statements want to determine the firm's ability to pay its bills as they come due. If a spa has little likelihood of being able to pay its bills, then suppliers will most likely not be interested in selling the spa their goods and services.

3. Assess the difference between the spa's net income and cash receipts and disbursements. The SCF allows a user to quickly determine the major net sources of cash and how much relates to the spa's operations. Investors, creditors, and other users generally prefer spas that are able to generate cash from operations (that is, from their primary purpose for being in business), as opposed to those generating cash solely from financing and investing activities (that is, activities that are incidental to the primary purpose).

4. Assess the effect of both cash and noncash investing and financing during the accounting period. Investing activities relate to the acquisition and disposition of noncurrent assets, such as property and equipment. Financing activities

relate to the borrowing and payment of long-term debt, deferred-revenue gift cards, and sale and purchase of capital stock. Noncash activities (that is, transactions involving no cash) include such transactions as the acquisition of a spa in exchange for stock or long-term debt.

The three major user groups of the SCF are management (internal), investors (external), and creditors (external). Management may use the SCF to (1) assess the spa's liquidity, (2) assess its financial flexibility, (3) determine its dividend policy, and (4) plan investing and financing needs. Investors and creditors will most likely use the SCF to assess the spa's (1) ability to pay its bills as they come due, (2) ability to pay dividends, and (3) need for additional financing, including borrowing debt and selling capital stock.

The SCF is related to other financial statements. The statement of retained earnings reflects results of operations and dividends declared, and reconciles the Retained Earnings accounts of two successive balance sheets. Net Income from the income statement is transferred to the Retained Earnings account when the temporary accounts (revenues and expenses) are closed at the end of the accounting period. In addition, Net Income is shown on the SCF when the SCF is prepared using the indirect approach (discussed later in this chapter). Finally, the SCF indirectly reconciles most accounts on the balance sheet other than Cash by showing the sources and uses of cash.

Classification of Cash Flows

The SCF classifies cash receipts and disbursements as operating, investing, and financing activities (both **cash inflows** and **cash outflows** are included within each category):

- *Operating activities.* This category includes cash transactions related to revenues and expenses. Revenues (cash inflows) include sales of services, membership dues, and retail products sold to guests, as well as interest and dividend income. Expenses (cash outflows) are for operational cash expenditures, including payments for salaries, wages, taxes, supplies, and so forth. Interest expense is also included as an operations cash outflow.

- *Investing activities.* These activities relate primarily to cash flows from the acquisition and disposal of all noncurrent assets, especially property, equipment, and investments. Also included are cash flows from the purchase and disposal of short-term investments (marketable securities).

- *Financing activities.* These activities relate to cash flows from the issuance and retirement of debt and the issuance and repurchase of capital stock. Cash inflows include cash received from issues of stock and both short-term and long-term borrowing and the sale of gift cards. Cash outflows include repayments of loans (although paying the interest expense portion of the debt is an operating activity) and payments to owners for both dividends and any repurchase of stocks as well as the redemption of gift cards. Payments of accounts payable, taxes payable, and the various accrued expenses, such as wages payable, are not payments of loans under financing activities, but they are classified as cash outflows under operating activities.

Finally, spas engage in noncash investing and financing activities, such as the exchange of capital stock for a building. Since this represents only an exchange, no cash transaction has occurred. Therefore, these noncash activities are not shown on the SCF. However, since a major purpose of the SCF is to include financing and investing activities, and since these activities will affect future cash flows, they must be disclosed on a separate schedule of the SCF. Thus, the user of financial information is provided with a complete presentation of investing and financing activities.

Generally, cash flows from operating activities are shown first. The indirect or direct approaches (to be discussed later) may be used to show cash flows from operating activities. Cash flows from investing and financing activities follow. Individual cash outflows and inflows are shown in each section. For example, Long-Term Debt may increase by $100,000 due to payment of $50,000 and subsequent borrowing of $150,000. Each cash flow should be shown separately, rather than netting the two flows. Finally, as stated earlier, a supplementary schedule of noncash investing and financing activities to the SCF must be included.

Conversion of Accrual Income to Net Cash Flows from Operations

A major purpose of the SCF is to show net cash flows from operations. The income statement is prepared on an **accrual basis**; that is, revenues are recorded when earned, not when cash is received from guests, and expenses are recorded when incurred, not necessarily when cash is disbursed. Consequently, there may be little correlation between net income and cash flow.

There are two methods of reporting cash flows from operations: the direct and the indirect methods. The **direct method** shows cash receipts from sales and cash disbursements for expenses. This method requires that each item on the income statement be converted from an accrual basis to a cash basis. An example of this conversion process for Any Spa is Payroll Expense. Assume that Any Spa reported $700,000 as Payroll Expense for 20X1, and its balance sheet's Accrued Payroll account at the beginning of the year showed $15,000 and at the end of the year showed $20,000. So even though payroll expense for the year totaled $700,000 as shown on the income statement, only $695,000 was disbursed during the year ($700,000 + $15,000 – $20,000 = $695,000). Some expenses shown on the income statement do not involve any direct cash disbursement and are simply ignored when the direct method is used. For example, depreciation expense is only an adjustment to help match expenses to revenues. Depreciation does not entail any cash, so it is ignored when the direct method is used. The same approach is taken for amortization expense and gains and losses on the sale of property and equipment.

Most spas use the indirect method because the information needed to prepare it is more readily available than that needed for using the direct method. For that reason, our major focus in this chapter will be on the indirect method.

The **indirect method** for determining net cash flows from operations starts with net income. Net income is then adjusted for noncash items included on the income statement. The most common noncash expense deducted to determine net income is depreciation. Therefore, since depreciation is subtracted to compute net income on the income statement, it is added back to net income to compute net cash flows from operating activities. Other items on the income statement that must be added or subtracted include amortization expense and gains and losses on the sale of noncurrent assets and marketable securities.

In addition, to determine the net cash flows from operating activities while using the indirect method, Any Spa's net income must be adjusted for sales and expenses that were recorded but transacted with cash during 20X1. These will be discussed in detail and illustrated in the next section.

Regardless of the method used, the result will show the same amount of net cash provided by operating activities. The Financial Accounting Standards Board (FASB) requires that firms using the indirect method report the amount of interest expense and taxes paid in separate disclosures.

Preparing the SCF

The principal sources of information needed for preparing the SCF are the income statement, the statement of retained earnings, and two successive balance sheets from the beginning and end of the accounting period, whether the accounting period is a month, quarter, year, or any other period selected. In addition, details of transactions affecting any change in noncurrent balance sheet accounts must be reviewed. For example, if a comparison of two successive balance sheets shows the Building account has increased by $500,000, the account must be analyzed to determine the reason(s) for the changes. Simply reflecting the net change of $500,000 on the SCF is generally not acceptable.

A four-step approach for preparing the SCF is as follows:

1. Determine the net cash flows from operating activities.
2. Determine the net cash flows from investing activities.
3. Determine the net cash flows from financing activities.
4. Present the cash flows by activity on the SCF.

The following paragraphs illustrate this four-step approach. The preparation of the SCF is illustrated using the indirect method for showing net cash flows from operating activities.

Step 1: Determining Net Cash Flows from Operating Activities. To determine the net cash flows from operating activities by using the indirect method, we focus first on the income statement (see Exhibit 1) by starting with net income of $184,400. Next, we need to adjust net income for items on the income statement that did not provide or use cash. In particular, depreciation expense and the gain on the sale of land are considered. Since depreciation was subtracted on the income statement to determine net income, it must be added to net income on the SCF to determine net cash flow from operating activities. Since the gain on the sale of land is not a cash flow (the proceeds from the sale of land of $300,000 are an investing activity on the SCF and will be discussed later), the gain of $100,000 must be subtracted

Exhibit 1 Any Spa Income Statement for the Year Ended December 31, 20X9

Net Revenue	
Massage	$1,446,000
Skin Care	523,000
Hair	206,000
Nail	199,800
Fitness	198,800
Food and Beverage	99,000
Memberships	174,000
Retail	515,600
Rental and Other Income	58,500
Other Operating Activities	–
Total Net Revenue	3,420,700
Cost of Goods and Direct Expenses	
Massage	874,000
Skin Care	340,500
Hair	125,900
Nail	115,000
Fitness	223,800
Food and Beverage	94,900
Health and Wellness	–
Retail	399,300
Other Operating Activities	–
Total Direct Expenses	2,173,400
Gross Margin	1,247,300
Indirect Expenses	
Indirect Operating Expenses	190,000
Indirect Support Labor	255,200
Total Indirect Expenses	445,200
Undistributed Operating Expenses	
Administrative and General	166,600
Marketing	99,100
Facility Maintenance and Utilities	128,000
Total Undistributed Operating Expenses	393,700
Income Before Fixed Charges	408,400
Fixed Charges	
Insurance	24,000
Management Fees	–
Rent	10,000
Real Estate/Personal Property Taxes	55,000
Total Fixed Charges	89,000
Income Before Depreciation, Amortization, Interest Exp. & Income Taxes	319,400
Depreciation and Amortization	82,000
Interest Expense	78,000
Gain on Sale of Property	(100,000)
Total	60,000
Income Before Income Taxes	259,400
Income Taxes	75,000
Net Income	$ 184,400

from net income on the SCF. Thus, the net cash flows from operating activities are determined at this point as follows:

Net Cash Flows from Operating Activities:		
Net Income		$184,400
Adjustments to Reconcile Net Income to Net Cash Flows from Operating Activities:		
Depreciation Expense	$ 82,000	
Gain on Sale of Investments	(100,000)	(18,000)
Partial Net Cash Flows from Operating Activities		$166,400

The second type of adjustment includes changes in current accounts from the balance sheet that affect operations. The balance sheets for Any Spa for December 31, 20X8 and 20X9 are shown in Exhibit 2. The Cash account is not considered, since we are essentially looking at all other balance sheet accounts to determine what caused the change in Cash for purposes of the SCF. The changes in the remaining current accounts and noncash current accounts are fully considered as follows:

	December 31 Balances		Change in	
Account	20X8	20X9	Account Balance	
Current Assets:				
Accounts Receivable	$310,179	$305,864	$ 4,315	(dec.)
Inventory—Retail	104,586	110,900	6,314	(inc.)
Inventory—Professional	21,564	23,000	1,436	(inc.)
Inventory—Other	2,541	2,091	450	(dec.)
Prepaid Expenses	45,127	55,130	10,003	(inc)
Deferred Income Taxes —Current	5,421	6,200	779	(inc.)
Other Assets:				
Deferred Income Taxes —NonCurrent	45,125	50,000	4,875	(inc.)
Other Assets	65,000	50,000	15,000	(dec.)
Current Liabilities:				
Accounts Payable	25,685	20,911	4,774	(dec.)
Sales Tax Payable	1,149	1,209	60	(inc.)
Gratuities Payable	2,856	4,567	1,711	(inc.)
Accrued Expenses	45,235	35,689	9,546	(dec.)
Income Taxes Payable	85,000	52,000	33,000	(dec.)
Customer Deposits	45,600	36,000	9,600	(dec.)

A brief explanation follows for each of the above current accounts, including how the change affects net cash flows from operating activities.

Accounts receivable relate directly to sales revenue, which was $3,420,700 for Any Spa for 20X9. Sales on account result in cash inflows when the guests pay their bills; however, under accrual accounting, the sale is recorded when services are provided. Most of the sales during 20X9 resulted in cash as the guests paid their accounts, but at year-end, the Accounts Receivable account balance was $305,864. The beginning of the year Accounts Receivable was $310,179, resulting in a decrease of $4,315. In preparing the SCF, we need to show a decrease in Accounts

Exhibit 2 Any Spa Balance Sheets for December 31 of 20X8 and 20X9

Assets

	Balance December 31, 20X8	Balance December 31, 20X9	Change in Assets—Increase (Decrease)
CURRENT ASSETS			
Cash in Bank	$ 245,600	$ 545,600	$ 300,000
Accounts Receivable			
Credit Cards	65,056	55,100	(9,956)
Members	200,000	210,897	10,897
Resort Guests	45,123	39,867	(5,256)
Total Acct's Receivable	310,179	305,864	(4,315)
Inventories			
Retail	104,586	110,900	6,314
Professional	21,564	23,000	1,436
Other	2,541	2,091	(450)
Prepaid Expenses	45,127	55,130	10,003
Deferred Income Taxes, Current	5,421	6,200	779
Other Current Assets	1,000	1,000	–
Total Current Assets	$ 736,018	$1,049,785	$ 313,767
PROPERTY AND EQUIPMENT			
Land	1,000,000	800,000	(200,000)
Buildings	4,500,125	4,500,125	–
Leaseholds and Leasehold Improvements	450,000	668,947	218,947
Construction in Progress	145,236	–	(145,236)
Furniture, Fixtures, & Equipment	1,546,000	1,600,000	54,000
Automobiles	46,851	46,851	–
Total Property and Equipment	7,688,212	7,615,923	(72,289)
Less: Accumulated Depreciation	(1,254,800)	(1,336,800)	(82,000)
Net Property and Equipment	6,433,412	6,279,123	(154,289)
OTHER ASSETS			
Security and Lease Deposits	65,000	65,000	–
Intangibles	100,000	100,000	–
Deferred Income Taxes, Noncurrent	45,125	50,000	4,875
Other Assets	65,000	50,000	(15,000)
Total Other Assets	275,125	265,000	(10,125)
TOTAL ASSETS	$7,444,555	$7,593,908	$ 149,353

(continued)

Exhibit 2 *(continued)*

Liabilities and Owners' Equity	Balance December 31, 20X8	Balance December 31, 20X9	Change in Liabilities—Increase (Decrease)
CURRENT LIABILITIES			
Accounts Payable	$ 25,685	$ 20,911	$ (4,774)
Sales Tax Payable	1,149	1,209	60
Gratuities Payable	2,856	4,567	1,711
Current Portion of Long-Term Debt	55,000	60,000	5,000
Income Taxes Payable	85,000	52,000	(33,000)
Accrued Expenses	45,235	35,689	(9,546)
Deferred Revenue—Gift Certificates	60,000	60,000	–
Customer Deposits	45,600	36,000	(9,600)
Other Current Liabilities	5,635	5,635	–
Total Current Liabilities	326,160	276,011	(50,149)
LONG-TERM LIABILITIES			
Notes Payable	1,555,000	1,500,000	(55,000)
Less: Current Portion—Notes Payable	(55,000)	(60,000)	(5,000)
Long-Term Deferred Revenue—Gift Cards	225,552	300,654	75,102
Less: Current Portion Deferred Revenue—Gift Cards	(60,000)	(60,000)	–
Total Long-Term Liabilities	1,665,552	1,680,654	15,102
OWNERS' EQUITY			
Common Stock	4,000,000	4,000,000	–
Retained Earnings	1,452,843	1,637,243	184,400
Total Owners' Equity	5,452,843	5,637,243	184,400
TOTAL LIABILITIES AND OWNERS' EQUITY	$7,444,555	$7,593,908	$149,353

Receivable of $4,315, which is added to Net Income as an increase in cash to determine net cash flows from operating activities.

The change in the balances of the inventory accounts is an increase of $6,314 in Inventory—Retail; and increase of $1,436 in Inventory—Professional inventory; and a decrease of $450 in Inventory—Other, amounting to a net total $7,300. The $7,300 increase in inventory is a result of purchasing inventory items that were not sold or consumed, resulting in a decrease in cash flows from operating activities.

The $10,003 increase in Prepaid Expenses represents cash payments in the excess of related items (such as insurance expense), which therefore results in a cash outflow.

The decrease in Other Assets could be the write-off on the income statement of this other asset. Thus, expense would be recorded for $15,000 without a related cash outflow this year and the expense must be added to net income to arrive at cash flow from operations.

The $4,774 decrease in Accounts Payable represents the difference between purchases on account and cash paid to suppliers during 20X9. A decrease in Accounts Payable means the amount of cash paid was more than the amount of purchases. Thus, the $4,774 increase in Accounts Payable must be deducted from the accrual basis net income to determine net cash flows from operating activities.

The $60 increase in Sales Tax Payable represents the difference between tax paid to the state and taxes collected. An increase in sales tax payable means the amount of cash paid was more than the amount collected from customers.

Gratuities Payable increased $1,711, representing tips that were collected from guests that were not paid to the technicians and must be added back to the accrual basis net income to determine net cash flows from operating activities.

The decrease in the Accrued Expenses account of $9,546 represents the difference between accrual basis costs and actual cash payments. Accrued Expenses include such expenses as payroll, etc.

The decrease of $33,000 in Income Taxes Payable represents the difference between the accrual basis income taxes of $75,000, shown on the condensed income statement of the Any Spa, and the taxes actually paid to the taxing authorities, adjusted for the changes in deferred taxes. The details of the account for deferred income taxes are beyond the scope of this text.

The decrease in Customer Deposits of $9,600 is a result of deposits being converted to sales revenue in 20X9 and must be deducted from net cash flow from operating activities.

Exhibit 3 shows the complete SCF for Any Spa. The net cash flows from operating activities section of that SCF reveals how the above information is handled.

In general, the rules for accounting for changes in current accounts in determining net cash flows provided by operating activities are as follows:

- A decrease in a current asset is added to net income.
- An increase in a current asset is deducted from net income.
- A decrease in a current liability is deducted from net income.
- An increase in a current liability is added to net income.

Step 2: Determining Net Cash Flows from Investing Activities. Step 2 of the four-step approach to preparing an SCF focuses on investing activities. In general, attention must be directed to noncurrent assets of Any Spa.

An analysis reveals a sale of land of $300,000 and a purchase of furniture, fixtures, and equipment in the amount of $54,000. Also, at the end of 20X8, Any Spa was in the process of adding additional building space, which was reflected as Construction in Progress—Building in the amount of $145,236. At the end of 20X9,

Exhibit 3 Any Spa Statement of Cash Flows for the Year Ended December 31, 20X9

Net Cash Flow From Operating Activities		
Net Income		$ 184,400
Adjustments to Reconcile Net Income to Net Cash Flows from Operating Activities		
Depreciation and Amortization	$ 82,000	
Gain on Disposal of Land	(100,000)	
Decrease in Accounts Receivable	4,315	
Increase in Retail Inventory	(6,314)	
Increase in Professional Inventory	(1,436)	
Decrease in Other Inventory	450	
Increase in Prepaid Expenses	(10,003)	
Increase in Deferred Income Taxes—Current	(779)	
Increase in Deferred Income Taxes—Non-Current	(4,875)	
Decrease in Other Assets	15,000	
Decrease in Accounts Payable	(4,774)	
Increase in Sales Tax Payable	60	
Increase in Gratuities Payable	1,711	
Decrease in Income Taxes Payable	(33,000)	
Decrease in Accrued Expenses	(9,546)	
Decrease in Customer Deposits	(9,600)	(76,791)
Net Cash Flow From Operating Activities		107,609
Net Cash Flow From Investing Activities		
Sale of Land	300,000	
Decrease in Construction in Progress	145,236	
Increase in Leasehold Improvements	(218,947)	
Purchase of Furniture, Fixtures, & Equipment	(54,000)	
Net Cash Flow From Investing Activities		172,289
Net Cash Flow From Financing Activities		
Payment of Long-Term Debt	(55,000)	
Increase in Deferred Revenue—Gift Cards	75,102	
Net Cash Flow From Financing Activities		20,102
Net Increase in Cash During 20X9		$ 300,000
Cash at the beginning of 20X9		245,600
Cash at the end of 20X9		$ 545,600

Supplementary Disclosure of Cash Flow Information

Cash paid during the year for:	
Interest	$ 78,000
Income Taxes	$ 102,346

the construction was completed and the construction in progress of $145, 236 plus the additional expenditures in 20X9 of $73,711 amounted to $218,947 in leasehold improvements placed in service.

Any Spa's final noncurrent account is Accumulated Depreciation, which increased by $82,000, the exact amount of depreciation expense for the year. Because depreciation does not affect cash, under the indirect method the $82,000 is added back to the accrual basis net income as discussed under Step 1. The change in no way affects investing activities of Any Spa.

Now that the noncurrent asset accounts of the Any Spa have been analyzed, look at the investing activities section of Exhibit 3.

Step 3: Determining Net Cash Flows from Financing Activities. To determine the net cash flows from financing activities, we must turn our attention to the noncurrent liabilities and owners' equity accounts. First, the change in the Long-Term Debt (LTD) account is a decrease of $55,000.

Any Spa did not borrow any additional funds; therefore, the $55,000 reduction in LTD had to be due to payment of LTD. The $55,000 payment is a cash outflow from financing activities.

The total of current portion and long-term portion of Deferred Revenue—Gift Cards should be used to calculate the amount of cash flow from the sale and redemption of gift cards. For the sake of simplicity, we have included both the current and long-term portion of Deferred Revenue—Gift Cards on the Any Spa balance sheet. The increase in Deferred Revenue—Gift Cards of $75,102 reflects the amount of cash generated from the sale of gift cards less redemptions and must be added to net cash flows from financing activities (see the financing activities in Exhibit 3).

Step 4: Presenting Cash Flows by Activity on the SCF. We now are ready to prepare the SCF based on the analysis in Steps 1 through 3. The three activities show cash flows as follows:

Operating activities provided cash	$107,609
Investing activities provided cash	172,289
Financing activities provided cash	20,102
Total	$300,000

The result is a bottom line of $300,000 cash inflow for Any Spa's operating activities, investing activities, and financing activities.

In the preparation of the SCF, the net increase in cash of Any Spa per the SCF is added to Any Spa's Cash account at the beginning of 20X8 to equal the Cash account at the end of 20X9. The $300,000 net increase in the Cash account per the SCF equals the $300,000 increase in cash per the Any Spa's successive balance sheets. This does not *prove* that the SCF is prepared correctly; however, if the $300,000 increase per the SCF had *not* been equal to the change per the successive balance sheets, we would know that we had improperly prepared the SCF. We would then need to locate our mistake and make the correction. Thus, this is at least a partial check on the SCF's accuracy.

Interpreting the Results. Any Spa's SCF lends insight to the user as follows:

- While net income increased by $184,400, cash flows from operations increased by only $107,609. The major differences are the depreciation expense of $82,000 and the gain on sale of land of $100,000.
- Cash flows from the sale of the land were sufficient to allow Any Spa to (1) pay off LTD of $55,000, (2) pay for leasehold improvements in the amount of $73,711, and (3) purchase $54,000 of furniture, fixtures, and equipment.
- The SCF reflects that $55,000 of debt was retired and that no additional funds were borrowed on a long-term basis. However, Deferred Revenue—Gift Cards increased in the amount of $75,102.

Accounting for Other Transactions

The preparation of the SCF for Any Spa was reasonably straightforward. Now we turn our attention to additional situations that may be encountered and that would have to be considered in preparing the SCF.

First, consider a possible sale of investments for $150,000 that originally cost $200,000. The result is a $50,000 loss on the sale. On the SCF, the $50,000 loss would be added into the cash flows from operating activities section, as the $50,000 loss on sale of investments would have been subtracted on the income statement to determine net income. Also, the proceeds of $150,000 received from the sale would be reported as sale of investments of $150,000 in the investing activities section of the SCF.

Second, consider the current asset account Marketable Securities. This account is used for investments with an expected life of less than one year. Still, the account reflects investments, and accounting for changes in this account would be the same as that for the Investment account. Proceeds from the sale of marketable securities or the cost of the purchase of marketable securities would be reported on the investing activities section of the SCF. Any gain or loss on the sale of marketable securities would be included in the operating activities section of the SCF.

Third, consider amortization expense. **Amortization expense** is the write-off of an intangible asset such as franchise costs or goodwill. Like depreciation, amortization is a noncash expense subtracted to determine net income; therefore, it must be added to net income to determine the net cash flows provided by operating activities.

Fourth, consider the sale of property and equipment. Assume a spa sells equipment for $500 and that the equipment originally cost $1,500 but had been depreciated over the years by $1,300. The gain on the sale would be $300, which is the difference between the proceeds of $500 and the net book value of $200. The gain on the sale would be reported on the income statement as an addition to income, yet the gain is *not* cash, and neither is the sale part of operations. Therefore, the gain on the sale must be subtracted from net income in the operating activities section of the SCF. In addition, the proceeds of $500 is an increase in cash that is included in the investing activities section of the SCF. If the equipment had been sold for only $100, however, a loss on the sale of $100 would have occurred. In this case, the loss on the sale of $100 would be added to net income in the operating activities section of the SCF and the proceeds of $100 reported in the investing activities section of the SCF.

Fifth, consider a firm's purchase of its own capital stock. Assume a spa pays $10,000 to purchase 1,000 shares of its common stock on the market. If the shares are retired, the Capital Stock account is debited. If the stock is held for future reissue, the Treasury Stock account is charged. Either way, the $10,000 expenditure would be included in the financing activities section of the SCF.

Sixth, consider the sale of stock. Assume a spa sells 300 shares of $10 par value common stock for $30 per share. Both the Common Stock and Additional Paid-In Capital accounts will be credited. The entire proceeds received should be reported in the financing activities section of the SCF as "proceeds from sale of common stock."

Finally, consider the borrowing of funds from a financial institution. Cash is received and a liability is incurred. The entire amount of cash borrowed would be shown as "proceeds from loan" in the financing activities section of the SCF. As the loan was paid off, the amount paid, excluding interest expense, would be reported in the financing activities section. Generally, amounts due within one year of the balance sheet date are reported on the balance sheet as Current Maturities of Long-Term Debt. This reclassification of long-term debt does *not* affect cash. Only the payment of the debt affects the cash flows. However, consider a spa's comparative balance sheet at December 31, 20X2, which reflects the following:

	Dec. 31	
	20X1	20X2
Current Maturities of Long-Term Debt	$ 20,000	$ 20,000
Long-Term Debt (LTD)	$800,000	$900,000

The Current Maturities account is a current liability account, while the LTD account is a noncurrent liability account. By definition, the amount of a current liability as of December 31, 20X1, must be paid during 20X2. If you had the above comparative information and nothing more, the analysis would reflect the payment of LTD of $20,000 and funds borrowed of $120,000.

The rationale is that the current maturities of LTD of $20,000 as of December 31, 20X1, *was paid* in 20X2. Remember, this was a current liability as of December 31, 20X1. Therefore, the $20,000 balance in current maturities of LTD as of December 31, 20X2, had to be a reclassification of LTD of $20,000 during 20X2. Finally, since the LTD account was reduced by $20,000 during 20X2, and the December 31, 20X2, balance was $900,000, we would assume the difference of $120,000 had to be due to the borrowing of funds on a long-term basis.

Summary

Cash is a very important asset for spa operations. Although it may not earn interest, cash is used to pay debts, make other disbursements, and facilitate guest/customer transactions. Management must try to minimize the operation's cash holdings by investing them in revenue-producing assets, while at the same time not jeopardizing its operations. This chapter highlighted a number of cash management tools including cash budgets, the treatment of other current assets, and an integrated cash system.

A fairly detailed discussion of gift card sales including the accounting for deferred current and noncurrent gift card liabilities was provided. Gift card breakage was defined and the accounting for breakage was illustrated.

Cash budgets are formulated to estimate the operation's future cash position. Two approaches, the cash receipts and disbursements approach and the adjusted net income approach, estimate the cash balance at the end of the period and give management the information necessary for planning.

The cash receipts and disbursements method is a direct approach that examines all cash inflows and outflows. Items found in this budget might include the amount of cash sales in the period, collection of accounts receivable, dividends and interest received, the operating expenses that were paid for during the period, and dividends paid. This type of budget is most useful for short-term periods because the estimates upon which it is based are less reliable the further the projections are made into the future.

The adjusted net income approach to cash budgeting is used for periods of over six months. The projected operations for each future year are adjusted to reflect cash flows. This approach also considers any expected changes in current accounts and any capital expenditures. Management should examine excess funds and determine the appropriate way to invest them.

Management must also monitor the activity in other current accounts in order to optimize the operation's liquidity position. Accounts receivable should be analyzed to ensure their timely collection. Inventory is expensive to store but is valuable to operations, so it should also be monitored. This is often done by analyzing the turnover ratio. Current liabilities should be studied with special consideration given to trade discounts. All of these procedures will aid management in cash control and overall operational efficiency.

The SCF is an FASB-mandated financial statement that must be issued with other financial statements released to external users. It reflects the inflow and outflow of cash for a period of time.

The SCF must show operating, investing, and financing activities. Operating activities reflect cash flows as they relate to revenues, expenses, and gift card sales and redemptions. Investing activities relate to changes in marketable securities and noncurrent asset accounts. Commonly included in these activities are the purchase and sale of property and equipment. Financing activities relate to payments of dividends payable and long-term debt, borrowing of long-term debt, and sale of capital stock. The net sum of the three activities shown on the SCF must equal the change in the cash amount shown on the two successive balance sheets.

There are two basic approaches to preparing the SCF—the direct and indirect methods. The difference between the two approaches is reflected only in the operating activities section of the SCF. The direct approach shows the direct sources of cash, such as cash receipts from sales, and direct uses of cash, such as disbursements for payroll. The indirect approach starts with net income and adjusts it to account for noncash transactions. Other adjustments for the indirect approach are the changes in current accounts related to operations. Most spas use the indirect approach because it is easier to prepare.

Key Terms

accrual basis accounting—System of reporting revenues and expenses in the period in which they are considered to have been earned or incurred, regardless of the actual time of collection or payment.

adjusted net income approach—One of two basic approaches to cash budgeting. It is generally preferable for budgeting cash for periods longer than six months.

amortization expense — The write-off of an intangible asset such as franchise costs or goodwill.

audit trail— A trail of documentation that is provided by an accounts payable voucher system.

bank reconciliation—A procedure that provides additional control over cash by finding and explaining any differences between the bank's cash balance and the cash balance (demand deposits) in the spa's books.

cash budget—Management's detailed plan for cash receipts and disbursements.

cash equivalents—Short-term, highly liquid investments such as U.S. Treasury bills and money market accounts.

cash float—The difference in the cash balance on the spa's general ledger cash account and the bank account.

cash flow—A stream of receipts (inflows) and disbursements (outflows) resulting from operational activities or investments.

cash inflows—Cash received.

cash management—The management of a spa operation's cash balances (currency and demand deposits), cash flow (cash receipts and disbursements), and short-term investments in securities.

cash outflows—Cash disbursed.

cash receipts and disbursements approach—One of two basic approaches to cash budgeting. It shows the direct sources of cash receipts and the direct uses of cash.

check request—Form used when items must be purchased within a shorter time frame than is available to generate a purchase order.

collection float—The time between when a spa deposits a guest's check (increasing its cash account on the books) and when the spa can use the funds (that is, when the bank receives the funds from the guest's bank).

direct method—One of two methods for converting net income to net cash flow from operations. This method shows cash receipts from sales and cash disbursements for expenses and requires that each item on the income statement be converted from an accrual basis to a cash basis.

disbursement float—See payment float.

effective cost—The true cost when all elements are considered.

electronic funds transfer (EFT)— A method of distributing cash electronically, without sending a hard copy of a check through the banking system's check-clearing process.

float—The time between the subtraction or addition of cash to the spa's books and the actual subtraction or addition to the spa's bank account.

gift card breakage—Term that refers to the issue of unused gift cards in the retail community.

imprest basis—Method of maintaining funds by replenishing the amount of disbursements since the previous replenishment.

income flow—Flow that results from operations generating revenues and incurring expenses. These flows are shown on the income statement and reflect the results of operations.

indirect method—One of two methods for converting net income to net cash flow from operations. This method starts with net income and then adjusts for noncash items included on the income statement.

lockbox system—A system used to speed the flow of cash from accounts receivable to the spa's bank accounts, consisting of a post office box from which bank personnel collect all incoming mail and deposit any checks directly in the spa's account with the bank.

net float—The difference between payment float and collection float.

payment float—The time between when a spa writes a check (decreasing its cash account on the books) and when the funds are actually deducted from the spa's bank account. Also called disbursement float.

petty cash—Small fund of cash used primarily to pay for miscellaneous expenditures.

statement of cash flows—A financial statement that explains the change in cash for the accounting period by showing the effects on cash of a business's operating, investing, and financing activities for the accounting period.

trade credit—Term for credit offered by suppliers who do not charge interest to hospitality operations for amounts owed in the normal course of business.

transaction motive—The reasoning that most operations maintain minimum balances in their checking accounts to cover checks drawn.

working capital—Current assets minus current liabilities. Also known as net working capital.

Review Questions

1. What are three items that exemplify the differences between income and cash flows?
2. What are the two different types of cash budget formats? In what circumstances would you use each one?

3. What are some informational items needed to prepare a cash budget using the cash receipts and disbursements approach?
4. What should management consider when investing excess cash?
5. Why must you analyze other current asset accounts when using the adjusted net income approach to cash budgeting?
6. How soon should you turn delinquent accounts receivable over to a collection agency? Why?
7. What is the value of a lockbox system to a hospitality operation?
8. Why are gift card sales not immediately accounted for as sales?
9. What is gift card breakage?
10. How do different users of the SCF use this statement?
11. What are the three major classifications of cash flows in the SCF?
12. How are changes in the various current balance sheet accounts shown on an SCF prepared using the indirect approach?

Chapter 10 Outline

Relationship of Capital Budget to Operations Budget
Types of Capital Budgeting Decisions
Time Value of Money
Cash Flow in Capital Budgeting
Capital Budgeting Models
- Accounting Rate of Return
- Payback
- Net Present Value Model
- Internal Rate of Return
- Comparison of NPV and IRR Models

Mutually Exclusive Projects with Different Lives
Capital Rationing
Use of Capital Budgeting Models in the Lodging Industry
Leasing
- Advantages and Disadvantages of Leases
- Provisions of Lease Contracts

Lease Accounting
- Classification of Leases
- Operating Leases
- Capital Leases
- Illustration of Accounting for Capital Leases

Leasehold Improvements
Leases and Their Effect on Financial Ratios
Choosing to Lease or Buy

Competencies

1. Explain the relationship of capital budgeting to operations budgeting and identify types of capital budgeting decisions. (pp. 315–316)
2. Calculate the time value of money. (pp. 316–323)
3. Describe the relevance of cash flow to capital budgeting. (pp. 323–326)
4. Describe and apply four capital budgeting models, and explain how the lives of projects affect capital decisions. (pp. 326–332)
5. Explain the need for and process of capital rationing. (pp. 332–335)
6. Describe leases and explain the function of a lease agreement. (pp. 335–336)
7. Describe some of the advantages and disadvantages of leases. (pp. 336–337)
8. Identify and describe common lease provisions. (pp. 337–338)
9. Differentiate between operating and capital leases and explain how they are accounted for. (pp. 338–345)
10. Define leasehold improvements and explain the effect that capital leases have on financial ratios. (pp. 345–346)
11. Select and use relevant information to make buy-or-lease decisions. (pp. 346–347)

10

Capital Budgeting and Lease Accounting

"ARE YOU READY to go to the movies?" Erica called out as she popped into her friend Monica's office at the Urban Day Spa. "Whoa! Guess not! What's up?"

Monica looked up from the spreadsheet she was working on, one finger still on the keypad of her calculator.

"I'm working on a justification for the purchase of a combination micro-current/light therapy unit for the spa," she explained. "The one I want costs more than $20,000, so the owner asked me to develop a ROI for the unit. I don't suppose you want to help."

"We're not going to have our girls' night out if you don't get this done, so why don't you talk me through it and I'll see if I have any insights to share," said Erica, pulling up a chair.

Monica sighed. "The owner always reminds me that she could just keep her money in a bank savings account," she said, "and that there is always risk when investing in a new piece of equipment. My payback analysis has to show that the purchase will generate sufficient payback and additional profit to prove to her that she should make the investment. She also wants to know if the spa could lease the equipment rather than buying it and whether that would be a better option."

Erica nodded. This was nothing she hadn't heard before. "Around the resort, we call our capital budget the 'Christmas list' or 'wish list,'" Erica said. "We have to submit all of our requests along with our budget for the next year. This year we included a similar piece of equipment along with some new fitness equipment for the gym. We also really need to renovate the couples relaxation lounge; it's beginning to look pretty worn."

Monica said, "I also submit my capital requests with the budget package to the owner, but she has had a chance to see a demonstration of a couple of optional pieces of equipment. So now, she wants me to update my payback analysis for the unit that I thought we had settled on before she gives me the green light to place the order. She also wants me to check out a lease option, so that she does not have to come up with $20,000 right away."

Erica explained that at the resort, the management agreement requires management to fund a capital reserve on a monthly basis, which is 2.5 percent of the resort's gross operating profit to be used for future capital projects.

"My problem," Erica said, "is that the spa has to compete for those limited funds with all of the other departments. The rooms division wants to renovate all of the suites, the kitchen wants a bunch of new equipment, and the laundry needs new washers, so it is hard for the spa to compete. The wish list is always more than the available reserves. We have to do an ROI justification for each item on our list, just as you are doing now. Ultimately, the resort general manager and the corporate office will review all of the requests and make the final recommendations to the owners. We just keep our fingers crossed, although I really think that the new equipment we requested has such a strong payback that it will be approved."

Monica nodded. "I guess I should feel lucky that I just have to deal with one owner, and not a whole corporate office, and that I don't have to compete with other departments for capital funds. I just have to figure out whether purchasing or leasing this piece of equipment is the better option. And you know what? I can let these numbers sit overnight while we make a capital decision about whether to spend our money on popcorn or candy bars at the movie."

Spas must purchase or lease property and various pieces of equipment in order to provide their services. There are virtually always limits on how much can be spent, so spa owners and managers must decide how best to use the limited resources available. Capital budgeting is the process of determining how much to spend on property and equipment and which assets to purchase. Leasing is often an alternative to purchasing that requires a much smaller initial outlay of cash. The choices of whether to purchase or lease items, and which items to purchase or lease, should be informed decisions. After reading this chapter, you should be able to answer the following questions:

1. What piece of equipment among several alternatives should be purchased?
2. What is meant by the time value of money?
3. How is cash flow computed from an investment?
4. How is payback computed?
5. What are executory costs in relation to leases?
6. How are leases classified for accounting purposes?
7. What are the criteria for capitalizing leases?
8. How are leasehold improvements amortized?
9. What is an incremental interest rate?
10. When should old equipment be replaced with new?

We will begin by comparing the capital budget with the operations budget and identifying various types of decisions involving capital budgeting. We will then focus on the concept of the time value of money and the computation of cash flow and payback from investments in property and equipment. Next, we will explain different models of capital budgets and see how they apply to choices among various kinds of projects. We will discuss leasing as an alternative to purchasing and examine the differences between operating leases and capital leases, as well as the guidelines for accounting for the different types of leasing arrangements. The chapter ends with a look at the question of leasing versus buying and how to make the better choice.

Relationship of Capital Budget to Operations Budget

The operations budget is a detailed operating plan that includes all revenues and expenses that appear on the income statement and related subsidiary schedules. Parts of it are used on a daily basis to help management plan and achieve goals.

By contrast, the capital budget is a plan for the acquisition of assets such as equipment and property. Spa ownership and management must carefully consider additions or changes in fixed assets in order to operate their businesses effectively. Most projects are evaluated based on their costs and corresponding revenues or cost savings. Projects that generate the most money for the spa should be accepted and the others may be rejected.

Capital budgeting is appropriate in a number of decision-making processes. It can be used when purchasing equipment to meet government standards or to replace existing equipment. It is also valuable when considering the purchase of equipment that could either increase the spa's revenues or decrease its costs. In each of these cases, budgeting is performed to determine if the revenues (or cost savings) generated by the equipment are greater than the corresponding expenditures, or to decide which option is best for the operation.

Preparing the operations budget is a prerequisite to capital budgeting for equipment. If the operations budget suggests that sales will increase beyond what the present number of stations is reasonably able to accommodate, then additional equipment must be planned for. If the utilization percentage for a specialized treatment room is significantly lower than for other treatment spaces, the spa should evaluate converting that room into a more financially productive treatment station. For example, if a spa routinely turns away pedicure appointment requests because there are too few pedicure stations, the capital budget will likely include additional pedicure units.

Capital budgets are prepared not only for the current year, but also for several years into the future. Construction projects undertaken by some resort properties with a spa may take up to 30 months to complete. Even though capital budgets may be prepared for several years, they must be reviewed annually to consider the impact of changing economic conditions. The capital budget should be adjusted as new information becomes available about changes in demand for the spa operation's goods and services, technological changes, and changes in the cost of providing goods and services. Evaluating past capital budgeting decisions in light of such current information can help determine whether those projects should be continued, expanded, reduced in scope, or possibly even terminated. Such current information may also affect the capital budgeting process itself.

Types of Capital Budgeting Decisions

There are several reasons for making capital budgeting decisions. These reasons include meeting government regulations, reducing operating costs, increasing sales, replacing equipment, and maintaining or increasing quality ratings.

For example, the Occupational Safety & Health Administration (OSHA) requires certain safety equipment. A spa operation may spend several hundreds or even thousands of dollars in order to upgrade equipment to meet OSHA's requirements. Regardless of the potential profit or cost savings (if any) from this upgrading of equipment, the government regulation forces the spa to make the expenditure.

A second capital budgeting decision is acquiring equipment to reduce the operation's costs. For example, a spa may have been processing laundry by contracting with an outside laundry service. By purchasing new, more energy efficient, or bigger washers and dryers, the spa might experience significant savings.

A third capital budgeting decision is acquiring property and equipment to increase sales. For example, a resort spa may see an opportunity to increase treatment revenues by adding treatment cabanas around the spa pool or on the beach. Another example is a spa that could increase retail revenues by adding a dedicated spa boutique rather than displaying merchandise in the spa reception area.

A fourth capital budgeting decision is replacing existing equipment. This replacement may be required because the present equipment is functionally obsolete; or a number of therapist workers' compensation claims suggest that the spa should replace its fixed massage beds with hydraulic tables to reduce back injuries for therapists; or perhaps the replacement is simply more economical.

A fifth capital budgeting decision is occasionally made for the spa to maintain its quality rating as judged by rating programs such as the Mobil Spa ratings. Examples would include capital projects such as remodeling the relaxation lounges and hospitality stations that have been used heavily and are beginning to show sign of significant wear or replacing key locks in the locker rooms with electronic entry systems.

All five kinds of capital budgeting decisions require significant expenditures for property and equipment. The return on the expenditures will accrue over an extended time. The more sophisticated capital budgeting models require a comparison of current cost expenditures for the property and equipment against a future stream of funds. In order to compare current year expenditures to future years' income, the future years' income must be placed on an equal basis. The process for accomplishing this comparison recognizes the **time value of money**.

Time Value of Money

The maxim, "$100 today is worth more than $100 a year from now" is true, in part because $100 today could be invested to provide $100 plus the interest for one year in the future. While economic cycles will result in significant variations in investment returns, it must be recognized that spa owners have assumed significant financial risk and are entitled to a reasonable return on the risks they have taken.

For illustration, if the $100 can be invested at 6 percent annual interest, then the $100 will be worth $106 in one year. This is determined as follows:

Principal	+	(Principal	×	Time	×	Interest Rate)	=	Total
100	+	(100	×	1	×	.06)	=	$106

Principal is the sum of dollars at the beginning of the investment period ($100 in this case). Time is expressed in years, as long as an annual interest rate is used. The interest rate is expressed in decimal form. The interest of $6.00 plus the principal of $100 equals the amount available one year hence.

A shorter formula for calculating a future value is as follows:

$$F = A(1 + i)^n$$

where F = Future Value

A = Present Amount

i = Interest Rate

n = Number of Years

One hundred dollars invested at 6 percent for two years will yield $112.36, determined as follows:

$$F = 100(1 + .06)^2$$

$$= 100(1.1236)$$

$$= \$112.36$$

An alternative to using this formula to calculate the future value of a present amount is to use a table of future value factors, such as that found in Exhibit 1. The future value factors are based on present amounts at the end of each period. For example, the future amount of $100 two years from now at 15 percent interest is $132.25. This is determined by finding the number in the 15 percent column and the period 2 row (1.3225) and multiplying it by $100.

The present value of a future amount is the present amount that must be invested at x percent interest to yield the future amount. For example, what is the present value of $100 one year from now when the interest rate is 6 percent? The formula to determine the present value of the future amount is:

$$P = F \frac{1}{(1 + i)^n}$$

where P = Present Amount

F = Future Amount

i = Interest Rate

n = Number of Years

Therefore, the present value of $100 one year from now (assuming an interest rate of 6 percent) is $94.33, determined as follows:

Exhibit 1 Table of Future Value Factors for a Single Cash Flow

$FV_{n,k} = (1 + k)^n$

Number of Periods	1%	2%	3%	4%	5%	6%	7%	8%	9%	10%	12%	14%	15%	16%	18%	20%	22%	24%	26%	28%	30%	35%
1	1.0100	1.0200	1.0300	1.0400	1.0500	1.0600	1.0700	1.0800	1.0900	1.1000	1.1200	1.1400	1.1500	1.1600	1.1800	1.2000	1.2200	1.2400	1.2600	1.2800	1.3000	1.3500
2	1.0201	1.0404	1.0609	1.0816	1.1025	1.1236	1.1449	1.1664	1.1881	1.2100	1.2544	1.2996	1.3225	1.3456	1.3924	1.4400	1.4884	1.5376	1.5876	1.6384	1.6900	1.8225
3	1.0303	1.0612	1.0927	1.1249	1.1576	1.1910	1.2250	1.2597	1.2950	1.3310	1.4049	1.4815	1.5209	1.5609	1.6430	1.7280	1.8158	1.9066	2.0004	2.0972	2.1970	2.4604
4	1.0406	1.0824	1.1255	1.1699	1.2155	1.2625	1.3108	1.3605	1.4116	1.4641	1.5735	1.6890	1.7490	1.8106	1.9388	2.0736	2.2153	2.3642	2.5205	2.6844	2.8561	3.3215
5	1.0510	1.1041	1.1593	1.2167	1.2763	1.3382	1.4026	1.4693	1.5386	1.6105	1.7623	1.9254	2.0114	2.1003	2.2878	2.4883	2.7027	2.9316	3.1758	3.4360	3.7129	4.4840
6	1.0615	1.1262	1.1941	1.2653	1.3401	1.4185	1.5007	1.5869	1.6771	1.7716	1.9738	2.1950	2.3131	2.4364	2.6996	2.9860	3.2973	3.6352	4.0015	4.3980	4.8268	6.0534
7	1.0721	1.1487	1.2299	1.3159	1.4071	1.5036	1.6058	1.7138	1.8280	1.9487	2.2107	2.5023	2.6600	2.8262	3.1855	3.5832	4.0227	4.5077	5.0419	5.6295	6.2749	8.1722
8	1.0829	1.1717	1.2668	1.3686	1.4775	1.5938	1.7182	1.8509	1.9926	2.1436	2.4760	2.8526	3.0590	3.2784	3.7589	4.2998	4.9077	5.5895	6.3528	7.2058	8.1573	11.032
9	1.0937	1.1951	1.3048	1.4233	1.5513	1.6895	1.8385	1.9990	2.1719	2.3579	2.7731	3.2519	3.5179	3.8030	4.4355	5.1598	5.9874	6.9310	8.0045	9.2234	10.604	14.894
10	1.1046	1.2190	1.3439	1.4802	1.6289	1.7908	1.9672	2.1589	2.3674	2.5937	3.1058	3.7072	4.0456	4.4114	5.2338	6.1917	7.3046	8.5944	10.086	11.806	13.786	20.107
11	1.1157	1.2434	1.3842	1.5395	1.7103	1.8983	2.1049	2.3316	2.5804	2.8531	3.4785	4.2262	4.6524	5.1173	6.1759	7.4301	8.9117	10.657	12.708	15.112	17.922	27.144
12	1.1268	1.2682	1.4258	1.6010	1.7959	2.0122	2.2522	2.5182	2.8127	3.1384	3.8960	4.8179	5.3503	5.9360	7.2876	8.9161	10.872	13.215	16.012	19.343	23.298	36.644
13	1.1381	1.2936	1.4685	1.6651	1.8856	2.1329	2.4098	2.7196	3.0658	3.4523	4.3635	5.4924	6.1528	6.8858	8.5994	10.699	13.264	16.386	20.175	24.759	30.288	49.470
14	1.1495	1.3195	1.5126	1.7317	1.9799	2.2609	2.5785	2.9372	3.3417	3.7975	4.8871	6.2613	7.0757	7.9875	10.147	12.839	16.182	20.319	25.421	31.691	39.374	66.784
15	1.1610	1.3459	1.5580	1.8009	2.0789	2.3966	2.7590	3.1722	3.6425	4.1772	5.4736	7.1379	8.1371	9.2655	11.974	15.407	19.742	25.196	32.030	40.565	51.186	90.158
16	1.1726	1.3728	1.6047	1.8730	2.1829	2.5404	2.9522	3.4259	3.9703	4.5950	6.1304	8.1372	9.3576	10.748	14.129	18.488	24.086	31.243	40.358	51.923	66.542	121.71
17	1.1843	1.4002	1.6528	1.9479	2.2920	2.6928	3.1588	3.7000	4.3276	5.0545	6.8660	9.2765	10.761	12.468	16.672	22.186	29.384	38.741	50.851	66.461	86.504	164.31
18	1.1961	1.4282	1.7024	2.0258	2.4066	2.8543	3.3799	3.9960	4.7171	5.5599	7.6900	10.575	12.375	14.463	19.673	26.623	35.849	48.039	64.072	85.071	112.46	221.82
19	1.2081	1.4568	1.7535	2.1068	2.5270	3.0256	3.6165	4.3157	5.1417	6.1159	8.6128	12.056	14.232	16.777	23.214	31.948	43.736	59.568	80.731	108.89	146.19	299.46
20	1.2202	1.4859	1.8061	2.1911	2.6533	3.2071	3.8697	4.6610	5.6044	6.7275	9.6463	13.743	16.367	19.461	27.393	38.338	53.358	73.864	101.72	139.38	190.05	404.27
21	1.2324	1.5157	1.8603	2.2788	2.7860	3.3996	4.1406	5.0338	6.1088	7.4002	10.804	15.668	18.822	22.574	32.324	46.005	65.096	91.592	128.17	178.41	247.06	545.77
22	1.2447	1.5460	1.9161	2.3699	2.9253	3.6035	4.4304	5.4365	6.6586	8.1403	12.100	17.861	21.645	26.186	38.142	55.206	79.418	113.57	161.49	228.36	321.18	736.79
23	1.2572	1.5769	1.9736	2.4647	3.0715	3.8197	4.7405	5.8715	7.2579	8.9543	13.552	20.362	24.891	30.376	45.008	66.247	96.889	140.83	203.48	292.30	417.54	994.66
24	1.2697	1.6084	2.0328	2.5633	3.2251	4.0489	5.0724	6.3412	7.9111	9.8497	15.179	23.212	28.625	35.236	53.109	79.497	118.21	174.63	256.39	374.14	542.80	1342.80
25	1.2824	1.6406	2.0938	2.6658	3.3864	4.2919	5.4274	6.8485	8.6231	10.835	17.000	26.462	32.919	40.874	62.669	95.396	144.21	216.54	323.05	478.90	705.64	1812.78
26	1.2953	1.6734	2.1566	2.7725	3.5557	4.5494	5.8074	7.3964	9.3992	11.918	19.040	30.167	37.857	47.414	73.949	114.48	175.94	268.51	407.04	613.00	917.33	2447.25
27	1.3082	1.7069	2.2213	2.8834	3.7335	4.8223	6.2139	7.9881	10.245	13.110	21.325	34.390	43.535	55.000	87.260	137.37	214.64	332.95	512.87	784.64	1192.5	3303.78
28	1.3213	1.7410	2.2879	2.9987	3.9201	5.1117	6.6488	8.6271	11.167	14.421	23.884	39.204	50.066	63.800	102.97	164.84	261.86	412.86	646.21	1004.3	1550.3	4460.11
29	1.3345	1.7758	2.3566	3.1187	4.1161	5.4184	7.1143	9.3173	12.172	15.863	26.750	44.693	57.575	74.009	121.50	197.81	319.47	511.95	814.23	1285.6	2015.4	6021.15
30	1.3478	1.8114	2.4273	3.2434	4.3219	5.7435	7.6123	10.063	13.268	17.449	29.960	50.950	66.212	85.850	143.37	237.38	389.76	634.82	1025.9	1645.5	2620.0	8128.55
40	1.4889	2.2080	3.2620	4.8010	7.0400	10.286	14.974	21.725	31.409	45.259	93.051	188.88	267.86	378.72	750.38	1469.8	2847.0	5455.9	10347.	19427.	36118.9	*
50	1.6446	2.6916	4.3839	7.1067	11.467	18.420	29.457	46.902	74.358	117.39	289.00	700.23	1083.7	1670.7	3927.4	9100.4	20797.	46890.	*	*	*	*
60	1.8167	3.2810	5.8916	10.520	18.679	32.988	57.946	101.26	176.03	304.48	897.60	2595.9	4384.0	7370.2	20555.	56348.	*	*	*	*	*	*

$^*FV_{n,k} > 99,999$

$$P = 100 \frac{1}{(1 + .06)^1}$$
$$= 100(.9433)$$
$$= \$94.33$$

The present value of $100 two years from now (assuming an interest rate of 6 percent) is $79.72, determined as follows:

$$P = 100 \frac{1}{(1 + .06)^2}$$
$$= 100(.8900)$$
$$= \$89.00$$

An alternative to using this formula to calculate the present value of a future amount is to use a table of present value factors, such as that found in Exhibit 2. The present value factors in Exhibit 2 are based on future amounts at the end of the period. For example, the present value of $100 a year from now at 6 percent interest is $94.34. This value is determined by finding the number in the 6 percent column and the period 1 row (0.9434) and multiplying it by $100. The present value of $100 today is simply $100.

Most capital investments provide a stream of revenues for several years. When the amounts are the same and at equal intervals, such as the end of each year, the stream is called an annuity. Exhibit 3 shows the calculation of the present value of an annuity (at 6 percent) of $10,000 due at the end of each year for five years. The present value factors used in the calculation are from the table in Exhibit 2.

The present value of an annuity will vary significantly based on the interest rate (also called the **discount rate**) and the timing of the future receipts. Everything else being the same, the higher the discount rate, the lower the present value. Likewise, everything else being the same, the more distant the revenues, the smaller the present value.

An alternative to multiplying each future amount by the present value factor from the present value table in Exhibit 2 is to sum the present factors and make one multiplication. This is illustrated in Exhibit 4. Thus, the $42,124 calculated in Exhibit 4 equals the calculation performed in Exhibit 3.

Rather than using the present values from Exhibit 2, present values for an annuity are provided in Exhibit 5. As a check on your understanding of the present value of an annuity table, locate the present value factor for five years and 6 percent. As you would expect, it is 4.2124. Thus, the present value for an annuity table is nothing more than a summation of present value factors from Exhibit 2. However, this table of present value factors for an annuity will save much time, especially when streams of revenues for several years must be calculated.

A problem that calls for the use of both present value factors (Exhibit 2) and present value factors for an annuity (Exhibit 5) is presented in Exhibit 6. This problem is solved by treating the stream of receipts as a $10,000 annuity and two separate payments of $5,000 and $10,000 due at the end of years two and four, respectively.

Exhibit 2 Table of Present Value Factors for a Single Cash Flow

$PV_{n,k} = 1/(1 + k)^n$

Number of Periods	1%	2%	3%	4%	5%	6%	7%	8%	9%	10%	12%	14%	15%	16%	18%	20%	22%	24%	26%	28%	30%	35%
1	.9901	.9804	.9709	.9615	.9524	.9434	.9346	.9259	.9174	.9091	.8929	.8772	.8696	.8621	.8475	.8333	.8197	.8065	.7937	.7813	.7692	.7407
2	.9803	.9612	.9426	.9246	.9070	.8900	.8734	.8573	.8417	.8264	.7972	.7695	.7561	.7432	.7182	.6944	.6719	.6504	.6299	.6104	.5917	.5487
3	.9706	.9423	.9151	.8890	.8638	.8396	.8163	.7938	.7722	.7513	.7118	.6750	.6575	.6407	.6086	.5787	.5507	.5245	.4999	.4768	.4552	.4064
4	.9610	.9238	.8885	.8548	.8227	.7921	.7629	.7350	.7084	.6830	.6355	.5921	.5718	.5523	.5158	.4823	.4514	.4230	.3968	.3725	.3501	.3011
5	.9515	.9057	.8626	.8219	.7835	.7473	.7130	.6806	.6499	.6209	.5674	.5194	.4972	.4761	.4371	.4019	.3700	.3411	.3149	.2910	.2693	.2230
6	.9420	.8880	.8375	.7903	.7462	.7050	.6663	.6302	.5963	.5645	.5066	.4556	.4323	.4104	.3704	.3349	.3033	.2751	.2499	.2274	.2072	.1652
7	.9327	.8706	.8131	.7599	.7107	.6651	.6227	.5835	.5470	.5132	.4523	.3996	.3759	.3538	.3139	.2791	.2486	.2218	.1983	.1776	.1594	.1224
8	.9235	.8535	.7894	.7307	.6768	.6274	.5820	.5403	.5019	.4665	.4039	.3506	.3269	.3050	.2660	.2326	.2038	.1789	.1574	.1388	.1226	.0906
9	.9143	.8368	.7664	.7026	.6446	.5919	.5439	.5002	.4604	.4241	.3606	.3075	.2843	.2630	.2255	.1938	.1670	.1443	.1249	.1084	.0943	.0671
10	.9053	.8203	.7441	.6756	.6139	.5584	.5083	.4632	.4224	.3855	.3220	.2697	.2472	.2267	.1911	.1615	.1369	.1164	.0992	.0847	.0725	.0497
11	.8963	.8043	.7224	.6496	.5847	.5268	.4751	.4289	.3875	.3505	.2875	.2366	.2149	.1954	.1619	.1346	.1122	.0938	.0787	.0662	.0558	.0368
12	.8874	.7885	.7014	.6246	.5568	.4970	.4440	.3971	.3555	.3186	.2567	.2076	.1869	.1685	.1372	.1122	.0920	.0757	.0625	.0517	.0429	.0273
13	.8787	.7730	.6810	.6006	.5303	.4688	.4150	.3677	.3262	.2897	.2292	.1821	.1625	.1452	.1163	.0935	.0754	.0610	.0496	.0404	.0330	.0202
14	.8700	.7579	.6611	.5775	.5051	.4423	.3878	.3405	.2992	.2633	.2046	.1597	.1413	.1252	.0985	.0779	.0618	.0492	.0393	.0316	.0254	.0150
15	.8613	.7430	.6419	.5553	.4810	.4173	.3624	.3152	.2745	.2394	.1827	.1401	.1229	.1079	.0835	.0649	.0507	.0397	.0312	.0247	.0195	.0111
16	.8528	.7284	.6232	.5339	.4581	.3936	.3387	.2919	.2519	.2176	.1631	.1229	.1069	.0930	.0708	.0541	.0415	.0320	.0248	.0193	.0150	.0082
17	.8444	.7142	.6050	.5134	.4363	.3714	.3166	.2703	.2311	.1978	.1456	.1078	.0929	.0802	.0600	.0451	.0340	.0258	.0197	.0150	.0116	.0061
18	.8360	.7002	.5874	.4936	.4155	.3503	.2959	.2502	.2120	.1799	.1300	.0946	.0808	.0691	.0508	.0376	.0279	.0208	.0156	.0118	.0089	.0045
19	.8277	.6864	.5703	.4746	.3957	.3305	.2765	.2317	.1945	.1635	.1161	.0829	.0703	.0596	.0431	.0313	.0229	.0168	.0124	.0092	.0068	.0033
20	.8195	.6730	.5537	.4564	.3769	.3118	.2584	.2145	.1784	.1486	.1037	.0728	.0611	.0514	.0365	.0261	.0187	.0135	.0098	.0072	.0053	.0025
21	.8114	.6598	.5375	.4388	.3589	.2942	.2415	.1987	.1637	.1351	.0926	.0638	.0531	.0443	.0309	.0217	.0154	.0109	.0078	.0056	.0040	.0018
22	.8034	.6468	.5219	.4220	.3418	.2775	.2257	.1839	.1502	.1228	.0826	.0560	.0462	.0382	.0262	.0181	.0126	.0088	.0062	.0044	.0031	.0014
23	.7954	.6342	.5067	.4057	.3256	.2618	.2109	.1703	.1378	.1117	.0738	.0491	.0402	.0329	.0222	.0151	.0103	.0071	.0049	.0034	.0024	.0010
24	.7876	.6217	.4919	.3901	.3101	.2470	.1971	.1577	.1264	.1015	.0659	.0431	.0349	.0284	.0188	.0126	.0085	.0057	.0039	.0027	.0018	.0007
25	.7798	.6095	.4776	.3751	.2953	.2330	.1842	.1460	.1160	.0923	.0588	.0378	.0304	.0245	.0160	.0105	.0069	.0046	.0031	.0021	.0014	.0006
26	.7720	.5976	.4637	.3607	.2812	.2198	.1722	.1352	.1064	.0839	.0525	.0331	.0264	.0211	.0135	.0087	.0057	.0037	.0025	.0016	.0011	.0004
27	.7644	.5859	.4502	.3468	.2678	.2074	.1609	.1252	.0976	.0763	.0469	.0291	.0230	.0182	.0115	.0073	.0047	.0030	.0019	.0013	.0008	.0003
28	.7568	.5744	.4371	.3335	.2551	.1956	.1504	.1159	.0895	.0693	.0419	.0255	.0200	.0157	.0097	.0061	.0038	.0024	.0015	.0010	.0006	.0002
29	.7493	.5631	.4243	.3207	.2429	.1846	.1406	.1073	.0822	.0630	.0374	.0224	.0174	.0135	.0082	.0051	.0031	.0020	.0012	.0008	.0005	.0002
30	.7419	.5521	.4120	.3083	.2314	.1741	.1314	.0994	.0754	.0573	.0334	.0196	.0151	.0116	.0070	.0042	.0026	.0016	.0010	.0006	.0004	.0001
35	.7059	.5000	.3554	.2534	.1813	.1301	.0937	.0676	.0490	.0356	.0189	.0102	.0075	.0055	.0030	.0017	.0009	.0005	.0003	.0002	.0001	*
40	.6717	.4529	.3066	.2083	.1420	.0972	.0668	.0460	.0318	.0221	.0107	.0053	.0037	.0026	.0013	.0007	.0004	.0002	.0001	.0001	*	*
45	.6391	.4102	.2644	.1712	.1113	.0727	.0476	.0313	.0207	.0137	.0061	.0027	.0019	.0013	.0006	.0003	.0001	.0001	*	*	*	*
50	.6080	.3715	.2281	.1407	.0872	.0543	.0339	.0213	.0134	.0085	.0035	.0014	.0009	.0006	.0003	.0001	*	*	*	*	*	*
55	.5785	.3365	.1968	.1157	.0683	.0406	.0242	.0145	.0087	.0053	.0020	.0007	.0005	.0003	.0001	*	*	*	*	*	*	*
60	.5504	.3048	.1697	.0951	.0535	.0303	.0173	.0099	.0057	.0033	.0011	.0004	.0002	.0001	*	*	*	*	*	*	*	*

*Rounds to zero

Exhibit 3 Present Value of a $10,000 Five-Year Annuity at 6 Percent

	Present Value	Years in Future 1	2	3	4	5
Amount		$10,000	$10,000	$10,000	$10,000	$10,000
	$9,434	.9434				
	8,900		.8900			
	8,396			.8396		
	7,921				.7921	
	7,473					.7473
Total	$42,124					

Exhibit 4 Shortcut Calculation of the Present Value of a $10,000 Five-Year Annuity at 6 Percent

Years from Today	Present Value Factors at 6%
1	.9434
2	.8900
3	.8396
4	.7921
5	.7473
	4.2124

4.2124 × $10,000 = $42,124

Similarly, to calculate future values of an annuity, it is simplest to refer to the table of future value factors for an annuity (Exhibit 7). For example, assume that a spa owner decides to invest $10,000 at the end of each year for five years at an annual interest rate of 10 percent, compounded annually. What will be the value of the investment at the end of year five? Using the factor for 10 percent and five periods from Exhibit 7, we can determine the answer as follows:

$10,000 × 6.1051 = $61,051

Exhibit 5 Table of Present Value Factors for an Annuity

$$PVA_{n,k} = \frac{1 - \frac{1}{(1+k)^n}}{k}$$

Number of Periods	1%	2%	3%	4%	5%	6%	7%	8%	9%	10%	12%	14%	15%	16%	18%	20%	22%	24%	26%	28%	30%	35%
1	0.9901	0.9804	0.9709	0.9615	0.9524	0.9434	0.9346	0.9259	0.9174	0.9091	0.8929	0.8772	0.8696	0.8621	0.8475	0.8333	0.8197	0.8065	0.7937	0.7813	0.7692	0.7407
2	1.9704	1.9416	1.9135	1.8861	1.8594	1.8334	1.8080	1.7833	1.7591	1.7355	1.6901	1.6467	1.6257	1.6052	1.5656	1.5278	1.4915	1.4568	1.4235	1.3916	1.3609	1.2894
3	2.9410	2.8839	2.8286	2.7751	2.7232	2.6730	2.6243	2.5771	2.5313	2.4869	2.4018	2.3216	2.2832	2.2459	2.1743	2.1065	2.0422	1.9813	1.9234	1.8684	1.8161	1.6959
4	3.9020	3.8077	3.7171	3.6299	3.5460	3.4651	3.3872	3.3121	3.2397	3.1699	3.0373	2.9137	2.8550	2.7982	2.6901	2.5887	2.4936	2.4043	2.3202	2.2410	2.1662	1.9969
5	4.8534	4.7135	4.5797	4.4518	4.3295	4.2124	4.1002	3.9927	3.8897	3.7908	3.6048	3.4331	3.3522	3.2743	3.1272	2.9906	2.8636	2.7454	2.6351	2.5320	2.4356	2.2200
6	5.7955	5.6014	5.4172	5.2421	5.0757	4.9173	4.7665	4.6229	4.4859	4.3553	4.1114	3.8887	3.7845	3.6847	3.4976	3.3255	3.1669	3.0205	2.8850	2.7594	2.6427	2.3852
7	6.7282	6.4720	6.2303	6.0021	5.7864	5.5824	5.3893	5.2064	5.0330	4.8684	4.5638	4.2883	4.1604	4.0386	3.8115	3.6046	3.4155	3.2423	3.0833	2.9370	2.8021	2.5075
8	7.6517	7.3255	7.0197	6.7327	6.4632	6.2098	5.9713	5.7466	5.5348	5.3349	4.9676	4.6389	4.4873	4.3436	4.0776	3.8372	3.6193	3.4212	3.2407	3.0758	2.9247	2.5982
9	8.5660	8.1622	7.7861	7.4353	7.1078	6.8017	6.5152	6.2469	5.9952	5.7590	5.3282	4.9464	4.7716	4.6065	4.3030	4.0310	3.7863	3.5655	3.3657	3.1842	3.0190	2.6653
10	9.4713	8.9826	8.5302	8.1109	7.7217	7.3601	7.0236	6.7101	6.4177	6.1446	5.6502	5.2161	5.0188	4.8332	4.4941	4.1925	3.9232	3.6819	3.4648	3.2689	3.0915	2.7150
11	10.3676	9.7868	9.2526	8.7605	8.3064	7.8869	7.4987	7.1390	6.8052	6.4951	5.9377	5.4527	5.2337	5.0286	4.6560	4.3271	4.0354	3.7757	3.5435	3.3351	3.1473	2.7519
12	11.2551	10.5753	9.9540	9.3851	8.8633	8.3838	7.9427	7.5361	7.1607	6.8137	6.1944	5.6603	5.4206	5.1971	4.7932	4.4392	4.1274	3.8514	3.6059	3.3868	3.1903	2.7792
13	12.1337	11.3484	10.6350	9.9856	9.3936	8.8527	8.3577	7.9038	7.4869	7.1034	6.4235	5.8424	5.5831	5.3423	4.9095	4.5327	4.2028	3.9124	3.6555	3.4272	3.2233	2.7994
14	13.0037	12.1062	11.2961	10.5631	9.8986	9.2950	8.7455	8.2442	7.7862	7.3667	6.6282	6.0021	5.7245	5.4675	5.0081	4.6106	4.2646	3.9616	3.6949	3.4587	3.2487	2.8144
15	13.8651	12.8493	11.9379	11.1184	10.3797	9.7122	9.1079	8.5595	8.0607	7.6061	6.8109	6.1422	5.8474	5.5755	5.0916	4.6755	4.3152	4.0013	3.7261	3.4834	3.2682	2.8255
16	14.7179	13.5777	12.5611	11.6523	10.8378	10.1059	9.4466	8.8514	8.3126	7.8237	6.9740	6.2651	5.9542	5.6685	5.1624	4.7296	4.3567	4.0333	3.7509	3.5026	3.2832	2.8337
17	15.5623	14.2919	13.1661	12.1657	11.2741	10.4773	9.7632	9.1216	8.5436	8.0216	7.1196	6.3729	6.0472	5.7487	5.2223	4.7746	4.3908	4.0591	3.7705	3.5177	3.2948	2.8398
18	16.3983	14.9920	13.7535	12.6593	11.6896	10.8276	10.0591	9.3719	8.7556	8.2014	7.2497	6.4674	6.1280	5.8178	5.2732	4.8122	4.4187	4.0799	3.7861	3.5294	3.3037	2.8443
19	17.2260	15.6785	14.3238	13.1339	12.0853	11.1581	10.3356	9.6036	8.9501	8.3649	7.3658	6.5504	6.1982	5.8775	5.3162	4.8435	4.4415	4.0967	3.7985	3.5386	3.3105	2.8476
20	18.0456	16.3514	14.8775	13.5903	12.4622	11.4699	10.5940	9.8181	9.1285	8.5136	7.4694	6.6231	6.2593	5.9288	5.3527	4.8696	4.4603	4.1103	3.8083	3.5458	3.3158	2.8501
21	18.8570	17.0112	15.4150	14.0292	12.8212	11.7641	10.8355	10.0168	9.2922	8.6487	7.5620	6.6870	6.3125	5.9731	5.3837	4.8913	4.4756	4.1212	3.8161	3.5514	3.3198	2.8519
22	19.6604	17.6580	15.9369	14.4511	13.1630	12.0416	11.0612	10.2007	9.4424	8.7715	7.6446	6.7429	6.3587	6.0113	5.4099	4.9094	4.4882	4.1300	3.8223	3.5558	3.3230	2.8533
23	20.4558	18.2922	16.4436	14.8568	13.4886	12.3034	11.2722	10.3711	9.5802	8.8832	7.7184	6.7921	6.3988	6.0442	5.4321	4.9245	4.4985	4.1371	3.8273	3.5592	3.3254	2.8543
24	21.2434	18.9139	16.9355	15.2470	13.7986	12.5504	11.4693	10.5288	9.7066	8.9847	7.7843	6.8351	6.4338	6.0726	5.4509	4.9371	4.5070	4.1428	3.8312	3.5619	3.3272	2.8550
25	22.0232	19.5235	17.4131	15.6221	14.0939	12.7834	11.6536	10.6748	9.8226	9.0770	7.8431	6.8729	6.4641	6.0971	5.4669	4.9476	4.5139	4.1474	3.8342	3.5640	3.3286	2.8556
26	22.7952	20.1210	17.8768	15.9828	14.3752	13.0032	11.8258	10.8100	9.9290	9.1609	7.8957	6.9061	6.4906	6.1182	5.4804	4.9563	4.5196	4.1511	3.8367	3.5656	3.3297	2.8560
27	23.5596	20.7069	18.3270	16.3296	14.6430	13.2105	11.9867	10.9352	10.0266	9.2372	7.9426	6.9352	6.5135	6.1364	5.4919	4.9636	4.5243	4.1542	3.8387	3.5669	3.3305	2.8563
28	24.3164	21.2813	18.7641	16.6631	14.8981	13.4062	12.1371	11.0511	10.1161	9.3066	7.9844	6.9607	6.5335	6.1520	5.5016	4.9697	4.5281	4.1566	3.8402	3.5679	3.3312	2.8565
29	25.0658	21.8444	19.1885	16.9837	15.1411	13.5907	12.2777	11.1584	10.1983	9.3696	8.0218	6.9830	6.5509	6.1656	5.5098	4.9747	4.5312	4.1585	3.8414	3.5687	3.3317	2.8567
30	25.8077	22.3965	19.6004	17.2920	15.3725	13.7648	12.4090	11.2578	10.2737	9.4269	8.0552	7.0027	6.5660	6.1772	5.5168	4.9789	4.5338	4.1601	3.8424	3.5693	3.3321	2.8568
35	29.4086	24.9986	21.4872	18.6646	16.3742	14.4982	12.9477	11.6546	10.5668	9.6442	8.1755	7.0700	6.6166	6.2153	5.5386	4.9915	4.5411	4.1644	3.8450	3.5708	3.3330	2.8571
40	32.8347	27.3555	23.1148	19.7928	17.1591	15.0463	13.3317	11.9246	10.7574	9.7791	8.2438	7.1050	6.6418	6.2335	5.5482	4.9966	4.5439	4.1659	3.8458	3.5712	3.3332	2.8571
45	36.0945	29.4902	24.5187	20.7200	17.7741	15.4558	13.6055	12.1084	10.8812	9.8628	8.2825	7.1232	6.6543	6.2421	5.5523	4.9986	4.5449	4.1664	3.8460	3.5714	3.3333	2.8571
50	39.1961	31.4236	25.7298	21.4822	18.2559	15.7619	13.8007	12.2335	10.9617	9.9148	8.3045	7.1327	6.6605	6.2463	5.5541	4.9995	4.5452	4.1666	3.8461	3.5714	3.3333	2.8571
55	42.1472	33.1748	26.7744	22.1086	18.6335	15.9905	13.9399	12.3186	11.0140	9.9471	8.3170	7.1376	6.6636	6.2482	5.5549	4.9998	4.5454	4.1666	3.8461	3.5714	3.3333	2.8571
60	44.9550	34.7609	27.6756	22.6235	18.9293	16.1614	14.0392	12.3766	11.0480	9.9672	8.3240	7.1401	6.6651	6.2492	5.5553	4.9999	4.5454	4.1667	3.8462	3.5714	3.3333	2.8571

Exhibit 6 Present Value of a Stream of Unequal Future Receipts

Problem:

Determine the present value of receipts from an investment using a 6 percent discount factor that provides the following stream of income:

Years Hence	Amount
0	$10,000
1	10,000
2	15,000
3	10,000
4	20,000
5	10,000

Solution:

Years Hence	Amount	Annuity	Excess of Annuity
0	$10,000	$10,000	$ 0
1	10,000	10,000	0
2	15,000	10,000	5,000
3	10,000	10,000	0
4	20,000	10,000	10,000
5	10,000	10,000	0

Calculation:

Present value of amount due today	=	$10,000
Present value of the $10,000 annuity for 5 years $10,000 × 4.2124	=	42,124
Present value of $5,000 due 2 years hence $5,000 × .8900	=	4,450
Present value of $10,000 due 4 years hence $10,000 × .7921	=	7,921
Total		$64,495

Cash Flow in Capital Budgeting

With most capital budgeting decisions, an investment should be made only when the future cash flow from the investment justifies the expenditure. Therefore, the concern is with the cash flow from the proposed investment.

From the spa operation's perspective, the incremental cash flows for the specific investment are the focus, rather than the overall spa's cash flow. **Incremental cash flow** is simply the change in the cash flow of the operation resulting from the investment. Cash flow relating to an investment includes the following:

- Initial cost of investment (cash outflow)
- Investment revenues (cash inflow)
- Investment expenses except depreciation (cash outflow)

Exhibit 7 Table of Future Value Factors for an Annuity

$$FVA_{n,k} = \frac{(1 + k)^n - 1}{k}$$

Number of Periods	1%	2%	3%	4%	5%	6%	7%	8%	9%	10%	12%	14%	15%	16%	18%	20%	22%	24%	26%	28%	30%	35%
1	1.0000	1.0000	1.0000	1.0000	1.0000	1.0000	1.0000	1.0000	1.0000	1.0000	1.0000	1.0000	1.0000	1.0000	1.0000	1.0000	1.0000	1.0000	1.0000	1.0000	1.0000	1.0000
2	2.0100	2.0200	2.0300	2.0400	2.0500	2.0600	2.0700	2.0800	2.0900	2.1000	2.1200	2.1400	2.1500	2.1600	2.1800	2.2000	2.2200	2.2400	2.2600	2.2800	2.3000	2.3500
3	3.0301	3.0604	3.0909	3.1216	3.1525	3.1836	3.2149	3.2464	3.2781	3.3100	3.3744	3.4396	3.4725	3.5056	3.5724	3.6400	3.7084	3.7776	3.8476	3.9184	3.9900	4.1725
4	4.0604	4.1216	4.1836	4.2465	4.3101	4.3746	4.4399	4.5061	4.5731	4.6410	4.7793	4.9211	4.9934	5.0665	5.2154	5.3680	5.5242	5.6842	5.8480	6.0156	6.1870	6.6329
5	5.1010	5.2040	5.3091	5.4163	5.5256	5.6371	5.7507	5.8666	5.9847	6.1051	6.3528	6.6101	6.7424	6.8771	7.1542	7.4416	7.7396	8.0484	8.3684	8.6999	9.0431	9.9544
6	6.1520	6.3081	6.4684	6.6330	6.8019	6.9753	7.1533	7.3359	7.5233	7.7156	8.1152	8.5355	8.7537	8.9775	9.4420	9.9299	10.442	10.980	11.544	12.136	12.756	14.438
7	7.2135	7.4343	7.6625	7.8983	8.1420	8.3938	8.6540	8.9228	9.2004	9.4872	10.089	10.730	11.067	11.414	12.142	12.916	13.740	14.615	15.546	16.534	17.583	20.492
8	8.2857	8.5830	8.8923	9.2142	9.5491	9.8975	10.260	10.637	11.028	11.436	12.300	13.233	13.727	14.240	15.327	16.499	17.762	19.123	20.588	22.163	23.858	28.664
9	9.3685	9.7546	10.159	10.583	11.027	11.491	11.978	12.488	13.021	13.579	14.776	16.085	16.786	17.519	19.086	20.799	22.670	24.712	26.940	29.369	32.015	39.696
10	10.462	10.950	11.464	12.006	12.578	13.181	13.816	14.487	15.193	15.937	17.549	19.337	20.304	21.321	23.521	25.959	28.657	31.643	34.945	38.593	42.619	54.590
11	11.567	12.169	12.808	13.486	14.207	14.972	15.784	16.645	17.560	18.531	20.655	23.045	24.349	25.733	28.755	32.150	35.962	40.238	45.031	50.398	56.405	74.697
12	12.683	13.412	14.192	15.026	15.917	16.870	17.888	18.977	20.141	21.384	24.133	27.271	29.002	30.850	34.931	39.581	44.874	50.895	57.739	65.510	74.327	101.84
13	13.809	14.680	15.618	16.627	17.713	18.882	20.141	21.495	22.953	24.523	28.029	32.089	34.352	36.786	42.219	48.497	55.746	64.110	73.751	84.853	97.625	138.48
14	14.947	15.974	17.086	18.292	19.599	21.015	22.550	24.215	26.019	27.975	32.393	37.581	40.505	43.672	50.818	59.196	69.010	80.496	93.926	109.61	127.91	187.95
15	16.097	17.293	18.599	20.024	21.579	23.276	25.129	27.152	29.361	31.772	37.280	43.842	47.580	51.660	60.965	72.035	85.192	100.82	119.35	141.30	167.29	254.74
16	17.258	18.639	20.157	21.825	23.657	25.673	27.888	30.324	33.003	35.950	42.753	50.980	55.717	60.925	72.939	87.442	104.93	126.01	151.38	181.87	218.47	344.90
17	18.430	20.012	21.762	23.698	25.840	28.213	30.840	33.750	36.974	40.545	48.884	59.118	65.075	71.673	87.068	105.93	129.02	157.25	191.73	233.79	285.01	466.61
18	19.615	21.412	23.414	25.645	28.132	30.906	33.999	37.450	41.301	45.599	55.750	68.394	75.836	84.141	103.74	128.12	158.40	195.99	242.59	300.25	371.52	630.92
19	20.811	22.841	25.117	27.671	30.539	33.760	37.379	41.446	46.018	51.159	63.440	78.969	88.212	98.603	123.41	154.74	194.25	244.03	306.66	385.32	483.97	852.75
20	22.019	24.297	26.870	29.778	33.066	36.786	40.995	45.762	51.160	57.275	72.052	91.025	102.44	115.38	146.63	186.69	237.99	303.60	387.39	494.21	630.17	1152.2
21	23.239	25.783	28.676	31.969	35.719	39.993	44.865	50.423	56.765	64.002	81.699	104.77	118.81	134.84	174.02	225.03	291.35	377.46	489.11	633.59	820.22	1556.5
22	24.472	27.299	30.537	34.248	38.505	43.392	49.006	55.457	62.873	71.403	92.503	120.44	137.63	157.41	206.34	271.03	356.44	469.06	617.28	812.00	1067.3	2102.3
23	25.716	28.845	32.453	36.618	41.430	46.996	53.436	60.893	69.532	79.543	104.60	138.30	159.28	183.60	244.49	326.24	435.86	582.63	778.77	1040.4	1388.5	2839.0
24	26.973	30.422	34.426	39.083	44.502	50.816	58.177	66.765	76.790	88.497	118.16	158.66	184.17	213.98	289.49	392.48	532.75	723.46	982.25	1332.7	1806.0	3833.7
25	28.243	32.030	36.459	41.646	47.727	54.865	63.249	73.106	84.701	98.347	133.33	181.87	212.79	249.21	342.60	471.98	650.96	898.09	1238.6	1706.8	2348.8	5176.5
26	29.526	33.671	38.553	44.312	51.113	59.156	68.676	79.954	93.324	109.18	150.33	208.33	245.71	290.09	405.27	567.38	795.17	1114.6	1561.7	2185.7	3054.4	6989.3
27	30.821	35.344	40.710	47.084	54.669	63.706	74.484	87.351	102.72	121.10	169.37	238.50	283.57	337.50	479.22	681.85	971.10	1383.1	1968.7	2798.7	3971.8	9436.5
28	32.129	37.051	42.931	49.968	58.403	68.528	80.698	95.339	112.97	134.21	190.70	272.89	327.10	392.50	566.48	819.22	1185.7	1716.1	2481.6	3583.3	5164.3	12740.
29	33.450	38.792	45.219	52.966	62.323	73.640	87.347	103.97	124.14	148.63	214.58	312.09	377.17	456.30	669.45	984.07	1447.6	2129.0	3127.8	4587.7	6714.6	17200.
30	34.785	40.568	47.575	56.085	66.439	79.058	94.461	113.28	136.31	164.49	241.33	356.79	434.75	530.31	790.95	1181.9	1767.1	2640.9	3942.0	5873.2	8730.0	23222.
40	48.886	60.402	75.401	95.026	120.80	154.76	199.64	259.06	337.88	442.59	767.09	1342.0	1779.1	2360.8	4163.2	7343.9	12937.	22729.	39793.	69377.	*	*
50	64.463	84.579	112.80	152.67	209.35	290.34	406.53	573.77	815.08	1163.9	2400.0	4994.5	7217.7	10436.	21813.	45497.	94525.	*	*	*	*	*
60	81.670	114.05	163.05	237.99	353.58	533.13	813.52	1253.2	1944.8	3034.8	7471.6	18535.	29220.	46058.	*	*	*	*	*	*	*	*

$^*FVA_{n,k} > 99{,}999$

Exhibit 8 Cash Flows from Spa Investment

Cost of combination ultrasonic microdermabrasion and light therapy unit =	$20,000
Life of machine	3 years
Tax rate	30%
Salvage value of machine	$1,000
Annual revenues	$34,500
Related annual expenses excluding depreciation and income taxes	$15,000
Method of depreciation	Straight-line

Cash Flow Calculations

	Years		
	1	2	3
Revenues	$34,500	$34,500	$34,500
Expenses except depreciation and income taxes	15,000	15,000	15,000
Income taxes	3,950	3,950	3,950
Salvage value	---	---	1,000
Cash flow	$15,550	$15,550	$16,550

Net cash flow is determined as follows:

Cash flows from above ($15,550 × 2) + $16,550 =	$47,650
Less: Cost of machine	–20,000
Net cash flow	$27,650

(1) Income taxes:

Pre-depreciation income	$19,500
Less: depreciation	6,333 (2)
Taxable income	13,167
Tax rate	× .30
Income taxes	$ 3,950

(2) *Annual depreciation* $= \frac{\text{Cost} - \text{Salvage Value}}{\text{Life in Years}} = \frac{\$20{,}000 - \$1{,}000}{3} = \$6{,}333$

Depreciation expense results from writing off the cost of the investment; however, it is not a cash outflow and, therefore, does not affect the capital budgeting decision. It is used in determining the income taxes relating to the investment since the IRS allows depreciation to be deducted when computing taxable income.

Exhibit 8 illustrates the relevant cash flows of the example discussed in the chapter's opening story. A combination ultrasonic microdermabrasion and light therapy unit costs $20,000. The annual additional revenue is estimated based on the assumption that there will be one upgraded 50-minute facial per day (increasing the price from $120 to $170) and one additional upsell per day of an 80-minute treatment (increasing the price from $200 to $265). Using 300 productive days a year, the increase in revenues would be 300 × $50 ($15,000) for the facial plus 300 × $65 ($19,500) for the upsell, for a total of $34,500.

The assumed salvage value for this machine is $1,000; that is, we assume at the end of three years the machine can be sold for $1,000. The annual expenses are $15,000, not including depreciation and income taxes related to the annual incremental revenues of $34,500.

The annual depreciation (using the straight-line method) is $6,333 based on the cost of $20,000, an assumed salvage value of $1,000, and an assumed life of three years. The annual cash flows are $15,550 for years one and two, and $16,550 for year three as shown in Exhibit 8. The net cash flow from this capital project is the sum of the cash flows for years one through three, less the cost of the machine. Thus, $47,650 less $20,000 results in a positive net cash flow of $27,650.

Capital Budgeting Models

Managers in most businesses may use up to four capital budgeting models in making capital budgeting decisions. The models vary from simple to sophisticated and afford various advantages and disadvantages, which will be discussed and compared. The simple models are **accounting rate of return (ARR)** and **payback**, while more sophisticated models, which require the discounting of future cash flows, are **net present value (NPV)** and **internal rate of return (IRR)**. Each model is discussed and an illustration is used to show the mathematics associated with each.

Accounting Rate of Return

The ARR model considers the average annual project income (project revenues less project expenses generated by the investment) and the average investment. The calculation of ARR is simply:

$$\text{ARR} = \frac{\text{Average Annual Project Income}}{\text{Average Investment}}$$

The average annual project income is the total project income over its life divided by the number of years. Average investment is project cost plus salvage value divided by two. The proposed investment is accepted if the ARR exceeds the minimum ARR required. For example, if the minimum acceptable ARR is 40 percent, a 52 percent ARR results in project acceptance.

The ARR model can be illustrated by using the Any Spa's proposed investment in the combination microdermabrasion/light therapy unit as shown in Exhibit 9.

The total project income over the three-year period is $27,651, which results in an average annual project income of $9,217. The average investment is $10,500, determined as follows:

Exhibit 9 Proposed Investment in Combination Ultrasonic Microdermabrasion and Light Therapy Unit

Investment
Cost = $20,000

Accept/Reject Criteria
ARR = 40%
Payback = 2 years
IRR = 12%
NPV = >0

Depreciation Consideration
Salvage value = $1,000
Life in years = 3
Straight-line method

Estimated Project Revenues and Expenses

	Years		
	1	2	3
Project revenues	$34,500	$34,500	$34,500
Project expenses			
Labor (30% of revenue)	10,350	10,350	10,350
Professional product costs	4,650	4,650	4,650
Depreciation	6,333	6,333	6,333
Income taxes	3,950	3,950	3,950
Project income	$ 9,217	$ 9,217	$ 9,217
Total project income	$27,651		
Cash Flow:			
Project income	$ 9,217	$ 9,217	$ 9,217
Add: depreciation	6,333	6,333	6,333
Salvage value	–0–	–0–	1,000
Total	$15,550	$15,550	$16,550

$$\text{Average Investment} = \frac{\text{Project Cost} + \text{Salvage}}{2}$$

$$= \frac{\$20{,}000 + \$1{,}000}{2}$$

$$= \$10{,}500$$

The ARR of percent is determined as follows:

$$\text{ARR} = \frac{\text{Average Annual Project Income}}{\text{Average Investment}}$$

$$= \frac{\$9{,}217}{\$10{,}500}$$

$$= 87.8\%$$

If this spa were to use this capital budgeting model, management would invest in this equipment since the project ARR of 87.8 percent exceeds the required minimum of 40 percent.

Some managers consider ARR to be useful because it relies on accounting income and, thus, it is easy to calculate and easy to understand. However, these advantages are offset by its disadvantages: ARR fails to consider cash flows or the time value of money.

Payback

The payback model compares annual cash flows to the project cost to determine a payback period. If the calculated payback period is equal to or less than the payback objective, then the project is accepted.

The payback model is reasonably popular because it is conceptually simple. Management or, in some cases, the spa owner(s) simply sets the payback period at the determined length of time required for the operation to get its money back from the project.

The payback model is often used as a screening device in conjunction with more sophisticated models, especially in high-risk situations. Some spa operators will not consider evaluating proposed projects using the NPV or IRR approaches unless their initial review using the payback model suggests that the proposed project is viable.

When the annual cash flows are equal, the payback period is determined as follows:

$$\text{Payback Period} = \frac{\text{Project Cost}}{\text{Annual Cash Flow}}$$

When the annual cash flows are not equal, the payback period is determined differently. First, subtract as many full-year cash flows as possible from the project cost. If the numbers do not come out evenly, divide the amount remaining after all full-year cash flows have been subtracted by the cash flow for the year directly following those full-year cash flows. The payback period equals the number of years (including fractional years if applicable) it takes for cash flows to equal project cost.

Using figures from Exhibit 9, the payback period for the spa's proposed investment in equipment can be calculated as follows:

Project Cost	=	$20,000
Less Year 1 Cash Flow	–	15,500
		$ 4,500
Year 2 Cash Flow	=	$15,500
Portion of Year 2 needed to balance project cash flows with project cost:	=	$ 4,500 ÷ $15,500 = .29
Payback Period	=	1.29 years

Since the payback period of 1.29 years is less than the accept/reject criterion of two years as stated in Exhibit 9, based on the payback model, the spa would invest in the proposed project.

Exhibit 10 Comparison of Two Mutually Exclusive Projects: Payback Model

Years Hence		Project Cash Flows	
		Project A	Project B
0	(cost of the projects)	$10,000	$10,000
1	(cash inflows)	5,000	3,000
2		4,000	4,000
3		3,000	5,000
4		2,000	6,000
5		1,000	7,000
Payback Period		2.33 years	2.60 years
Excess Cash Flow: Cash flow generated beyond payback period		$5,000	$15,000
Present value of all cash inflows discounted at 6%		$13,127	$20,572

Disadvantages to the payback model that require careful consideration are that it fails to consider either the time value of money or the project flows after the payback period. The latter disadvantage is readily apparent when comparing two mutually exclusive projects (A and B) as shown in Exhibit 10. Based on the payback method, project A would be accepted rather than project B, because the payback period of 2.33 years for project A is less than 2.6 years for project B. However, the excess cash flow is $10,000 larger for project B. The calculation of the present value of all cash flows of $13,127 and $20,572 for projects A and B, respectively, is convincing. If this is not readily clear, it will be as we now turn to consider the net present value model.

Net Present Value Model

Both the NPV and IRR models overcome the weaknesses of the previous models in that they consider the time value of money over the projected life of the capital project. The NPV approach discounts cash flows to their present value. The net present value is calculated by subtracting the project cost from the present value of the discounted cash flow stream. The project is accepted if the NPV is greater than zero. If the capital budgeting decision considers mutually exclusive alternatives, the alternative with the highest NPV is accepted and other alternatives are rejected.

The advantage of the NPV model over the ARR model is the consideration of cash flows and the time value of money. The advantage of the NPV model over the payback model is the time value of money consideration with NPV.

Some managers have suggested that a disadvantage of the NPV model is its complexity. This argument may have been convincing to business operations in the past, but as the spa industry continues to mature, the best methods of capital budgeting must be used to optimize decision-making. Furthermore, the use of

Exhibit 11 Illustration of NPV Proposed Purchase by Spa

Years Hence	Cash Flows	Present Value Factors (6%)	Present Value of Cash Flow
0	($20,000)	1	(20,000)
1	15,500	0.94339623	14,623
2	15,500	0.88999644	13,795
3	16,500	0.83961928	13,854
	Net Present Value		$22,271

electronic spreadsheet programs, such as Excel, greatly simplifies the mathematical calculations required with the NPV model.

Using the proposed investment in a combination ultrasonic microdermabrasion and light therapy unit as an illustration (Exhibit 9) and assuming a discount rate of 6 percent, Exhibit 11 shows the net present value to be $22,271. Therefore, based on the NPV model, the spa should make the proposed investment, because NPV is positive.

The NPV may be easily determined using a spreadsheet program. The formula is simply:

$$= \text{NPV}\,(k, \text{CF}_1\text{:CF}_n) + \text{C}$$

where k = interest rate
CF = cash flows resulting from the investment
C = cost of the investment

The cost of the investment must be entered in a cell as a negative amount.

Internal Rate of Return

The IRR model is a capital budgeting approach that considers cash flows and the time value of money, then determines the rate of return earned by a proposed project. In determining IRR, the net present value of cash flows is set at zero and the discount rate is determined. The formula is as follows:

$$0 = \frac{CF_1}{1+r} + \frac{CF_2}{(1+r)^2} + \dots + \frac{CF_n}{(1+r)^n} - C$$

where CF = Annual Cash Flow
r = Internal Rate of Return
C = Cost of investment

The proposed spa project costs $20,000 and is expected to yield a cash flow stream of $15,500 for each of years one and two and $16,500 for year three. The internal rate of return is 58.93 percent, which can be demonstrated as follows:

$$0 = \frac{\$15,500}{1.5893} + \frac{\$15,500}{(1.5893)^2} + \frac{\$16,500}{(1.5893)^3} - \$20,000$$

$$0 = 0$$

Using the IRR model, a project is accepted if the IRR is equal to, or greater than, the established minimum IRR, which is commonly called the **hurdle rate** by seasoned financial managers. Therefore, since the IRR exceeds the accept/reject criteria for the IRR method of 12 percent, as stated in Exhibit 9, the equipment should be purchased.

Like the NPV model, the IRR model is superior to the ARR and payback approaches because it considers the time value of money. The IRR is also superior to the ARR model because it considers cash flows. When there is a capital budgeting decision involving mutually exclusive projects, results from the IRR model may conflict with the NPV approach. This conflict may occur because of the IRR's assumption that all project cash flows are reinvested at the internal rate of return. Since operations normally invest in the most profitable projects first, one should not assume that other projects would result in the same return. This conflict will be discussed in greater detail later in this chapter.

The IRR for considering whether the spa should purchase the equipment may be easily determined using Excel. Pull up an Excel worksheet and enter the cost and cash flows for the proposed equipment purchase by a spa in cells 7C through 10C as follows:

Cell	Amount
7C	–20,000
8C	15,500
9C	15,500
10C	15,000

Then, in cell 11C type "= IRR(" (without the quotation marks). After the left parenthesis, highlight the values in cells 7C–10C and hit enter. The result of 57 percent (or .5717 if cell 11C is formatted to four decimal points) is the IRR.

Comparison of NPV and IRR Models

As discussed previously, the NPV and IRR models are preferred to the simplistic ARR and payback models. However, which is preferred, NPV or IRR? The NPV and IRR models, when applied in most situations, provide the same solution whether the situation considers a single project or mutually exclusive projects. However, in some of the latter situations, the NPV could suggest one project while the IRR model suggests a different project. This outcome results from the assumed reinvestment rates of each model. The NPV model assumes reinvestment at the discount rate used (6 percent in the spa problem), while the IRR model assumes reinvestment at the computed IRR (57.17 percent in the spa problem). Even if the superior projects are first selected, it is doubtful that reinvestment would be at the calculated IRR. Reinvestment will likelier be at a lower rate. Therefore, when mutually exclusive projects are considered, the NPV approach is more useful.

The NPV is generally easier to compute than the IRR. However, computers and calculators have reduced the laborious calculations of the IRR model. Many industry financial managers prefer the IRR model because the results are easier to interpret.

Mutually Exclusive Projects with Different Lives

To this point in our discussion, capital expenditure discussions have been assumed to have the same useful life. In reality, many mutually exclusive projects do not have equal lives. In such situations, three approaches to decision-making are as follows:

1. Assume that the shorter-lived capital investment is followed with another purchase and that the combined lives of the two projects equal the life of the mutually exclusive longer-lived project.
2. Assume that the longer-lived project is disposed of at the end of the shorter-lived project's life.
3. Ignore the differences in lives of the two mutually exclusive projects.

The third approach is reasonable only if the lives of both projects are long and the differences are insignificant. For example, a difference of one year for proposed projects with 14- and 15-year lives may be immaterial.

The first approach is illustrated in Exhibit 12. In this example, a spa is considering whether to replace its treadmills with a less expensive treadmill B, which has a three-year life and no salvage value, or with a more expensive Treadmill A, which has a six-year life and no salvage value. At the end of the useful life of Treadmill B (three years), the spa will purchase a replacement Treadmill C, again with a three-year life and no salvage value. In both alternatives, the treadmills are expected to provide services resulting in $3,000 of net cash flows each year. Treadmill A costs $8,500, while Treadmill B costs $5,000 and three years later Treadmill C will cost $6,000. The capital budgeting model and discount rate used are NPV and 6 percent, respectively.

The results suggest that Treadmill A should be purchased now rather than Treadmills B and C as part of alternative B.

The second approach, that of assuming the longer-lived project is disposed of at the end of the short-lived project's life, is illustrated in Exhibit 13. The same situation is assumed as in Exhibit 12, except the comparison is only for three years as Treadmill B is totally used at the end of year three. In addition, at the end of year three, Treadmill A is assumed to have a salvage value of $1,500. The NPV of Treadmills A and B are $2310.20 and $4550.80, respectively. Therefore, based on the available information, Treadmill B would be purchased.

Obviously, there are other considerations when comparing mutually exclusive capital decisions, such as estimated repair costs, the relative warranty claim rates for each of the options, and the guest satisfaction level. However,it is important to understand the financial analysis process when making these kinds of capital decisions.

Capital Rationing

Up to this point, no limit on capital projects has been discussed as long as the project returns exceeded the reject criteria. In reality, there are almost always limited funds available for capital improvements. For example, the spa owner may limit funds, or a corporation may limit funds provided to a division. This concept of

Exhibit 12 Comparison of Machine Acquisitions with Different Lives: Approach #1

	Cash Flows		
	Alternative A	Alternative B	
Years Hence	Treadmill A (1)	Treadmill B (2)	Treadmill C (3)
0	($8,500)	($5,000)	
1	3,000	3,000	
2	3,000	3,000	
3	3,000	3,000	$(6,000)
4	3,000		3,000
5	3,000		3,000
6	3,000		3,000

NPV—Alternative A

NPV = $3,000 (4.9173) − $8,500
NPV = $6,251.90

NPV—Alternative B

NPV = $3,000 (4.9173) − $5,000 − $6,000 (.8396)
NPV = $4,714.30

(1) Treadmill A costs $8,500 and provides a project cash flow of $3,000 per year for its six-year life.

(2) Treadmill B costs $5,000 and provides a project cash flow of $3,000 per year for its three-year life of years 1 through 3.

(3) Treadmill C (purchased to replace Treadmill B) costs $6,000 at the end of year three and provides project cash flow of $3,000 per year for its three-year life of years 4 through 6.

Exhibit 13 Comparison of Machine Acquisitions with Different Lives: Approach #2

Treadmill A costs $8,500 and provides project cash flow of $3,000 per year for five years and then may be sold for $1,500 at the end of year three. Treadmill B costs $5,000 and provides project cash flow of $3,000 per year for three years. At the end of three years, the Treadmill B is worthless.

	Cash Flows	
Years Hence	Treadmill A	Treadmill B
0	$(8,500)	$(5,000)
1	3,000	3,000
2	3,000	3,000
3	4,500	3,000

NPV—Machine A

NPV = $3,000 (3.1836) + $1,500 (.8396) − $8,500
NPV = $2,310.20

NPV—Machine B

NPV = $3,000 (3.1836) − $5,000
NPV = $4,550.80

limiting funds for capital purposes, regardless of the expected profitability of the projects, is called **capital rationing**. Under capital rationing, the combination of projects with the highest net present value would likely be selected.

Exhibit 14 Capital Rationing: Five Proposed Projects

Project	Project Cost	NPV
A	$10,000	$ 8,000
B	10,000	9,000
C	5,000	6,000
D	20,000	15,000
E	15,000	12,000
Combinations	**Total Investment**	**Total NPV**
A, B, & C	$25,000	$23,000
A & E	25,000	20,000
C & D	25,000	21,000
C & E	20,000	18,000

Exhibit 14 considers five proposed projects and calculates four possible combinations and their NPVs. In this illustration, projects B and E are considered to be mutually exclusive, and only $25,000 is available for capital projects.

The optimum combination is projects A, B, and C, because this yields the highest combined NPV. Other feasible combinations result in a lower NPV. In the combination where all funds would not be spent on projects, excess funds would be invested at the going interest rate; however, the present value of the return on the excess funds would be the amount invested, thus there would be no related NPV on these excess funds. (This assumes that the going interest rate is equal to the discount rate.)

Thus far, our discussions have been limited to the capital purchases of new equipment for the spa. In the chapter's opening story, one of the desired capital projects was the renovation of the couples relaxation lounge. For the sake of discussion, let's assume that the relaxation lounge renovation includes replacement of the carpeting, the purchase of new lounge sofas and chairs, and replacement of the simple side table (used for the complimentary teas and fruit display) with a custom buffet that includes refrigeration, a cold well, and a granite counter top. The total project expense estimate is $20,000. Clearly, it would be difficult to assign any hard dollar revenue increases or payback for a project such as this. The justification for the capital expenditure might include considerations such as:

- The spa has earned a *Forbes Travel Guide* (formerly the *Mobil Travel Guide*) four-star rating for the past two years, but would be in jeopardy of losing a star.
- New competition has entered the market with beautiful relaxation areas, so the spa could expect to lose market share to the competing spa as the result of an inferior guest experience.
- The spa utilizes a guest experience feedback rating system and over the past year, the most frequent criticism by the guest has been the relaxation lounge quality.

- Business has increased over the past couple of years to the point that there is insufficient seating in the relaxation space for all the guests waiting for appointments.

In such cases, the spa will make financial assumptions on loss of market share and revenues.

This example also brings up the discussion of capital expenditure versus maintenance expense. Spa managers typically want to capitalize as much as possible, as the cost of the project does not directly reduce the operating profitability as an expense. On the other hand, owners and corporate offices frequently want to treat these kinds of projects as maintenance and pay for them out of operating funds rather than capital. For example, if the decision was made to re-upholster the relaxation lounge furniture rather than purchasing new furniture, the owners may insist that the cost of re-upholstering is an operating expense and not a capital improvement. Renovation/repair projects that extend either the life or the earning power of the spa should be capitalized. From a capital budgeting perspective, one would compare the present value of the relevant future cash flows to the cost of the project. A positive NPV suggests the spa should make the change while a negative NPV suggests letting it be.

This example points to the importance of setting very specific parameters for what dollar amount and useful life criteria will be used to determine what purchases are to be capitalized The owner or corporate officer might, for example, set a minimum of $2000 for expenditures that should be considered for capitalization. All lesser amounts would automatically be expensed.

Use of Capital Budgeting Models in the Lodging Industry

For spas in a hotel or resort, it is noteworthy that a survey of the 150 largest lodging chains revealed that 74 percent of the respondents use IRR, while 66 percent, 55 percent, and 32 percent use payback, NPV, and ARR, respectively.[1] These results differ significantly from a similar survey in 1980, which showed that only 33 percent of hospitality businesses used IRR, while 71 percent and 36 percent used payback and NPV, respectively.[2] The more recent survey did not request reasons for the changes, but it seems likely that computer usage is a major reason. Calculations of NPV and IRR are virtually child's play for a computer.

Leasing

Leasing entitles a spa to use equipment, land, or buildings without buying them. Leasing often provides a way to use resources when purchasing them is not possible or desirable. For example, a day spa may lease land in a desirable location because that land is not for sale. Day spas typically lease space in a commercial development to develop a new spa project. With respect to leasing equipment, major spa equipment suppliers have said that new resort/hotel spa projects almost never use leases to equip the spa. By contrast, perhaps as many as a third of day spa development projects will have arranged with a bank or other lending institution for leasing the equipment to open the spa. The rest of this chapter will address a number of issues about lease accounting, including:

- The advantages and disadvantages of leasing resources
- Executory costs in relation to leases
- How leases are classified for accounting purposes
- The criteria for capitalizing leases
- How to amortize leasehold improvements
- Incremental interest rates
- Common provisions of lease agreements
- How cash flows are discounted

In addition, we will focus on the differences between operating leases and capital leases, and present guidelines for accounting for the different types of leasing arrangements. We will investigate the effects that leases may have on a day spa's or hotel/resort's financial statements and ratios. Finally, we will consider the lease-versus-buy question and provide a model for making a reasonably objective decision.

A **lease** is an agreement conveying the right to use resources (equipment, buildings, and/or land) for specified purposes and a limited time. The **lessor** owns the property and conveys the right of its use to the **lessee** in exchange for periodic cash payments called **rent**. Lease agreements govern the parties to the lease, usually the lessor and the lessee.

From an operational perspective, the resource, whether leased or purchased, is available for use; the spa's therapists and support personnel generally have little concern whether the spa owns or leases it. Leasing is popular in the United States with businesses in general, but international businesses use it much less often.

Advantages and Disadvantages of Leases

The following list presents some of the advantages of leasing.

- Leasing conserves working capital because it requires little or no cash deposit; cash equal to 20 to 40 percent of the purchase price is required when purchasing property and equipment. For the cash-strapped spa, leasing may be the only way to obtain the desired property or equipment.
- Leasing often involves less red tape than buying with external financing. Although a lease agreement must be prepared, it usually is less complicated than the many documents required to make a purchase, especially when long-term financing is involved.
- Leasing allows more frequent equipment changes, especially when equipment becomes functionally obsolete. However, the lessee cannot expect this flexibility to be cost-free. The greater the probability of technological obsolescence, the greater the lease payment (all other things being the same).
- Leasing generally places less restrictive contracts on a lessee than financial institutions often place on long-term borrowers.
- Leasing has less negative impact on financial ratios, especially when the leases are not capitalized. Equipment acquired for use through an operational lease

is not shown on the balance sheet. Future rent obligations also do not appear on the balance sheet, although some footnote disclosure may be required. For this reason, leases are often referred to as **off-balance-sheet financing**.

- Operating leases may allow an operation to obtain resources without following a capital budgeting process.

Therefore, in many cases, leasing may be a lower overall cost alternative for many spas. However, there are also disadvantages of leasing, including:

- Any residual value of the lease equipment benefits the lessor unless the lessee has the opportunity to acquire the leased property at the end of the lease.
- The cost of leasing in some situations is ultimately higher than purchasing. This is especially true when there are only a limited number of less-than-competitive lessors.
- Disposal of a financial lease before the end of the lease period often results in additional costs.

Provisions of Lease Contracts

Each lease is a unique product of negotiations between the lessor and lessee that, ideally, meets the specific needs of each party. However, all lease contracts normally contain certain provisions. The following list presents some of these common provisions.

1. Term of lease. The term of a lease may be as short as a few hours or a single day (usually for equipment needed for a special function being held at the spa) or as long as several decades (as is common with real estate). Leases should be long enough to ensure a proper return on the investment for leasehold improvements and other costs.
2. Purpose of lease. This provision generally limits the lessee to using the property for certain purposes. For example, a lease may state, "The lessee shall use the leased premises as a Day Spa and Salon and for no other purpose without first obtaining the written consent of the lessor."
3. Rental payments. The lease specifies the amount of rental payment and when it is due. It also indicates any adjustments; for example, adjustments for inflation are often based on the consumer price index for a given city. **Contingent rent** may also be specified. For example, a lease may stipulate that contingent rent equal to three percent of all annual treatment and retail sales in excess of $700,000 is due the fifteenth day of the first month after the end of the fiscal year.
4. Renewal options. Many leases contain a clause giving the lessee the option to renew the lease. For example, a lease may provide "an option to renew this lease for an additional five-year period on the expiration of the leasing term upon giving lessor written notice 90 days before the expiration of the lease."
5. Obligations for property taxes, insurance, and maintenance. Leases, especially long-term leases, specify who shall pay the **executory costs**—property

taxes, insurance, and maintenance costs—on the leased property. A lease in which the lessee is obligated to pay these costs in addition to the direct lease payments is commonly called a **triple-net lease**.

6. Other common lease provisions include:
   - The lessor's right to inspect the lessee's books, especially when part of the lease payment is tied to revenues or some other operational financial figure.
   - The lessor's obligations to restore facilities damaged by fire, tornadoes, and similar natural phenomena.
   - The lessee's opportunity to sublease the property.
   - The lessee's opportunity to make payments for which the lessor is responsible, such as loan payments to preclude default on the lessor's financing of the leased property.
   - Security deposits, if any, required of the lessee.
   - Indemnity clauses protecting the lessor.

Lease Accounting

Historically, leases were accounted for simply as executory contracts; the rental expense was generally recognized with the passage of time. Leases were not capitalized as assets, nor were liabilities recognized for the lessee's obligations under lease contracts. However, as leases have become more sophisticated and economically similar to sale/purchase transactions, many accountants have argued for a change in lease accounting.

The Accounting Principles Board, the former accounting rule-making body, issued four opinions on the topic of lease accounting. The Financial Accounting Standards Board (FASB), the current rule-making body, has issued more than ten statements relating to lease accounting. A major result of these rules is that many long-term leases are now capitalized (recorded as fixed assets with recognition of a liability).

Most of the remainder of this section presents lease accounting guidelines for lessees. Lease accounting for lessors is beyond the scope of this section. Our discussion is meant to cover the major elements of lease accounting and is certainly not exhaustive. The reader interested in further study of lease accounting should consult an intermediate accounting text and/or FASB statements.

Classification of Leases

In general, lessees classify leases for accounting purposes as either *operating leases* or *capital leases*. At the extremes of what is essentially a continuum, operating leases differ substantially from capital leases. Depending on their specific provisions, however, they can also be hard to distinguish.

Operating leases (also called *service leases*) are normally (but not always) of relatively short duration, and the lessor retains the responsibility for executory costs. They can usually be canceled easily. **Capital leases** (also called *financing leases*) cover relatively long periods, and the lessee often assumes responsibility for executory costs. In addition, they are generally noncancelable or at least costly to cancel. Capital leases are capitalized; operating leases are not.

The FASB has established four capitalization criteria for determining the status of noncancelable leases. If a noncancelable lease meets *any* of the four criteria, the lessee *must* classify and account for the lease as a capital lease. Noncancelable leases that don't meet any of the four criteria are accounted for as operating leases. The FASB criteria are as follows:

1. The property is transferred to the lessee by the end of the lease term, referred to as the **title transfer provision**.
2. The lease contains a bargain purchase option, referred to as the **bargain purchase provision**.
3. The lease term is equal to 75 percent or more of the estimated economic life of the leased property, referred to as the **economic life provision**.
4. The present value of minimum lease payments (excluding executory costs) equals or exceeds 90 percent of the excess of fair market value of the leased property over any investment tax credit retained by the lessor, referred to as the **value recovery provision**.

The bargain purchase option (criterion #2) means that the purchase price at the end of the lease period is substantially less than the leased property's expected market value at the date the option is to be exercised. The bargain price is generally considered substantially less than the market value only if the difference, for all practical purposes, ensures that the bargain purchase option will be exercised. The "economic life" (criterion #3) refers to the useful life of the leased property. The following list explains several terms in the value recovery provision (criterion #4):

- *Minimum lease payments* consist of minimum rental payments during the lease term and any bargain purchase option. If no bargain purchase option exists, the minimum lease payments include any guaranteed residual value by the lessee or any amount payable by the lessee for failure to renew the lease. Minimum lease payments do not include contingent rent (such as a percentage of sales). Executory costs are also excluded in determining minimum rental payments when the lease specifies that lease payments include these costs.
- *Fair market value* represents the amount the leased item would cost if it were purchased rather than leased.
- *Investment tax credit* was a credit that the federal government used to allow a deduction against the federal income tax liability of the business. When it was allowed, up to 10 percent of the cost of qualifying equipment could typically be taken as a credit. The credit generally applied to personal property (such as equipment), but not to real property (such as land and buildings). Investment tax credits are no longer allowed by current tax laws; however, if they are reinstated, they would be treated as indicated by criterion #4. Note that, when there is no investment tax credit, criterion #4 in effect states that if the

present value of minimum lease payments (excluding executory costs) equals or exceeds 90 percent of the fair market value of the leased property, the lease must be capitalized.

- *Residual value* refers to the estimated market value of the leased item at the end of the lease term. When the residual value is guaranteed by the lessee, then the lessee is ultimately liable to the lessor for the residual value.

Operating Leases

Operating leases are accounted for as simple rental agreements, and the expense is generally recognized when the rent is paid. For example, if a spa leases storage space for $200 per month and pays rent on the first day of each month, the monthly rental payment would be recorded as follows:

Account	Debit	Credit
Rent Expense	$200	
Cash		$200

When rent is paid in advance, it should be recorded in a Prepaid Rent account. For example, if the spa had paid three months' rent in advance, the proper entry would be:

Account	Debit	Credit
Rent Expense	$200	
Prepaid Rent	400	
Cash		$600

This accounting entry recognizes rent expense for the current month and delays recognition of rent for the following two months (based on the matching principle).

In the event rent is paid for a period beyond 12 months from the balance sheet date, the rental payment should be recorded as Deferred Rent and shown as a deferred asset on the statement. Any rent paid for future periods is recognized during the period to which it relates by an adjusting entry. In the example above, the adjusting entry to recognize the second month's rent would be:

Account	Debit	Credit
Rent Expense	$200	
Prepaid Rent		$200

Capital Leases

A capital lease is similar to the purchase of a fixed asset. Therefore, the accounting for capital leases recognizes an asset and applicable liabilities. The amount to be recorded as an asset and a liability is the present value of minimum lease payments, as defined earlier in relation to the fourth capitalization criterion. The lease payments are discounted using the lessee's incremental borrowing rate, or, if known, the lessor's implicit rate of interest in the lease—but only if the implicit rate is lower than the lessee's incremental borrowing rate. The former is used more often because the lessee does not usually know the lessor's implicit interest rate in the lease. The lessee's **incremental borrowing rate** is the rate of interest the lessee would have to pay if financing the purchase of the leased item.

Executory costs included with the lease payments must be excluded in determining the present value of minimum lease payments. However, a bargain purchase option or a lessee's guaranteed residual value must be included. For example, a lease agreement may require a monthly payment of $1,000, of which $200 is for maintenance. This $200 cost is excluded in determining the present value of minimum lease payments. On the other hand, if the lessee guarantees a residual value of $2,000 for the leased item, the present value of $2,000 (which might have to be paid at the end of the lease) should be included in determining the present value of minimum lease payments.

When the lessee makes subsequent lease payments, the lease obligation (the liability account) is reduced by the difference between the lease payment (excluding executory costs) and the interest on the lease obligation. The interest is calculated by using the effective interest method, which results in a constant rate of interest throughout the lease term. This is accomplished by multiplying the interest rate used in discounting the minimum lease payments by the lease obligation for the lease period. For example, assume that a lease payment for a day spa located in a commercial mall is $5,000 for the month, including $500 for property taxes, and the lease obligation for the period (related liability) is $480,000. Further assume that the lessee's incremental borrowing rate is 10 percent. The entry to record the lease payment for the month is as follows:

Property Tax Expense	$ 500	
Interest Expense	4,000	
Lease Obligations	500	
Cash		$5,000

The interest expense of $4,000 is determined as follows:

$$\text{Interest} = \text{Lease Obligation} \times \text{Incremental Borrowing Rate} \times \text{Time (In Years)}$$

$$= \$480{,}000 \times .10 \times \frac{1}{12}$$

$$= \underline{\underline{\$4{,}000}}$$

Therefore, the lease obligation is debited by $500, determined as follows:

$$\text{Reduction in Lease Obligation} = \text{Lease Payment} - \text{Executory Costs} - \text{Interest Expense}$$

$$= \$5{,}000 - \$500 - \$4{,}000$$

$$= \underline{\underline{\$500}}$$

We will now provide an example to further illustrate accounting for capital leases.

Illustration of Accounting for Capital Leases

Assume that the Any Spa signs a lease agreement with the manufacturer for the use of the combination microdermabrasion/light therapy equipment discussed earlier in the chapter. Provisions of the lease agreement and other relevant facts for classifying the lease are as follows:

1. The term of a lease is three years, commencing on January 1, 20X1. The lease is noncancelable.
2. The first annual payment of $9,900 is due at the beginning of 20X1, while the next two annual payments are due on December 31, 20X1 and 20X2.
3. The leased equipment has a fair market value of $20,000 at January 1, 20X1.
4. The estimated economic life of the unit is three years, and there is a expected residual value of $1,000
5. The Any Spa is to pay all executory costs directly except for annual maintenance costs of $1,200, which are included in the annual lease payments.
6. The lease contains no renewal or bargain purchase options, and the equipment reverts to the lessor at the end of the lease period.
7. The Any Spa's incremental borrowing rate is 6%.
8. The Any Spa depreciates its equipment on a straight-line basis.
9. The lessor's implicit rate of return on leasing the equipment to the spa is unknown.
10. There are no tax credits applicable to this situation.

The Any Spa must determine whether the lease should be capitalized by comparing the lease provisions to the FASB lease capitalization criteria. Exhibit 15 illustrates this comparison. As the exhibit indicates, the lease should be capitalized, based on criteria #3 and 4, because the term of the lease is equal to the useful life of the equipment (criterion #3) and the present value of lease payments, excluding executory costs, exceeds 90 percent of the fair market value of the leased equipment (criterion #4). The calculations are as follows:

Fair market value of leased equipment	$ 20,000
90 percent factor	× .9
	$ 18,000
Present value of lease payments (see Exhibit 15)	$ 24,651
Excess of PV of lease payments	$ 6,651

The journal entry to record the capitalization of the leased equipment accompanied by the first payment of $9,900 is as follows:

Exhibit 15 FASB Lease Capitalization Criteria

Lease Capitalization Criteria	Equipment Lease Provisions		Capitalize Yes/No
1. Title transfer provision	Item 6 states the "equipment reverts to the lessor at the end of the lease."		No
2. Bargain purchase provision	Item 6 states the lease contains no bargain purchase options.		No
3. Economic life provision	$\frac{\text{Life of lease}}{\text{Useful life of equipment}} = 3/3 = 100\%$		Yes
4. Value recovery provision	\$8,700 (2.8334)* =	\$24,651**	Yes
	\$20,000 (.9) =	(18,000)	
	excess of PV of lease payments over 90% of FMV is	\$ 6,651	

Present value factor for initial payment at the *beginning* of the first year	1.0000
Present value factor at 6% for lease payments 2 and 3 due on the last day of years	1.8334
Total PV factor	2.8334

* For the derivation of this factor, see below.

** This amount is actually \$24,650.58; however, the detail of cents is dropped here and throughout the rest of this illustration.

Leased Equipment Under Capital Leases	\$24,651	
Prepaid Maintenance	1,200	
Cash		\$ 9,900
Obligations Under Capital Leases		15,951

This single entry consists of the capitalization of the lease at \$24,651 (the present value of the two lease payments of \$9,900 less \$1,200 related to maintenance), the recognition of the related liability at \$15,951, the initial payment of \$9,900, and \$1,200 related to maintenance.

The single entry could have also been recognized in two parts.

(1) Capitalization of lease

Leased Equipment Under Capital Leases	\$24,651	
Obligations Under Capital Leases		\$24,651

This entry simply records the present value of the two lease payments.

(2) Lease payment

Obligations Under Capital Leases	$8,700	
Prepaid Maintenance	1,200	
Cash		$9,900

This entry records the initial cash payment of $9,900, the $1,200 executory payment, and the reduction in the Obligation account of $8700.

The prepaid maintenance would be written off throughout the year by a monthly entry of $100 (1⁄12 of the annual payment):

Maintenance Expense	$100	
Prepaid Maintenance		$100

Future payments will result in the recognition of interest expense, the reduction of the obligation under capital leases, and prepayment of maintenance for the next year.

The Any Spa would record its second lease payment on December 31, 20X1, as follows:

Interest Expense	$ 957	
Obligations Under Capital Leases	6,843	
Prepaid Maintenance	1,200	
Cash		$9,900

The Interest Expense of $957 results from multiplying the $15,951, recorded as Obligations Under Capital Leases through the year, by the spa's incremental borrowing rate of 6 percent. The reduction in the liability Obligations Under Capital Leases of $6,873 is the difference between the net lease payment of $8,700 and the Interest Expense of $957.

The leased equipment should be depreciated over its lease term of three years. The annual entry for depreciation expense (based on the straight-line method) would be as follows:

Depreciation Expense	$8,217	
Accumulated Depreciation—Capital Leases		$8,217

This entry assumes a zero salvage value because the equipment reverts to the lessor at the end of the lease term. At the end of the three-year term, the leased equipment is returned to the lessor and the two accounts, Leased Equipment Under Capital Leases and Accumulated Depreciation—Capital Leases, each at $24,651, are reduced to zero:

Accumulated Depreciation—Capital Leases	$24,651	
Leased Equipment Under Capital Leases		$24,651

Throughout the three-year period, the following expenses related to the leased item were incurred:

Maintenance—$1,200/year	$ 3,600
Depreciation—the capitalized cost of the lease	24,651
Interest Expense—the sum of the three net lease payments less the capitalized cost of the lease ($26,100 − $24,651):	1,449
Total Expense	$29,700

Notice that the total expense equals the three annual payments of $9,900.

Leasehold Improvements

Buildings or space within a commercial retail center that are leased for several years often require extensive improvements before operations begin. Often, the space leased is not capitalized since none of the capitalization criteria is met. However, any improvements to the space must be capitalized as **leasehold improvements**. For example, the cost of walls, ceilings, carpeting, and lighting installed in leased space is capitalized. The leasehold improvement is recognized as an intangible asset, and the cost must be amortized against revenue over the life of the lease or the life of the leasehold improvement, whichever is shorter. For example, assume that the Any Day Spa leased 8,000 square feet of space in a new strip shopping center and spent $1,000,000 or $125 per square foot to build out the space with interior walls, ceilings, floor coverings, electrical and lighting, sounds systems, water features and zoning heating ventilating and air-conditioning to transform the empty space into a tranquil spa environment. Further assume that the life of the improvement is 10 years, while the space was leased for 20 years. The annual amortization of the leasehold improvement would be 1/10 of the cost—$100,000 per year for ten years. This expense is generally recognized monthly (1/12 of annual amortization) as follows:

Amortization of Leasehold Improvement	$100,000	
Leasehold Improvement		$100,000

Leases and Their Effect on Financial Ratios

Whether a leased item is accounted for as a capital lease or an operating lease can have a major impact on the financial statements, especially the balance sheet. Therefore, several financial ratios are also affected. Property leased under an operating lease is not shown on the balance sheet, while property leased under a capital lease is. The statement's disclosure of capital leases includes both assets and liabilities. Therefore, most financial ratios involving noncurrent assets and long-term liabilities are affected by how leases are accounted for. Four financial ratios affected by capitalizing leases are shown in Exhibit 16.

In general, capitalizing leases negatively affects these ratios; the ratios suggest a less desirable financial situation than they would if the leases had been accounted for as operating leases. For example, if a lease is capitalized, assets and

Exhibit 16 Financial Ratios Most Affected by Lease Accounting

Ratio	Ratio Formula	How capital lease affects ratio
1. Asset turnover	revenue ÷ average total assets	Capitalizing leases results in increasing the average total assets, therefore reducing the asset turnover ratio.
2. Return on assets	net income ÷ average total assets	Increased average total assets will also assets reduce the return on assets.
3. Debt-equity ratio	total debt ÷ total equity	Capitalizing leases results in increasing the total debt, therefore increasing the debt-equity ratio.
4. Number of times interest earned	earnings before interest and taxes ÷ interest expense	Capitalizing leases results in increased interest earned ratio interest expenses, therefore reducing this ratio.

liabilities increase. This means the net income must also increase in order to maintain a constant return on assets. Thus, some spas prefer not to capitalize leases. They often negotiate lease provisions so that the lease does not qualify as a capital lease under any of the FASB's four capitalization criteria.

Choosing to Lease or Buy

Should a spa lease or buy property? The elements to consider when answering this question include the effect of the decision on taxes, whether funds to finance the purchase must be borrowed, and the time value of money.

Suppose the management of Any Spa is deciding whether to buy or lease the two treadmills in response to members' complaints that the gym has insufficient cardio equipment. Assume these treadmills will have a five-year life. Assume that the suggested retail cost of the two treadmills at $8,500 each for a total cost of $19,000, while the annual lease payments would be $5,000 for the first year and $4,565 for the next four years (paid at the end of years one through four). Because the lease payments total $23,260, the apparent advantage to Any Spa of buying over leasing is $4,260.

However, we must not forget to consider the time value of money. Assume that Any Spa would have to borrow funds at 6 percent if it were to finance the purchase of the two treadmills this is the lessee's incremental borrowing rate. As stated earlier, lease payments must be discounted by this rate (or, less commonly, by the lessor's implicit rate of interest in the lease) for financial accounting purposes. Therefore, the future cash flows covering the lease payments for years one through four should be discounted as follows:

Present value of first payment:	$ 5,000
Present value of next four (annuity) payments:	
$4,565 ($PVA_{n=4, k=10}$) = $4,565(3.4651)	$15,818
Total	$20,818

This result suggests that leasing the treadmills would cost $1,818 more ($20,818 – $19,000) than buying it.

However, there are yet other considerations—in particular, taxes and the salvage value of the treadmills at the end of the five years. Tax considerations for the purchase option involve depreciation expense each year; those for the lease option involve treating the lease payment as an expense each year. Salvage value also must be considered since, under the buy alternative, the salvage value provides cash.

Assume that, based on discussions about the treadmills, Any Spa's owner estimates that the salvage value of each of the two treadmills will be $500; that is, the two treadmills can be sold for $1,000 at the end of year five. Further assume that the discount rate is still 6 percent, that Any Spa's marginal tax rate is 25 percent and that the spa uses straight-line depreciation. Exhibit 17 presents the effects of considering taxes and salvage value. Buying again appears to be less costly than leasing, but this time by $1,444, which is a lesser difference than the $1,818 shown before.

Still our analysis is incomplete. Repairs would certainly be the responsibility of Any Spa if they purchased the treadmills but might be paid by the lessor if the treadmills are leased, which would favor leasing. Also, a different salvage value could change the final numbers in either direction. Using accelerated depreciation rather than straight-line depreciation would reduce the cost of buying since depreciation and thus cash flows would be speeded up (and therefore discounted less). Further, financing the purchase rather than paying cash, could also affect the final cost.

From a financial point of view, when all relevant factors of who covers repair costs, borrowing, taxes, salvage value, and the time value of money are considered, there may be little difference between leasing and buying. In a truly competitive environment, there *should* be little difference between the costs of leasing and buying. However, truly competitive environments most likely exist only in major metropolitan areas. In noncompetitive markets, a smaller number of lessors will have greater economic power.

Summary

Spa owners, corporate officials of branded spas, and spa managers must carefully consider many necessary additions or changes in fixed assets over time to operate their spas effectively. Projects are evaluated based on their costs and corresponding revenues. Generally, projects that generate the most money for the spa should be accepted. This process is called capital budgeting.

Capital budgeting is appropriate in a number of decision-making processes. It can be used when purchasing equipment to meet government standards, to comply with spa quality rating criteria, or to add to or replace existing equipment. It is also valuable when considering the purchase of equipment that could either increase revenues or decrease costs. In each of these cases, budgeting is

Exhibit 17 Discounted Cash Flow Payments—Considering Tax Effects and Salvage

	Years					
	0	1	2	3	4	5
Purchase Option						
Purchase price	19,000					
Salvage Value						–$ 1,000
Depreciation tax shield[1]	–0–	–$ 900	–$ 900	–$ 900	–$ 900	–$ 900
Net purchase cost						
Annual cash flows	19,000	–900	–900	–900	–900	–1900
Discount factors	× 1	× .9434	× .8900	× .8396	× .7921	× .7473
Present value of cash flows	$19,000	$ 846	–$ 801	–$ 756	–$ 713	–$ 1,420

Total present value of cash flows for purchase option = $14,464

	0	1	2	3	4	5
Lease Option						
Lease	$ 5,000	$ 4,565	$ 4,565	$ 4,565	$ 4,565	–0–
Lease tax shield[(2,3)]		–1,250	–1,141	–1,141	–1,141	–1,141
Annual cash flow	5,000	335	3,424	3,424	3,424	1,141
Present value factors	× 1	× .9434	× .8900	× .8396	× .7921	× .7473
Present value of cash flows	$ 5,000	$ 3,127	$ 3,047	$ 2,875	$ 2,712	–$ 853

Total present value of cash flows from lease option = $15,908
Difference—apparent advantage of buying: $ 1,444

(1) Depreciation expense × tax rate = depreciation tax shield

Depreciation expense:

$$\frac{\$19{,}000 - \$1{,}000}{5} = \$3{,}600$$

$3,600(0.25) = $900

(2) $5,000 (0.25) = $1,250

(3) $4,565 (0.25) = $1,141

performed to determine if the revenues (or cost savings) generated by the purchasing the equipment are greater than the corresponding expenditures, or to decide which option is best for the spa. By using capital budgeting models, management actively works to maximize the spa's profits.

Four capital budgeting approaches were examined in this chapter: accounting rate of return, payback, net present value, and internal rate of return. ARR is defined as the average project income divided by the average investment. Although it is a simple method, it does have a number of deficiencies and is, therefore, not used frequently. The payback method is also simple and is used more frequently than the ARR. It examines the cash flows generated by the equipment and determines the number of years of cash flows required to recover the investment. The NPV approach looks at the cash flows relating to the project and discounts them to their present value. A project with NPV greater than zero is accepted. The final approach discussed, IRR, examines cash flows to determine the rate of return the investment generates. In other words, it sets the project NPV equal to zero and calculates the discount rate.

The NPV and IRR methods are more complex than the ARR and payback approaches, but they also provide more valuable results. They both examine cash flows and recognize the time value of money. Using Excel can greatly reduce the tedious calculations to determine the NPV and IRR. The major difference between the two is that IRR somewhat unrealistically assumes that the project cash flows will be reinvested in projects that generate the same return. Thus, when mutually exclusive projects are analyzed, the NPV method is preferred over the IRR.

Leasing is sometimes an alternative to capital expenditure. Leasing is a special type of financing. By entering into a lease agreement, the lessee acquires the right to use specific resources for a limited time and a specific purpose. The advantages for the lessee include the conservation of working capital, the benefits of tax deductions that might not otherwise be available, and, in some cases (when the lease is accounted for as an operating lease), a favorable effect on the balance sheet ratios. In exchange for these advantages, the lessee must make some sacrifices. In many instances, the residual value of the property remains with the lessor, there may be substantial penalties for termination of the lease contract, and the cost of leasing may be higher than purchasing the leased item. The spa operator contemplating a lease arrangement must weigh the advantages and disadvantages before entering into the contract.

When deciding between leasing and purchasing an asset, many businesses consider how the agreement will affect the financial statements. Depending upon its terms, a lease will either be capitalized (recorded on the balance sheet as an asset and liability) or treated as an operational lease (expensed as the payments are made). If capitalized, certain financial ratios can be negatively affected. Some managers avoid capital leases because of this effect.

In addition to accounting for the initial lease, leasehold improvements must be recorded and subsequently amortized over either the life of the lease or the life of the improvement, whichever is shorter.

Management should study all the variations of the lease agreement before signing any contract. Establishments judged solely on their financial ratios will probably be more interested in whether a lease is capitalized. Other establishments may value the difference between the total lease payments and the benefits of having a present cash flow.

To determine whether it is better to lease or buy a certain resource, calculate the total cost of each option. Consider the time value of money with regard to both lease payments and, if appropriate, loan payments. Also, consider the tax effects of both options (including the effect of using straight-line or accelerated depreciation) and the fact that the purchase option might provide salvage value. In competitive markets, there should be little difference between the final costs of leasing and buying.

Endnotes

1. Raymond S. Schmidgall and James W. Damitio, "Hotels and Long-Term Investment," *The Bottomline*, August–September 1990.

2. James J. Eyster, Jr., and A. Neal Geller, "The Capital-Investment Decision: Techniques Used in the Hospitality Industry," *The Cornell Hotel and Restaurant Administration Quarterly,* May 1981, pp. 69–73.

Key Terms

accounting rate of return (ARR)—An approach to evaluating capital budgeting decisions based on the average annual project income (project revenues less project expenses) divided by the average investment.

annuity—A stream of funds provided by a capital investment when the amounts provided are the same and at equal intervals (such as the end of each year).

bargain purchase provision—One of four Financial Accounting Standards Board capitalization criteria for determining the status of noncancelable leases. If a lease has a bargain purchase option, the lessee must classify and account for the lease as a capital lease. A bargain purchase option gives the lessee the option to purchase the leased property at the end of the lease at a price substantially lower than the leased property's expected market value at the date the option is to be exercised.

capital leases—Lease agreements that are of relatively long duration, generally noncancelable, and in which the lessee assumes responsibility for executory costs. For accounting purposes, capital leases are capitalized in a way similar to the purchase of a fixed asset (that is, recorded as an asset with recognition of a liability).

capital rationing—An approach to capital budgeting used to evaluate combinations of projects according to their net present value (NPV).

contingent rent—Rent based on specified variables, such as a percentage of revenues above a given amount.

discount rate—The term used for *k* when finding a present value.

economic life provision—One of four Financial Accounting Standards Board capitalization criteria for determining the status of noncancelable leases. If the lease term is equal to 75 percent or more of the estimated economic life of the leased property, the lessee must classify and account for the lease as a capital lease.

executory costs—Obligations for property taxes, insurance, and maintenance of leased property.

hurdle rate—The established minimum internal rate of return that must be met or exceeded for a project to be accepted under the internal rate of return model of capital budgeting.

incremental borrowing rate—The rate of interest a lessee would have to pay if financing the purchase of the item to be leased.

incremental cash flow—The change in cash flow of an operation that results from an investment.

internal rate of return (IRR)—An approach to evaluating capital budgeting decisions based on the rate of return generated by the investment.

lease—An agreement conveying the right to use resources (equipment, buildings, and/or land) for specified purposes for limited periods of time. The lessor owns the property and conveys the right of its use to the lessee in exchange for periodic cash payments called rent.

leasehold improvements—Renovations or remodeling performed on leased buildings or space prior to the commencement of operations. For accounting purposes, all leasehold improvements are capitalized (that is, recorded as an asset with recognition of a liability).

lessee—Party that makes periodic cash payments called rent to a lessor in exchange for the right to use property.

lessor—Party that owns property and conveys the right of its use to the lessee in exchange for periodic cash payments called rent.

net present value (NPV)—An approach to evaluating capital budgeting decisions based on discounting the cash flows relating to the project to their present value; calculated by subtracting the project cost from the present value of the discounted cash flow stream.

off-balance-sheet financing—Term sometimes applied to operating leases, because property acquired for use through such leases is not shown on the balance sheet. Future rent obligations also do not appear on the balance sheet, although some footnote disclosure may be required.

operating leases—Lease agreements that are usually of relatively short duration, easily canceled, and in which the lessor retains responsibility for executory costs. For accounting purposes, operating leases are not capitalized, but simply recognized as an expense when rent is paid.

payback—An approach to evaluating capital budgeting decisions based on the number of years of annual cash flow generated by the fixed asset purchase required to recover the investment.

rent—Cash payments made by a lessee to a lessor.

residual value—With regard to leasing, the estimated market value of a leased item at the end of the lease term.

time value of money—The process of placing future years' income on an equal basis with current-year expenditures in order to facilitate comparison.

title transfer provision—One of four Financial Accounting Standards Board capitalization criteria for determining the status of noncancelable leases. If the property is transferred to the lessee by the end of the lease term, the lessee must classify and account for the lease as a capital lease.

triple-net lease—A form of lease agreement in which the lessee is obligated to pay property taxes, insurance, and maintenance on the leased property.

value recovery provision—One of four Financial Accounting Standards Board capitalization criteria for determining the status of noncancelable leases. If the present value of minimum lease payments (excluding executory costs) equals or exceeds 90 percent of the excess of fair market value of the leased property over any applicable investment tax credit retained by the lessor, the lessee must classify and account for the lease as a capital lease.

Review Questions

1. What is capital budgeting?
2. What are four situations that might require capital budgeting?
3. Why is one dollar today worth more than one dollar a year from now?
4. How is the payback method of capital budgeting performed?
5. What is project cash flow?
6. What are the disadvantages of using the payback method of capital budgeting?
7. How can two mutually exclusive projects with different lengths of lives be analyzed?
8. What role does the accept/reject criterion play in the NPV and IRR methods of capital budgeting?
9. Which method of capital budgeting is the most effective? Explain your choice.
10. What is capital rationing?
11. What are three major advantages to the lessee of lease financing?
12. What are some provisions common to most leases?
13. What are the FASB's four criteria for determining if a lease is a capital or an operating lease?
14. What major effects do capital leases (compared to operating leases) have on an operation's balance sheet?
15. What are leasehold improvements?
16. What are lease executory costs and how do they influence the determination of whether a lessee should capitalize a lease?
17. What is meant by guaranteed residual value? How does it affect the present value of lease payments?
18. At what value is a capitalized lease recorded?

Chapter 11 Outline

Competencies

1. Discuss the importance of business plans, explain the significance of an executive summary, and distinguish between the two different summary types. (pp. 357–360)
2. List considerable factors in identifying and inspecting a potential spa site, and outline information that should be included in a spa positioning statement. (pp. 360–364)
3. Describe how to develop a market analysis. (pp. 364–375)
4. Describe how to develop a demand analysis. (pp. 375–380)
5. Discuss the elements of a financial forecast, including pricing, revenues, and expenses. (pp. 380–399)
6. Summarize the recommendations provided for spa projects. (pp. 400–401)

11

Business Plan Development

ERICA LOOKED AROUND THE BUSY WINE BAR, hoping to see her friend Monica. Monica had called her earlier that day and, with a voice brimming with excitement, had insisted that they meet that night so she could share some great news.

When Erica saw Monica walk through the door, she could see the huge smile on Monica's face. "This must be big," she thought. Once they placed their order, Erica said, "Okay, Monica, what's the big news?"

Monica explained that she had had a long meeting with the owner of the Day Spa that morning. The owner had been wanting to expand her spa business for some time and told Monica that she had found some wonderful lease space in Dana Point, about 14 miles from the current Day Spa location. The new location was in a strip center currently under construction. Putting in all of the water, sewer, and electric supplies needed for a spa was going to be a lot easier than if existing space were converted into a spa. The owner believed the available space was just the right size; plus, it was located on Pacific Coast Highway at the end of downtown, so a ton of traffic would drive by the location each day. When the owner started the original Day Spa, she and her husband were able to use the money they had invested over the years to design and open the spa. Even though the Day Spa had done very well over the past five years, the owner would still need to identify an investor or obtain bank financing to secure the lease and pay for the build-out costs and necessary equipment to open a second spa location.

"She has asked me to help her do the market analysis and write the business plan for the project. Isn't that exciting?" Monica said.

Although she was thrilled for her friend, Erica asked whether Monica had ever written a business plan before. Monica replied, "No, but the owner still has the original business plan she did when she was planning the original Day Spa. That should help, right?" Monica went on to say that the owner had a really great idea for the new spa to include an open room that could seat about 20 to 30 people so the spa could host educational programs every week. "She wants to engage the clients so they feel that the spa is not simply a place where you go to have a massage or get your nails done, but a place whose mission is to improve your wellness and create a sense of community," Monica explained.

Erica cleared her throat. "That is a great idea. But you should be careful with the business plan, because I have seen business plans and pro formas that have been developed for resort spas where I've worked. They require a tremendous amount of effort, because they lay the business blueprint for years to come." Erica went on to tell the story of a dreadful business plan that had been developed for a spa where Erica was part of the opening management team. The hotel had engaged an inexperienced consultant, who had the mix of treatment rooms all wrong. "He had three hydrotherapy tub rooms and even a scotch hose room that no one wanted to experience, but no nail area. He said that nail services did not belong in a true spa," Erica recalled.

Not only that, but the consultant assumed that because the hotel was forecasted to run 62 percent occupancy in the first year, the spa should easily be able to achieve a 62 percent treatment room utilization rate. Plus, the consultant had simply taken the spa menus from other resorts in the region and calculated an average of the prices for the various services on the other menus to determine first-year revenues. He had said that as the new and best spa, they would be able to achieve the market average treatment rate plus 10 percent for pricing.

"What a disaster!" Erica continued. "Our first-year budget was based on the consultant's projections and the management team ended up re-forecasting the remainder of the year almost every month. At the end of our first year, the spa had to undergo major renovations to provide the mix of treatment spaces that the guests wanted. I wouldn't want to go through that again," Erica exclaimed. "Monica, the only advice I have for you is that you should really do your homework and take your time to get all of your data and assumptions just right. Bankers and investors look at business plans all day long. You will want yours to be so professional that it distinguishes itself from all the others they see or you will not get the financing to make the second spa location a reality. Who knows, if you do a great job, you could end up overseeing two spas. How cool would that be?"

Many people have had good business ideas during their lives, but to translate an idea into reality requires a well-conceived and well-presented business plan that will articulate the vision and goals of the entrepreneur to secure the necessary financing for the project. This chapter will discuss the many components needed to create a strong spa business plan.

Long before a new spa opens, a good business plan should be developed. The discussion of a business plan in this chapter should provide answers to the following questions:

1. What is meant by a business plan?
2. What are the common elements of a business plan?
3. Generally, how many years are covered by a business plan?
4. What is included in the executive summary?
5. How many treatment rooms are proposed?

6. What is the mix of potential leisure, group, business, and local guests of a proposed hotel spa?
7. What is the projected revenue by revenue department for the first year of operations?
8. What are the expected changes in revenues by department in years two through five?
9. What is the expected hotel guest spa capture rate over the five-year projection period?
10. What is the treatment room utilization rate over the first five years?

What Is a Business Plan?

In order to create a successful business plan, it is important to understand its function and purpose. A business plan is simply what its name implies: it is a roadmap detailing the spa concept, the goals of the spa, how ownership/management intends to achieve those goals, and, most importantly, the specific data needed to support the financial objectives for the business. In most cases, a bank will require a business plan before granting the owner/developer a loan, while other investors or venture capitalists will demand one to determine whether or not to provide capital to finance the spa. Remember, however, that while a business plan may be required by outside sources, the greatest beneficiary of the planning process required to write a business plan is the spa operator.

Sometimes business plans are called feasibility studies; the terms are often used interchangeably. For our purposes, however, we will make a distinction between the terms. This chapter will use the term "business plan" when discussing the development process for a day spa and the term "feasibility study" when discussing the development process for spas developed in conjunction with hotels and resorts.

The vast majority of day spas are developed as sole proprietorships or limited partnerships. There are, of course, exceptions for major day spa brands such as Red Door Spas. When a new resort is being developed, the spa is part of a much larger project that will include hotel rooms, meeting space, perhaps a golf course, certainly restaurants, and, in today's world, either residential property or an interval ownership component. The spa feasibility study will be a component of a much larger development package that will either seek capital for the entire project from private equity companies or institutional investors or attempt to structure the ownership with independent investors owning a proportional share in the entire development. Again, of course, there will be exceptions as hospitality corporations such as Hyatt and Marriott may take an ownership position in the property, although in most cases entities such as institutional funds, REITs, and independent owners will own the entire project and contract with a major brand to manage the property.

In the case of a hotel/resort development, the developers will typically contract with a spa specialty consulting company. This company will develop a feasibility study for the spa component that will be included in the financing package along with separate studies for other facility components. One of the challenges today for spas being developed within hotel/resorts is the likelihood that the project developers will develop an initial pro forma for the entire project that includes assumptions about spa revenues and profitability *before* the spa's strategic positioning and market research have been completed. These developers may even develop an initial site plan for the entire project, assuming a square-footage allowance for the spa, without the supporting market research and strategic positioning.

It has become a reality for a resort or hotel that aspires to be a four- or five-star luxury resort to include a spa. Before the developer contracts with a spa specialty consulting firm, he or she must have already established the size and placement of the spa within the entire resort project, perhaps even the number of treatment rooms, salon location, and fitness space allocation. Assumptions with respect to revenues and departmental profit contribution expectations need also be established as part of the initial project concept. After doing so, the developer should approach a specialty spa consulting firm to confirm that these initial assumptions are reasonable.

During the "dot com" explosion of the 1990s, the economy was booming, the Internet was spawning thousands of new enterprises, and capital for new ventures was easily obtained. At the same time, spas were also rapidly expanding, having in the United States grown from just a few hundred in the early 1980s to over 18,000 in 2008, according to the 2008 International SPA Association (ISPA) research. A lot has changed since then. Investors are much more cautious about their investments and carefully scrutinize new ventures; the financial expectations placed on entrepreneurs and developers are higher, which makes due diligence necessary. It is more important than ever to have a strong, compelling business plan.

The ultimate purpose of creating a business plan is to end up with a successful business. While many may view the process as a demanding chore, it is actually an opportunity. Gathering the data and information necessary to develop an accurate business plan will minimize the possibility of failure and maximizes the likelihood of success. Preparing a business plan requires time and effort; the resulting package will most likely include the specifics on the spa industry, the markets and customers it serves, how the spa will be marketed, how operations are conducted, and what resources are required to ultimately achieve the financial goals.

This chapter will cover the following common elements of the business plan/feasibility plan process:

- Executive summary
- Project parameters and research objectives
- Opportunity analysis
- Demand analysis and financial forecast
- Spa project recommendations

The chapter will also highlight the distinctions between those plans developed for a free-standing day spa and a spa project in conjunction with the development of a hotel/resort.

Executive Summary

While the executive summary appears first in a business/feasibility plan presentation, it is actually written last. It may take several months of data collection and business concept development to reach the point when it is time to write the executive summary, but, without a doubt, the most important component of a business/feasibility plan is the executive summary. The cold facts are that bankers, venture capitalists, corporate hospitality executives, and other investors are very busy people. They may receive hundreds of proposals and business plans each year and can dismiss a poorly conceived or constructed plan after reading just the executive summary if it is not direct, concise, and compelling. It is essential that the executive summary makes a positive impression in those critical first couple of pages to spark the readers' interest to go through the entire plan. An executive summary highlights the key fundamentals and financial objectives for the proposed business.

There are several things that the executive summary must convey in as little as one to three pages, including:

- The fundamental spa concept
- That the spa's operation has been thoroughly planned
- That the research demonstrates that there is sufficient market demand for the spa to be successful
- That the spa incorporates significant competitive advantages
- That the financial projections presented in the plan are realistic and attainable
- That potential investors will receive an appropriate return on their investment and that the return on capital is achievable within the expected time period or that repayment presents little risk

For a small day spa project, the executive summary will end with brief details of what the financing request involves, such as a request for a loan or a capital investment in the project. If the capital required is substantial, it is advisable to present a more detailed financial proposal separately following the executive summary. The information contained within a financing proposal would typically include:

- The amount and use of the funds requested as a loan or direct investment into the spa.
- The specific preferred financing package. The proposal should indicate whether borrowed funds (debt) or invested capital (equity) is desired.
- An explanation of when and how the financing will be used.
- What type of financing will be required, i.e., short-term, intermediate-term, or long-term financing.
- A timetable suggesting when and at what amounts the lender will be repaid.
- If debt financing is sought, a description of the type and market value of assets that can be pledged as collateral, thus reducing the risk for the lender.
- An indication of the owner's personal investment.

For a hotel/resort spa, the executive summary must answer the fundamental questions of whether a spa is financially feasible to be included with the property and how much space should be allocated to the spa. The amount the developers can expect as a spa departmental profit contribution to the overall gross operating profit of the hotel/resort must also be covered. Additionally, the summary should include the amount of additional room revenue that will be generated by having a spa through a projected increase in room nights, double occupancy and average daily rate, and competitive advantages.

Types of Executive Summaries

The summary should be written in one of two ways: a synopsis, sometimes referred to as a topical summary, or a narrative summary.

The most straightforward and easiest executive summary to prepare is the synopsis/topical summary as it simply relates, in abbreviated form, the essential points and conclusions of each section of the complete plan. Writing the narrative summary is like telling the reader the story of the spa project. Obviously, it requires a talented writer, and it can be very effective for a spa concept that is new or for an existing spa that is seeking a second location, which has developed a unique competitive advantage within the market. If done well, the narrative style conveys the spa's message in such a way that it offers a better chance to engage the reader than the topical summary. The narrative summary writer must, however, be careful to avoid superlatives, as the experienced reader can quickly identify hyperbole used to create positive initial perceptions from factual descriptions and specific information. As a general rule, the synopsis/topical summary is easier to write, and presents less risk than creating a stimulating narrative.

Finally, understand that the executive summary is the most critical part of any business/feasibility plan, as it must motivate the reader to consider the plan in its entirety. The executive summary should be reviewed before submission and perhaps modified with the specific reader in mind. To be successful, the summary should attempt to respond to the issues and questions that a specific reader may have. This requires a thorough understanding of the target reader's frame of reference and potential issues.

Project Parameters and Research Objectives

When developing a spa feasibility/business plan, the first step is to conduct market research and to refine the spa's concept to determine the revenue potential and opportunities within the market for that particular spa concept. The information gathered from the market research will guide recommendations for the spa's **program of space**. "Programming" is an architectural term used by facility designers when allocating space and determining adjacencies of spa functions, circulation, and unique design characteristics. The program of space outlines the minimum square footage allocated to every component of the spa facility, from the janitor closet to the reception lobby. The program will include space allocations and placement of a retail shop, locker areas, relaxation areas, and the desired number of treatment rooms, hair and nail stations, and any other spa features such as fitness space, pools, wet lounges, etc. Even small details such as the minimum space required for treatment product dispensary, linen storage, and offices must be included. This research is critical to the success of the project in order to properly position the spa as functional and highly desirable for travelers and/or local residents, while also distinguishing it from competitors.

Potential Site Identification and Inspection

With the recent explosion of the spa industry, it is extremely unlikely that there are any perfect spa sites that are devoid of any competition within the demographic composition predisposed to be frequent spa-goers. Thus, the identification of the spa's location may be the most critical first step in the business plan process. It would simply be unrealistic for any feasibility study/business plan to indicate the absence of competition for the proposed spa project. In fact, statements suggesting that the developer believes their project has no competition would be viewed by lenders or investors as uniformed and naïve. Strategic opportunity or competitive advantage does not exist because of an absence of competition—it is the result of having a clearly identifiable concept and unique service platform that directly appeal to a specific target market.

In selecting the location for a new day spa, there are really only three possibilities: to purchase land and build the spa; to take over existing space and reconstruct the space for use as a spa; or to identify a new development that could include a spa facility. For a hotel/resort spa, location has almost universally been predetermined by the developers of the overall hotel/resort project. In these cases it is typical for the property developers to invite a spa consultant to visit the project location in order to define the spa parameters and to examine its key elements in order to better facilitate the final recommendation. This initial visit will include:

- A review of the physical plant and grounds.
- A review of the proposed spa location within the resort/hotel project, square footages, and adjacencies.
- An examination of the proposed spa location relative to access points for both hotel guests and local spa patrons.
- A meeting with the development team to determine to what extent the spa's concept and positioning have been determined.

The principal factors in evaluating a location for a day spa include:

- Cost of the land or lease cost in cases where the day spa is part of a multi-unit shopping center or a free-standing existing building
- Zoning regulations
- Auto and pedestrian traffic and general site visibility
- Site appearance
- Related and complementary businesses
- Customer convenience

- Parking
- Area demographics within the spa's potential market
- The relative proximity to competition
- Access to the site
- Available labor market and transportation

Questions that need to be taken into consideration when placing a spa at a hotel/ resort location include:

- Can the spa site be easily accessed by hotel guests?
- How visible is the spa to hotel guests?
- Does the site have a separate entrance for use of local spa guests?
- Is there ample and convenient parking for local spa clients?
- Are the hotel fitness facilities accessible to spa guests and will they be accessible by hotel guests when the spa is closed?
- Does the location allow clean and soiled linens to be discreetly transported to the hotel laundry?
- Is there easy access for supply deliveries and support services?
- Does the location allow for access to private outdoor spa gardens or pools?

Spa Positioning Statement

Once the site has been determined, or potential sites for a day spa have at least been examined, and the information relative to the site has been prepared for the business plan/feasibility study, it is time to focus on the business itself. The business description or positioning statement follows the potential site examination in a business plan. The positioning statement is one of those exercises that is best to write first and then rewrite later, because it is a good idea to attempt a rough draft of the positioning statement before writing the entire plan. Doing so allows the person preparing the statement to better articulate his or her understanding of the spa and the adequacy of the research and planning. Once finished, the rough draft will allow for a better understanding of where additional information or planning is needed before proceeding with the entire plan development, and will provide clues as to what evidence will be required to support the initial vision for the spa. After the entire plan has been developed within the rough draft, it should be rewritten. The positioning statement is a synopsis of the entire concept—the final version must address all issues that are important, and a rewrite helps to ensure that every necessary point is covered.

Typically this section of the business/feasibility plan would start with a description of spa industry trends. The fact is that no spa operates in a vacuum. Each new spa development is part of the larger, overall spa industry and the trends and purchasing climate that impact the spa and wellness-oriented industries will inevitably affect the new spa project as well. An overview of the overall spa industry will increase the owner/developer's knowledge of the key factors that contribute to the project's success and demonstrate to potential lenders or investors that the external industry conditions that would contribute to the project's success have been researched and are understood.

The International SPA Association publishes annually the results of an industry trends study that includes the industry revenues, number of spa locations, number of employees, number of customer visits, and square footage. There are an increasing number of other studies available to include in the plan's recounting of the exponential growth of spas globally over the past 20 years. In addition to this brief macro-description, the plan should also provide a short micro-description of the industry trends of the market in which the proposed spa will operate, including the history of other spas in the target market. There have also been consumer studies such as Lifestyles of Health and Sustainability (LOHAS) that could be useful to highlight, as it is important to demonstrate the growth in consumer acceptance of the spa as an important element of their personal sense of well-being. Once an overview of the spa industry has been provided, other important topics should be covered such as the following:

- The history of the proposed spa project and progress as to what has been accomplished thus far in the spa's development. If the plan is being written for an expansion to an additional location for an existing spa business, this section should give a brief description of the significant events and milestones of the firm's history. This historical perspective must indicate why the existing spa has been successful to this point, including any major episodes in the spa's financial history and any evolutionary changes that the spa has undergone. If this section is written for a new spa venture, the plan should outline the spa's stages of development and explain what has been accomplished and what remains to be accomplished before the spa is operational.
- The spa project's vision statement. It is critical for the plan to articulate and clarify the vision and philosophy of the project. Vision statements are not simply creative exercises, but rather the principles and objectives that will guide all other aspects and activities of the spa. The plan should be able to describe the basic vision and objectives of the spa in just a few sentences that encapsulate the foundation for the concept, its guiding principles, its financial goals and culture, and strategic positioning within the marketplace. The vision should not be limited to just the opening of the spa, but should include projections as to where the spa is expected to be next year, three years from now, and five years from now as measured by growth indicators such as profits, sales, and market share.
- The spa's legal structure and organization; e.g., identify whether the spa will be a sole-proprietorship, partnership, or corporation.
- Whether the name of the spa has been selected and registered, and whether Internet domain sites have been secured.
- The spa's products and scope. This can be a brief description or, in some cases, a separate section unto itself, that describes the number of treatment rooms, hair and nail stations, etc., along with any other features that will distinguish the spa.

- The spa's services. It is not necessary to present an entire spa treatment menu of services, but this section should describe what services the proposed spa will offer and highlight those that are distinct within the market.
- Profiles of the principals involved with the spa project and a brief outline of their special experiences, qualifications, or knowledge that will help ensure the spa success.
- The financial requirements of the project. It is also advised to offer a brief synopsis of the financial status of the company; for example, the reader will want to know how the project has been funded thus far and if there are any pre-existing financial obligations.

Opportunity Analysis

It is absolutely necessary to complete a competitive market analysis and to include the results of the research in the business/feasibility plan. For a day spa project, while there is no scientific research to confirm the adage that 80 percent of the spa's business will come from a five-mile radius of the spa's location, there is sufficient antidotal evidence to support this assumption that the preparer of the business plan could begin his or her research within this radius. For a hotel/resort spa feasibility study, the preparer will need to conduct the research that would be done for a day spa project, plus evaluate the hotel/resort development data. This is because a hotel/resort spa simply cannot rely solely on the hotel guests to ensure the spa's financial success and must also compete with day spas within the market for local support.

With respect to the unique process of defining the served market for a hotel/resort spa facility, it is not just other hotels and resorts within the spa's immediate area that might be included in the competitive market. For example, a resort that is being developed in Fort Lauderdale, Florida, may determine that properties in Miami or Boca Raton or Palm Beach may be direct competition. Before the competitive market research is started, it is critical to meet with the resort ownership and development team to reach consensus as to what properties should be included in the spa's competitive market. Typically, the competitive set would range in size from eight to twelve properties; however, some properties may not be located in the immediate geographic market, but in different geographic regions. The feasibility study should include two sections: one discussing the other hotel/resort spas in the competitive set for travelers and a second focused on the competitive set for local clients.

Market Analysis

There are two important aspects necessary to research the market for a spa project within a hotel/resort. The first is to identify what the owners and developers of the project anticipate the property's positioning and market to be, and the second is to identify the competing hotel and resort spas to determine opportunities for differentiation and competitive advantage.

To prepare a feasibility plan, one must fully understand the overall project assumptions because they will impact the financial projections for the spa facility.

The types of questions that must be answered to begin the market research process would include:

- What is the projected occupancy, average daily rate, and percentage of double occupancy anticipated for each of the first five years for the hotel? The feasibility study must make assumptions with regard to the number of potential guests who will use the spa facility. For example, the forecasted average daily rate will help establish the relative positioning of the project to those properties within the competitive market. If it is anticipated that the resort/hotel project will be the market leader in average daily rate, the study may make the assumption that the guest demographics will be more likely to purchase spa treatments and services. On the other hand, if the project will be positioned at the lower end of the competitive set, the plan would want to consider that in its projections.
- What is the projected guest mix for the hotel or resort? What percentage of the guests will be group guests and what percentage will be staying at the property on vacation as leisure guests? The spa capture rate will be forecasted based on factors derived from the guest mix, average length of stay, occupancy, and average daily rate.
- What assumptions relating to group occupancy have been made with respect to the types of groups who will be booking the hotel/resort? What percentage of the group room nights will be for corporate groups, incentive business, national and regional associations, and from the tour and travel segment? The feasibility plan will want to address the group business composition by segment, as group guests staying at the hotel on an award or incentive trip will be much more likely to use the spa than guests attending a state association meeting.
- What are the national and international feeder markets for the property?
- If a resort development project includes amenities such as a golf course, an extensive tennis program, or an expansive fitness facility, what types of membership programs have been designed and what is the projected membership sales pace expected to be?
- If the property is a major hospitality brand such as Marriott or Hilton, what are the hotel guest capture rates and the overall revenue and expense histories for other properties?
- Will the hotel participate in a brand marketing group such as Preferred Hotels & Resorts or Small Luxury Hotels of the World? What Internet marketing and distribution systems will drive additional occupancy?
- Does the hotel project include a residential component and what is the projected price per square foot and sales pace for the residences? Will residents be given any spa privileges with their resident status?

Both a feasibility plan and a business plan will also require a competitive market study. A careful study of the target market may lead you to make changes to the features and character of the spa project, along with services modifications, advertising, pricing assumptions, and perhaps even location and size of the spa facility. In the long run, the market analysis will save money, as the leg work done in assembling the data for the competitive market study will help refine the spa concept. A market analysis may seem like a marketing plan, but it differs in that a feasibility/business plan analysis enables you to identify and understand your customers while a marketing plan describes how you are going to reach your customers.

In developing the competitive market study, there are many pieces of information you will want to gather on each individual spa in the competitive set. This requires the same process used to analyze day spas within the market or other hotel/resort spas. Research on individual competitive spas would include:

- The location and proximity of the competitive spa establishment to your project.
- The size and allocation of space within the spa, including the number of treatment rooms by type; the number of hair and nail stations; and the amount of space devoted to locker areas, relaxation lounges, wet lounges, retail, and other revenue-generating spaces.
- The number of years the spa has been in business.
- The ownership structure for the existing spa facilities.
- The products and services offered, such as:
    - Treatment menu and services.
    - Exercise programs and classes.
    - Educational/nutritional/lifestyle classes.
    - Food and beverage offerings.
    - Sports and recreation activities.
    - Hair and nail services offered.
- A description of the spa's concept.
- The spa's signature therapies/treatments/programs.
- Regionally inspired products and services the spa carries.
- The spa's architectural and interior design theme and concept.
- The professionalism of the spa staff.
- A product and service mix evaluation.
- A treatment menu composition.
- Advertising and marketing programs.
- Pricing averages for spa products, services, and packages.
- Existing membership programs.
- The strength of retail display and quality of merchandise.
- The spa's ambience.

- A quality assessment of the spa's linens, guestwear, grooming area supplies, and any complimentary hospitality offerings.
- A description of the sense of arrival and parking situation.
- A description of the spa's overall exterior and interior cleanliness.
- A description of the spa's overall service experience levels.

When evaluating the competition in a feasibility/business plan it is also important to include any announced or anticipated spa openings. New competition enters markets all the time and sometimes current competitors will close. Should a spa prove successful, someone will want to take a piece of that market from you. Besides a description of likely new competitors, the plan should forecast how long the competitive landscape will exist as it does at the time of writing. A forecast of the competitive climate over the next five years or so should be based on logical conclusions from specific evidence, such as the opening dates of existing competition and the number of new spas that have entered the market in recent years. This information will give potential investors a better sense of the long-term financial sustainability of the spa project.

The next item that needs to be considered is the process of collecting the information needed to complete a competitive market study. It is critical that this component of the plan be completed methodically and comprehensively; it is essential to both acquire and demonstrate an objective and thorough understanding of the spa in the competitive set. Obviously, the person(s) preparing the plan will have to visit each competitive spa, perhaps several times; however, it should be kept in mind that he or she is not there solely to experience a treatment, but with the mission of objectively studying each competitor, including its facilities and service levels. The types of information that should be collected include things such as:

- Total number of treatment rooms/spaces including:
    - Massage rooms.
    - Skin care rooms.
    - Wet rooms.
    - Hydrotherapy rooms.
    - Signature treatment rooms such as a couple's suite.
    - Hair stations.
    - Manicure and pedicure stations.
- The amount of square footage devoted to retail merchandise.
- The total square footage of the spa facilities.
- An estimated number of parking spaces.
- If the spa has any food service:
    - The number of seats.
    - The menu description.

- If the competitor has a fitness component:
    - The number of cardiovascular machines.
    - The number of stations in a resistance circuit.
    - Free weight area.
    - Number and size of movement studios.
- If the competitor has locker rooms:
    - The number of lockers.
    - The number and types of showers.
    - Whether there is a sauna, whirlpool, or other wet lounge features.
    - The number of seats in any relaxation areas.
- If there is a dedicated spa pool or outside relaxation gardens:
    - The size.
    - The number of seats.

It is suggested that this section of the plan include a half- to one-page profile of each spa within the competitive set that provides both a quantitative description and a qualitative description of the spa. Additionally, it is very helpful to the reader of the plan to include a chart such as the one shown in Exhibit 1.

The next discussion within the competitive market study should be based on personal visits to the spa as a guest, again to collect data and to evaluate the service levels. It is best to again illustrate your findings in a chart, one that lists each competitor on the horizontal axis and qualitative measures for each service component. The chart could use a rating system from 1–10, for example, with 1 representing unacceptable service and 10 indicating highly or extremely competent service. The types of service attributes that could be rated might include:

- Reservation process and confirmation protocol
- Sense of arrival
- Reception at the registration desk
- Introduction to the spa facilities and locker and relaxation areas
- Cleanliness and housekeeping standards
- Professional product lines used by the spa
- Quality of the spa's robes, sandals, terry, and locker display
- Quality of relaxation area and hospitality station if available
- Greeting by the therapist and introduction to the treatment room
- Quality of the treatment room including temperature, music, and other atmospheric features
- Quality of pre-treatment conversation with the therapist
- Quality of treatment delivery and service protocols

Exhibit 1 Competitive Spa Data Chart

	Competitor #1	Competitor #2	Competitor #3
Total Spa Square Footage			
Number of treatment rooms			
Number of Hair Stations			
Number of Nail Stations			
Total Number of Fitness Equipment Pieces			
Number of Cardio Fitness Equipment Pieces			
Number of Free Weights			
Number of Strength-Training Machines			
Square Footage of Retail Space			
Number of Saunas			
Number of Steam Rooms			
Number of Whirlpools			
Number of Relaxation Spaces			
Square Footage of Movement Studio			
Capacity Estimate of Movement Studio			
Number of Parking Spaces			

- Retail sales suggestions by therapist or sales support in the spa's retail area
- If attending fitness classes, quality of instruction and attendance
- If using a personal trainer, an evaluation of professionalism
- Check-out and departure procedures
- Overall rating

This list is not intended to be definitive, as each individual spa plan would customize the areas to be rated. The point of this exercise, however, is to allow the person(s) preparing the plan to evaluate their own facility and service expectations, which would allow for refinement of the projected spa concept and scope.

The next step in preparing the competitive analysis is to access the financial and marketing strengths of the other spas in the market. The ideal process is to interview the owners or members of the leadership team of each competitive spa to learn as much as possible about their operation. They will, of course, have a vested interest in hearing about the spa project for which the plan is being prepared, since it will be a new entrant into the market. It is natural that leaders of other spas will want to protect their market share, but during this time of explosive growth of spa globally they will likely realize that new spa facilities will enter the market and it is to their advantage to share their perspective on the market's ability to absorb an additional spa facility. The person interviewing these owners should not expect that they will provide their actual financial results, although some may be very open to sharing general operating statistics. This is especially likely if the interview is opened with a statement explaining that the research is being conducted for a proposed spa project and that the results of the research would be shared with those spas that participate. These other spas in the competitive set should not be named, but results should be provided in a summary fashion that would allow each spa to measure its own financial results against other facilities in the served market. In most cases, leadership will be unwilling to share specific financial information generally because of the potential problems and violations of the Sarbanes Oxley regulation, which prevents publicly traded companies from sharing financial data or performance statistics with potential competitors. It is essential, however, that the person preparing the plan complete exhaustive research of information that is publicly available that will convince the interviewee that he or she has a good understanding of that particular competitive spa, including its concept and positioning within the market. Sources for this type of information would include:

- The spa's menu of services.
- Current marketing pieces and brochures.
- The spa's website and/or other social websites such as Facebook.
- Industry magazines
- Acquaintances who may have used the spa
- Spa membership programs
- The spa brand if it is branded

After the preparer of the plan has gathered as much information as possible on each of the spas in the competitive set, one-on-one interviews with each of the competitive spa principals can be conducted. Even if they are unwilling to share specific financial information, there are open questions that can be asked that will give clues about the financial performance of the spa, which can be used in the process of developing revenue forecasts and operational assumptions, such as:

- Are there days of the week that you are routinely fully booked?
- What would be your busiest days and how busy might you be?
- What are your slowest days?
- On your slowest days, how many treatments might you provide?
- On a mid-week day, would you say that you average around 50 percent utilization?
- What treatments sell out first?
- Do you maintain any overall treatment room utilization percentages?

For a hotel/resort spa, ask about the business by market segment:

- Approximately what percentage of your business is from leisure hotel guests? Group guests?
- Do you do much local business? About what percentage of your total treatment sold does it contribute?
- If there is a membership program, how strongly do the members support the spa treatment departments?

Ask questions about their employees and compensation program, such as:

- How do you compensate your therapists?
    - Base wage
    - Commission percentage of service revenue
    - Fee for service
    - Retail commissions
    - Other incentives
    - Are there automatic service charges or gratuities? If so, how are they distributed?
    - Do you provide a benefits package?
    - Do you have any independent service contractors
    - Do you have any "booth or station" renters?
    - When was the last time you changed your compensation structure?
- What positions do you have for your leadership team?
- How many employees do you have, and how difficult has it been to hire new employees?
- In the ISPA Foundation's *Compensation Workbook,* it is suggested that in order to have financial sustainability, a spa's overall labor cost including benefits should be in the range of 45–60 percent. Would you say that your spa operates within that range?
- Do you track your retail sales per treatment or per customer, and approximately what are you able to achieve?
- What do pay new employees who work as support personnel, such as guest reception agents, as an entry wage rate?
- Do you waive your daily use fee for the spa facilities if the guest is having a treatment?
- For your fitness classes and personal training, how many people would you say you average for each class, and how do you compensate your class instructors and personal trainers?

Again, this list of possible questions is not intended to be definitive, but rather a guide in establishing a list of specific questions applicable to an individual spa business plan. In a case where one or more competitive spas in the market will not agree to an interview, someone might have to simply observe the traffic at the spa and extrapolate estimates of how much business the spa is doing. This can be done on a spot-check basis, where the number of people entering and leaving the spa is observed at various hours on various days of the week. Acquaintances who have been a guest at the spa might be able to provide information about how busy the spa was when they were there and how easy it was for them to book an appointment. Test calls can also be made to the spa to determine treatment availability at various times of the week. Surveys can be a very useful tool in evaluating the overall consumer perception of the spa market. The surveys can be conducted by phone, by mail, or on the Internet, and can be useful in spotting trends and assessing consumer's needs and desires. Focus groups may also be useful and are a popular form of research. There are, of course, market research firms that conduct focus group discussions, but even if there are no funds to hire a market research firm, a focus group can still be assembled, such as a group of potential customers; however, do not use people who are personally acquainted with those preparing the business/feasibility plan for any organized focus group discussions. The point is that understanding the spa's competition is too important to dismiss, should gathering the data be difficult. Once the market leaders have been determined by personal experience ratings and interviews, it will come to light that some spas are more directly competitive than others due to the fact that they command a large percentage of market share. These spas may not necessarily be the largest or have the most luxurious interiors, and they may not provide the best treatments or products at the best price, but they nevertheless represent a crucial component in evaluating your competitive position.

The next step in the process, which will be very closely examined by a potential lender or investor, is addressing the question of whether the demographics and market conditions are strong enough to ensure sufficient market share to be financially successful. This section is used for both a day spa project and for the assumptions for local support for a hotel/resort spa. Thus, the research results will be included in both feasibility studies and business plans. While there is a growing body of research as to what a hotel/resort spa may assume for capture rates and treatment room utilization averages and many experienced hotel/resort consultants who have over time developed spa revenue assumptions from the many projects with which they have been involved, there has been almost no industry research done on market dynamics for a day spa that would provide industry standards for demographic data to be translated into revenue assumptions. There has been limited research done by the International SPA Association as well as some studies published by The Day Spa Association, the Professional Beauty Association, the Salon & Spa Association, and consultants who specialize in day spa developments, but the fact is that the preparer of a day spa business plan will have to demonstrate to the lender or investor that he or she has carefully studied the market and can present adequate evidence of understanding of the spa's customer base and the size of the potential market for the spa.

There have been a number of consumer research studies completed to describe the "spa-goer," which have even categorized spa users into categories including core, peripheral, and non-spa user. According to the International Spa Association

2006 "Spa-Goer Study," while many spa-goers are male (31 percent of U.S. spa-goers; 29 percent of Canadian spa-goers), the typical spa-goer is female (69 percent of U.S. spa-goers; 71 percent of Canadian spa-goers); non-minority (85 percent of U.S. spa-goers; 70 percent of Canadian spa-goers); and in her early to mid 40s (average age of spa-goers in both countries is approximately 44). She has been going to spas for over a year, but not as long as nine years (60 percent of U.S. spa-goers; 55 percent of Canadian spa-goers), and her first spa visit was to a day spa (49 percent of U.S. spa-goers; 60 percent of Canadian spa-goers). On that first visit, she had a body massage (68 percent of U.S. spa-goers; 45 percent of Canadian spa-goers) or a facial (13 percent of U.S. spa-goers; 20 percent of Canadian spa-goers). Over time she has added other services, especially manicures (in the past year: 57 percent of U.S. spa-goers; 54 percent of Canadian spa-goers), pedicures (56 percent of U.S. spa-goers; 52 percent of Canadian spa-goers) and deep-tissue massages (48 percent of U.S. spa-goers; 33 percent of Canadian spa-goers).

The business plan must present a preponderance of evidence showing there is a sufficient customer base within the targeted demographic data to ensure that the spa project is economically viable. While there has been no exact study, there is ample antidotal evidence that a day spa should anticipate that 80 percent of its customers will come from within a five-mile radius, so research for the plan should principally focus on the immediate area surrounding the spa. There are exceptions in areas with an extremely low density of day spa facilities; however, it is advisable to be conservative when describing the spa's intended market radius. The reader of the plan will expect to see solid supporting documentation and not personal opinion, which means the plan's preparer must resist the natural tendency to be excited about the spa's concept and services and to assume that the consumers in the market will be equally enthusiastic. Thus, this section should begin with a definition of the primary geographic area the spa will serve, highlight the critical density of the area, and identify whether the spa will be located in a mall, strip center, business district, etc., or function as a stand-alone facility. It is recommended to include a detailed map of the five-mile radius surrounding the spa's location with concentrations of spa consumers identified on the map. It should also pinpoint any of the projected spa competition within the five-mile radius, including highlighted areas signaling overlap within the market. Begin the narrative by describing the demographic composition of the market in terms of the most basic, objective aspects of the customer base. The content must frame the narrative to fit within those characteristics of the spa's target market that meaningfully relate to the interest, need, and ability of the population to become customers of the spa. The following are sources that plan writers can use to collect relevant data to include in the narrative:

- *The Internet.* The Internet is the best, easiest, and least expensive place to gather data and conduct research of the industry and local market. Use search engines to find trade or industry studies or publications that are available online along with articles, statistics, surveys, and other relevant material.
- *U.S. Census Bureau reports.* The U.S. Census Bureau produces a report every ten years that provides a wealth of comprehensive demographic data. The report includes key data such as age income distribution, household

numbers, and ethnic group concentrations. The U.S. Census Bureau website, www.census.gov, contains a large amount of information including census data, publications, and population projections. Additionally, the U.S. Census Bureau conducts an economic census every five years and publishes statistical information gathered, which covers spa-related industries such as retail trade, Census of Selected Service Industries, and a Census of Women-Owned Businesses.

- *The local Chamber of Commerce.* The local Chamber of Commerce is a good source of data relating to both the business climate in the immediate area and growth and population trends.
- *Economic development offices.* Some areas have an economic development office whose mission is to attract businesses into the area and to study business trends important to those considering bringing a new business to the area.
- *State and local government agencies.* These organizations will be useful in determining sales tax collection trends, local ordinances that would affect the spa development, and population, income, and business trends.
- *Service Core of Retired Executives (SCORE).* Many areas of the country have a chapter of SCORE whose mission is to provide entrepreneurs with information and expertise on the small business environment of the local area.
- *Local Realtors' organizations and major realty offices.* These organizations and agencies will be the best source for information about home values, income levels, residential growth in the area, new communities entering the market area, and the general health of the local residential economy.
- *Local bank offices.* Banks are oftentimes useful sources for information on the local business environment and population statistics. They will want the new spa as a commercial account and will therefore be receptive to helping the plan preparer identify usable data.
- *Nearby colleges and universities.* These are frequently overlooked as a source of market data. Research bureaus and academic departments housed in schools of business administration will typically gather and evaluate various industries and the service sectors of the surrounding market area, as well as publish periodicals or reports containing updates of the economic environment and forecasts of activity in the market.
- *Merchants' associations.* Some areas will have formal merchants' groups that can be a source of information about the strength of the retail market and future developments that may enhance or impact the project spa.
- *Interviews with managers/owners of related businesses with similar customer demographic profiles.* These interviews can provide insight into their perceptions of the market, e.g., its strengths and challenges. When selecting a site for the project spa, it is important to choose an area where the spa's desired customers already go to shop. For example, it would be better to be near a Whole

Foods Market than a discount grocer, or in a strip center with unique high-end boutique shops than next to a franchise sub shop or hardware store. The managers of these similar businesses will be able to provide insight on revenue trends over the past several years and their perceptions of the consumer market strength.

- *Managers of surrounding office buildings.* Employees of nearby offices are also an important source of information, even if they live outside the five-mile radius. They will be able to provide information on the types of tenants, the total number of persons working in the building, and whether the demographics are a close match to the spa project's target market.
- *Area hotels without spas.* If there are quality hotels in the nearby area without spas, interview the front office manager or concierge staff to find out if they have spa service requests from guests to determine if business could be generated from their guests.
- *Vendors.* Vendors can be an important source of information about the strength of the market area. A skin care company, for example, is not going to share its sales information with a specific competitor, but it will certainly be able to discuss the strength of the market relative to other areas or regions as well as its growth or decline, and will clearly have an opinion regarding the ability of the market to support an additional spa facility.
- *Fitness clubs.* If the spa is not going to include a gym, it would be valuable to meet with the managers of local health and fitness clubs to ascertain membership trends, and to find out if they have existing relationships with competitive spas and whether their members support spas in the local area.
- *Medical clinics and hospitals.* The plan should include any evidence that doctors, such as dermatologists, refer patients to local spas for skin care treatments. Local physicians can recommend pre- and post-surgical massage treatments for their patients. Local hospitals attract patients from outside the immediate area, whose families visit and may be looking for opportunities to relax during the stressful time of a hospital visit.

There are dozens of other market research sources, e.g., libraries, trade associations, and groups such as professional women's groups, and the market study should cite each source used for research to illustrate the work required to develop this important section. The reader of the plan will carefully review the presentation of the plan's market data as evidence of the preparer's due diligence in assembling not just a brief overview of the spa project's market, but a thorough study of the project's target market as well.

Demand Analysis and Financial Forecast

The ultimate purpose of researching the spa industry trends, the competition, and the served market is to gather information necessary to construct a realistic revenue forecast. This forecast is the single most critical piece of information contained in the feasibility/business plan, as profitability is the most obvious indicator of success. The assumptions prepared for the revenue forecast will be carefully evaluated by the reader of the plan. An overly aggressive sales forecast can create suspicion about the plan's financial claims.

Forecasting is the art of estimating what is likely to happen based on an assumed set of conditions. This process, unfortunately, is not an exact science; rather, good forecasting is a blend of relevant information about the past and future, quality market research, the judgment of the entrepreneur, and the experience that comes from historical operations. In order for the sales forecast to be viewed as credible, the assumptions on which the forecast is built must be supported by the associated research.

Generally, financial forecasting will present detailed five-year projections for spa sales and operating expenses. Demand indicators will be based on the findings of the market research in areas including competitive set, market area supply, future developments, and long-term positioning of the spa project. Areas in which projections will be made include the following:

1. Revenue departments:
   - Massage and bodywork
   - Skin care
   - Hair
   - Nails
   - Fitness
   - Retail
   - Other revenue departments (e.g., health and wellness, food and beverage, etc.)
2. Labor costs and staffing guidelines based on spa size and projected revenues:
   - Spa management
   - Therapists/estheticians
   - Support staff
   - Dedicated retail and fitness personnel
3. Spa operating expenses

To illustrate the basic information contained in a financial forecast, the chart in Exhibit 2 displays a basic income statement showing Revenue, Cost of Sales, Payroll, and Operational Expenses for a five-year forecast period.

Demand Analysis for a Hotel/Resort Spa

In order to forecast spa revenues for a hotel/resort feasibility study, the source of spa revenues needs to be derived from usage by the hotel guests. The chart below indicates that this particular hotel project has 186 guest rooms and is forecasted to

Exhibit 2 Five-Year Forecast Profit and Loss Statement

	Year 1		Year 2		Year 3		Year 4		Year 5	
Revenue										
Treatment	$1,041,689	84.0%	$1,200,476	84.0%	1,404,794	84.0%	1,519,510	84.0%	1,585,422	84.0%
Retail	197,921	16.0%	228,091	16.0%	266,911	16.0%	288,707	16.0%	301,230	16.0%
Total Spa Revenue	1,239,610		1,428,567		1,671,705		1,808,217		1,886,652	
Cost of Sales										
Treatment Supplies & Product	51,792	4.2%	59,686	4.2%	69,845	4.2%	75,548	4.2%	78.825	4.2%
Retail Cost of Goods Sold	108,857	8.8%	125,450	8.8%	146,801	8.8%	158,789	8.8%	165,677	8.8%
Total Cost of Sales	160,649	13.0%	185,136	13.0%	216,646	13.0%	234,337	13.0%	244,502	13.0%
Payroll										
Wages and Salaries	538,333	43.4%	591,944	41.4%	658,312	39.4%	700,971	38.8%	730,958	38.7%
Related Payroll	80,750	6.5%	88,792	6.2%	98,747	5.9%	105,146	5.8%	109,644	5.8%
Total Payroll & Related	619,083	49.9%	680,736	47.7%	757,059	45.3%	806,117	44.6%	840,602	44.6%
Operational Expenses										
Spa	181,221	14.6%	201,502	14.1%	225,142	13.5%	222,694	12.3%	232,310	12.3%
Retail	12,865	1.0%	14,826	1.0%	17,349	1.0%	18,766	1.0%	19,580	1.0%
Total Operational Expenses	194,086	15.7%	216,328	15.1%	242,491	14.5%	241,460	13.3%	251,890	13.3%
Total Spa Profit	265,792	21.4%	346,367	24.2%	455,509	27.2%	526,303	29.1%	549,658	29.1%

run 76 percent occupancy in its first year of operation, growing to 78 percent by the fifth year:

	Year 1	Year 2	Year 3	Year 4	Year 5
Guestroom Inventory					
Guestrooms	186	186	186	186	186
Total Annual Guestrooms Available	67,890	67,890	67,890	67,890	67,890
Annual Occupied Guestrooms					
Guestrooms	51,596	51,596	52,275	52,275	52,954
Total Annual Occupied Guestrooms	51,596	51,596	52,275	52,275	52,954
Occupancy %					
Guestrooms	76.0%	76.0%	77.0%	77.0%	78.0%
Average Occupancy %	76.0%	76.0%	77.0%	77.0%	78.0%

Next, an assumption must be made to reflect the number of qualified guests that will occupy each sold guestroom. A **qualified guest** is defined as anyone over the age of 18 who could be a potential spa user. Urban hotel locations will generally have a double occupancy rate of approximately 1.1 potential spa guests per occupied room, while resort locations generally would experience a double occupancy percentage in the range of 1.5–2.2. Guest mix is also an important factor when considering the potential users of the spa. Thus, an estimate of guest distribution between those traveling on leisure and those traveling for business must be established as shown on the chart in Exhibit 3.

Once the potential hotel guest population has been calculated based on the market segment of group and leisure guests, a capture rate of each guest mix

Exhibit 3 Guest Mix Chart

Guest Mix	Year 1	Year 2	Year 3	Year 4	Year 5
Guests per Occupied Room	1.3	1.3	1.3	1.3	1.3
Annual Property Guests Available	67,075	67,075	67,958	67,958	68,840
Hotel Guest Mix %					
Group %	15%	15%	15%	15%	15%
Transient %	85%	85%	85%	85%	85%
Total Guest Mix					
Group Guests	10,061	10,061	10,194	10,194	10,326
Transient Guests	57,014	57,014	57,764	57,764	58,514

assumption must be set. To do this, the preparer of the spa feasibility study should discuss the various types of groups the property will attract with the property developers. Incentive groups staying at the property will be more likely to use the spa facilities than those staying for business because those guests will most likely have less time to use the spa due to their more extensive schedules. Almost always, the spa will achieve a higher capture rate of transient guests, as these guests are at the resort to rest, relax, and renew themselves. The spa capture rate assumption chart is illustrated in Exhibit 4.

Additionally, a hotel/resort feasibility plan will make assumptions with respect to other direct hotel/resort demand generators for spa usage if the project includes a membership component. Increasingly, hotels are being developed with a residential component whereby the hotel would, for example, occupy the first twelve floors of a urban hotel, while the remaining four floors would be occupied by private residents. Again, in meeting with the overall project owners/developers, the spa consultant or other plan preparer would need to ascertain the projected pace of membership program sales and/or the sales pace of residential units, as the people in both groups would be expected to be spa users. A chart illustrating these demand generators can be found in Exhibit 5.

The last assumption that must be made is the number of treatments sold to local residents. The number of local clients who use hotel/resort spas ranges from near zero for those few properties that do not allow any local patronage to as high as 60–75 percent for those properties located in areas with very high populations of spa-goer demographic residents and a comprehensive marketing strategy to attract local customers. Although there has been no specific research conducted that has studied hotel/resort spa average capture rates for local guests, it is estimated that hotel/resort spas average approximately 30 percent of local market contribution. An increased capture of local spa guests can greatly enhance the overall success of the spa by off-setting weekly and seasonal fluctuations and stabilizing utilization to drive yield. Once the hotel guest and related hotel demand estimates have been calculated it is advisable to do a quick calculation of the assumptions made thus far to test the reliability of the data presented in the feasibility study. Thus, for our small 186-room hotel example, we will assume that the local market usage will grow from 30 percent in the first year to 40 percent by the fifth year.

Exhibit 4 The Spa Capture Rate Assumption Chart

Spa Capture	Year 1	Year 2	Year 3	Year 4	Year 5
Hotel Guest Capture					
Group	5.0%	5.9%	6.5%	7.1%	7.1%
Transient	10.0%	11.5%	12.7%	13.7%	13.7%
Group	503	594	662	724	733
Transient	5,701	6,557	7,336	7,914	8,016
Hotel Spa Guests	6,204	7,151	7,998	8,638	8,749
Hotel Guest Spa Capture	9.3%	10.7%	11.8%	12.7%	12.7%
Spa Capture per Occupied Room	12.0%	13.9%	15.3%	16.5%	16.5%

Exhibit 5 Other Hotel Demand Generators

	Year 1	Year 2	Year 3	Year 4	Year 5
Number of Members	80	120	160	200	200
Membership Spa Monthly Usage (times per member)	0.8	0.8	0.9	0.9	1
Annual Member Treatments	768	1,152	1,728	2,160	2,400
Residential Units Sales Pace	60	90	100	100	100
Resident Spa Monthly Usage (times per member)	1.3	1.3	1.4	1.4	1.5
Annual Resident Treatments	936	1,404	1,680	1,680	1,800
Total Member/Resident Annual treatments	1,704	2,556	3,408	3,840	4,200

There have been surveys of treatment room utilization that suggest that treatment room utilization/occupancy averages from the low 30 percent to 40 percent range. Exhibit 6 reflects the utilization progress of the spa over the first five years based on the assumptions made up to this point. (The calculations used to establish local market demand in Exhibit 6 will be covered later in the chapter.)

The quick validation test presented in Exhibit 6 would seem to give credence to the assumptions made thus far as the spa in its infancy would be expected to achieve a utilization rate lower than industry averages and then to achieve industry averages by its third year of operation. By the fifth year, the spa is expected to perform at a higher utilization percentage.

It should be noted that all of the assumptions and calculations thus far have dealt specifically with a hotel/resort spa project. The next step in the demand analysis, however, is to address the local market contribution to spa revenues, which should be done by both the spa feasibility plan and the business plan. It is the most difficult type of forecasting to ascertain, as there has yet to be a significant spa industry study to establish industry trends for local contribution. Thus, the assumptions used in the plan will be determined based on the quality of the

Exhibit 6 Spa Treatment Utilization Assumption Test

Assuming there is available ten appointment hours each day, 365 days a year, for twelve treatment spaces, which equals a total of 43,800 available annual treatment hours (10 × 365 × 12 = 43,800).

	Year 1	Year 2	Year 3	Year 4	Year 5
Hotel Guest Group	503	594	662	728	737
Hotel Guest Transients	5,701	6,557	7,336	7,914	8,016
Total Hotel Guests	6,204	7,151	7,998	8,642	8,753
Members	768	1,152	1,728	2,160	2,400
Residents	936	1,404	1,680	1,680	1,800
Total Hotel Demand	7,908	9,707	11,406	12,482	12,953
Local Market Demand	30%	33%	35%	38%	40%
Local Contribution	2,372	3,203	3,992	4,741	5,180
Total Treatments	10,280	12,910	15,398	17,223	18,133
Utilization Percentage	23.47%	29.47%	35.16%	39.31%	41.39%

preparer's market analysis and the art of using supporting data that will give the reader a sense of confidence in the evidence presented to support the financial projections.

Forecasting Local Demand

Forecasting local demand for a second location is easier than doing so for an initial location. In forecasting local demand for a second location for an existing day spa operation and for a hotel/resort brand with several other spa operations, the preparer of the plan can extrapolate data from similar market conditions and past sales histories to use as the basis for local market revenue projections, even if the additional locations are in different regions. For example, for a day spa plan for a second location, the preparer can compare the demographic data for the five-mile radius of the existing operation with the demographic data for the proposed site. Then, accounting for variances in demographic composition, the preparer can extrapolate from the historical experience from the first location to set the assumptions for the new project. Likewise, in the case of a hospitality-branded hotel/resort spa development, the study preparer should be able to gather the local market contribution from other spa locations, and again extrapolate from the historical data and base the assumptions for the new project off that information. This does not mean, however, that a consultant doing work for a hotel brand with forty spas that average 38 percent local contribution can simply assume a 38 percent local market for the spa being developed. It would be important to research the residential and business demographics of other locations and base the spa's demand forecasts on the most similar locations.

There is an inherent caution that must accompany the extrapolation of information. It is clear that for any extrapolated forecast, regardless of the level of technical sophistication employed, the assumptions implicitly assume that the conditions causing historical sales patterns will continue into the future. Since any forecast is only as good as its underlying assumptions, a revenue projection will be realistic if the market conditions are comparable and if the past is a reliable indicator of the future. Where circumstances are changing, any extrapolations of sales should be used as a starting point for projecting revenues for the new project.

The most difficult potential market assumptions to make are for an initial day spa project because it does not have a directly comparable spa from which to base its sales forecast. In the most basic terms, financial success will be determined by the demographic population within the served market. Following meetings with the competitive spas within the market and personal observations, the plan preparer should be able to construct a model of sales projections for the other spas based on the data collected. The goal of this exercise is to gain an estimate of the number of treatments, treatment room/service area utilization percentages, and average revenue per treatment within each of the revenue departments, which can then be compared to the sales forecast for the new spa project so adjustments can be made if necessary.

The model would also include a profile of each of the competitive spas that would say, for example:

> Competitor One: In discussions with the spa's manager, through personal observation, and in conversation with the therapist during shopping tests of the spa, I attempted to learn if there were days of the week when the spa is always fully booked. The manager stated that the spa is fully booked every Saturday and nearly always booked on Fridays. When asked to identify the slowest days of the week, the manager responded that Sundays were hit and miss, with some Sundays having about half of the appointment times booked, while other Sundays had only about 10 percent of the appointment times booked. When asked about weekday volume, the manager's description of customer traffic suggested that Mondays were the quietest day of the week and that no hair services were booked for Mondays. Business would then build during the week with Tuesdays being about 20 percent booked, while on Wednesdays and Thursdays about one third of the appointment times are reserved, although Thursdays can sometimes be a stronger day.

Additionally, if the competitive research included any personal customer count observations at different times and different days of the week, the plan would also include that information.

After this brief competitive narrative, the model would provide an outline of the estimates of business volume such as the one found in Exhibit 7. This exhibit would suggest that Competitor One would generate approximately 22,000 treatments/services during a year, which is calculated by multiplying the 440 services by 50 weeks. By using 50 weeks instead of 52 weeks, the forecast would take into account those anomalous weeks during the year, such as the days immediately preceding or following a holiday or when there is bad weather, when the spa will experience very low sales that cannot be forecasted.

The plan should include a brief narrative and chart such as the one found in Exhibit 7 for each competitor. It should also include a table listing each competitor and their respective utilization estimates, along with the project spa's

Exhibit 7 Estimated Business Volume for a Spa Project

Competitor One

Size:

Massage Rooms	6
Skin Care Rooms	2
Hair Rooms	4
Nail Rooms	4

	Operating Hours	Utilization Estimate	Number of Services
Monday	8	15%	20
Tuesday	10	6%	10
Wednesday	10	13%	20
Thursday	10	25%	40
Friday	10	50%	80
Saturday	10	75%	120
Sunday	10	94%	150
Total		**40.44%**	**440**

Note: This utilization estimate does not factor in any seasonal changes; in some markets the chart may include additional columns for seasonal sales variations and utilizations percentages during different times of the year.

utilization estimates so that the reader of the plan can see at a glance how the new spa development's revenues are being forecasted relative to the competitive market. It should be noted, however, that this information is only intended to illustrate the market and provide an evidentiary reference for the sales projections for the new spa project, and should be used as a test for the data and assumptions. If these charts were the only market research data shown for the spa project's revenue assumptions, the potential lender/investor would be naturally skeptical of the new spa project's success in gaining full market share.

The most common method used for forecasting sales is the **market sales build-up method,** which uses the market research data collected to project customer contributions. The market build-up method involves identifying potential spa customers both within and outside the market and estimating their contribution to spa treatment usage.

Overall Demographic Assumption. Remember in the market research discussion the statement, "It is all about the demographics" is largely true. The summary description of the population, number of households, average and medium home values, age, income levels, gender, new residential and commercial developments, and the potential buyers' assumption will receive the most scrutiny and require the most evidence in the potential market and revenue forecast.

Other Market Demand Generator Assumptions. The plan also needs to discuss other specific sources of potential spa users and treatment/service volume assumptions such as follows:

> There are three office buildings within two blocks of the spa project site. Building has x number of square feet with 24 tenants totaling 850 employees. Management would estimate that 30 percent of the employees earn $75,000 plus and 70 percent reside outside the five-mile radius of the building. Interviews were conducted with the three major tenants: a large law firm, a realtor office, and an accounting services firm. The office manager at the realtor office expressed that he could see a few of the employees using the spa, while the two firms suggested that they would use spa gift certificates for employee incentive programs and there would be additional support if the employees were given a preferential discount. (Buildings B and C would need a similar description prepared, and an assumption as to the total number of treatments the three buildings would generate would need to be provided).

The plan should list the number of offices within the five-mile radius along with the amount of people employed in each, as well as summarize the office's estimated income and businesses profile. It would not be necessary to present a profile for each office building in the area, but the plan should highlight any significant demand generator companies, such as a software development company that routinely provides their employees with a spa experience. The plan would present several assumptions for the remaining offices.

The plan might also include hotel properties within the five-mile radius that do not have their own spa, and medical clinics or physician offices within the area, particularly if there are plastic surgeons or dermatological offices. Assumptions would need to be made as to how many treatments these places would generate.

Unique concepts that will stimulate additional sales should also be included in this section. For example, if the spa plans on doing a Thursday after-work champagne and manicure/pedicure program for the women working in the nearby offices, it would be appropriate to include an assumption of the number of services that this program is anticipated to generate.

The plan would next provide an exhibit of the total number of treatments forecasted for the project spa on an annual basis, including the number of treatments anticipated by each demand generator. The total would be compared with the other spas in the competitive set.

Once the total number of annual treatments has been forecasted, two additional assumptions must be presented to determine revenues by department. There is a wide range in sources of data regarding revenues and mix of business between a hotel/resort spa and a day spa. There has been sufficient research conducted over the past few years to suggest that the industry averages for a hotel/resort spa would be:

Massage and Bodywork Department	55%
Skin Care Department	20%
Hair Department	10%
Nail Department	15%

It must be considered, however, that there are two principal types of day spas. The first type is the salon/day spa, where there is a large hair and nail emphasis with a predominance of hair and nail stations, but a limited number of spa treatment rooms. The second type sells only spa services and perhaps has a nail area, but no hair stations. Thus, there is no definitive day spa industry research for mix of business for the many variations in day spas, but the following model reflects antidotal studies and is intended to illustrate the significant variations that can occur:

	Day Spa w/o Hair & Nail	Salon/Day Spa
Massage	45%	18%
Skin Care	55%	20%
Hair	0%	50%
Nail	0%	12%

For the purpose of this chapter discussion, the spa project is neither a salon/day spa with heavy emphasis on hair and nail stations nor a day spa that does not have hair services. The owner/developer of a day spa in reality would set the number of treatment room/stations based on the spa concept and market conditions. For simplicity's sake we will assume the following mix of business and a first-year total of 15,000 treatments for our day spa project:

Source/Mix of Business Assumption

Department	Percentage of Treatments	Number of Treatments
Massage and Body	40%	6,000
Skin Care	25%	3,750
Hair	15%	2,250
Nail	20%	3,000
Totals	100%	15,000

Pricing/Revenue per Treatment

Until recently, there was little discounting and almost no price premiums for peak demand appointment times used in hotel/resort spas. Day spas, on the other hand, have widely distributed coupons and special promotions to attract new clients. Thus, for those consultants preparing hotel/resort feasibility studies, it was common practice to simply use the suggested printed prices from the competitor's spas as a guide to the revenues projections of the spa under development. Meanwhile, most professionally managed day spas will track the amount of discounts from published pricing, which could be as high as 30 percent for some spas, in an effort to build a loyal client base. During the competitive analysis for a day spa, it is important to ask for an estimate of how much business it discounts. In the case of either a hotel/resort spa or a day spa, an exhibit should be presented in the plan displaying the market pricing dynamics, such as:

Treatment Pricing Comparison

Spa Name	50-Min Massage	50-Min. Facial	50-Min. Body Scrub	Spa Manicure	Spa Pedicure	Hair Cut/Style	% Disc.
Comp 1	120	130	120	35	50	55	20%
Comp 2	100	110	na	30	45	50	25%
Comp 3	125	130	130	35	45	na	20%
Average	115	123	125	33	47	53	22%

Next the plan would discuss the average treatment revenue assumptions and promotional discount marketing. For example, the plan may suggest that the percentage of business to be discounted or special promotions given in the first year be 30 percent, and lowered in succeeding years as a loyal customer base is established:

Gross Treatment Sales Model

Treatment	Percentage of Mix	Number of Treatments	Average Treatment Price	Revenue
Massage and Body	40%	6,000	$110	$660,000
Skin Care	25%	3,750	120	$450,000
Hair	15%	2,250	50	$112,500
Nail	20%	3,000	40	$ 120,000
Totals		15,000	$89.50	$1,342,500

The plan would then adjust the projected revenues to reflect the promotions and discounts. For illustration purposes, assume that the average discount is 18 percent. Thus, for massage and body revenues, $660,000 would be multiplied by 30 percent, which equals $198,000, and then multiplied by 18 percent to determine what the discount amount would total, resulting in a projected first year's revenues of $660,000 less $35,640 for a total of $624,360. The same calculation would be done for each treatment department resulting in the following:

Year One Treatment Revenue Forecast with Discounts

Treatment	#Treatments	Avg. Treatment Revenue	Revenue
Massage	6,000	$104.00	$624,360
Skin Care	3,750	$114.00	$425,700
Hair	2,250	$47.00	$106,225
Nail	3,000	$38.00	$113,520
Totals	15,000	$84.65	$1,269,805

Retail Revenues Forecast

Retail revenue is a significant contributor to spa revenue and profitability. The associated labor cost for retail sales and high margins can significantly increase profitability. The feasibility/business plan should describe the spa's retail strategy and establish retail revenue assumptions based on the specific concept for the project. Retail revenues are projected in two ways: as a fixed dollar amount per treatment or as a percentage of treatment revenues. Some plans will choose to be very detailed in their retail assumptions, knowing that a customer who is at the spa for a facial is much more inclined to buy skin care products than a client who is at the spa to have her nails done. For example, if the plan is projecting retail revenues as fixed dollar amounts, it might reflect retail revenues of $35 per skin care treatment and $5 for a nail treatment.

The other retail revenue projection method makes an assumption of retail revenues as a percentage of overall treatment revenue. A luxury resort with a dedicated spa retail shop and highly trained sales staff may achieve between 20 and 30 percent in retail revenues as a percentage of treatment sales, while a smaller day spa without a dedicated retail store and limited merchandise displayed in the reception area may experience retail revenues between 10 and 15 percent. The plan establishes the retail revenue assumptions based on the specific concept for the project.

The plan would then go through the same process for any other revenue departments. If the spa concept includes a membership department, for example, the plan preparer would need to make a series of assumptions (and provide rationale for these assumptions) including:

- The number of memberships.
- The initiation fee and whether it will be tiered.
- The dues structure.
- The pace of attracting members.
- The retention rate for members.
- The daily use fee available for non-members (if applicable).

Once these assumptions were decided, the plan would present a revenue forecast for the department. The same process would be done until the first-year revenues for all departments were identified.

Once all of the first-year revenue forecasts have been established and the underlying evidence and assumptions outlined, the plan should present a five-year revenue projection. There should be an accompanying narrative that discusses the justifications for the forecast of revenues made as the spa matures from its infancy in the first year through growth cycle years and reaches stabilization in revenues in the fourth or fifth year of operation. It would be expected that the spa would experience accelerated revenue growth in the second and third years as it builds brand loyalty, with the rate of growth slowing over time. For example, the five-year projections might assume a growth rate of 10 percent in year two, 7 percent in year three, 5 percent in year four, and 3 percent in year five.

Other underlying factors should also be discussed in the five-year revenue projection, such as the forecasted discount percentages. Potentially significant influences, such as a new office tower being completed in year three directly across the street from the spa or a large new residential community opening during year two just a mile away from the spa, should be included as well. Exhibit 8 presents a five-year projection for the example spa.

Spa Project Marketing

How does one approach a revenue forecast for a spa project for which the location has not been decided? In cases where a day spa developer has defined a spa

Exhibit 8 Sample Five-Year Revenue Projection

Five-Year Revenue Projections					
Revenue Departments	**Year 1**	**Year 2**	**Year 3**	**Year 4**	**Year 5**
Treatment Revenues:					
Massage	$ 624,300	$ 693,000	$ 749,000	$ 786,000	$ 809,000
Skin Care	425,700	473,000	511,000	536,000	551,000
Hair	106,200	118,500	128,200	135,000	139,800
Nail	113,500	126,000	136,000	142,500	146,500
Total Treatment Revenues	1,269,700	1,410,500	1,524,200	1,599,500	1,646,300
Retail Revenues	194,000	282,100	304,800	319,900	329,300
Total Spa Revenues	$1,463,700	$1,692,600	$1,829,000	$1,919,400	$1,975,600

concept that he or she feels would be in high demand and is creating a business plan to seek funding or investors before a specific location has been identified, the revenue forecasting becomes more difficult. The plan cannot include a detailed analysis of the served market, so it should instead provide a detailed description of the demographic characteristics of the location that will be selected in the concept narrative and profile of the spa's customers. The required space, terms of the lease, and build-out costs will be based on assumptions, while the calculations of demand drivers from actual research will be replaced with assumptions provided in a marketing section of the business plan.

If the intention is to seek external funding, the preparer must realize that the potential investors will study the marketing plan section very carefully. They will want to be assured that the project has a realistic strategy to attract customers to the spa. The marketing section of the business plan will need to articulate, first and foremost, the spa's core message and how the spa's positioning will motivate consumers to experience the spa. Traditional marketing experts emphasize the following elements, known as "the Four P's," which influence customers to buy:

1. Product: The tangible aspects of the service experience.
2. Price: The cost/value advantage.
3. Place: The desired location's convenience and design.
4. Promotion: The amount and nature of the marketing activities.

Most marketing strategies agree that consumers buy benefits, not features. Potential customers are more concerned with how a purchase will benefit them than about how the spa achieves that result. The marketing section must tell the reader what the clients can expect to receive, such as an enhanced self-image or emotional and educational engagement, rather than just give detailed descriptions of what the spa includes. The bottom line is that the marketing section should end with the five-year revenue projections based on the assumptions outlined in the marketing strategies.

Payroll and Staffing Guidelines

Payroll is a spa's largest expense. In North American and Western European spa operations, depending on the geographical location, payroll expense can range from 30 percent to 70 percent of gross revenues. The ISPA Foundation's *Compensation Workbook for the Spa Industry* targets a total labor cost (wages plus taxes and benefits) between 45 and 60 percent for a spa to sustain financial success. Of course, payroll levels are also dictated by the availability of skilled labor and experienced therapists and regional labor laws. A well-conceived plan will generally include an exhibit of the competitive wage rates in the served market that can be determined during the meetings with the competitive spa or separately as a local area wage survey. Spas are generally willing to participate in these surveys, providing the results are shared with the participants without identifying the names of any specific spa operations. The plan should establish a proposed compensation structure with supporting assumptions including:

- A therapist compensation program, such as base wage and commission, fee per service, straight commission, etc.
- Entry-level and experienced rates for support staff including guest receptionists, reservationists, spa attendants, and concierge or hostess personnel.
- Potential benefit offerings and the corresponding benefits cost percentage assumption.
- A management compensation program.

Competent management stands out as the most important ingredient in business success. Thus, it will add strength to the plan if the owner/operator or other key leadership personnel are identified, including a brief description of their prior experience and previous spa successes. This can inspire confidence in the reader.

It is advisable to include an organizational chart in this section. In the case of a small spa project, the chart can simply list the owner/operator, with a couple of supervisory positions and the number of service providers for each revenue department. The organizational chart for an expansive hotel/resort spa, on the other hand, might include the spa director and assistant director; other managers such as the sales coordinator, guest registration and reservations manager, fitness manager, retail manager, lead therapists in each treatment discipline; other staff members such as attendants and housekeepers; and titles of the various line positions along with the wage rates and number of staff. In either case, the plan should give the reader an overview of the staffing and organization of the spa.

Direct Payroll and Related Expenses for Treatment Departments

In accordance with the *Uniform System of Financial Reporting for Spas (USFRS)*, the first calculations of payroll and expense would be to make assumptions regarding direct labor cost percentages and the cost per treatment for professional products and supplies for the massage and bodywork, skin care, and hair and nails treatment revenue centers. Typically, a business plan would present the direct labor costs as a percentage of revenues. The ISPA compensation study recommends that total labor cost be in the range of 45 to 60 percent. The therapist payroll is the most

Exhibit 9 Direct Labor and Professional Product and Supplies

For the sake of simplicity, this exhibit uses a 25 percent direct labor cost percentage for the massage and skin care departments and a 40 percent commission assumption for the hair and nail departments.

	Revenue	# of Treatments	Direct Labor	Product & Supply	Contribution
Massage & Bodywork Department	$624,300	6,000	$156,075	$30,000	$438,225
Skin Care Department	$425,700	3,750	$106,425	$45,000	$274,275
Hair Department	$106,200	2,250	$ 42,480	$22,500	$ 41,220
Nail Department	$113,500	3,000	$ 45,400	$24,000	$ 44,100

significant component of overall labor costs because availability of qualified staff is essential in any market.

It is also likely that the labor cost percentage will not be identical for all treatment departments. For example, in many markets hair and nail technicians will be paid a higher commission percentage than the massage therapists due to competition with salons and nail businesses or a shortage of qualified technicians within the market. In this case, the plan might use a labor percentage of 25–30 percent for the massage department and a labor percentage of 30–40 percent for the hair and nail department.

The professional products and supplies will also vary for different treatment departments. It should be obvious, for example, that the professional product and supply expense for a Swedish massage would be lower than the expense for a facial. The business plan should present costs based upon the number of treatments as costs per treatment, not percentages of department revenues. Exhibit 9 gives an illustration of how these expenses should be presented in a business plan. For illustration purposes, we will use an average of:

- Massage and Bodywork $5
- Skin Care $12
- Hair $10
- Nails $8

Indirect Support Labor and Indirect Operating Expenses

This section of the plan will discuss the support staff necessary to operate the spa. Small spas can employ as few as one to two staff members to work guest reception and reservations; a host(ess) to serve clients beverages and keep the waiting area tidy on the busy days; and a housekeeper. On the other end of the spectrum, a large hotel/resort spa may have several reception stations with a base staff of two employees on quiet days and four to five on a busy weekend; a separate concierge desk in the reception lobby requiring at least one employee; a back office reservations area with several employees; one or more locker room attendants in both the men's and women's areas; a daytime housekeeping staff composed of several employees; and a nighttime cleaning staff to deep clean the entire spa. In either case, the plan should list the staff positions and outline the fixed staffing minimum number of hours staff must work, average rate of pay, and added expense for benefits for each position. It should also describe the staffing assumptions used to calculate the total cost of each support staff position for the year. For example, the plan might say that the spa will operate for ten hours per day, with the base staff at the reception desk consisting of one employee who works for ten hours. On busier days with more than fifty appointments, the staffing guide would add one swing-shift receptionist working from 11 A.M. to 7 P.M. Finally, on the weekend, the desk could staff two employees for all operating hours plus an additional employee to work a mid-day shift for a total of 28 hours on those days. If we assume that the average wage for the guest reception staff is $12.00 and the spa is operating with minimum staffing on Sundays and Mondays, one swing position on Tuesdays through Thursdays, and a full staff on Fridays and Saturdays, it would total:

Sundays and Mondays: 10 hours × $12.00× 52 weeks =	$6,240
Tuesday–Thursdays: 18 hours × 12.00 × 52 weeks =	$11,232
Friday and Saturdays: 40 hours × $12.00 × 52 weeks =	$24,960
Salaried Guest Reception Manager:	$35,000
Total Guest Reception Payroll:	$77,432

Of course, a percentage for benefit expenses would be added to this total based on the intended benefit package and qualification requirements.

The same process of developing a staffing assumption and average wage rate would be used for each support labor position and an exhibit would be prepared to illustrate the total cost of the spa's support labor.

The indirect operating expenses are expenses for the spa treatment departments that are not specific to an individual department. Guests receiving a spa service or services from one or more of the treatment departments use these expenses as part of the treatment experience. The items will vary according to the needs and requirements of individual spas, and the line items would be the specific line items shown in the *USFRS*. The Indirect Operating Expenses schedule includes:

- Ambience—the cost of providing the sensory environment.
- Contract Services—outsourced service such as janitorial work or window washing.
- Dues and Subscriptions—the cost of memberships, such as ISPA and the local Chamber of Commerce.
- Equipment Rental—the cost of equipment rented for use in the spa.
- Guest Clothing—items such as robes and sandals, salon smocks, etc.
- Guest Supplies—the cost of the spa locker room area supplies and amenities that are provided on a complimentary basis.
- Hospitality—the cost of bottled water, fresh fruit, teas, and other items provided to the guest at no cost.

- Laundry—the cost of processing linens by either an outside laundry service or the cost of cleaning the linens in-house.
- Licenses and Fees—the costs of all federal, state, and municipal licenses.
- Linen—Items such as sheets, terry cloth, blankets, and treatment table covers.
- Operating Supplies—a general account for expenses such as cleaning supplies, printed forms, facial tissue and toilet paper, office supplies, and similar expenses in the spa.
- Professional Development—the costs of training spa employees outside of the employee's time.
- Telecommunications—the cost of items such as monthly telephone charges, cell phones, and pagers.
- Uniforms—the cost or rental of uniforms for employees.
- Other—the cost of spa expenses that do not apply to the accounts listed previously.

The plan should include a brief description of each item and an annual forecast of the expense of each, which would be shown on an exhibit depicting all indirect operating expenses. For example, the spa may plan on becoming a member of ISPA and the local Chamber of Commerce, plus provide the guest with reading materials in the relaxation areas at a cost of $100 per month. The preparer would simply total those three expenses and record that amount under Dues and Subscriptions on the exhibit.

Other Operating Departments

While it may seem as though the feasibility/business plan is now complete, there is still considerable work remaining. While all spas will include a retail department, there are many medium and large spas that will have a number of other operating departments, which could include:

- Fitness
- Food and beverage
- Spa café
- Health and wellness
- Membership
- Rentals and other income
- Smaller, specialized operating departments such as:
    - Art programs
    - Adventure experiences
    - Pool/beach services
    - Guided hiking programs
    - Equestrian

- Children's camps
- Tennis
- Additional retail shops

The *USFRS* has schedules for each of these other operating departments (schedules 5–11), which can be used as a guide in preparing this portion of the plan. It is necessary to go through the same exercise with each of these departments, just as assumptions were described, payroll calculations were determined, and operating expenses were forecasted for each spa treatment department in the previous sections. It would not, however, be expected that a fully developed schedule for each of the other operating departments be included.

An expansive retail operation, for example, would include in the plan a cost of goods sold assumption along with a brief description of any dedicated retail staff positions, including retail manager and sales clerks. In a small operation, retail sales are often handled by the guest reception staff. Finally, an estimate of the retail operating expenses would be included. All of this information would result in an abbreviated table such as the following, as well as a short narrative that discusses each of the assumptions used in the exhibit with regard to revenues, cost of goods sold, labor costs, and other retail expenses:

Retail Department Assumptions	
Revenues:	$194,000
Cost of Goods Sold:	$93,000 (based on 48% COGS)
Gross Margin:	$101,000
Retail Labor Expense:	$25,000 (based on one working supervisor)
Other Retail Expenses:	$10,400 (based on 5.4% of revenues)
Retail Departmental Income:	65,600 (33.8% retail profit)

The plan should not simply indicate one combined revenue number for each of the other operating departments, but instead should discuss the assumptions used to build the revenues. For example, the plan would not simply state "Fitness Department Revenues: $100,000," but would discuss the fitness concept and articulate the assumptions with regard to personal training revenues, group exercise revenues, fitness evaluation revenues, and any other relevant revenues. The membership department would likewise discuss the methodology for calculating forecasted Daily Facility/Guest Fees, Initiation Fees, and Membership Dues revenues.

Undistributed Overhead Expenses

Once each of these other operating departments is analyzed and the projections exhibited, the financial calculations should be summarized to illustrate the spa project's Income before Undistributed Expenses. This point marks the end of the commonalities between the hotel/resort feasibility study and the day spa business plan.

The *USFRS* has established the industry standard for reporting these expenses as shown on spa schedules 14—Administrative and General, 15—Marketing, and 16—Facility Maintenance and Utilities (see Exhibits 10, 11, and 12). There are a total of sixty-seven different line items listed on the three schedules, making it

Exhibit 10 Spa Sub-Schedule 14: Administrative and General

	Current Period
Payroll and Related Expenses	
Management Salaries	$
Administrative Salaries and Wages	______
Total Salaries and Wages	
Payroll Taxes and Employee Benefits	______
Total Payroll and Related Expenses	
Accounting Expenses	
Audit and Other External Expenses	
Payroll Processing Expenses	
Other Accounting Expenses	______
Total Accounting Expenses	______
Other Expenses	
Bank Charges	
Cash Over/Short	
Contract Services	
Corporate Office Charges	
Credit and Collection	
Credit Card Commissions	
Donations	
Dues and Subscriptions	
Human Resources	
Information Systems	
Legal and Professional	
Licenses and Fees	
Loss and Damage	
Meals and Entertainment	
Operating Supplies	
Postage	
Professional Development	
Provision for Doubtful Accounts	
Security	
Telecommunications	
Travel	
Other	______
Total Other Expenses	______
Total Administrative and General Expenses	$ ______

highly impractical to do a detailed analysis and set of assumptions for each line item. Adding to the difficulty is the fact that there has not been any meaningful research done that establishes industry standards for each line item. The business plan preparer should highlight those line items of which he or she has specific knowledge. For example, if the spa will have a position dedicated specifically to sales and marketing, the plan should discuss the reasoning behind this choice and indicate the intended pay for that position. Yet another example might be that the spa has received an estimate for the cost of heating, ventilation, and air conditioning (HVAC) equipment from a company with which the owner/developer of the spa has a relationship from previous business dealings; this relationship should be mentioned, as well as the specific licenses and fees if known. Other than a few

Exhibit 11 Spa Sub-Schedule 15: Marketing

	Current Period
Payroll and Related Expenses	
Salaries and Wages	$
Payroll Taxes and Employee Benefits	
Total Payroll and Related Expenses	
Other Expenses	
Advertising Broadcast	
Advertising Print	
Agency Fees	
Collateral Materials	
Complimentary Guests	
Contract Services	
Direct Mail	
Dues and Subscriptions	
In-House Promotions	
Meals and Entertainment	
Postage	
Professional Development	
Special Events	
Telecommunications	
Trade Shows	
Travel	
Other	
Total Other Expenses	
Total Marketing Expenses	$

specific line item expenses, however, the plan would have to make a tremendous number of assumptions if it were to include an annual dollar amount for each of the sixty-seven line items. Although the number of expense lines can vary based on the specific needs of the spa, it is still a daunting task to reasonably make so many assumptions. Additionally, the reader of the plan might be skeptical if it were to contain too much detail listing specific dollar amounts for items such as postage or direct mail or the annual locks and keys expense.

Undistributed Overhead Expenses in Hotels/Resorts. In the hotel world, Income before Undistributed Expenses is the same as the spa's Departmental Profit. In all hotel/resort revenue centers, the principle of accountability has been in place since the creation of the *Uniform System of Accounts for Hotels* in the 1920s and has essentially remained the same for nearly ninety years. In hotel/resort operations, the categories of expenses within the undistributed overhead expenses include Administrative and General, Sales and Marketing, Property Operation and Maintenance, and Utilities. These expenses are considered costs to the overall property; to assign or allocate each of these costs to the various operating departments would be arbitrary and would create a situation where individual department management would be focused on their shares of the allocations and constantly arguing or attempting to justify lower allocations, rather than focusing on the expenses directly in their control.

Exhibit 12 Spa Sub-Schedule 16: Facility Maintenance and Utilities

	Current Period
PAYROLL AND RELATED EXPENSES	
Salaries and Wages	$
Payroll Taxes and Employee Benefits	
Total Payroll and Related Expenses	
OTHER EXPENSES	
Facility Maintenance Expenses	
Building	
Contract Services	
Dues and Subscriptions	
Equipment Rental	
Equipment Repair	
Grounds and Landscaping	
Heating, Ventilating, and Air Conditioning	
Licenses and Fees	
Locks and Keys	
Operating Supplies	
Sauna, Steam, and Pool Supplies and Repairs	
Trash Removal	
Uniforms	
Other Repairs and Maintenance	
Total Facility Maintenance Expenses	
Utility Expenses	
Electric	
Gas	
Water	
Other Fuels	
Total Utility Expenses	
TOTAL OTHER EXPENSES	
TOTAL FACILITY MAINTENANCE AND UTILITIES EXPENSES	$

Undistributed Overhead Expenses in Day Spas. A day spa, as an independent business unit (IBU), must account for all of the Administrative and General, Marketing, Energy and Facility Maintenance expenses. Therefore, in the preparation of the business plan, a day spa project must deal with these categories of expenses in the plan's financial projections. With the limited number of surveys that have been conducted, there have been statements made concerning appropriate ranges for each of the undistributed overhead expenses. These statements suggest, as a test for a spa project's sustained profitability, that total Administrative and General expenses could fall between 8 and 12 percent of total spa revenues, Marketing could be projected to be between 5 and 7 percent of total revenues, and Utilities and Maintenance expenses could amount to 3–5 percent of total revenues.

The narrative for this section of the plan should also include trend assumptions over the five-year Statement of Income (see Exhibit 13). For example, the marketing strategy for the spa project might call for a higher percentage of revenues to be spent on marketing in the first couple of years as the spa is gaining awareness within the market and then project reduced assumptions for years three, four, and five, as the spa's presence becomes more established. Likewise, the maintenance cost for equipment will be lower in the first year, as most of the equipment will be under warranty; as the equipment ages, the expenses will increase.

Estimating Fixed Charges

Once the day spa business plan's Undistributed Operating Expense assumptions have been finalized, a table summarizing all of the financial projections made in the development of the plan needs to be created, with the table's bottom line identifying Income Before Fixed Charges. **Fixed charges** relate, for the most part, to the facility itself, including both the building and equipment and the financing thereof. They include insurance coverage, taxes, depreciation, rent (when applicable), and interest.

Property insurance coverage includes the cost of insuring the building and its contents, including equipment, against damage or destruction caused by fire, weather, sprinkler breakage, boiler explosion, plate glass breakage, or any other cause. Spas typically also purchase liability insurance, which usually amounts to 2–4 percent of the spa's total revenue.

Real estate taxes include all taxes assessed against the real property of the spa by state or political subdivisions such as county, city, or township. Personal property taxes include personal property taxes on furnishings, fixtures, and equipment. These taxes will vary widely depending upon the spa's location, thus it would be inappropriate to offer a typical range in the plan.

Depreciation of the spa's buildings and improvements is based on the cost, the estimated salvage value, and the expected life of these facilities. These factors are also the basis for the depreciation for furnishings and equipment. Amortization expenses are associated with leaseholds and leasehold improvements. These costs are written off against revenues over the shorter of the life of the lease or the life of the improvement.

Rent, if any, is the cost of leasing facilities and equipment.

Interest is the cost of borrowing funds to finance the spa facility and equipment. The formula used to calculate interest expense is:

$$\text{Interest Expense} = \text{Loan Amount} \times \text{Annual Interest Rate} \times \text{Loan Payment Period}$$

For example, say a spa borrowed $1 million to finance its building and makes a single payment a year. Assume the $1 million was borrowed on January 1, 20X1, and the annual interest rate is 8 percent. The interest expense for the 20X1 would be:

$$\text{Interest Expense} = 1{,}000{,}000 \times .08 \times 1$$
$$\text{Interest Expense} = \$80{,}000$$

For purposes of the feasibility business plan, the fixed charges must be estimated based on expected plans.

Estimating Initial Capital Investment

Capital investment estimates should be based on professional recommendations from spa consultants and financial planners. These estimates include building

Exhibit 13 Projected Five-Year Statement of Income

Revenue	**Year 1**	**Year 2**	**Year 3**	**Year 4**	**Year 5**
Massage	$ 624,300	$ 693,000	$ 741,500	$ 786,000	$ 825,300
Skin Care	425,700	473,000	506,100	536,500	563,300
Hair	106,200	118,500	126,800	134,400	141,100
Nails	113,500	126,000	134,800	142,900	150,050
Retail	194,000	282,100	301,850	320,000	336,000
Total	1,463,700	1,692,600	1,811,050	1,919,800	2,015,750
Cost of Sales and Direct Expenses:					
Massage	186,072	206,548	221,000	234,300	246,000
Skin Care	151,425	168,250	180,000	190,800	200,350
Hair	64,980	72,506	77,600	82,300	86,400
Nails	67,000	74,379	79,600	84,400	88,600
Retail	128,400	186,709	199,800	211,800	222,400
Total	597,877	708,392	758,000	803,600	843,750
Gross Margin	865,823	984,208	1,053,050	1,116,200	1,172,000
	59%	58%	58%	58%	58%
Indirect Expenses:					
Operating Expenses	81,300	92,700	97,300	101,200	104,200
Support Labor	109,200	124,500	130,700	136,000	140,000
Total	190,500	217,200	228,000	237,200	244,200
Undistributed Operating Expenses:					
Administrative & General	71,300	81,300	85,400	88,800	91,500
Marketing	42,500	48,500	50,950	53,000	54,600
Facility Maint. & Utilities	54,750	62,400	65,500	68,100	70,150
Total	168,550	192,200	201,850	209,900	216,250
Income before Fixed Charges	506,773	574,808	623,200	669,100	711,550
Insurance	10,250	10,550	10,900	11,250	11,600
Real Estate and Personal Property Taxes	23,500	24,200	24,950	25,700	26,500
Depreciation	180,000	180,000	180,000	180,000	180,000
Interest	124,800	122,072	119,126	115,944	112,507
Income before Income Taxes	168,223	237,986	288,224	336,206	380,943
Income Taxes	48,785	69,016	83,585	97,500	110,473
Net Income	$ 119,438	$ 168,970	$ 204,639	$ 238,706	$ 270,470
Profit margin	8.16%	9.98%	11.30%	12.43%	13.42%

costs, land and equipment costs, pre-opening expenses, initial working capital, and interest on construction financing. The building costs include the cost of the physical building and professional fees paid to architects, designers, and attorneys. The pre-opening expenses include the costs of hiring and training staff prior to opening, marketing efforts prior to opening, any grand-opening parties, and the estimated initial working capital that will be required during the first months of the spa operation. The initial working capital is used to provide cash for transactions and to purchase opening inventories of supplies and retail inventory. The interest on construction financing is the cost of borrowing funds during the construction period. After the completion of the construction, the construction loan will be converted to a mortgage loan with the facility as collateral.

The estimated capital investment for the day spa illustration is $2,952,710, detailed as follows:

Land	$200,000
Building	2,000,000
Equipment	600,000
Pre-Opening Expenses	30,000
Initial Working Capital	40,000
Interest on Construction Financing	82,710
Total	$2,952,710

The total capital investment of $2,952,710 is divided into debt and equity sources as shown in the following table. In this example, the equipment, pre-opening expenses, initial working capital, and interest on construction financing are all financed using equity:

		Total	Debt	Equity
Land	(80% debt and 20% equity)	$200,000	$160,000	$40,000
Building	(70% debt and 30% equity)	2,000,000	1,400,000	600,000
Equipment		600,000	0	600,000
Pre-Opening Expenses		30,000	0	30,000
Initial Working Capital		40,000	0	40,000
Interest on Construction Financing		82,710	0	82,710
		$2,952,710	$1,560,000	$1,392,710

The debt and equity investment schedule shown in Exhibit 14 shows the timing of the required cash flows for the purchase of land ten months prior to the opening and the amount of debt/equity financing over the ten-month construction period. The construction financing is based on an interest rate of 1 percent per month of the cumulative debt outstanding. Thus, the cumulative debt of $174,000 at the beginning of the tenth month prior to opening results in $1,740 of construction financing interest for the tenth month.

The loan amortization schedule shown below reflects the amount of the debt financing for the building and land as $1,560,000. The annual debt payment is based on an annual interest rate of 8 percent and a loan amortization period of 20 years. The projected interest expense of $124,800 shown is for the first year of the spa operations; it should also be shown on the projected income statement for the first year:

Year	Payment	Interest	Debt Reduction	Loan Balance
0				$1,560,000
1	$158,900	$124,800	$34,100	1,525,900
2	158,900	122,072	36,828	1,489,072
3	158,900	119,126	39,774	1,449,298
4	158,900	115,944	42,956	1,406,342
5	158,900	112,507	46,393	1,359,949

Exhibit 14 Debt and Equity Investment Schedule

Months Before Opening	Debt Amount	Cumulative Debt	Equity Amount	Land	Building	Equipment	Construction Financing Interest	Pre-Opening Expense	Initial Working Capital
10	$ 174,000	$174,000	$ 47,740	$200,000	$ 20,000		$ 1,740		
9	35,000	209,000	17,090		50,000		2,090		
8	105,000	314,000	48,140		150,000		3,140		
7	175,000	489,000	79,890		250,000		4,890		
6	210,000	699,000	96,990		300,000		6,990		
5	210,000	909,000	99,090		300,000		9,090		
4	210,000	1,119,000	101,190		300,000		11,190		
3	210,000	1,329,000	113,290		300,000		13,290	10,000	
2	140,000	1,469,000	404,690		200,000	300,000	14,690	10,000	20,000
1	91,000	1,560,000	384,600		130,000	300,000	15,600	10,000	20,000
Totals	$1,560,000		$1,392,710	$200,000	$2,000,000	$600,000	$82,710	$30,000	$40,000

Note: Construction interest is based on 1 percent per month.

The following depreciation schedule reflects the amount of annual depreciation for the equipment and building for years one through five. The equipment cost of $600,000 is depreciated over five years using the straight-line method of depreciation and assuming no salvage value at the end of the fifth year. The building is depreciated over thirty years at 3 percent per year of the cost of the building, including construction period interest, less the estimated salvage value of $282,710:

Year	Equipment	Building	Total
1	$120,000	$60,000	$180,000
2	120,000	60,000	180,000
3	120,000	60,000	180,000
4	120,000	60,000	180,000
5	120,000	60,000	180,000

The following table shows the spa's five-year projected annual cash flows. Depreciation, a non-cash expense, is added to net income and the debt reduction amounts for each year, as previously shown on the loan amortization schedule, are subtracted to provide the estimated annual cash flows. The projected cash flow for the first year is $265,338, and projected to increase to $404,077 by the fifth year:

	Year 1	Year 2	Year 3	Year 4	Year 5
Net Income	$119,438	$168,970	$204,639	$238,706	$270,470
Add: Depreciation	180,000	180,000	180,000	180,000	180,000
Less: Debt Reduction Payments	34,100	36,828	39,774	42,956	46,393
Projected Cash Flow	$265,338	$312,142	$344,865	$375,750	$404,077

These very positive cash flows suggest the mortgage payments can be paid and cash may also be available to distribute to the spa owners.

Feasibility Study Recommendations

Considering all the market research and assumptions that must be made, it is easy to understand why the vast majority of hotel/resort developers will engage a spa consulting company to develop a spa feasibility study. Very few hotel/resort developers have the skills and experience or even the time necessary to conduct a complete analysis for a spa. Even major hospitality brands do not generally have the resources to conduct their own market research; even if they *have* developed general design standards and guidelines, they will still probably ask the ownership/development team to contract with a spa consulting company to validate their preliminary assumptions. In addition to the market research, concept development, and financial projections, the contract should require that the consultant include other recommendations such as:

- *A final spa positioning strategy.* It is important to inform the owner/developer where the spa will be situated within the market and how the spa should position itself to become an effective force within the competitive marketplace. The final positioning strategy should explain how to incorporate the spa concept and the local surroundings to create a unique and memorable experience for each spa guest.
- *A service menu and programming recommendations.* The plan will identify opportunities within the local market that will provide the spa with an advantage in developing strategic marketing initiatives. The spa's service menu must deliver a range of services that clearly unite the spa concept, the expected experience, and types of treatments provided. Layering the service menu with basic core services, such as massage and facials, along with special signature services and alternative therapies will provide maximum capture per guest. Recommendations will provide a solid foundation for the development of an appropriate and profitable spa program. Examples of typical recommendations might include:
    - Treatment opportunities.
    - Value-added service opportunities.
    - Professional product lines.
    - Additional revenue opportunities.
    - Marketing recommendations.
- *Facility and design parameters.* The plan could include a description of how the spa will provide a relaxing, luxurious, and yet embracing ambience. This description should also discuss how special features or gracious amenities will be included that appeal to the type of guest that the spa has identified in its customer profile.
- *An architectural program.* Based on the demand analysis, revenue projections, and staffing requirements, the feasibility study would likely include recommendations for the architectural program of space (see Exhibit 15) that would include:

Exhibit 15 Sample Architectural Program

SPA FACILITY PROGRAM—SUMMARY

AREA	Total Square Feet	Total Square Meters	% of Total Interior Spaces
1.00 Arrival	444	41.2	5%
2.00 Administration	299	27.8	3%
3.00 Retail	435	40.4	5%
4.00 Men's Locker Room	1,031	95.8	11%
5.00 Women's Locker Room	1,206	112.1	13%
6.00 Coed Relaxation	720	66.9	8%
7.00 Treatment Rooms	1,725	160.3	19%
8.00 Nails—Women's Grooming	516	47.9	5%
9.00 Hair Stations—Men's Grooming	324	30.1	3%
10.00 Fitness	825	76.6	9%
11.00 Support	1,248	115.9	14%
12.00 Circulation	460	42.7	5%
TOTAL INTERIOR SPACES	9,233	857.7	100%

SPA FACILITY PROGRAM—SUMMARY

AREA	Total Square Feet	Total Square Meters
13.00 Energy	828	76.9
14.00 Duet Treatment	300	27.9
TOTAL EXTERIOR SPACES	1,128	104.8

- Overall required space to meet demand projections.
- Square foot allocations.
- Number of treatment rooms/stations by type.
- Circulation allocation of square footage.
- Fitness facilities.
- Signature spaces and features.
- Support spaces.
- Program brief that outlines all assumptions and rationales used in developing the program.

Summary

This chapter starts with the premise that a feasibility/business plan is required to secure financing for a new spa project. After thoroughly examining the process of creating a feasibility/business plan, it should be evident how much time and effort is required to make a plan successful. While the funding is critical, the real beneficiary of the feasibility/business plan process is the entrepreneur who has a vision of owning a spa facility. Gone are the days when spas were of low density in the major markets and only a very small percentage of resorts and hotels had a spa as an amenity of the property. The landscape of the industry has changed as the number of spas just in the United States has grown from a few hundred in the 1980s to more than 18,000 in 2008. It is no longer a matter of simply adding a couple of treatment rooms to a salon and changing the name on the sign out front to include "Spa," or for a hotel or resort to convert some storage space alongside a fitness center, add a couple massage rooms, and suddenly reposition the property as a resort and spa. In today's more competitive landscape, it is critical to prepare a detailed feasibility/business plan to ensure the financial sustainability of the project.

This chapter addressed the common elements of a feasibility plan for a hotel/resort and a business plan for a day spa, i.e., the executive summary; project parameters and research objectives; opportunity analysis; demand analysis and financial forecast; and project recommendations. The executive summary can be written as a synopsis or a topical summary, but it must be direct, concise, and compelling, as readers of the plan will read no further if their interest is not sparked initially.

The section on project parameters and research objectives included information about potential site identification/inspection and spa concept positioning.

The opportunity analysis of the feasibility/business plan includes first identifying the property's positioning and market and, second, identifying the expected competing spas. The characteristics of the expected competing spas, as well as their financial and marketing strengths, must be determined.

The demand analysis and financial forecast must result in a realistic revenue and expense forecast over the first five operating years. This forecast includes all revenues and related expenses for the spa departments and other operating departments. In addition, the indirect expenses for the spa departments along with the undistributed operating expenses must be forecast. The five-year financial plan must also show fixed charges and initial capital investment estimates. This is a tedious and critically important process; if the financial forecast fails to show positive, realistic results, the dreams of the spa developer and owners will end.

Key Terms

capital investment estimates—Expenses including building costs, land and equipment costs, pre-opening expenses, initial working capital, and interest on construction financing.

fixed charges—Expenses that relate, for the most part, to the facility itself, including both the building and equipment and the financing thereof.

forecasting—The art of estimating what is likely to happen based on an assumed set of conditions.

market sales build-up method—Method used to forecast sales that uses collected market research data to project customer contributions.

program of space—Outlines the minimum square footage allocated to every component of the spa facility.

qualified guest —Anyone over the age of 18 who could be a potential spa user.

Review Questions

1. What are the two different types of executive summaries and how do they differ?
2. What are the differences between a business plan and a feasibility plan?
3. What are the three possibilities in selecting the location for a new day spa?
4. What issues must be considered when evaluating whether a spa can be successful at a hotel/resort location?
5. What information should be included in a spa positioning statement?
6. What is a major purpose of the opportunity analysis section of a business plan?
7. What should be the final result of a business plan's demand analysis and financial forecast?
8. What are considered to be a spa's fixed charges?
9. How does the debt financing of a proposed spa impact the projected expenses over the first five years of operation as shown in a business plan?
10. What elements are included in the feasibility study recommendations?

Index

F

G

H–I

J–L

S

T

U

V–Z